PRURIENT INTERESTS

COLUMBIA STUDIES IN CONTEMPORARY AMERICAN HISTORY

WILLIAM E. LEUCHTENBURG AND ALAN BRINKLEY,

GENERAL EDITORS

Columbia Studies in Contemporary American History
William E. Leuchtenburg and Alan Brinkley, General Editors

PRURIENT INTERESTS

Gender, Democracy, and Obscenity in New York City, 1909–1945

Andrea Friedman

Columbia University Press

NEW YORK

Columbia University Press

Publishers Since 1893

New York   Chichester, West Sussex

Copyright © 2000 Columbia University Press

All rights reserved

Library of Congress Cataloging-in-Publication Data

Friedman, Andrea.

Prurient interests : gender, democracy, and obscenity in New York City, 1909–1945 /
Andrea Friedman.

p. cm. — (Columbia studies in contemporary American history)

Includes bibliographical references and index.

ISBN 0-231-11066-9 (cloth : alk. paper) — ISBN 0-231-11067-7 (pbk. : alk. paper)

1. Erotica—Social aspects—New York (State)—New York—History—20th century.

2. Sex in popular culture—New York (State)—New York—History—20th century.

3. Obscenity (Law)—New York (State)—New York—History—20th century.

4. Censorship—New York (State)—New York—History—20th century. 5. Arts—
Censorship—New York (State)—New York—History—20th century. 6. Vice control—
New York (State)—New York—History—20th century. 7. New York (N.Y.)—Moral
conditions—History—20th century. I. Title. II. Series.

HQ472.U6 F75 2000

363.4′7′09747109041—dc21   99-089010

Printed in the United States of America

c 10 9 8 7 6 5 4 3 2 1

p 10 9 8 7 6 5 4 3 2 1

For my parents

CONTENTS

ACKNOWLEDGMENTS

In the years that I have been working on this study my debts, for kindnesses large and small, have mounted precipitously. I owe much to teachers, colleagues, and friends who have given generously of their time from this project's earliest stages. I am grateful to Linda Gordon, my dissertation director, whose high standards and insistence that I rethink yet again profoundly shaped and greatly improved this book. I'd also like to thank Paul Boyer, Julie D'Acci, Carl Kaestle, and especially Steve Stern for their guidance and encouragement at the dissertation stage. My fellow students at the University of Wisconsin, particularly those in the Women's History Dissertation Group, offered close readings, challenging questions, and a passion for doing history that matters. They made all the difference. Thanks especially to Karen Booth, Katherine Dresher, Joyce Follet, Jennifer Frost, Laura McEnaney, Lesa Meyer, Leslie Reagan, Bethel Saler, and Susan Smith for reading above and beyond the call of duty. For valuable comments on conference papers and chapters, I am grateful to Nicola Beisel, Peter Buckley, Varda Burstyn, Jill Dolan, Dirk Hartog, and Mariana Valverde. I also appreciate the suggestions of four anonymous reviewers for the *Journal of American History.* More recently, Henry Berger, Casey Blake, and Derek Hirst read the entire manuscript and offered incisive critiques and helpful suggestions. I am especially indebted to Frank Couvares, Dirk Hartog, and Leisa Meyer, each of whom provided meticulous readings and much appreciated encouragement. Whatever its remaining flaws, this book is immensely better for their guidance.

A number of institutions generously granted funds for research and writing. For support during the dissertation stage, I am grateful to the Woodrow Wilson National Fellowship Foundation for a Women's Studies Research Grant, to the Rockefeller Archive Center of the Rockefeller University and the Center for the Study of Philanthropy of the Graduate Center, City University of New York for research funds, and to the Department of History and the Graduate School of the University of Wisconsin. Washington University in Saint Louis provided a semester's leave and generous financial assistance for research and writing. I would also like to thank those friends, and friends of friends, who gave me a temporary home during research trips, including Audrey Fried and Faith

Ruderfer, Cindy Hecht, Brenda Marston, Darlene Mitera, Adela Oliver, Sue Reynolds, and Leslie Schwalm.

Among the many archivists whose assistance was invaluable, several deserve special mention. I am indebted to the staff of the Rare Books and Manuscripts Division at the New York Public Library for their patience with my predilection for microfilming large quantities of material. Thanks also to the employees at the New York Municipal Archives, in particular Evelyn Gonzalez. She provided encouragement, advice, and assistance at several stages of this project. I am especially grateful for her suggestions — and the efforts of several city employees — in my fruitless hunt for records of the New York City Department of Licenses, which, unfortunately, it appears, have not been preserved.

I would also like to thank the staff at Columbia University Press for their patience in introducing a novice to the intricacies of publishing. Thanks to James Burger for answering my many questions in a timely manner, to Susan Pensak for her careful editing, and especially to Kate Wittenberg for being always encouraging and infinitely flexible. Nancy Taylor generously agreed to compile the index, and I will be forever grateful.

For general moral support, encouragement, and entertainment over the years, I am indebted to my parents, Elynore Friedman and Harold Friedman, and to Nicky Gullace, Wendy Kline, Leisa Meyer, and Rachel Schurman. Thank you to my St. Louis friends who have helped me to feel at home there, especially Leslie Brown and Annie Valk, Kathy Morris and Gwen-Marie Lerch, and K. and Lisa Mandel. Thanks also to Lisa for the photos. My colleagues at Washington University, including Nancy Berg, Iver Bernstein, Howard Brick, Mary Ann Dzuback, Helen Power, and Liann Tsoukas, have been supportive during the last stages of this project. I also wish to thank Leila Rupp, who early in my academic career convinced me not only that I could be a historian, but that I wanted to be one. Finally, my greatest debt is to Kate Dresher, who, through it all, helped me face my fears, taught me to keep my eye on the ball, and, most important, made me laugh.

PRURIENT INTERESTS

INTRODUCTION

H
ow should modern citizens manage the "exploitation of pleasure?" This was the question that Michael Davis, an investigator for the Russell Sage Foundation, sought to answer in 1911 when he published a study of commercial recreations in New York City. The need for such a study arose, Davis argued, out of the imperatives of city life and industrial development as well as out of the necessity of a well-founded public policy. His conclusion set out a brief "historical" survey of responses to the problem of commercial amusements:

> In the past, the attitude toward recreation in America has been either that of the Puritan or of *laissez-faire*. To the Puritan, joy is danger, and the pleasure side of life should be reduced to the lowest possible point. American public men, however, and American governments during this generation, have regarded recreation less from the standpoint of the Puritan than as a side of life which the individual would naturally take care of for himself. . . . [But] the city masses the recreational activities of large groups of people so as to create a public problem instead of merely a series of countless individual ones, and calls therefore upon the local government for appropriate communal action. We are learning, in a new field, what was taught by the economic world a generation ago; like industry, *recreation has become a matter of public concern; laissez-faire* can no longer be the policy of the State.

Davis conceded that "the community cannot tolerate a situation which leads to the economic and moral exploitation of its children," but, he warned, "public policy must not be Puritanical but thoroughly democratic." He recommended that New York enact legal regulation to enforce minimum standards of health, safety, and morals and that voluntary agencies and state government engage in "constructive action" to establish desirable recreational alternatives outside of the commercial sphere.[1]

The publication of *The Exploitation of Pleasure* suggests the concern with which many Progressive-era New Yorkers viewed the problem of regulating entertainment. In the city, reformers and municipal authorities feared, children were subject to countless dangers in the busy streets, the unwholesome candy shops, the dark nickelodeons; overcrowding and despair sent too many adult men into saloons in search of relief from their drab lives; adolescent boys and girls likewise escaped the "human pressure" of the city by seeking refuge within billiard parlors and dance halls, respectively. As leisure activities increasingly took commercial forms — in motion picture theaters springing up across the city, in burlesque theaters controlled by national "wheels," in taxi-dance halls and amusement parks — older styles of supervising the recreation of children and controlling that of adults seemed insufficient. Parents appeared helpless to protect their children against the temptations of city life. Vice societies lacked the resources to patrol the growing numbers of recreational venues. And blue laws and similar repressive measures, many Progressive activists believed, ignored the reality that city dwellers needed outlets that rural life had more naturally provided.[2]

As leisure changed, the politics of regulating leisure changed as well. The rapid growth of commercial culture brought new participants to the debates about how to solve the problems posed by recreation in the modern heterogeneous city. The Protestant middle-class women and ministers who had constituted the core of nineteenth-century moral reform movements were now joined by social workers like Michael Davis, by rabbis and Catholic clergy, by municipal authorities who had begun increasing their regulatory powers in numerous areas of urban life, by owners, employees, and consumers of the new cultural industries, and, ultimately, by civil libertarians. Some of these agreed with Davis on the need for constructive alternatives to commercial recreation; others continued to plead for the "repressive" strategies that Davis had termed Puritan; still others contended that laissez-faire was sufficient, questioning whether the growth of commercial culture posed a problem at all. Further, as spectatorship became an increasingly important characteristic of urban recreation, more of these citizens turned their attention to the particular problem of the obscene.[3] From the first decade of the twentieth century through World War II, New Yorkers debated how to regulate obscenity; by the 1950s their concerns were being echoed in a national arena, where they have remained to this day. In disputes about whether and how to control what city residents could see on the motion picture screen or on the stage, and what they could read in books and magazines, New Yorkers contended not only about the nature of obscenity and the appropriateness of censorship but also about the legitimacy of moral authority, the value of democracy, and the character of the nation. These debates, and their consequences, are the subject of this book. It is my argument that by focusing on local disputes over particular media — and here I concentrate on motion pictures, burlesque shows, and the legitimate theater — we can detect the emergence of a modern regime of obscenity regulation in the United States in the fifty years before it was codified by the U.S. Supreme Court.

$\sim$

In New York, as in much of the nation, anti-obscenity activism had flourished in the late nineteenth century. The most conspicuous of these activists were men like Anthony Comstock, the white, middle-class, and elite Protestant men who constituted the membership of the New York Society for the Suppression of Vice and like organizations. Vice society personnel had greater access to the resources of the state than did other moral reformers; indeed, in New York they were awarded quasi-state status. Comstock was empowered to make arrests of those who violated the federal law named after him; legislation required that local officials aid his enforcement activities. In cities other than New York male investigators also sought out obscene materials and assisted state authorities in making arrests and obtaining convictions.[4]

The vice societies' easy access to government power may have made them the most visible members of the anti-obscenity coalition, but their efforts were endorsed and augmented by Protestant clergymen and female activists. These latter groups became increasingly prominent within anti-obscenity organizing, reflecting their important role in the broader social purity movement that arose in the late nineteenth century. Seeking to enforce an ideal of marital procreative sexuality pegged to a critique of the sexual "double standard" and male profligacy, social purists battled prostitution, waged age-of-consent campaigns, and validated a wife's right to abstain from intercourse if she so chose. Active both in the broader social purity movement and anti-obscenity campaigning were the members of the Woman's Christian Temperance Union, who founded a Department for the Suppression of Impure Literature in 1883. For these women and for anti-obscenity activists generally, preventing the arousal of lust required that a single sexual standard be honored not only in behavior but also in cultural representations of sexuality.[5]

Nineteenth-century anti-obscenity activism was linked to the larger social purity movement by a shared belief in moral absolutism. Moral absolutism had several components: the assertion that morality (including sexual morality) was both knowable and timeless, that it was ordained by God and essential for public and private order; the belief that social authority derived from one's position at the top of a moral hierarchy, determined by religion, age, class, race, and gender; and agreement that the moral standards established by those at the top of this hierarchy should be enforced upon the larger society through public policy. The ideology of moral absolutism provided the foundation for claims to social, cultural, and political authority by late-nineteenth-century moral reformers. This foundation was especially crucial in enabling the activism of white middle-class women, whose profession to moral authority permitted them to assert both the responsibility and the right to help shape public policy, despite their disfranchisement. As historian Peggy Pascoe has argued, the assertion of female moral authority underlay a wide range of activism by white middle-class women in the late nineteenth and early twentieth centuries.[6]

Yet the precepts of moral absolutism, and the claims to authority that it made possible, were subject to challenge. Working-class and immigrant people had long questioned whether economic privilege afforded the right to judge moral behavior.[7] And by the beginning of the twentieth century a growing number of middle-class women and men also spurned the presumptions of social hierarchy and a divinely ordained, unchanging morality. Repudiating the valuation of self-control that underlay moral absolutism and choosing to emphasize self-expression and pleasure seeking as individual and social goods, these individuals exchanged what they saw as an outmoded "Victorianism" for an identity as "moderns." As substantial numbers of Americans debated the idea of the modern, *modern* became a term by which they heralded or critiqued specific conceptions of the relationship between individual and community, the desirability of change, the fixedness of morality, and the nature of authority. Americans who identified as modern understood authority to be based in the knowledge that derives from individual experience. Because every individual's experience was equally valuable and productive, modernity was bound up with a new valuation of democracy as well. Thus, the challenge to moral absolutism in the cultural arena, and particularly in twentieth-century debates about regulating obscenity, took the form of a search for a new kind of moral authority — one in tune with the values of a modern age.[8]

Beginning in the early twentieth century, then, an increasing number of New Yorkers, including Progressive-era social workers, members of the entertainment industry, and the civil libertarians who created the ACLU-affiliated National Council on Freedom from Censorship in the 1930s, opposed the continuing efforts to police obscenity under the old terms of moral absolutism. They created a language of public policy that I call democratic moral authority, which became widely accepted by the end of World War II. The concept of democratic moral authority provided a structure for determining *what* representations of sexuality might be proscribed by government, and *how* they might be proscribed. Two precepts comprised its core: that whether a representation of sex was obscene ought to be judged according to the standards of the "average person" and that regulation of that content must occur only in accordance with carefully defined democratic processes. In articulating a democratic moral authority and, finally, convincing New Yorkers of its value, opponents of censorship helped to shape a modern regime of obscenity regulation.[9]

The process by which democratic moral authority came to furnish the dominant paradigm for American obscenity law was complicated and contentious, and it had often unintended consequences. Even as some New Yorkers became increasingly skeptical of vice agents, anti-obscenity activists redoubled their efforts to counter an expanding commercial culture industry focused in large part around the commodification of sexuality. They reshaped their arguments and proffered strategies to offset the growing influence of a discourse emphasizing democracy, often seeking to present their regulatory efforts as consonant with democratic values. The ability to cast the anti-obscenity movement as democratic was abetted by early anticensorship activists' willingness to endorse voluntary regulation and self-regulation. Into the 1920s censorship opponents offered a wide range of strategies intended to obviate state control, with the result that they actually contributed to the expansion of private or quasi-public regulation. By the 1930s, however, they had recast the relationship between democratic control and government, championing instead a state-centered system of criminal prosecution with the guaranteed right to trial by jury. This system, which not only rejected "voluntary" censorship mechanisms and the legitimacy of anti-obscenity activists' interventions but also limited the arsenal of regulatory weapons available to municipal authorities, was accepted, more or less enthusiastically, by city officials and growing numbers of New York residents by the end of World War II.

Anti-obscenity activists also reacted to the growing influence of democratic moral authority by offering a more precise elaboration of the dangers posed by sexual portrayals. In order to demonstrate the necessity of circumventing democratic safeguards, they sought to create a vulnerable public whose need for protection outweighed citizens' rights to govern themselves. This elaboration depended upon linking specific audiences to specific genres. For example, anti-obscenity activists argued that movies catered to an audience overwhelmingly composed of children and therefore were "cradles of corruption" deserving of government censorship, that burlesque caused some in its audience to rape and murder women and children and therefore should be banned from the city, that the proliferation of lesbian-themed plays on Broadway mandated new regulatory strategies in order to prevent the vulnerable young women in the audience from being seduced into lesbian relationships. The dangers that they enumerated — the effect of sexually explicit materials upon children, the allegation that obscene depictions caused sexual violence against women, and the spread of homosexuality — would remain prominent within anti-obscenity discourse into the late twentieth century, when they came to constitute the bogeymen of the debates about pornography.

The influence of democratic moral authority is evident not only in the changing mechanisms of regulation and in the arguments offered by foes of obscenity but also in shifting configurations of leadership, especially among anti-obscenity activists. In her study of New York cultural life during the 1920s, Ann Douglas argues that the white and African American New York "moderns" of that decade struggled to create a democratic culture through opposition to the "Titaness": "the powerful white middle-class matriarch of the recent Victorian past" whose authority as arbiter of the nation's culture constituted an apparent "block to modernity." Douglas's analysis highlights the ways that moderns of all sorts — including the anticensorship activists studied here — perceived certain forms of female moral authority as an impediment to establishing a system of sexual and cultural democracy.[10] As I will show, they formulated democratic moral authority, at least in part, in order to blunt the power of public policy initiatives advanced by the white middle-class women who represented the forces of female moral authority in the cultural arena.[11] Their success facilitated the marginalization of such women within the leadership of anti-obscenity campaigns and within the emerging regulatory regime for obscenity. It is both ironic and, perhaps, inevitable, that at the moment of their formal entry to national citizenship with the passage of the Nineteenth Amendment, the possibilities of a "woman's voice" on the issue of obscenity were forestalled. Ironic, as well, was the movement of clerics and male religious layworkers into the forefront of anti-obscenity campaigns during these years. Male religious anti-obscenity activists were much more adept than were either the men of the vice societies or the white middle-class women of the club movement at accommodating to the changing discourse of obscenity regulation. By cultivating an interfaith movement for the suppression of obscenity by the 1930s, religious leaders were able to portray themselves as representatives of the people of New York.

This development, too, contributed to the creation of a masculinized discourse about, and system of, obscenity regulation.

As the foregoing suggests, the political contests over the sexual content of commercial culture were conflicts among white middle-class women and men as frequently as they were attempts by middle-class reformers to control working-class consumers. Much of the literature on commercial culture and its regulation has focused on the ways in which such regulation provided opportunities for enforcing or resisting the hegemony of the middle class, but close examination of the locales and timing of debates about obscenity reveals the limitations of this approach.[12] These debates often raged most fiercely — and the regulatory apparatus was frequently expanded most successfully — around entertainment forms patronized by middle-class consumers. State censorship of motion pictures in New York was accomplished in 1921, long after the movies had expanded beyond their original working-class audience; Broadway's dangers reached no further than the middle-class New Yorkers who filled its theaters; even burlesque — a quintessentially working-class medium — became the focus of reformers' attention only when it threatened to draw a middle-class audience. The social conflicts examined here, about culture and sex, democracy and authority, were predominantly conflicts within the middle class, even if they also furthered middle-class hegemony.

To a surprising degree, perhaps, in an era that most scholars have characterized as the locus of a standardized, corporatized, and nationalized popular culture embodied in the mass media,[13] the processes through which a modern obscenity regime emerged operated at the local level. Even into the 1940s individual consumers participated in a world of entertainment that mixed elements of the local and the national. For example, mass culture such as motion pictures existed side by side with burlesque shows, which became increasingly localized during the 1920s and 1930s as the national burlesque "wheels" faltered. Just as important, mechanisms for regulating the content of both mass and local media functioned at the state and local levels, and these localized regulatory strategies were frequently interwoven. The enactment of a state motion picture censorship law structured the antiregulatory strategies pursued by advocates of free speech on the stage; local and state court rulings concerning New York City's license commissioner's powers regarding Broadway helped shape debates about the regulation of burlesque. New York's obscenity debates also remind us that we must direct our gaze to the state in order to understand fully the complexities of modern American cultural history. During the twentieth century citizens have increasingly turned to government to articulate their concerns about culture, and government officials have often proved willing mediators of those concerns. Indeed, whether they took an anti-obscenity or an anticensorship stance, New Yorkers agreed upon the necessity of making government a powerful arbiter of culture in modern society. In sum, examining cultural politics at the local level reveals the limits of focusing too narrowly on the supposedly hegemonic control exercised by the institutions of mass culture and their owners.

≈

In debates about obscenity New Yorkers contended not only about forms of moral authority and the shape of state regulation but also over the outlines of modern sexuality. By modern sexuality, I refer to the constellation of ideas and behavior identified by John D'Emilio and Estelle Freedman as "sexual liberalism," which included

> the new positive value attributed to the erotic, the growing autonomy of youth, the association of sex with commercialized leisure and self-expression, the pursuit of love, the visibility of the erotic in popular culture, the social interaction of men and women in public, the legitimation of female interest in the sexual

as well as the increasing visibility of homosexual communities.[14] New York's plays, movies, and burlesque performances reflected back to city residents the ways in which their sexual behavior was changing to accord with and create this new sexual system. These entertainment forms also popularized new ideologies about sexuality, making them available to new audiences, and commercial culture venues offered a site for participating in the emergent sexual culture as well. It is because theater and motion pictures not only mirrored but also propelled changes in the sexual ideology and behavior of a wide spectrum of urban residents that these mainstream cultural forms, rather than more narrowly defined "pornography," provided a focal point for concern in these years.

While the three media discussed here differed from each other in many respects, the representation of sexuality was at the core of each, and the similarities in that representation are perhaps more significant than the differences. During the first half of the twentieth century, plays, burlesque shows, and motion pictures shared a number of characteristics in their treatment of sexuality. First, the display of women's bodies increased. This is most obvious in the case of burlesque, which became identified with the striptease during the 1930s. But controversies during the 1910s over motion pictures featuring female nudity and almost yearly denunciations of 1920s Broadway revues for their chorus lines of "girls with no clothing above the waist and little below" indicate the pervasiveness of female sexual display within all of these media.[15]

Also common to these media was the assertion of women's sexual desire. In the movies, Theda Bara's sexually voracious and vengeful "vamp" was an extreme representation, but in general the portrayal of women's sexual passion was much less ominous and more endemic to motion pictures than the attention paid to Bara might suggest. Young women characters were generally virtuous, but nonetheless they flirted outrageously, danced with wild abandon, and responded to men's kisses, often despite censors' instructions to the contrary.[16] On Broadway and in burlesque shows women were even more forward in asserting their passionate nature. From the wife in one 1920s comedy who fell in love with her husband only after (and only because) he performed so well in consummating their marriage, to the society matron in another who raced with two young women to see who could first deflower a college student, to every woman who appeared on a burlesque stage during the 1930s, women of all classes and ages were assumed to be sexual beings.[17]

Each of these media also offered an acknowledgment of sexual diversity within American society, especially regarding homosexuality. Gay men were most frequently the object of comedy. In motion pictures, plays, and numerous burlesque sketches the effeminate homosexual stereotype maintained the ubiquity of the heterosexual norm at the same time that it reminded New Yorkers of exceptions to the universality of heterosexual desire. Lesbians, on the other hand, were always portrayed as the subject of tragedy and made their appearance almost exclusively on the Broadway stage. Few of these portrayals of gay men or lesbians offered a serious challenge to clichéd understandings of homosexuality; indeed, in most cases they cultivated and sustained such clichés. Yet the appearance of homosexuals in mainstream media was nonetheless a new and noteworthy phenomenon.[18]

Engaging in anti-obscenity activism did not simply mean that an individual *opposed* the emergence of a new sexual system. During the 1910s, when anti-obscenity campaigners devoted most of their attention to motion pictures, they fought hard against the expression of sexual liberalism in movies, condemning the portrayal of female passion, discussions of birth control, and representations of youthful independence from parental authority and identifying motion picture theaters, quite rightly, as a site for adolescent sexual education and experimentation. Beginning in the 1920s, and increasingly in the 1930s and 1940s, however, anti-obscenity activists focused their attention on defining and maintaining the boundaries of sexual liberalism. While among obscenity opponents some preferred that sexuality of any kind not be portrayed on the stage or in movies, nonetheless in New York City most attempts to regulate the content of commercial culture in the decades after World War I focused upon identifying what was beyond the pale. Their targets were, increasingly, uncontrolled male sexual desire, as represented in burlesque theaters, and the enhanced visibility of lesbians and gay men, as represented on the Broadway stage.[19] Indeed, we can learn a good deal about the meanings of anti-obscenity campaigns by paying attention to forms of sexuality that they did not target. For the most part, for example, cultural forms that were focused around the portrayal of African American sexuality escaped the wrath of those concerned about obscenity. A likely explanation for their neglect of the burgeoning Harlem nightclubs and the Negro revues that appeared on Broadway during the 1920s is that the presumption of black "primitivism" and hypersexuality that underlay many of these productions presented no challenge to the racial and sexual beliefs of the white New Yorkers who engaged in these campaigns. On the other hand, when Broadway plays such as *Aphrodite* (1919) or *All God's Chillun Got Wings* (1924) gave any hint of interracial sexuality, they quickly attracted condemnation, because of their intimation of sexual desire (and sexual sameness) between whites and blacks.[20] In deciding which representations to oppose, tolerate, or defend, anti-obscenity activists and their foes participated in defining the parameters of sexual liberalism and in shaping the regulatory mechanisms that helped maintain those parameters.

∾

Exposed female bodies, an affirmation of women's sexual passion, the increasing visibility of gay men and lesbians — each of these are specific examples of a changing urban sexual culture that New Yorkers saw reflected, larger than life, in their commercial culture. And in part it was because commercial culture played such an important role in the life of New York City that many of the city's residents devoted so much attention to that reflection in debates about obscenity. Indeed, early-twentieth-century New York's importance as a national center for commercial culture virtually ensured the eruption of political struggles over policy concerning the entertainment industry at the same time that it gave these local struggles national importance. New York City was the unrivaled theatrical center of the nation. It boasted of a vibrant legitimate theater as well as numerous vaudeville and burlesque houses. Further, touring companies brought New York's theatrical productions to Americans in other cities. The motion picture industry got its start in New York, and during the first decade of the century almost all U.S. films were produced in or near the city. Even after film production moved to the West Coast, New York remained the commercial and manufacturing center of the industry. The city also contained a vast array of other forms of commercial culture including amusement parks, dance halls, restaurants, and dime museums, and it was home to the nation's publishing industry as well. In *The Exploitation of Pleasure* Michael Davis tried through quantification to convey a sense of the vast influence commercial culture exercised over New Yorkers: in Manhattan alone he counted 7 burlesque theaters, 36 vaudeville theaters with an estimated weekly attendance of almost 1.4 million, and 30 "high-priced" theaters that were patronized by about 160,000 people a week. He estimated (very conservatively) that there were approximately 400 motion picture theaters in the city as a whole, drawing hundreds of thousands of customers every day. No other city in the nation came close to the variety and abundance of commercial culture offered by New York.[21]

New York's position as the nation's cultural mecca, and the important role played by entertainment industries in the city's economy, made the conflicts over obscenity that occurred there unique in their importance to municipal life. Furthermore, the demography of New York shaped these debates in particular ways. One scholar has estimated that in 1900 New York City's population was 47 percent Catholic, 39 percent Protestant, and 12 percent Jewish.[22] As a result, the influence of Protestant clergy in anti-obscenity campaigns was probably less pronounced in New York than in other cities and towns throughout the nation, at the same time that Catholics and Jews were more prominent.[23] Indeed, the substantial role played by Jews in New York's entertainment industries made debates about obscenity especially important to many Jewish leaders. The city's position as cultural capital also facilitated the creation of a strong anticensorship coalition, for many residents perceived that their ability to make a living was threatened by attempts to regulate commercial culture too strictly. Yet the battles that were writ large in New York occurred in other cities and towns across the nation, from Chicago and Boston and Los Angeles to places like Spokane and Rochester, New York.[24] Moreover, because individuals throughout the country perceived the city as a symbol of modern culture they attached a great deal of importance to the political debates over obscenity in New York, arguing that their outcomes would affect similar struggles elsewhere in the nation. Finally, the modern obscenity regime whose emergence I trace in New York City in the years prior to World War II became the nation's obscenity regime by the 1950s, formalized in a series of U.S. Supreme Court rulings by mid decade. Despite the city's singularity, analysis of anti-obscenity campaigns and resistance to them in New York City reveals much about the issues occupying other Americans also concerned with the transition from a Victorian to a modern culture.

This study is divided into two sections. Part 1 examines the ways in which specific regulatory strategies were fashioned in relation to both the particular representations of sexuality featured within each entertainment form and the audience associated with each. Chapter 1 focuses on the role of the New York-based National Board of Censorship of Motion Pictures in shaping a system of municipal film regulation in the years prior to 1921, when a state censorship law was enacted. Chapter 2 describes the successful campaign during the 1930s and 1940s to rid New York of burlesque performance, while chapter 3 is concerned with efforts, spanning more than twenty years, to legitimate censorship on Broadway by playing on fears of the lesbian predator. Emphasizing the opportunities and constraints embedded in the articulation of democratic moral authority, this first section reveals that, while regulatory strategies expanded during the first decades of the twentieth century, by the World War II era the range of acceptable sanctions against sexually explicit entertainment had narrowed considerably.

Part 2 takes a more integrative approach, considering who was involved in these debates and the ways in which these New Yorkers refigured understandings of moral authority and government authority. Chapter 4 examines the shifting contours of the anti-obscenity coalition, paying special attention to the growing importance of Catholic men in leading anti-obscenity campaigns as well as the complex nature of Jews' participation in the debates about obscenity. Chapter 5 explores more directly the ways in which the construction of democratic moral authority operated to displace middle-class white women from the modern system of obscenity regulation. The conclusion describes the national debate about obscenity and pornography that developed after World War II, emphasizing the contradictions embedded within a system of obscenity regulation articulated through the concept of democratic moral authority.

∾

At the center of the American obscenity regime has been — and remains — one immutable axiom: that obscene speech may be prohibited by the state.

Nonetheless, the definition of obscenity has changed substantially, as have the permissible mechanisms for regulating it. Gauging the depths of that change, and the significance of twentieth-century developments, requires an examination of the origins and evolution of U.S. obscenity law.

While the federal government did not pass effective, enforceable national legislation governing sexual portrayals in commercial culture until after the Civil War, there existed an earlier tradition of more local regulation. Encompassing common law, statutory prohibitions of obscenity, and the licensing of entertainments, these efforts initially betrayed a concern with upholding church and state authority rather than opposition to sexual portrayals per se. All the American colonies enacted statutes criminalizing heresy and/or blasphemy, including Massachusetts, which in 1711 passed a law prohibiting the "composing, writing, printing or publishing of any filthy obscene or profane song, pamphlet, libel or mock-sermon, in imitation of preaching, or any other part of divine worship."[25] The wording of this law suggests that in British North America, as in Europe, early obscene writings and pictures offered a forum for articulating religious and political criticism.[26]

In addition to enacting statutes prohibiting speech — sexual or otherwise — opposed to the maintenance of public order, colonists passed a variety of laws forbidding or regulating theatrical entertainments. These too derived from a religious sensibility, as William Penn's Frame of Government reveals:

> That as careless and corrupt administration of justice draws the wrath of God upon magistrate, so the wildness and looseness of the people provoke the indignation of God against a country: therefore . . . all prizes, stage plays, cards, dice, may-games, masques, revels, bull-baitings, cock-fightings, bear-baitings and the like, which excite the people to rudeness, cruelty, looseness and irreligion, shall be respectively discouraged, and severely punished.[27]

By the eighteenth century, mirroring developments in England, the giving of stage plays by professional companies was not prohibited outright (indeed, these previous legislative efforts had rarely met with success, frequently being voided by the Crown) but performances were required to be licensed by local authorities. The presumption behind licensing was that the contemplated act (in this case, producing theatricals) had the potential to undermine public order or to otherwise cause social harm; the issuing of licenses by government authorities was intended to prevent these potential harmful consequences. While a more thoroughgoing antitheatrical bias continued to hold sway among some even after the War of Independence — the Contintental Congress, for ex-

ample, implored "the several states, to take the most effectual measures for
. . . the suppressing of theatrical entertainments, horse racing, gaming, and
such other diversions as are productive of idleness, dissipation, and a general
depravity of principles and manners" — licensing became the principal form of
theatrical regulation in the new republic.[28] Lacking the requirement that prohibited representations violate some standard of the obscene, licensing permitted public officials a wide discretion to govern sexual portrayals.

By the early 1800s a growing commerce in materials that were sexually explicit, but not blasphemous or overtly political, gave rise to a search for new
regulatory strategies. In the first two decades of the century, states such as Massachusetts and Pennsylvania successfully prosecuted purveyors of obscene
paintings and books on the argument that "whatever outrages decency and is in-
jurious to public morals" was prohibited by the common law. Soon a number of
states enacted statutes prohibiting the publication of obscene books and pictures, giving more substantive form to this common law principle. In 1842 federal lawmakers took up the issue as well, passing a customs law that prohibited
the importation of obscene material. Concern about obscenity remained relatively muted, however, until the outbreak of the Civil War, when reports that
Union soldiers were receiving sexually explicit pictures prompted members
of Congress to pass a law barring "obscene . . . vulgar and indecent" publications from the mail.[29]

That it was anxiety about young men on the front lines that made possible a
more concerted attack upon the obscene was no accident. The experience of
Union soldiers — who were so evocative of the future of the republic, yet so vulnerable to death, disfigurement, and disease — was merely an extreme example
of the dangers that life in the rapidly changing nation presented to all youth.
These dangers included the loosening of ties to family, church, and community,
the temptations of strong drink and gambling dens, the lure of bad companions
and the ruin of reputation, in short, the perils thought to accompany rapid urbanization.[30] Such fears gave rise in the last quarter of the nineteenth century
to an active social purity movement of which the crusade against obscenity was
merely a part.

That crusade began in earnest merely one year after the war's end, when
members of the New York City Young Men's Christian Association charged that
"vile" and "licentious" publications were readily available at the city's newsstands, warning that "the debasing influence of these publications on young
men cannot be over-estimated."[31] They sought to meet this threat by urging the
state legislature to pass a statute outlawing obscenity, and after campaigns in

both 1866 and 1868 they succeeded. It was under this law that Anthony Comstock, the nation's most notorious smut fighter, caused his first arrest when he
conducted the police to a bookseller who, he claimed, had "led astray and corrupted" a friend of his by selling him an improper book.[32] The youthful Comstock is often given credit for singlehandedly beginning the nation's war against
obscenity (he was twenty-eight years old when, in 1872, he became the agent of
the YMCA's newly formed Society for the Suppression of Vice), but it is well to
remember that even the 1873 federal law that bore his name merely strengthened earlier Congressional enactments. Comstock, himself a Civil War veteran,
may be most profitably understood not only as a leader of antivice campaigns
but also as a representative of that generation of young people whose protection furnished the raison d'être of the anti-obscenity laws passed during the
nineteenth century.[33] As much as he was seeking to control others, he was also,
at least at the beginning of his career, seeking to save himself and his peers.

The desire to protect youth was at the center of nineteenth-century understandings of the dangers posed by obscenity. It was articulated not only by
Comstock, in books like *Traps for the Young*, but also by the gentlemen of the
New York YMCA who joined him in initiating the vice society movement and
their compatriots in cities such as Cincinnati, St. Louis, and Boston. The latter
city's Watch and Ward Society, for instance, engineered the passage of a Massachusetts law outlawing the sale of material "manifestly tending to corrupt the
morals of youth."[34] The concern for youth was shared as well by the members
of the Woman's Christian Temperance Union. Anticipating arguments that participants in the broader women's club movement would make in the early twentieth century, the women of the WCTU voiced their concerns about obscenity's
dangers to young people at the same time that they highlighted another theme
of antivice activism: that public displays of sexuality represented "organized
disrespect toward women." For example, in an 1890s campaign to suppress so-
called living pictures on the commercial stage, the New York WCTU drafted a
bill that would prohibit "demoralizing" tableaux vivants in order to "better protect public morals, defend the health and happiness of youth, prevent the degradation of women and girls, and preserve the honor and respect due to woman."
Discussing the bill, WCTU President Frances Willard observed that "it is inevitable that women should condemn public amusements that involve a moral
taint in their sons and daughters." As Alison Parker has demonstrated, the connection between protecting children and protecting "the respect due to
woman" was an obvious and unavoidable one for the WCTU women, who
framed their cultural activism generally as a social expression of their mother-

ing role.[35] Anti-obscenity activists of the late nineteenth century, whether the men of the vice societies or the women of the social purity organizations, agreed that protection of children, home, and family was their main concern.

Reformers' concern for protecting youth was mirrored in the legal definition of the obscene that prevailed in the United States from almost the moment that national attention was directed toward this issue. This definition derived from an 1868 British decision, *Regina v Hicklin*, that was first endorsed by American courts in 1879. In *United States v Bennett* the court upheld the conviction of newspaper publisher D. M. Bennett for advertising Ezra Heywood's free love tract *Cupid's Yokes, or the Binding Forces of Conjugal Life*. First Heywood then Bennett were prosecuted by Anthony Comstock, convicted under the Comstock Act, and imprisoned. When Bennett appealed, the court incorporated *Hicklin* into American law by proclaiming that the test for obscenity was "whether the tendency of the matter charged . . . is to deprave or corrupt those whose minds are open to such immoral influences, and into whose hands a publication of this sort may fall." While this wording did not explicitly focus on youth, the trial judge's formulation revealed the presumptions behind the test: obscene materials were those that would have a bad effect upon "the young and inexperienced." Further, determining whether or not a publication was obscene did not require that the work be considered as a whole; a single word or isolated passage would be enough to condemn it. This so-called Hicklin Rule was almost uniformly upheld by courts throughout the nation until well into the twentieth century and not explicitly repudiated by the U.S. Supreme Court until 1957. In practice it established as the standard for obscenity the potential effect of written or visual material upon children, who were perceived to be society's most impressionable and vulnerable members.[36]

"To deprave or corrupt": this language betrays the belief, shared by the nation's moral reformers, legislators, and judges, that obscenity left unchecked would pollute and contaminate the entire nation, beginning with the children. Comstock, the movement's most eloquent publicist, gave voice to the fears of many when he declared that

> this cursed business of obscene literature works beneath the surface, and like a canker worm, secretly eats out the moral life and purity of our youth. . . .
> It breeds lust. Lust defiles the body, debauches the imagination, corrupts the mind, deadens the will, destroys the memory, sears the conscience, hardens the heart, and damns the soul. . . . This traffic has made rakes and libertines in society — skeletons in many a household. The family is polluted,

home desecrated, and each generation born into the world is more and more cursed by the inherited weakness, the harvest of this seed-sowing of the Evil one.[37]

Comstock, who saw his antivice activism as a religious mission and privately compared his work with that of Jesus, may have been more sensationalist than other opponents of vice when he charged that Satan was directly responsible for the traffic in obscenity. Nonetheless, his vivid description of the effects of "lust" captured well the beliefs of his colleagues that obscenity threatened the social order.

A broad range of materials fell under the rubric of the obscene in the late nineteenth century. The Comstock Law prohibited carriage by mail of any

> obscene, lewd, or lascivious book, pamphlet, picture, paper, print or other publication of an indecent character, or any article or thing designed or intended for the prevention of contraception or the procuring of abortion, [or] any article or thing intended or adapted for any indecent or immoral use or nature, [or] any . . . book, pamphlet, advertisement or notice of any kind giving information, directly or indirectly, where, or how, or of whom, or by what means either of the things before mentioned may be obtained or made.[38]

"Little Comstock" laws passed by many states often went farther, criminalizing the sale or purchase of such materials. But what exactly was characterized as an obscene work? To Comstock's mind, at least, any public reference to sexual desire or sexual practice qualified as obscene, because it violated the boundary between the private life of the family, to which any sexual expression ought to be confined, and public life. In the courts, as Rochelle Gurstein has argued, this impulse was expressed in two ways. The obscene was variously defined as material that was "indecent" — that is, material bringing "that which is 'unfit to be seen or heard'" into public sight or hearing — and as material that aroused lust in its consumer. This dual emphasis on both the inherent attributes and the effects of sexually explicit matter made possible the successful prosecution of serious works of social criticism, sex education tracts, advertisements for contraceptives, and outright pornography alike.[39]

The desire to encompass so much within the category of obscenity was one response to the growing commodification of sexuality in the nation's urban culture. Indeed, one scholar has described the mid-nineteenth century as "the halcyon years of commercialized sex" in New York City, and this characterization undoubtedly held true for many cities.[40] Commercial sex was not limited to the expansion of prostitution. Concert saloons, dance halls, and restaurants all offered public spaces for expressing sexual desire and for arranging extramarital liaisons. Images of nude or seminude women could be purchased at cigar stores, were displayed in saloons and pool halls, and could be found in national media like the *Police Gazette*.[41] Even marital sexuality was drawn into the commercialization of sex, as married women perused advertisements for contraceptives and "female remedies" and availed themselves of the services of professional abortionists.[42] This sexual commodification, already well underway in the mid-nineteenth century, only intensified as the century came to a close. The "cheap amusements" that came to dominate urban commercial culture — dance halls and dime museums, amusement parks and vaudeville theaters, burlesque halls and, finally, the nickelodeons that mushroomed after the turn of the century — all appealed to their patrons by emphasizing the pleasures not only of heterosocial leisure but also of heterosexual, and occasionally homosexual, desire.[43]

Nineteenth-century anti-obscenity crusaders sought to dam the flood of sexual commerce that, they believed, threatened the nation's future. Their campaigns were defensive, and, as a result, the obscenity regime that they erected was an unstable one from its beginnings, always vulnerable to assault and erosion. The first attacks came not primarily from the purveyors of commercial sex, however, but from political radicals. From the 1870s into the 1890s freethinkers, free-lovers, and some birth control advocates battled against enactment and enforcement of obscenity statutes, charging — accurately — that such laws were frequently used to suppress critiques of the prevailing sexual, religious, or political order. Few of these men and women completely opposed the regulation of obscenity, however; free love advocate Ezra Heywood, for example, bemoaned the "alarming increase of obscene prints and pictures."[44] In their romantic understanding of sexuality as an expression of individual autonomy and spiritual union, free-lovers, like antivice activists, rejected "commercialized vice"; the difference between the two groups came in their definition of what constituted commercialized vice. Free-lovers included the institution of marriage, which they called "the legalized slavery of women," while excluding serious discussions of contraception or human sexual relations; the views of antivice activists were exactly opposite. Yet both movements were responding, in different ways, to the commodification of sex.[45]

In the early twentieth century the attack on the nation's obscenity laws took new forms. In 1902 a small group of what we would now call free-speech absolutists formed the Free Speech League in New York City. Having founded the group in response to government suppression of anarchist speech in the wake of the assassination of President William McKinley, participants in the Free Speech League quickly expanded their mission to oppose government suppression of obscenity as well, declaring that it was their purpose to "make it possible for anybody to say anything anywhere."[46] The group's most active member was iconoclast lawyer Theodore Schroeder, who argued in numerous publications that it was "as true of obscenity, as of every witch, that it exists only in the minds of those who believe in it."[47] Schroeder was joined in his endeavor by such men as Edward Bond Foote, a physician whose resistance to the Comstock Act extended back into the 1870s, and journalist Lincoln Steffens; radicals Emma Goldman and Margaret Sanger also had close ties to the league.[48]

At the same time, a broader spectrum of citizens had begun to reproach Anthony Comstock for his excesses, even as they continued to support the vice society movement generally. In the first decade of the twentieth century Comstock undertook several campaigns that brought him widespread ridicule and resentment. In 1906, for example, he raided the offices of New York's Art Students' League. The vice reformer confiscated their catalog, which contained a number of nude studies, and arrested the young female bookkeeper who had sold it to him. Comstock claimed that he was moved to act by the complaint of a mother whose daughter had received the catalog, and he justified his action as always: "These pictures are improper and immoral. They are hurtful to the rising generation." Comstock prevailed in court, and the offending catalogs were destroyed. But, just as worthy of note, Comstock was censured not only by the city's artists (the lawyer for the Art Students' League called him "a degenerate blind to the beauties of life") but also by ordinary New Yorkers, who criticized him both for arresting a nineteen-year-old woman and for proceeding against "legitimate" art. Even such steadfast supporters of the Comstock Act as the editors of the New York Times could offer only diffident endorsement of his behavior, noting that it was "absurd for Mr. Comstock or any one else to say that the magazine was, in the words of the law, 'obscene, indecent, filthy, and disgusting.' . . . But some of its illustrations were thoughtlessly chosen. The incident, disagreeable as it is, and sure to be misinterpreted, may serve to make those conducting the magazine more cautious in the future."[49] Other defenses of Comstock excused his "possible excess of zeal" by citing the higher good — the necessity of a war against impurity.[50] Such half-hearted endorsements refracted the more common response of outrage.

The attack on Comstock might be seen merely as a response to the vice fighter's poor judgment in proceeding against reputable artists and organizations rather than the "pornographers" and sex radicals who served as his earlier targets. But several unsuccessful prosecutions of allegedly obscene plays suggest that a wider assault on the legal regime governing obscenity was underway, even if it was still in its infancy. In 1900 New York police closed *Sapho* after journalists and others, including the president of the New York Mothers' Club, complained about the Broadway production. They arrested Olga Nethersole, whose portrayal of a prostitute allegedly crossed the line of decency when she allowed herself to be carried into her bedroom by a man to whom she was not married and who, the staging made clear, spent the entire night.[51] Significantly, the presiding judge's charge to the jury deviated from the standards that had been set out in the nineteenth century. Among his instructions came the warning:

> You must remember that you are not the guardians of the morals of this community, or the participants in a crusade against vice. . . . In regard to the suggestiveness of the play, you must not consider whether or not it is suggestive, but whether it is a positive offense to public decency; not whether it would shock the modesty of an innocent young girl, but whether it shocks the sensibilities of the people at large.[52]

The jury deliberated for only fifteen minutes before acquitting Nethersole, to the cheers of New York City suffragists. Similarly, the producer of George Bernard Shaw's prostitution-themed play *Mrs. Warren's Profession* was cleared of violating obscenity statutes in 1906. In announcing their 2-1 decision in favor of acquittal, the judges of New York's Court of Special Sessions laid out the test for obscenity to be "whether a production is naturally calculated to excite in the spectator impure imagination and whether the other incidents and qualities, however attractive, are merely accessory to this as the primary or main purpose of the representation." Justice Olmstead contended that the play did not meet that test, for "the unlovely, the repellent, the disgusting in the play are merely accessories to the main purpose of the drama, which is an attack on certain social conditions relating to the employment of women."[53]

In both cases the two primary precepts of the Hicklin Rule were rejected by the courts. The star of *Sapho* was acquitted because the judge's charge had replaced the vulnerable child with the "people at large," and while the hint of extramarital sex might indeed corrupt an innocent young girl it was unlikely to do the same to the average New Yorker. The legal vindication of Shaw's play rested upon a rejection of the doctrine that a work could be found obscene on the basis of an isolated passage, without regard for the intention of the author.

Rulings such as these were not the order of the day, even in New York City. They suggest, however, the extent to which the presumptions underlying the nineteenth-century obscenity regime had already begun to erode, at the same time that they provide a hint of new directions. These changes were also reflected in the creation, in 1909, of the National Board of Censorship of Motion Pictures, a New York-based organization that offered the first institutional articulation of the principles underlying democratic moral authority. It is with the National Board of Censorship that this study begins.

PART I

Moral Panics and Moral Panaceas

CHAPTER 1

"To Protect the Morals of Young People": Regulating Motion Pictures

On Christmas Day, 1908, New York City mayor George McClellan gave the city's Christian clergy a gift when, in response to their complaints, he revoked the licenses of every nickelodeon in New York. Motion picture exhibitors greeted the mayor's action with outrage and lawsuits, but other New Yorkers thanked him for protecting children's moral and physical safety. Among those praising McClellan was one parent who only wished that the mayor had acted more quickly. This parent's daughter had been spending every Sunday at a motion picture theater and as a result, it seems, had run away from home. Although she had since returned, her parent lamented that she was "ruined, and will never be the same child again."[1] The charge that the "pictures" had ruined the morals of New York youth had already become a common refrain, just several years after nickelodeons sprouted up around the city.

Mayor McClellan's assault upon the city's nickelodeons was merely the first skirmish in a coming struggle over the regulation of motion picture content. From 1908 until 1921 New York City reformers, politicians, and representatives of the motion picture industry debated whether to implement "voluntary" or government control of the movies. One result of these debates was the creation of the National Board of Censorship of Motion Pictures, a Progressive-era experiment in voluntarism and industrial self-regulation, the purpose of which was to arrest the movement toward expanded state authority over the movies. Ultimately the experiment failed, for in 1921 legislators created an official board that censored every motion picture shown in the state until 1968.

Before the enactment of state censorship, however, a complex local system for film regulation developed. Within the debates about local regulation can be heard early articulations of the vocabulary that would come to dominate public debate about obscenity for the remainder of the century, a vocabulary focused around the conflicts between adult rights and children's needs, between guarding democracy and protecting the vulnerable. At the center of New York's system of control was the National Board of Censorship of Motion Pictures, which, because of its location in the city, fundamentally shaped local film politics despite its national moniker. The members of the National Board used the language of democracy to create a voluntaristic scheme of motion picture control, in the process taking an important step toward a system of democratic moral authority that obviated a wide range of state regulatory mechanisms for cultural representations of sex. Ironically, however, their efforts to avoid state control facilitated its expansion, especially over those movies that challenged the sexual and gender status quo. Their failure to make voluntary regulation work can be traced to a number of factors, including their foes' ability to link movies to a child audience, the contradictions between the board's democratic rhetoric and its less-than-democratic reality, and the organization's continuing dependence upon state authority for enforcement of its rulings. The debates about local film regulation reveal important fissures among New York's elite regarding the best way to shape twentieth-century urban culture.[2]

CRADLES OF CORRUPTION:
THE PROBLEM OF THE MOTION PICTURES

In 1900 there were fewer than 50 motion picture theaters in New York City. By 1908 this number had grown to over 500. Between 200,000 and 400,000 New Yorkers attended the movies daily, and one-quarter of the city's population went to at least one picture show a week. Admission prices of ten cents for adults and five cents for children made motion pictures particularly attractive to the immigrant and working-class audiences who comprised the bulk of early moviegoers, although even in the first decade of the twentieth century some middle-class New Yorkers also embraced the "pictures." Children were especially visible among moviegoers, constituting a substantial minority of the audience. In a 1911 study of children in New York City 16 percent claimed daily attendance at the movies, while 62 percent stated that they attended at least once a week. The study's authors estimated that, in Manhattan alone, each week 225,000 children under sixteen years old viewed motion pictures.[3]

Such numbers fueled concerns about the unwholesome effects of city life upon urban youngsters, to which Progressive-era reformers devoted immense attention. They bemoaned the "disorganization" of family life among the poor, attacked child labor practices, fretted about immorality and inadequate fresh air within crowded tenements, unsupervised play, and juvenile crime. Motivated both by altruism and the desire to mold the behavior of city residents, they created a network of institutions to resolve such problems, ranging from family and juvenile courts, to organized playgrounds and more standardized schools, to the Boy Scouts and working girls' clubs.[4] They counted so-called commercial recreation, which included nickelodeons, amusement parks, dance halls, vaudeville theaters, and the like, among the most menacing influences of city life, because it offered children and adolescents opportunities for entertainment away from the eyes of parents. More significant, perhaps, than the possibility of autonomous recreation, the commercial nature of these amusements meant that their proprietors were governed not by regard for the moral well-being of their customers but by the desire for profits.[5]

Concern for guarding "innocent" youth from exposure to the immorality of commercial culture predated the Progressive era, of course, and was enshrined in the Hicklin Rule's injunction to protect the most vulnerable individuals.[6] Anxiety about movies' hazards to children encompassed a wide variety of potential problems. Social workers and health experts speculated that too frequent attendance might result in eyestrain and nervousness (the latter from a combination of overstimulation by the larger-than-life images on the screen and the lack of physical exercise). Still, the most outspoken critics focused their attack upon the moral consequences of the medium. The content of motion pictures gave them special cause for concern, and they condemned nickelodeons as "cradles of corruption" upon whose screens children saw drinking, close dancing, and women wearing tights.[7]

Indeed, many early films did challenge middle-class notions of morality and respectability. In 1908, for example, a visitor to one of New York City's nickelodeons might see *How a Pretty Girl Sold Her Hair Restorer*, in which a beautiful young woman walked through the streets, accumulating a caravan of gawking men as she made her way to her shop. There, of course, she sold them her remedy for baldness. *The Piker's Dream*, another typical film, depicted a man who fell asleep in an opium den and dreamt of winning big at the race track. The high price of ill-chosen love was also a popular theme. *Romance of a Gypsy Camp* was representative of such films; in it a gypsy girl committed suicide after discovering that the middle-class young man whom she loved was engaged to another.[8] Such films focused the viewers' attention upon women's sexuality, made drug use and gambling the object of humor, and idealized "inappropriate" romantic relationships. Critics of the new entertainment form argued that such pictures set children on a downward path from which they might never escape.[9]

Moving pictures also were condemned for endangering children's morality, especially that of young girls, in more concrete and immediate ways. Much of the criticism of movies focused upon the risks arising from children's unsupervised presence in the nickelodeon. The Reverend H. A. Stimson, for example, asserted that children's association with "degraded" people in the theaters would prove to be the source of their later immorality. Some feared that adolescents would take advantage of the darkened auditorium to practice the kissing and caressing that they saw on the movie screen. Others saw a more serious threat to girls from the male youth and adults who also frequented the theaters. E. Fellows Jenkins of the Society for Prevention of Cruelty to Children warned that girls would be susceptible to sexual advances from their elders: "The darkened rooms, combined with the influence of pictures projected on the screens, have given opportunities for a new form of degeneracy." His colleagues at the Society for the Prevention of Crime warned of a "terrible tale of ruined maidenhood and blighted lives" that followed upon the admission of unescorted young children to the pictures. Such complaints, which combined concerns about the sexual exploitation of girls with opposition to young women's sexual experimentation and expression, suggested that motion picture theaters were "cradles of corruption" in more ways than one.[10]

By 1907 and 1908 these fears led Protestant and Catholic clergymen and representatives of child-saving organizations to pressure city officials to act against the movies. Especially vocal were the Protestant clergy who belonged to the Interdenominational Committee for the Suppression of Sunday Vaudeville, which campaigned for the enforcement of laws against live theater performances on the Christian Sabbath. When these ministers turned their attention to motion pictures, they widened their attack to argue that movies were immoral in general. This enabled them to broaden their coalition to encompass Catholic clergy who did not advocate Sunday closing and other reformers concerned with commercial culture, including members of antivice and child protection societies.[11] As a result of this pressure the New York City police commissioner investigated motion pictures, but he reported that his inspectors found no "lewd or salacious" films and that the new medium posed no threat to the morality of either adults or children. This conclusion was also offered by two reform organizations, the Women's Municipal League and the People's Institute, whose members cooperated in a similar investigation. They spoke in glowing terms of the essential purity of the movies. Contending that the frequency of indecent pictures was negligible, these reformers argued that "the moving picture show is a constructive influence, meeting a genuine need in the people."[12]

Despite these reports that motion pictures presented no moral harm, opposition to the movies continued to mount, especially among clerics. Ignoring the results of his police department's investigation, Mayor McClellan convened public hearings on the movie problem. Although McClellan declared at the outset that he was concerned only with the questions of Sunday closings and the physical safety of movie patrons, much of the testimony by clergy and child advocates detailed the "demoralization," "corruption," and "contamination" of children by the movies.[13]

Seeking to defend their burgeoning industry from these attacks, New York's motion picture exhibitors questioned the motives of movie critics and suggested that, far from posing a threat, motion pictures benefited the morality of children and adults alike. One exhibitor proclaimed that movies made working-class men and boys more virtuous, by diverting little boys from gambling in the streets, and their fathers from the saloons. They denied that the nickelodeon provided a particularly conducive arena for sexual activity; as a witness at the hearings noted, if young people didn't "take advantage of the darkness in the theatres[,] they will do it in the parks." At the same time, they sought to defuse testimony that immoral activities took place in the darkened auditoriums by pointing to a few "bad" theaters and demanding action against them. Using racial stereotypes to emphasize the differences between their own theaters and these bad ones, industry representatives asked the mayor to close one theater, which, they alleged, contained an audience of "twenty four Chinamen and seventeen young girls and three or four adults" on a recent visit.[14]

At the same time that motion picture exhibitors and producers, as well as a few allies, challenged the view that movies in general threatened children, they suggested that the nickelodeon's critics were trying to enforce a moral code that had no place in a cosmopolitan city like New York. One industry representative warned that "you can't make a Sunday school out of New York City." Another picture fan charged that those calling for action against the movies were "using innocent children as a subterfuge to conceal the real motive of their opposition." He did not name their "real" motive, but he may have been implying that critics of the movies were being manipulated by vaudeville theater owners who feared competition from the new entertainment form. Throughout this testimony ran the theme that it was the motion picture exhibitors, rather than clergy and reformers, who articulated the will of New York's population.[15] The suggestion that critics of the motion pictures were "undemocratic" would become a prime strategy in the upcoming battles to prevent government censorship of movies in New York City.

Despite these attempts to defray criticisms of the movies, Mayor McClellan's

action at the close of the hearings proved the effectiveness of condemning motion pictures in the name of saving children. It had been widely predicted that
the mayor would prohibit Sunday exhibition of motion pictures and close a few
dozen theaters that were unsafe or showed especially racy films. But, to the surprise of many, the mayor ordered the revocation of the licenses of every nickelodeon in New York, over 550 in all.[16] His claim that he was motivated by concern for the physical safety of filmgoers reflected the limitations of the licensing
laws, which permitted revocation only under specified conditions that did not
include immoral exhibitions. But concerns about morality had furnished the
public pressure that prompted his action.[17]

Mayor McClellan's dramatic move changed the complexion of film regulation in New York City and elsewhere in the nation. In one sense the license revocation proved no solution to the motion picture problem. New York's motion
picture exhibitors immediately secured injunctions to keep their theaters open,
and McClellan's order was overturned in the courts. Nonetheless, the revocation
had other, more long-term effects.[18] Most important, it convinced New York
City's motion picture exhibitors that they must defuse criticisms of the industry
or face continued harassment from city officials and reformers. The exhibitors'
association asked the People's Institute to create a censorship mechanism that
would regulate the moral content of motion pictures. The institute, coauthor of
the recent report exonerating the industry, was a prominent educational and
cultural organization. It sponsored a variety of adult educational projects, including a popular lecture series that attracted an immigrant, working-class, and
often left-leaning audience, and also sought to encourage constructive cultural
productions. One of its programs supported "clean" legitimate theater productions by offering free or subsidized tickets to poor theatergoers.[19] In March 1909
the members of the institute established the association that would soon become
known as the National Board of Censorship of Motion Pictures. For the next
twelve years the presence of this regulatory agency, more than any other factor,
shaped the debates about the motion picture problem.[20]

REPRESENTING PUBLIC OPINION: THE NATIONAL BOARD
OF CENSORSHIP OF MOTION PICTURES

The Board of Censorship created by the People's Institute in 1909 was conceived
as a purely local effort to protect motion picture exhibitors from financial loss.
Through voluntary cooperation with an unofficial censorship organization, the

exhibitors hoped to demonstrate their goodwill and avoid future license revocations or criminal prosecutions, while placing the blame for immoral pictures upon film producers. In the original plan board representatives were to inspect films while they were showing in local theaters, informing exhibitors which films were acceptable and which were not. The Association of Moving Picture Exhibitors of New York agreed to require that its members refuse to exhibit any film that was disapproved by the Board of Censorship. Further, the association would fund the board's activities for three months.[21]

Even before the board began its activities, however, the People's Institute had enlisted the support of the Motion Picture Patents Company (MPPC), a trust organization of film manufacturers that endeavored to establish a monopoly over motion picture production in the United States. The manufacturers, also fearing the effect of continued public criticism upon the industry, agreed to provide film viewing facilities for the actual censoring work, enabling members of the board to view the master prints of films before they were released for exhibition. By June, the MPPC was providing much of the board's funding as well.[22]

When film producers agreed to cooperate with the Board of Censorship, it was fundamentally transformed. Now the board's censors could do more than approve or condemn a complete motion picture that had already been exhibited in a theater. They could also order the elimination or alteration of offensive scenes, and they could prevent condemned films from ever being shown. Further, its access to films before distribution meant that the Board of Censorship's influence extended beyond New York City to the rest of the nation. By early 1910 the board's name had officially been changed to the National Board of Censorship of Motion Pictures, and its members claimed widespread control over motion pictures exhibited throughout the U.S.[23]

The National Board of Censorship embodied many of the premises as well as some of the contradictions of Progressive-era reform. Its founders sought to control and tame city amusements through the creation of a bureaucratic organization that combined the principles of industrial self-regulation and "disinterested" voluntarism. Their reasons for committing to such an organization varied. Motion picture entrepreneurs likely believed that the censorship board would provide a more tractable, more lenient, or at least more consistent form of regulation than that which might be instituted by municipal authorities subject to political pressures. The social reformers who set up the board, on the other hand, seized the opportunity to create a rationalized system for shaping the urban environment, one that was operated by professional social workers and volunteer "experts" rather than by municipal officials who might be corrupt. Both groups asserted that the purpose of this combination of self-regulation and voluntarism was to help the motion picture become a constructive force in modern life. They aimed not for "negative" repression but for "positive" creation of commercial culture. The National Board of Censorship constituted an attempt by industry members and Progressive activists to preempt state regulation by inventing for themselves the responsibility of controlling the movies.[24]

Nonetheless, if the voluntary model was to work, the board's self-regulatory aspect must be minimized, for censorship by an unofficial board had to have the confidence of those interested in the question of public amusements, including clergy, reformers, and government officials. Because it was essential that the board appear to be an autonomous organization, one not subject to the whims of the industry it regulated, a respected social service institution organized the board, and its supervisory governing board included representatives of such groups as the Children's Aid Society, the Public Education Association, and the Women's Municipal League. The people who staffed the board were similarly "objective." Professional social workers — men such as John Collier, who began his career working with immigrants and later served as the nation's commissioner of Indian affairs, and Orrin Cocks, a Presbyterian minister who was employed by the YMCA and the New York Federation of Churches before coming to the National Board — constituted its paid staff. Its volunteer censors, who ranged in number from five, at the very first censoring session, to over three hundred in the 1920s, were mostly white middle-class and upper-middle-class women and men. Many of them were either professionals — educators and social workers — or otherwise involved in Progressive reform, for instance, as clubwomen.[25]

The personnel of the National Board promoted their organization as a demonstration of the possibilities of cooperation between industry and social welfare institutions. National Board members maintained that their own interests and the interests of the moviegoing public were identical with those of moviemakers. Because audiences craved moral, educational, and artistic films, they argued, motion picture exhibitors' and producers' profits would rise if they offered "clean" motion pictures. Implicit in this argument was the belief that voluntary censorship of films could make movies palatable to a larger, and presumably middle-class, audience. The role of the National Board of Censorship was to represent this "concurrence of interests between the public and the film business."[26]

Despite these assertions of harmonious interests, internal contradictions plagued the structure and purpose of the National Board of Censorship. The board actually obscured the relationships between the motion picture industry, government officials, regulators, and entertainment consumers, weaving all of these into relations of interdependence while presenting the illusion of separateness. The National Board maintained the appearance of objective voluntarism, but its financial dependence upon the motion picture industry reinforced its self-regulatory aspect, leaving it open to criticism on these grounds. While their organization was created to circumvent a movement for government censorship, board members themselves engaged in preexhibition censorship. Technically the National Board avoided the taint of state-sponsored censorship, but by empowering their volunteers — persons outside of the motion picture industry — to take scissors to film, the organization seemed to endorse the *idea* of censorship: that an authority beside the filmmaker ought to make decisions about what was morally acceptable content.[27] Although board members constantly portrayed their organization as a democratic one that represented the interests of the consumer, they simultaneously constituted themselves as a group of experts who possessed the authority to regulate entertainment. Finally, over time the personnel of the National Board came to depend upon state mechanisms to enforce their decisions, yet they championed the idea that the state was not and should not be involved in censorship. From 1909 until the early 1920s, the censorship board's success in defusing demands for government censorship had a direct relationship to its ability to mask these dependencies. Board members' primary strategy for reconciling these contradictions — one imagines, both to themselves as well as to their wider audience of reformers, consumers, and government officials — was to develop a language of democratic moral authority.

This language reflected the strong influence of democratic thought within the Progressive ethos. Historians who agree that there was no one coherent ideology uniting those who called themselves Progressives acknowledge nonetheless that many activists perceived themselves as working on behalf of *the people* or, if they shied away from the potentially radical meanings of that term, a more broadly defined common weal. Seeking to reunite a society that they believed was increasingly fragmented by ethnicity and religion, hoping to avoid class warfare by ameliorating the worst effects of industrial capitalism, Progressives spoke the language of democracy even if, sometimes, they also engaged in profoundly antidemocratic strategies for reforming the nation's cities. Settlement workers especially embraced an ethic of cultural pluralism, praising the innocence and the ambition to "improve" themselves that they saw in the immigrants in whose neighborhoods they lived, at the same time that they cited that innocence as need for their own protective activities and advocated assimilation of the nation's newest residents to American institutions. Social workers and Progressive activists who positioned themselves on the left of the political spectrum believed that their authority lay to a large degree in their respect for the values, and their protection of the interests, of the people among whom they lived and worked. Those who created the National Board of Censorship, especially the staff of the People's Institute, had close ties to this liberal wing of Progressive reform. They defined themselves as cultural arbiters rather than censors and presented their organization as the people's democratic alternative to state regulation.[28]

The National Board of Censorship devised a theory of democratic morality that rejected the idea of a single higher moral standard to which all Americans should be held, an idea that underlay demands for government censorship. Board members traced the organization's authority over the motion picture industry not to the volunteer censors' moral superiority but to their ability to articulate public opinion to filmmakers. Doing so was more democratic, board personnel thought, because it required sensitivity to variation in "standards of taste" among Americans. They proclaimed that, unlike advocates of government censorship, they respected the morals of the average American:

> The principal reason . . . for the existence of the National Board is that it is the agent of public opinion in the moral regulation of photoplays. Public opinion is not represented by professional uplifters and reformers — the collection of moralists generally — but is represented by the thoughtful and intelligent attitude of the great mass of mankind which is not greatly affected with "isms" of any sort.

The women and men who made up the National Board of Censorship tried to "embrace multitudinous points of view and concepts of morality," meshing the many diverse voices of Americans into one democratic voice that would advise the motion picture industry on what it could and could not portray on the screen.[29]

Board members contrasted their "editing" and advising services with government censorship, which they viewed as a despotic imposition of moral absolutism upon the people. They charged that state-appointed censors were likely to enforce "the opinions of . . . one class or group"; unlike the National Board, they "would pass upon films arbitrarily and autocratically as individuals without consulting local public opinion."[30] By identifying themselves as the true representatives of the people, board members tried to pull off the tricky maneuver of simultaneously criticizing and engaging in preexhibition censorship, delegitimizing state control over the representation of sexuality in films while affirming that the movie industry was being regulated in a democratic manner. Not accidentally, advocacy of a democratic moral authority also justified granting greater latitude in movie standards, because it rested upon both the perception and the reality that immigrant and working-class New Yorkers tolerated a wide range of sexual portrayals on the screen.[31]

The leaders of the National Board tried to constitute themselves the true representatives of the people in several ways. Occasionally they conveyed the impression that the personnel of the board themselves embodied the class diversity of the American people, for example when they described board members as citizens "from all walks of life."[32] More often board representatives declared themselves the champions of the poor. Sometimes reflecting the same paternalism they attributed to their opponents, they proclaimed their respect for the morality of

the vast army of the common people, among whom were the toilers, the submerged, the life-wearied, defeated and starved, who had found, in the little nickelodeons where the magic screen with its moving shadows was hung, food for their spiritual hunger and a blessed means of recreation.

They condemned those puritans who sought to "restrict the amusements of the poor."[33] In its usage by National Board members, *the people* was an elastic term. Often it clearly conveyed advocacy of the interests of the working class; at other times it seemed to include anyone who was not a "reformer" (National Board members saw themselves as "public spirited," not as reformers). Nonetheless, it served as a legitimating term, signaling the democratic values of these motion picture "editors."

The class composition of the National Board gave this democratic rhetoric a hollow ring, for the board included few, if any, working-class New Yorkers. Rather, the censoring committees as well as the board's leadership were composed of middle-class city residents who imagined themselves "liberal-minded" friends of the people: "cultured men and women, trained to look on the activities of life from the broad viewpoint of their social significance . . . in sympathy with the best life and aspiration of the people."[34] Yet, despite this paternalism and the domination of the board by white elite New Yorkers, the significance of their language of moral authority remains undiminished. The women and men of the National Board sought to establish their authority by positing not their own superior morality but their ability to interpret and articulate the moral standards of a variety of individuals in different social positions in order to "represent public opinion" to film manufacturers. Their assertion of a democratic moral authority thus constituted a direct attack upon an ideal of moral superiority that provided the cornerstone of the culture of moral absolutism. It also offered the middle-class activists of the National Board a language — one that claimed an amorphous class position ranging from identification with working-class interests to an alliance with a ubiquitous *people* — with which they could counter the efforts of other middle-class activists to structure the state.

FIRE IN THIS WORLD AND THE WORLD TO COME: MUNICIPAL REFORM AND THE MOVIES

The creation of the National Board of Censorship did not solve the problem of the motion pictures but it did complicate it. At the same time some reformers remained skeptical that a voluntary censorship board could provide adequate protection for children's morality, National Board personnel tried to redefine the problem by seeking to emphasize physical rather than moral safety of moviegoers. Maintaining that their organization had already improved the content of the movies, they began pressing for a "rationalization" of the licensing laws governing motion picture exhibition. These laws were quite lax, and the vast majority of movie theaters in New York City faced little in the way of requirements for construction, ventilation, fireproofing, or emergency exits.[35] While the campaign to upgrade the building codes for new motion picture theaters was framed as a way of protecting patrons from the risk of fire and other hazards, it would also benefit the industry by making new theaters more attractive to middle-class audiences.[36]

When National Board staff succeeded in having legislation introduced in the Board of Aldermen to establish licensing requirements for New York's movie theaters, critics of motion pictures' morality saw an opportunity for advancing their own ideas about what was wrong with movies and how to make it right. Such reformers as Canon William S. Chase, rector of Brooklyn's Christ Church, and the members of the antivice Society for the Prevention of Crime and the Women's Municipal League (a good-government group) believed that the purpose of government licensing ought to include guarding the purity as well as the physical safety of moviegoers, especially child patrons.[37] As one woman who contended that moral stewardship should be the city's first priority wrote to the editor of the New York Times, "Fire protection and proper ventilation are good things, but of what avail is it to insure against fire in this world and invite it for the world to come. . . . By all means let us remove the impure air, but remove also the impure picture."[38] Thus, National Board members' attempt to upgrade physical standards for movie theaters offered an occasion for their opponents to advocate the expansion of state authority over the content of the pictures. The discussion about ventilation requirements and exit signs became a debate about whether or not to establish government censorship of the movies.

The contest over licensing motion picture theaters that raged from 1911 to 1913 was framed by participants sometimes as a debate about children's needs and adult rights, sometimes as a debate about corruption and democracy, but the terms of the debate camouflaged important economic and political struggles as well. Vaudeville entrepreneurs lobbied for the institution of strict construction and safety requirements that would raise the costs of operating motion picture theaters and thus limit the competition that the movies posed to the cheap theater. Conversely, some nickelodeon managers opposed any legislative requirements that would increase their expenses. At the same time, Tammany Democrats, Republicans, and independent politicians battled among themselves for political advantage and, some observers suggested, for graft money paid by the theater entrepreneurs whose interests they represented. Finally, volunteer censors and antivice reformers fought to legitimate particular strategies for regulating an emerging mass entertainment industry and, in so doing, to structure a relationship between themselves, the motion picture industry, and the state.[39]

These immediate material interests became submerged in a two-year struggle over the shape of licensing legislation in which the adequacy of the National Board of Censorship's protection of children's morality emerged as the fundamental question. Because a number of government officials, including Mayor William Gaynor, argued that the existence of the board effectively prevented the exhibition of immoral motion pictures, discrediting the organization was one of the key strategies for advocates of government censorship.[40] Shortly after National Board members began agitating for an overhaul of licensing laws, the reformers of the Women's Municipal League set out to accomplish this task. In previous years the league had been perceived as friendly to the motion picture industry. Its members had collaborated with the People's Institute in the 1908 investigation exonerating the movies, and the league was an early supporter of the National Board of Censorship. But its relationship with the board soured in 1911, when Mrs. Gilbert Montague, chair of the group's Committee on Motion Pictures, charged that board members hid the fact that the Motion Picture Patents Company supported the board financially. In November Mrs. Montague publicly accused the board of "catering to trade interests," claiming that the board's reliance on industry support as well as its lack of legal authority made it inefficient and too lenient. She concluded that "the National Board of Censorship does not satisfactorily perform the work for which it was organized, and that this work cannot be satisfactorily performed without the exercise of authority which lawfully can be vested only in some branch of the local government."[41] Led by Mrs. Montague, the Women's Municipal League demanded that the new licensing laws include government censorship of motion pictures.[42]

Although members of the National Board of Censorship immediately denied that they had hidden anything, the league's allegations cemented the shift of public debate away from concern about physical safety and toward the question of municipal censorship.[43] The Women's Municipal League succeeded in placing the necessity of film censorship at the center of debates about licensing by attacking board members' objectivity and assailing the board's credibility as a Progressive institution, showing it to be not disinterested but corrupt. The effect of the league's attack was to bring to the surface those economic relationships that were obscured by the board's presentation of itself as a voluntary, democratic regulatory institution.

In the next eighteen months New York City aldermen introduced at least six different sets of ordinances regulating motion picture theaters, and every piece of legislation offered contained a clause on motion picture morality.[44] Most of the proposed ordinances sought to create preexhibition censorship of motion pictures, variously empowering as censor the police commissioner, an unnamed member of the License Bureau, or teachers and other employees of the municipal Department of Education.[45] Even the ordinance advocated by members of the National Board of Censorship, known as the Folks ordinance (after Alderman Ralph Folks, who introduced it), provided for "Motion Picture Inspectors" who would be empowered to examine the "character of exhibitions" at theaters. Since no funds to hire such inspectors were contemplated, the provision was intended to mean little. But the clamor for preexhibition censorship was so great that National Board staff member John Collier felt compelled to justify the clause on the grounds that it gave city officials "the inquisitorial and arbitrary power of the original Roman censor."[46]

Because reform mayor William Gaynor supported the Folks ordinance, it became the centerpiece of the debates about licensing overhaul. Mayor Gaynor, a former municipal judge and something of a maverick, opposed all proposed ordinances that created preexhibition motion picture censorship on the grounds that such laws would violate constitutional guarantees of free speech, a position that exceeded even the arguments against censorship articulated by National Board members. Warning, "Once revive the censorship and there is no telling how far we may carry it," Gaynor insisted that only the Folks ordinance could appropriately protect children's needs for physical safety while also protecting adults' rights, for its "morality" clause permitted inspection of films only after they had been released for public exhibition.[47] A variety of organizations such as the Citizens' Union, the New York Federation of Churches, and the City Club also pressed for enactment of the Folks ordinance, holding that censorship, if it was necessary, should come later. The most immediate need was for the protection of the physical safety of the children who went to the movies.[48]

"Reform sentiment" was not unified on the question of motion picture regulation, however, and the members of the Women's Municipal League and the Society for the Prevention of Crime led a campaign to defeat the proposed law because it lacked official preexhibition censorship.[49] While league members continued to concentrate their attack upon the objectivity of the National Board, their allies contrasted the needs of children and the rights of adults, arguing that "freedom of speech . . . is not to be construed as of higher authority than freedom . . . of the child to grow up in an atmosphere free from immoral suggestions." Ultimately, however, Mayor Gaynor's insistence that no licensing reform include preexhibition censorship prevailed, probably because he vetoed every law that did not meet his standards. In July 1913 an exhausted Board of Aldermen passed the Folks ordinance.[50]

Although censorship advocates had succeeded in defining the terms of the debate over licensing motion pictures, they did not accomplish their goals. The reasons for their failure were not limited to Mayor Gaynor's persistent opposition. The February 1913 deaths of two women trying to escape a movie theater in a fire panic helped to make the arguments of those advocating protection of physical safety seem more pressing than concern over fire "in the world to come."[51] More important, the disagreements among reformers about how to control the movies revealed competing visions of Progressivism: one that envisioned an increase in private, voluntary regulatory mechanisms that were purportedly free from the taint of corruption believed to accompany big-city politics and another that looked to the state as the only repository of power strong enough to control industries of mass production and mass communication.

The Folks ordinance may have ultimately succeeded because it combined these two visions, making the state responsible for the physical and, to a lesser degree, the moral safety of movie patrons but also leaving spaces within which voluntary organizations such as the National Board of Censorship could operate.

Far from ending debate over movies' morality the passage of the Folks ordinance shaped the contours of future conflict over motion pictures, permitting the National Board to retain its authority over their content but also laying the foundation for an expansion of state authority. The section of the law empowering motion picture inspectors to monitor film morality made the commissioner of licenses, to whom the inspectors would report, potentially the single most powerful government authority in relation to the movies. At the same time, the fact that the law did not set forth a specific censorship procedure continued the obligation of the police and courts to enforce laws prohibiting obscene performances. The law therefore reinforced the claims of each of these arenas of state authority to power over motion pictures. And the absence of a preexhibition censorship provision permitted members of the National Board of Censorship to continue to claim a role in the regulation of film. The stage was set for increasing conflict between the National Board, state officials, and critics of movie "immorality" over the question of motion picture content.

THE RECOGNIZED STANDARDS OF SEX MORALITY: CENSORSHIP AND SEXUAL REPRESENTATION

Having constructed a role for themselves as experts uniquely qualified to determine whether a film met the standards of the community, after the question of municipal regulation was settled National Board personnel turned their attention to defining those standards. Their success in convincing officials, activists, and film consumers that the standards they devised and enforced, while democratic, nonetheless provided adequate protection to movie audiences was crucial to the National Board's continuing project of preventing government censorship at not only the local but also the state and federal levels. But the board's financial relationship with the motion picture industry qualified its ability to create and enforce such standards. Motion picture studio personnel pressured National Board staff to allow them as much freedom as possible in film production, believing such freedom essential to profits. The members of the National Board tried to reconcile these contradictions when establishing standards.

Therefore, just as they argued for a democratic review process that reflected the values of the "average" person rather than the reformer, board personnel sought to create standards that would protect the adults rather than the children in the audience. Despite the fact that most critics of the movies continued to focus on their effects on youth, National Board staff consistently resisted demands that films be made safe for anyone, from a child of five to an adolescent of fifteen to an adult of fifty. They disputed the contention that children constituted the majority of the audience, estimating their numbers at no more than a quarter of moviegoers. Board members assured the public that in censoring films they tried to keep in mind that children comprised a substantial minority of the audience. But the preponderance of adults, they argued, justified their decision to "never [review] pictures for children alone." Board members believed that judging films by the lowest common denominator would be a "calamity" to the motion picture as an art form.[52]

To offset criticism of this policy, National Board members developed special advisory standards for young people that were intended to help parents decide which motion pictures their children should see. The standards defined representations that were too "gruesome" or frightening for small children and also warned against the portrayal of crime methods or cruelty against animals, reflecting allegations that young boys, especially, learned to engage in such behaviors by watching the movies. "Love-making" was acceptable if it conveyed respect for women and upheld the sanctity of marriage. For example, leers, winks, and suggestive glances were barred, but kissing was permissible if it was not shown with "objectionable detail."[53] The development of children's standards constituted a strategy by which National Board members meant to protect the standards they had created for the film industry in general. By offering guidelines that placed the burden of supervising children's recreation on their parents, National Board members could continue to defend motion pictures as an adult genre.[54]

Rather than establishing standards higher than those of the "general conscience and intelligence of the country," then, board members sought to identify an "irreducible minimum." Until 1914 that was defined in only the most general of ways; for example, board representatives proclaimed that they absolutely forbade "obscenity and obscene suggestions" and eliminated "elements which tend to degrade moral standards or which are in repulsively bad taste."[55] By 1914 the growing number of motion picture producing companies, the increase in film output, the new importance of longer and complex feature films, and a consequent need for more volunteer censors required that the board publish a comprehensive and specific statement of its standards.[56] The document re-stated board personnel's commitment to setting standards at the level of public opinion: "The members of the National Board . . . try to reflect what the people of the United States would think about any given picture were they sitting *en masse* to view" it. It described board prohibitions and guidelines concerning such subjects as insanity, suicide, murder, and the use of narcotics, all of which came under the broadly defined rubric of "morality." However, questions of sexuality figured most prominently in the board's articulation of standards, and thus the statement of standards contained sections on "prolonged passionate love scenes," "insufficient clothing," "infidelity and sex problem plays," "dance halls and objectionable dancing, vulgar flirtations, questionable resorts," and "the social evil."[57]

In general, the members of the National Board maintained that it was not the mere portrayal of sex but the effect upon the spectator of such portrayals with which they were concerned. Indeed, the board's critics were most irritated by its stance that such subjects as dance halls, love scenes, or infidelity had a legitimate place in motion pictures. Board personnel asserted that these subjects had to be handled in a "wholesome" and reserved manner. Board policy curtailed "those prolonged love scenes which are ardent beyond the strict requirements of the dramatic situation," but also maintained that there was a "difference between expressions of affection and sensuality"; it was only the latter that came under special scrutiny. On the other hand, scenes of dance halls were to be presented in such a way that "their sordid nature must be kept in the minds of the spectators."[58]

Despite the effort to set out specific standards, these guidelines often remained vague. In regard to "infidelity and sex problem plays," for instance, National Board members at first merely insisted "that the recognized standards of sex morality be upheld." And in the attempt to censor for the adult audience while still offering a modicum of protection to children, the board's instructions must have led to much confusion. For example, board standards cautioned motion picture producers against, but did not prohibit, the portrayal of saloons, dance halls, and brothels because it was so difficult to achieve the desired effect: such scenes must be "made intellectually suggestive without being made physically stimulating and suggestive." Further, "the Board requires that when these scenes are produced they be made unintelligible to children and innocuous to adolescents."[59]

Slapstick films presented a special problem for the National Board because bodies, and therefore sex, constituted the heart of their comedy. Board members issued a special bulletin on comedies, warning that it would cut scenes that portrayed

> suggestive rolling on women; suggestive placing of legs over the knees of women; . . . smelling of women's underclothes and night clothes (or rubbing face on such); excessive and suggestive wriggling of the body of a man or woman; girls putting hands in man's pants pockets; . . . man and wife or people of opposite sex in bed together; suggestive actions when sitting on lap of man or woman; lustful looks at women's figures, legs, etc., in a way to attract attention to display of person.

The evidence from the records of the board's censoring committees indicates that such scenes were abundant, and repeated warnings to film producers suggest that they continued to be a problem throughout the teens. In 1915, for example, National Board members protested the costume of one film comedian whose trousers were so ill-fitting that "it seems every minute that his person will be exposed." And when members of the censoring committee viewed *Agonies of Agnes* in 1918, they found it necessary to cut out a scene in which a woman and man rolled on top of each other during a fight.[60]

That "suggestive actions" and "lustful looks" remained in motion pictures passed by the National Board suggests that the nature of the organization constrained its members' efforts to uphold stricter standards. Because the board's only punishment to recalcitrant producers was withholding its seal of approval, enforcement was sometimes difficult. Furthermore, the cooperative relationship between the board and the film industry was reflected in the censorship process. This process often involved negotiation between board censors and filmmakers and, in the case of any particular motion picture, specific standards might end up being very loosely applied.

These difficulties are apparent in the censors' inability to control the portrayal of male homosexuality in films. Despite their warnings that the depiction of "degenerates" as the object of humor constituted objectionable vulgarity and bad taste,[61] comic films featuring "sissified" men became increasingly common in the mid-teens. Such films used sexual innuendo and stereotypes about homosexual men to amuse and titillate audiences. *A Pair of Queens*, for example, depicted two "female impersonators"; *The Rogue* portrayed a "feminine" butler afraid of a mouse; and in *Jerry's Winning Way* a female-garbed Jerry "wiggled" his buttocks against the groin of another man.[62] Consequently, in late 1916 or early 1917 the board issued a special bulletin notifying motion picture producers that "any picture given over entirely to the comedy presentation of the sexual pervert will be condemned and that any part of a picture in which such a character is shown with intention to burlesque will be eliminated." They justified this ruling by appealing to the motion picture industry's self-interest, implying that the portrayal of homosexuality would cost the industry the middle-class audience it desired: "For Motion Picture producers to attempt its presentation on the screen is to court loss of prestige as well as time and money."[63]

These warnings often went unheeded, however, and characters who were deemed objectionable by the board continued to appear in films. Throughout the decade the censors ordered the elimination of scenes in which effeminate men appeared or in which one man, dressed as a woman, flirted or danced with another man.[64] The history of one of these films, *Caught with the Goods*, is especially well documented in the board's files. It reveals the process of negotiation between censors and filmmakers that produced a motion picture expressing standards quite different from those originally envisioned by the censors.

Caught with the Goods tells the story of Alice, whose father owns a department store, her fiancé, Harry, and Ray, a store employee who is in love with Alice. Having been spurned by Alice, Ray seeks to win her by framing Harry for shoplifting. When Alice breaks her engagement with Harry, it seems that he will succeed, but finally the scheme is revealed, Ray is arrested, and Harry and Alice reconcile. Incidental to the story, but present in a number of scenes, is a "nance" character — a clerk who is intended to provide comic relief as he sprays himself with perfume, fawns over Harry, Ray, and other assorted men, and prances about the set. In accordance with board policy, the censoring committee that viewed this film ordered the producers to eliminate all scenes portraying this "effeminate clerk." However, the character appeared in so much of the film that if he had been completely excised very little would remain. Triangle Film Corporation appealed these eliminations to the National Board's General Committee. Triangle's representative explained that the company agreed that "those scenes in which the actions of this character suggested that he was a pervert should be eliminated," but nonetheless believed it wrong to assume that "in the minds of the public, every male character who was effeminate was necessarily perverted."[65]

Triangle's argument reflected contemporary instabilities in the definition of perversion, for during the first few decades of the twentieth century medical and popular discourses increasingly emphasized "inappropriate" sexual object choice rather than inappropriate gender role display as the primary indicator of male homosexuality.[66] The Triangle Corporation representative skillfully manipulated this instability as well as the board's commitment to representing public opinion for, after discussion, the General Committee members decided not to remove every scene in which the offending character appeared. Accepting the reasoning that an "effeminate" man was not necessarily a "perverted" one, they voted to eliminate only those parts of the film showing the clerk flirting with another man, stroking and attempting to kiss the hand of the store detective, and trying to embrace Ray. Despite these eliminations, in the revised film the clerk appears enamored of every man who crosses his path. It is likely that many members of the audience would have recognized the clerk as a stereotyped homosexual, a fact upon which Triangle Films undoubtedly counted.[67] Thus, the process of negotiation with filmmakers foiled National Board members' attempts to exclude "sexual perverts" from American motion pictures.

The board's formulation and enforcement of policies on female nudity presented a different set of difficulties. The board's 1914 statement of standards offered a nuanced stance toward the question of costuming or its lack. Noting that "frank exposure of the person is much less objectionable than the exposure which is partly hidden and partly revealed," board members suggested that decisions about costuming could only be made contextually. It would not necessarily be immoral to display what they called "savages" in their native dress, even if this involved nudity; but a picture that showed (presumably white) women "almost wholly dressed, but yet displaying a lavish amount of lingerie" would be condemned. Another statement of the board's standards, issued at about the same time, maintained that there was "nothing innately immoral or indecent in nudity."[68]

However, critics throughout the nation continued to voice complaints about the indecency of women's dress in motion pictures. In early 1916 the board proclaimed that, as a result of the increasing occurrence of female nudity in films, as well as unfavorable public opinion, all motion pictures featuring nude figures would be given "the most critical consideration." Barely five months later, this new policy was put to the test when the Mutual Film Corporation submitted *Purity* to the board for censoring. Starring Audrey Munson, a famous artist's model, the film contained a number of scenes in which Miss Munson could be seen "undraped."[69]

In the case of controversial films, board members often sought to gauge public opinion by exhibiting the motion picture to persons whom they considered to be "representative citizens" — prominent social workers or educators, for example. Expecting controversy over *Purity*, the National Board sponsored a special showing of the film for fifty-four invited guests. While a majority of these approved the film for exhibition to "adult" audiences, there was less agreement as to whether the film should be released for general exhibition. After considering the results of this survey, and viewing the film themselves, the board's General Committee members decided that they could not pass the film, as they had no policy permitting them to approve a picture with the requirement that children be excluded from the audience. But, in line with their policy that nudity was not inherently immoral, neither did they wish to condemn it. Believing that it was "impossible for the National Board to seek to render a decision which would be satisfactory to the entire country," they made no recommendation on the film at all.[70]

Outside New York City the articulated response to *Purity* was almost exclusively shock and outrage. In Kansas City and Dallas municipal authorities banned the film. In other cities its exhibition prompted calls for local censorship. The National Board, always basing its claim to legitimacy in its role as an agent of public opinion, was compelled to change its policy. Late in 1916, and acting in concert with a newly formed group of motion picture producers who declared their intention to fight calls for state and federal censorship by making morally acceptable films, the board added a section on female nudity to its standards. Although they continued to insist that there was nothing innately wrong in nudity, board members reluctantly recognized that "custom and prudery" had made it taboo. Therefore, as "a reflector of public opinion" the board would cease to approve any picture containing the female nude, no matter how "artistically and unsuggestively it may be presented." By April 1917, board members recast their assessment of public opinion, issuing a statement that cited opposition to the nude as an indicator of the "wholesomeness of the sentiment of the people of the United States."[71]

Despite this change in policy, there is evidence that in the next several years board censoring committees continued to recommend that representations of nude women be permitted in some pictures.[72] For example, a 1919 film, *The Girl Alaska*, chronicled the adventures of Mollie McCrea, who journeys to Alaska disguised as a boy, seeking her fortune and her father who disappeared there years previously. Mollie meets Phil Hadley, a handsome young man with whom she stakes a claim, shares a cabin, and falls in love. Phil's belated discovery that Mollie is really a woman comes only during a lengthy scene in which he spies her cavorting naked on the beach. While Mollie is filmed from a distance and little detail can be discerned, she appears to be nude — or at least costumed so as to seem nude to the viewer. The continued portrayal of nude or seminude women in motion pictures throughout the 1910s and 1920s — which reflected both pressure from filmmakers and National Board members' lingering belief that nudity was not immoral — ensured that such criticisms of movies would not abate.[73]

Thus contradictions within the National Board of Censorship — the necessity for its members to satisfy both film producers and film critics as well as its reliance on "expert" judgment concurrent with a self-justification as a "democratic" institution — compromised the construction and implementation of standards by which motion pictures were to be evaluated. However, even had these standards been strictly enforced, the formulation of standards for the adult audience rarely satisfied the most vocal critics of motion pictures, who continued to assert that children's moral safety was the key issue. As a result, formulating standards for an adult audience was less than successful as a strategy for allaying concerns about motion pictures.

The board's failure to prevent censure of the movies through the creation and enforcement of standards resulted in a campaign by New York City officials to expand their own authority over motion picture content. The surge in "sex problem" films provided the immediate impetus. These films, many of which were produced by social hygienists or feminists, explored questions relating to sexuality, especially but not only women's sexuality: prostitution, birth control, and venereal disease. Despite the fact that such movies were generally aimed at adult audiences, here too children were invoked as the justification for expanding the state's control over sexual representation.

NOT FIT FOR PUBLIC DISPLAY:
THE DEBATE ABOUT SEX PROBLEM FILMS

Municipal authorities began their attempts to assert authority over motion pictures when a spate of "white slave" films appeared beginning in 1913. In that year New York City, along with the rest of the nation, was in the throes of a white slavery panic.[74] While public concern about the extent of prostitution dated from the latter years of the nineteenth century, the idea that innocent young girls were being kidnapped and coerced into sexual servitude had captured the national imagination since an exposé of Chicago prostitution was published in 1908. In New York these fears were substantiated by a 1910 grand jury investigation that uncovered police protection for procurers and resulted in fifty-four indictments for trafficking in women. Vice investigations in cities across the nation, prosecutions under the Mann Act of 1910, and the publication of lurid revelations of the traffic in women kept alive the rumors of girls, fresh from the countryside, who were pricked by a dope-filled hypodermic needle wielded by a foreign-looking man and sold into degradation and, ultimately, death.[75]

With the proliferation of speech about white slavery, in newspapers, magazines, novels and plays, it was perhaps inevitable that the white slave should make her appearance in motion pictures as well. Indeed, short films about white slavery were produced as early as 1904. But it wasn't until 1913, when Universal Studio's feature film *A Traffic in Souls* packed theaters across the nation, that the number of white slave films exploded. These motion pictures began to attract attention from censors and municipal authorities throughout the United States, including those in New York City.[76]

Because white slave films were often conceived and always marketed as a purposeful attack upon the conspiracy of silence allegedly shrouding discussion of sex problems, their production invited controversy. Social hygienists and feminists argued that such problems as venereal disease and prostitution would be solved only if they were talked about, and if the underlying causes of white slavery (among which the feminists, at least, counted low wages for women, the double standard, and the profit accruing to men from prostitution) were revealed. Motion pictures provided one very public site for breaking the silence. Many cultural traditionalists opposed these portrayals, however, contending that such subjects were not fit for public discussion and that such discussions, no matter what their form, were by nature obscene. In New York City the staff of the National Board of Censorship embraced the former of these viewpoints, arguing that portrayals of prostitution and other sexual issues, if they abided by certain standards, should be permitted. Municipal authorities increasingly took the traditionalist position. Using concerns about children's safety — this time, the vulnerability of adolescent girls to the "traffic" in women — New York officials moved to strengthen government power to prohibit these films.

The appearance of white slave films did not at first create conflict among city officials and National Board members. Indeed, municipal authorities and volunteer censors cooperated in 1913 in suppressing an early feature film about white slavery, *The Inside of the White Slave Traffic*. This motion picture was produced by Samuel London, who claimed to base the film upon his experiences as a vice investigator. The story is loosely structured around the experiences of one young working woman who is drugged and seduced by a white slaver; her fate is sealed when her old-fashioned father banishes her from his house, and she becomes a prostitute. Much of the picture shows the methods allegedly used by procurers to entrap young women, to trade them around the nation, and to keep them in prostitution against their will. When the film opened at the Park Theatre on December 8, 1913, several hundred patrons had to be turned away. Newspaper reports indicated that the audience was two-thirds female and included many young women aged sixteen to eighteen. Police responded to complaints about the film, including one lodged by Alice Edith Abell and Marjorie Dorman of the Wage-Earners' Anti-Suffrage League, by raiding the theaters at which it was playing.[77] Ultimately, Samuel London and one theater manager were convicted of giving an immoral exhibition. The vigorous campaign against this motion picture affected other sex problem films as well; when the police began an investigation of A Victim of Sin, the exhibitor "voluntarily" canceled its run.[78]

Despite their earlier approval of another white slave film,[79] National Board of Censorship personnel supported the city's campaign against the picture by refusing to approve The Inside of the White Slave Traffic. The censorship organization's hostility toward this film was due in part to the fact that the production company released it for public exhibition before submitting it to the National Board, thus threatening the board's credibility. When board censors did view the motion picture, they determined that it transgressed the boundaries they had established for sex problem films. Not only did it offer detailed, lengthy portrayals of brothels, including a scene showing prostitutes in negligees. More worrisome, board members thought, was the fact that the motion picture did not show the lives of prostitutes as "disagreeable." As one stated, the film ought to show "what happened to the girl in the end; her becoming a drug-fiend hag, a sufferer of venereal disease; a suicide; a specimen for the doctor's dissecting table; and finally filling a grave at Potters Field." Nor was the trafficker punished for his crimes.[80] Members of the National Board endorsed a policy of permitting films about white slavery, but they required that those films depict what they perceived to be the "reality" of prostitution. In addition, such pictures must have a good effect. "Instead of pointing a moral," they argued, The Inside of the White Slave Traffic merely "points to an easy method of obtaining money by both men and women." Even after the producer made some of the suggested changes board members condemned the film, which, they believed, provided "an illustration rather than an education."[81]

Some New Yorkers had a different reaction to The Inside of the White Slave Traffic, heralding it as a frank portrayal of the sexual exploitation of women.

Suffragists Carrie Chapman Catt and Alva Belmont, as well as social hygienists Dr. William J. Robinson and Dr. Ira S. Wile, testified in favor of the film in court. Inez Milholland Boissevain, a lawyer and feminist, was a defense attorney for the film's producer. Declaring that she and her allies acted from a belief in freedom of speech in all media, she affirmed in particular the importance of "frank, scientific . . . discussion and presentation of all subjects pertaining to sex" that would destroy "the murky, unclean, timid and defiled mental attitudes [which make sex a] matter of shame, secrecy, uncleanness and dirty jokes."[82] While National Board policy indicates that many members of the organization agreed with her principles, their perception that *The Inside of the White Slave Traffic* was neither scientific nor truthful — and its producer's lack of deference to the board — united them with municipal officials in opposition to the film.

In the wake of the controversy over this film, National Board members formulated a general policy on "social evil" films that, they hoped, would strike a compromise in the debate over the public discussion of sexual matters. They declared that the board would support films that "present facts in a sincere, dramatic way leading to repression or to the removal of the causes of commercial or sub-rosa prostitution." Board censors would pass those films "which arouse fear in the minds of both sexes, which develop a hatred on the part of the audience of this ancient evil, which stimulate efforts to rescue the prostitute, and which indicate sensible and workable methods of repression or suppression." These standards focused not upon the question of whether a film showed too much flesh, or too many "disorderly resorts," but upon the effect of the film on its viewers: whether or not it would prevent young women from becoming prostitutes and young men procurers, inspire the audience to rise up against the social evil, or lead to government efforts to end the traffic in women. Members of the National Board thus supported the view that public discussion of sexual problems could be a good thing — but that talk about sex for its own sake was harmful.[83]

At the same time that the proliferation of white slave films prompted National Board members to create standards for evaluating these films it also inspired municipal authorities to expand their control over motion picture content. In 1914 government officials reorganized the municipal bureaucracy in order to put the regulatory mechanism envisioned in the Folks ordinance to work, transforming the underfunded, relatively powerless License Bureau into a department and hiring inspectors to monitor the establishments it licensed. Simultaneously, George Bell was appointed the new commissioner of licenses, and he quickly moved to enlarge his role in the regulation of motion pictures.

In June 1914 Bell and the National Board set up a formal system of cooperation to ensure that films that had been condemned by the board were not shown in New York City. In addition, Bell began reviewing the decisions of the board more closely.[84]

Bell's efforts to enlarge his role may have been a response to the difficulties municipal authorities encountered in their criminal prosecution of the producer of *The Inside of the White Slave Traffic*. Although they ultimately obtained a conviction, it was a lengthy process, requiring hearings before two magistrates (one of whom failed to sustain the charges), a grand jury indictment, the vacating of an injunction obtained by London to protect the film, and a jury trial. In contrast, the Folks ordinance empowered the license commissioner simply to revoke the license of a motion picture theater for a variety of offenses that included showing "immoral" films. In keeping with legal precedent giving wide discretion in the performance of their duties to administrative officials, the license commissioner's decision was reviewable by the courts only on questions of his good faith, not on questions of fact. As long as the commissioner could cite a cause for the revocation of a license, he was not required to prove that cause.[85] It seemed likely that the license commissioner could act much more quickly and effectively than police officials.

Cooperation with municipal authorities was in the interests of the National Board, whose members were concerned about the number of films that either were never submitted to them or were shown in theaters even after they were condemned by the board, as *The Inside of the White Slave Traffic* had been. In June 1914 board members agreed to inform License Commissioner Bell when New York City theaters showed films they had rejected. For his part, Bell was to notify the owners of the theaters exhibiting such motion pictures that if they did not comply with the orders of the National Board he would take steps to revoke their license. These arrangements formalized a system of regulation under which state and voluntary authority reinforced and depended upon each other. They also had the effect of increasing the license commissioner's role in controlling the content of motion pictures.[86]

For two years this system functioned relatively smoothly, but in 1916 Commissioner Bell moved once again to expand his power over motion pictures.[87] In February a group of disgruntled women, including the president of the National Board's old nemesis, the Women's Municipal League, complained to Bell about some of the films being approved by the board. They included in their protest films about venereal disease and birth control as well as vamp films.[88] As a result, Commissioner Bell scolded National Board representatives for their laxity and increased his surveillance of their activities, appointing license bureau employees to screen controversial films that board censors had approved.[89] Not satisfied with these measures, Bell also launched a new campaign against "sex problem" films, including motion pictures about childbirth, birth control, prostitution, and abortion. That campaign led to serious friction between city authorities and the National Board and resulted in a substantial increase in the use of the licensing power to ban films in New York City.[90]

Commissioner Bell instituted his drive against sex problem films in the midst of heightened anxiety about the health and safety of New York's children. During the summer of 1916 city residents were enduring the uncertainties of an ongoing infantile paralysis epidemic. At the same time, another investigation of white slavery was launched, and police officers as well as procurers had been indicted. To complicate matters, that fall Margaret Sanger opened her first birth control clinic in Brooklyn, and New York officials arrested Emma Goldman for lecturing on the same topic. In September the polio crisis lessened, and city officials lifted a ban on children's attendance at motion pictures, which had been adopted as a public health measure. It was in the context of the return of children to the movies and continuing revelations about organized prostitution and police corruption that the white slave film *Is Any Girl Safe?* came to New York City. It was approved for exhibition by National Board censors in line with their endorsement of educational antiprostitution films.[91]

Commissioner Bell responded by inviting a number of concerned citizens, including John Sumner of the New York Society for the Suppression of Vice and Frederick Whitin of the antiprostitution Committee of Fourteen, to view the film. When these men and women offered the "unanimous opinion . . . that it was not a fit film for public display," Bell prohibited its exhibition under threat of revoking the theater's license. He notified the National Board that he intended to use all his power to ensure that no white slave films would be shown in New York. Chastising the board for passing the film, he asserted that all such films had "a thoroughly bad effect. I have time and again sat in audiences when such pictures were shown, and have found from the comments of those about me, particularly boys and girls from 16 to 22 or 23 years of age that this is so." One New York man, recently convicted on vice charges, told city authorities that many motion picture theaters were operated for "the purpose of recruiting young girls to the white slave traffic," which gave added force to Commissioner Bell's concerns.[92]

When the film producer took Bell to court for prohibiting the movie's exhibition, the commissioner of licenses' authority to supervise motion picture morality under the Folks ordinance was affirmed. New York Supreme Court Justice Cohalan ruled that Commissioner Bell indeed had the power to prevent the exhibition of *Is Any Girl Safe?* in New York City. Citing a number of letters and affidavits opposing the film, many of them from people "experienced in the work of setting proper standards for moving picture houses . . . and in protecting the morals of society, particularly the young members thereof," he ruled that the picture appealed to sensuality and offended public decency. Further, he argued that, even if there was no open immorality in the motion picture, it did contain immoral suggestion, which was even more dangerous, for "the more that is left to the imagination[,] the more subtle and seductive is the influence." Finally, the Supreme Court justice affirmed that, in any case, it was within the license commissioner's discretion to revoke a theater license if he believed the motion picture was immoral.[93]

The 1916 campaign against *Is Any Girl Safe?* brought to fruition the promise of expanding government power implicit in the Folks ordinance passed three years earlier. The pattern established by Commissioner Bell in this case would be repeated many times in the next several years. Opponents of sex problem films regularly condemned them for the dangers they posed to children and adolescents, whom they deemed "more open to the demoralizing influences of indecent pictures than are adult persons." Among these dangers were the fears that white slave pictures would turn girls into prostitutes and boys into procurers. City officials then used the licensing power to suppress such films. Initially Commissioner Bell was satisfied merely to prohibit the attendance of children at sex problem films, as was the case with the eugenics-themed *Where Are My Children?* in 1916. Ultimately, however, he and his successor totally banned the commercial exhibition of such films in New York. In this process, city officials and reformers who opposed discussion of sexual problems in motion pictures used concerns about children to widen government power that would determine what all New Yorkers, adult and child, could see on the movie screen.[94]

Emboldened by court decisions upholding his powers, Commissioner Bell went on to ban an ever widening range of subjects from the city's theaters. He prohibited white slavery films such as *It May Be Your Daughter* and *Protect Your Daughter* as well as movies advocating the liberalization of birth control laws, including Margaret Sanger's *Birth Control* and Lois Weber's *The Hand That Rocks the Cradle*. One motion picture that came under prohibition, *The Sex Lure*, was targeted not because of harmful content but because of its racy title.

The commissioner claimed that he received complaints from parents who said that although they could keep their children from seeing it in the theater, they "could not prevent their being on the streets of the city" where they saw indecent posters advertising the show.[95]

When George Bell's tenure as commissioner of licenses ended, his successor, John Gilchrist, continued the campaign against sex problem films, prohibiting a number of films approved by National Board censors. For example, in June 1918 Gilchrist banned *The Finger of Justice*, produced by a San Francisco minister to publicize his efforts to stamp out prostitution. An advertisement for the film called it "a sympathetic and wholesome dramatization of the program of vice repression and of mercy toward the erring Magdalen." The National Board passed the film in accordance with its policy permitting white slave pictures that were "strictly propaganda . . . produced obviously for social betterment." However, the license commissioner opposed the film because he believed that it would injure "youthful and impressionable minds." This decision, too, was ultimately upheld in court.[96]

Commissioners Bell and Gilchrist were supported in this campaign against sex problem films by a number of local reform organizations, including the antiprostitution Committee of Fourteen, the Catholic Theatre Movement, which monitored Broadway shows, the Hebrew Educational Society, and the New York Society for the Suppression of Vice. John Sumner, secretary of the NYSSV, urged the National Board of Censorship to follow municipal authorities' lead, arguing that white slave pictures merely aroused young people's curiosity about vice. Even if sex problem films did not contain scenes that would be held obscene by a court, he declared, when they showed the ways in which girls were enticed into prostitution they provided "a thorough education in this line of crime to young, unmoral male persons of whom there are entirely too many in all of our cities."[97]

Similar sentiments were voiced by Ellen O'Grady, the fifth deputy commissioner of police, who was a leading advocate of motion picture censorship. Mrs. O'Grady had become a probation officer in 1907 when, newly widowed, she had to go to work to support her three daughters. In 1918 she was appointed the first woman deputy police commissioner in New York City. Her special charge was "welfare work," and she was concerned not just with movie censorship but also with dance halls, prostitution, and the sexual exploitation of women.[98] Immediately after her appointment as police commissioner she joined in the campaign against sex problem films. O'Grady condemned *The Finger of Justice*, for example, because she believed it had a bad effect on both the impressionable and the general public. The "young girl on the downward path" as well as the "loafer of evil mind" would see nothing but allurement and potential profit in the film's portrayal of the prostitute and the procurer. The rest of the audience would receive "the impression that all city officials are dishonest and depraved, and, consequently los[e] respect for authority." Further, O'Grady claimed that the efforts of the film's hero to eliminate the horrors of prostitution could not allay the effects of the "filth" that the audience witnessed in the picture. She suggested that, rather than show films of this kind, motion picture exhibitors ought to project the Ten Commandments on the movie screen every night to inspire the audience to reflection.[99]

The concern articulated by Ellen O'Grady and shared by others over the portrayal of sex in the movies increased with the end of World War I. In 1919 a number of films about venereal disease, most of which were originally training films for military personnel, were released for commercial exhibition. At the same time, filmmakers continued to turn out other sex problem films as well, such as *The Solitary Sin*, which warned that masturbation led to insanity. Again, the National Board and the license commissioner disagreed over how these motion pictures should be regulated. While not passing all films of this kind, National Board members approved some of them, provided they were to be shown to adult audiences only, a policy they had instituted in 1916 as a means of protecting such films. Commissioner Gilchrist, on the other hand, was determined to prohibit all discussion of such matters in motion pictures. He declared in particular that no movies about venereal disease could be shown in New York. Through use of his licensing powers, Gilchrist successfully banned v.d. films from New York commercial theaters, without ever obtaining a conviction for violation of anti-obscenity statutes.[100]

This campaign did not ensure that depictions of sexuality were never projected onto New York City's motion picture screens after 1916. The license commissioner sometimes did not proscribe sex problem films until after they appeared in local theaters, and anecdotal evidence suggests that once a movie was proclaimed immoral by city officials or reformers attendance soared until authorities succeeded in banning the film. Further, in a city as large as New York it was impossible to police every motion picture theater. Nor were all other portrayals of sexuality abolished from New York's theaters. Municipal authorities rarely chose to prohibit the exhibition of films that could be classified more purely as entertainment, such as the vamp and crime films that provoked much condemnation among clergy, women's organizations, and others across the nation.

The focus on sex problem films by New York licensing authorities suggests that there was more to their concern about dangers to children than meets the eye. Films about white slavery, birth control, and venereal disease were marketed to a particular audience. They were usually lengthy feature films; in order to be profitable, they were exhibited at theaters with relatively high admission prices — perhaps a dollar instead of ten or twenty cents. Furthermore, at the National Board's insistence, after 1916 theater owners prohibited children under eighteen from the audience for these movies. Since children were unlikely to view sex problem films, it seems likely that it was not only children whose protection was at issue in these cultural battles. But because the audiences for such movies were, by and large, middle class, it is not enough to presume, as have other scholars, that children functioned as a kind of cultural code for immigrant and working-class adults, over whom middle-class reformers and officials sought control. In the case of sex problem films, concern for children was indeed symbolic, but it served to stifle debate within the middle and upper classes about urban sexual policy and practice.[101]

Sex problem films were entertainment, certainly, but they were also political, and they articulated controversial ideas. A relatively high proportion of banned films criticized the sexual double standard. Some of them were produced by women; many were self-consciously feminist. Producers of birth control and white slave films attacked the sexual subordination of women, using the new medium to reach an audience much greater than the readership of Margaret Sanger's *The Woman Rebel* or Emma Goldman's *Mother Earth*. It was exactly this political content that justified the exhibition of such films in the minds of National Board representatives, who approved of "strictly propaganda pictures produced obviously for social betterment."[102] In so doing, they asserted not only that motion pictures ought to be judged in accordance with public opinion but also that they ought to provide an arena for the formulation of public opinion — in other words, that the movies be properly understood as a forum for the democratic discussion of public policy. And it was exactly this political content that New York's license commissioners quashed, countering the National Board's language of democratic moral authority with an ever more vociferous emphasis upon the child audience. Because protection of the vulnerable provided the bedrock of the legal regime governing obscenity, and because movies had already been linked with children in the public perception, government authorities and their allies found articulating concerns about children to be an effective strategy for control, even when they were mostly absent from the audience. The underlying reasons for their opposition to such films may be lost to history — political considerations, antifeminism, sensitivity to criticism of authority all seem probable — but the outcome is not: a silencing of the feminist-inspired debate on the sexual and gender order.

TO REMEDY A GREAT EVIL:
THE ARRIVAL OF STATE CENSORSHIP

Throughout the late teens the National Board's authority was being eroded by increasingly assertive municipal officials who resisted its attempts to censor for the average person. At the same time, concerns about the moral and physical safety of children continued to mount. The entry of the United States into World War I gave rise to fears that children, lacking the supervision of mothers who were joining the workforce or fathers who were off to war, would fall prey to any number of traps, of which motion pictures were only one. Increasingly, the dangers to children posed by the movies depended on their sex. Reformers cited instances of young boys who learned criminal methods from films and became arsonists, armed robbers, even murderers. Boys were not victimized by motion pictures, but learned to victimize others.[103] On the other hand, warnings that the movies turned girls and young women to sexual delinquency were articulated more vociferously than ever. For example, one city magistrate cautioned that "there are not snares for the catching of young girls like the motion picture shows," while another claimed that "ninety-five [percent] of the motion picture places in New York City are dens of inequity. More young women are led astray there than in any other way."[104]

The end of the war brought a new wave of reports of the connections between juvenile delinquency and motion pictures, and demands for government censorship increased. Despite New York license commissioners' successful campaign against sex problem films, many critics of motion pictures desired to create a more systematized and broader regulatory regime, and in 1919 they renewed the attempt to pass a municipal censorship law for New York City. This legislation would have required that Department of Licenses personnel view every film before it was exhibited. Exhibition permits were to be denied to all films that were "immoral or obscene, indecent or suggestive," defamed any religious belief, or tended to corrupt morals or disturb the peace. Ellen O'Grady, the most prominent champion of the legislation, argued that films contributed to the criminality of youth and gave immigrants the wrong idea about American institutions as well.[105]

The members of the National Board of Censorship and their allies in the motion picture industry succeeded in engineering the defeat of the legislation by focusing on adults' rights to freedom rather than children's vulnerability. At a public hearing on the ordinance, Dr. Everett Martin, chairman of the National Board, argued that censorship advocates wanted "to prevent the poor from having a good time," while a board employee reiterated the organization's position "that the people themselves shall decide what they shall see through the process of selection." After this hearing, the Board of Aldermen declined even to vote on the legislation, concluding that the suggested censorship was "far more inimical to our institutions than the evil sought to be corrected." That every campaign waged for municipal preexhibition censorship in New York City went down to defeat indicates that the discourse of democracy could be effectively used in the city's heterogeneous political culture, even if it was not strong enough to overcome the license commissioners' opposition to sex problem films.[106]

In the face of the apparent impossibility of passing municipal censorship legislation, local activists who blamed movies for the downfall of the day's youth shifted their attention to a campaign for statewide censorship. As early as 1915 the New York legislature considered creating an official censorship board to pass upon all films shown in the state. In 1916 both houses of the legislature endorsed such a bill. Its proponents, among whom were included the Woman's Christian Temperance Union, the Humane Society, various Sunday school associations, and numerous clergymen, argued that the legislation was "essential for the proper protection of the morals of the young." After heavy lobbying by the National Board, however, New York's governor vetoed the legislation.[107] Nor did several subsequent efforts to enact state motion picture censorship succeed. Indeed, a writer for the trade publication *Moving Picture World* declared state censorship "a dead letter" when, in 1920, a committee convened by the New York State Conference of Mayors, and containing a number of members of the National Board, concluded that "state censorship in any form is undesirable." But these predictions of censorship's death were greatly exaggerated, for in 1921 New York state legislators enacted a preexhibition censorship law.[108]

A return to the strategies employed a decade earlier by the members of the Women's Municipal League helped make possible the passage of this law. During the winter of 1920–1921 Frederick Boyd Stevenson, a reporter for the *Brooklyn Daily Eagle*, launched an attack upon the National Board of Censorship, severely undermining its credibility. Stevenson, proclaiming himself shocked by the portrayals of sex and crime that he found in films passed by the board, investigated the organization and uncovered evidence suggesting that its staff members, whose salaries were paid by the motion picture producers, exercised influence over the volunteer censors and that at least one of those volunteers had a financial stake in the motion picture industry. His investigation offered a measure of concrete proof that the National Board was not as disinterested as its members had professed, undermining its claim to be the people's representative. As a result of Stevenson's campaign, Brooklyn legislators introduced a bill creating a three-member motion picture commission that would inspect and license every film intended for exhibition in the state. Similar commissions existed in several other states, including Kansas, Pennsylvania, and Ohio; they had been upheld as a constitutional form of motion picture regulation by the U.S. Supreme Court in 1915.[109]

From the first, the campaign to pass this bill was undertaken in the name of children. Reflecting the changing tenor of concerns about children's safety, however, most advocates of the law cited concern about children's susceptibility to criminality rather than their sexual vulnerability. Having resigned from the police department because, she charged, the police commissioner limited her authority to act against motion pictures, Ellen O'Grady became one of the most vocal promoters of the proposed law, renewing her claims that motion pictures caused juvenile delinquency. John Sumner, of the New York Society for the Suppression of Vice, offered censorship advocates ammunition when he warned that crime in New York City was "but a ripple on a mill pond compared to what we shall have if we continue to permit our children to be demoralized by a lawless and immoral aggregation of sordid and sensual defilers of the screen." Still others appealed for the protection of children but urged that different vulnerable groups would also be assisted by censorship. As one of the bill's sponsors told the legislature, "This censorship bill before us is drawn in the interest of the children of New York State. It aims to protect the morals of young people, and likewise womanhood."[110]

Opponents of the legislation, as they had in the past, tried to focus on the effect of censorship on adults as well as on its undemocratic nature. Sidney Cohen, a New York City resident and president of the Motion Picture Theatre Owners of New York State, questioned the motives of those who wanted to censor, calling them bigots who desired to be "paid dictators and custodians of the public morals." Cohen asserted that "the people" were moral and demanded good pictures themselves.[111] Representatives of the National Board offered their habitual argument that adults constituted the appropriate audience for discussing the effects of motion pictures and motion picture censorship. But they also sought to address the concerns of those who wanted to protect children, asserting that government censorship was actually harmful to children because it created a false sense of security, lulling parents into believing that their children were protected by the state. According to a board representative, in those states where censorship already existed the censors realized that "any number of pictures must be passed by the state board of censorship which were not suitable . . . for young people." Renewing an old refrain, National Board members argued that only direct parental supervision of children's film choices — "selection, not censorship" — would protect impressionable youth.[112]

These arguments failed, however, in the wake of heightened anxiety about juvenile delinquency and the succession of assaults upon the National Board's authority by New York's license commissioners, local journalists, and reformers. In May 1921 Governor Charles Whitman signed the censorship bill into law, calling it "the only way to remedy . . . a very great evil." The bill outlawed any film or part of a film that was "obscene, indecent, immoral, inhuman, sacrilegious, or is of such a character that its exhibition would tend to corrupt morals or incite to crime."[113] A number of factors permitted the enactment of this bill where others had failed. Differences in local and statewide politics in New York played an important role. In general, the New York state legislature, dominated by upstate lawmakers representing small-town and rural constituents, was more conservative than the New York City Board of Aldermen. Advocates of censorship were better organized in small towns, where churches and women's clubs had more influence. Fears that small-town children would be corrupted by big-city movies also helped mobilize sentiment in favor of the law.[114]

The successful campaign for this law owed much to national trends as well. During World War I and the years following, government officials throughout the nation expanded their authority to control and penalize allegedly dangerous speech. Increased acceptance of government censorship of political ideas may also have facilitated the growth of a nationwide movement for censorship of motion pictures, which was at its height in 1921. Finally, the motion picture industry and its allies, perhaps overconfident that this proposal would be defeated, as had previous film censorship laws in New York, put very little effort into opposing the bill. When they realized that it might pass, their lobbying was too little and too late.[115]

The creation of the New York State Motion Picture Commission concluded local struggles over municipal regulation of motion picture content at the same time that it effectively ended the National Board of Censorship's role as a censor of films. In the wake of the law's passage, members of the motion picture industry began casting about for new strategies to avert demands for state and federal censorship of the movies.[116] The National Board's failure to establish and enforce film standards that satisfied the medium's critics had limited its usefulness to the industry that helped create it. Its members were forced to abandon their regulatory role for the less central one of fostering appreciation of motion pictures as an art form.

In their quest to represent public opinion to filmmakers, the members of the National Board of Censorship tried to create a democratic system of cultural regulation that would obviate the demand for local, state, or federal censorship. They succeeded in introducing the concept of the average person to these debates but ultimately were unable to substitute this figure for that of the child in need of protection. Nor could their presence as volunteer censors stop New York's license commissioners or, finally, its state legislators from claiming the right to censor motion picture content. As a result, the National Board's brand of censorship, which for all its faults was geared to adult sensibilities and sought to allow the movies a role in fostering discussion of controversial sexual issues, was replaced by a system of government regulation that took the protection of the child as its raison d'être but directed much of its energies toward controlling adults.

CHAPTER 2

"The Habitats of Sex-Crazed Perverts": Campaigns Against Burlesque

In 1942 New York City's license commissioner finally achieved victory in a decade-long crusade against the city's burlesque theaters when he refused to renew their licenses, forcing them to close. The proprietors of the Gaiety Theatre sued Commissioner Paul Moss, but their hopes were dashed when a New York Supreme Court justice ruled that the commissioner's action was justified. Rejecting the plaintiffs' contention that Moss acted in a manner that endangered "due process, democratic procedure, [and] free expression," he reflected that

> some of us may feel, by reason of self-deception or superior endowments, that any attempt at protection against the alleged hazards and evils of lewd exhibitions is both futile and unnecessary. This smug attitude, however, overlooks the essential function of government in democracy and its service to all the people, including the lowliest. It does not follow that because regulation in this field is in the first instance vouchsafed to one man, this becomes a government of men rather than laws.

To Justice Levy it was clear that burlesque patrons' and owners' belief that they could escape its corrupting effects — not "one-man censorship" — was the real threat to a democratic culture.[1]

During the 1930s, anti-obscenity activists focused their attention upon low-priced entertainment forms that prospered as a result of the economic crisis. Nationally, both motion pictures and cheap magazines came under increased scrutiny when the Catholic hierarchy organized the Legion of Decency and the National Organization for Decent Literature. In New York City municipal officials and opponents of "smut" launched occasional campaigns against the cheap "art" and horror magazines read by teenage boys. They railed most loudly against burlesque shows, which during the Depression moved beyond working-class areas of the city to Times Square. Their campaign against burlesque was among the most successful of all attempts to control the content of New York's entertainment industry in the first half of the twentieth century.

Burlesque had long been a thorn in the side of New York's antivice activists, but it was a thorn exceedingly difficult to remove. The staff of the New York Society for the Suppression of Vice regularly visited the city's burlesque theaters from the 1910s through the early 1940s, reporting that the shows were "suggestive," "indecent," "smutty," "filthy," "very bad," and "getting worse." Occasionally they observed that performances were "tamer," following adverse publicity or infrequent arrests and convictions. Very common in the NYSSV's internal reports was the notation that "there was nothing in the show to which successful legal exception could be taken." Antivice crusaders found burlesque "thoroughly degrading," but they recognized that it did not meet the legal standards for obscenity, at least as they were usually applied by New York's judges and juries. It was only when city officials again turned to their licensing powers that they succeeded in banishing burlesque from New York's stages.[2]

The difficulty in obtaining convictions against burlesque, which was the most sexually suggestive and sexually explicit of all of New York's popular media,[3] points to a contradiction in the existing obscenity regime. The Hicklin Rule's emphasis upon a text's potential tendency to "corrupt those whose minds are open to such immoral influences, and who might come into contact with it" focused attention upon the audience as much as the text. Usually, this accent on those vulnerable viewers open to immorality facilitated obscenity prosecutions, making the definition of the obscene very broad indeed.[4] But when the vulnerable viewer was absent from the audience, and unlikely to come into contact with the suspect material, obtaining a conviction paradoxically could become very difficult, especially when those in the audience — adult men, frequently working-class men — were presumed to be beyond corruption. This difficulty grew during the interwar years, when white men's sexual behavior came once again to be accepted as a standard for human sexual experience rather than, as during the heyday of social purity movements, a weakness to be overcome.[5] And it was especially great in the case of burlesque, which unlike the underground pornography that was usually successfully prosecuted, used sexual suggestiveness rather than simple explicitness to appeal to its audience.

Anti-obscenity activists escaped this conundrum by arguing that burlesque *did* corrupt its already "low" audience in new ways, and that their corruption presented a horrible threat to the community's vulnerable women and children. The varying contours of this threat were elaborated more precisely than ever before in the years between 1932 and 1942. Opponents of burlesque articulated a logic of male sexuality that reflected the economic conditions and political imperatives attending the Great Depression and the wartime boom. During times of economic crisis they described an escalating trajectory of male sexual danger, as they moved from asserting that burlesque *attracted* men who were likely to harass female passersby to arguing that it *incited* them to rape and murder. With the Depression's end burlesque opponents abandoned the effort to link burlesque to aggressive male sexuality, instead contending that burlesque drained masculine virility and therefore undermined the war effort, endangering in new ways the women and children entitled to protection.

The position that burlesque theaters had become the "habitats of sex-crazed perverts" can also be traced to continued efforts to articulate a democratic defense of sexual representation in commercial culture. Indeed, the Depression-era debates about burlesque may be productively analyzed as a debate about democracy, class, and culture in modern America.[6] Within the context of the Great Depression burlesque's threat to the social order, long asserted by its critics, took on a new form. Catering at the beginning of the decade to an audience predominantly composed of working-class men, produced by entrepreneurs and performers who were themselves largely of immigrant or Jewish working-class origin, burlesque was emblematic of a particular kind of mass culture, denoted as such not because of an oligopolistic structure but because of its traditional status as "poor man's theater." When it escaped its confines in working-class areas of the city and was embraced by some middle-class New Yorkers, it seemed to betoken an assault upon the newly precarious economic and social order. In the ensuing debates about burlesque's expansion, competing descriptions of its audience functioned as texts about both the "eruption of class difference"[7] and the extent to which the members of that audience were captured by the entertainment they consumed. As burlesque's defenders argued that its audience of "average citizens" had the wherewithal to control their responses to its provocations, their foes reciprocated with the assertion that burlesque's incitements led inexorably first to disorderliness, then to violence, and finally to debility. Thus, the debate about burlesque was ultimately a debate about danger and desire in a democratic culture.

A WORLD OF ILLUSION: THE CULTURE OF BURLESQUE

It is the burlesque of the 1930s — the decade in which striptease became the predominant feature of burlesque and strippers such as Ann Corio and Gypsy

Rose Lee became stars — that has shaped most popular conceptions and nostalgic remembrances of the genre, but America's original burlesque shows differed greatly from their Depression-era descendants.[8] Burlesque arrived in the U.S. in 1868, when Lydia Thompson and her "British Blondes" traveled from England to perform in New York City. Thompson productions and the host of imitators that followed featured women performers scantily clad in above-the-knee skirts and pink tights or, alternatively, women dressed in the clothing and taking the prerogatives of men. The performance itself consisted of a lengthy sketch that played on and with a popular legitimate theater production of the day. The Thompson troupe incorporated the two qualities — a focus on the "spectacular female performer" and performances that transgressed sexual, gender, and class norms — that historian Robert C. Allen contends defined the genre of burlesque.[9]

By the end of the nineteenth century burlesque performances had been transformed in both structure and content, owing to the influence of American entertainment forms such as the minstrel show. The long burlesque sketch was broken up into several disconnected brief comic "bits," interspersed with musical numbers and variety acts, thus creating a formal structure very similar to that of vaudeville. But vaudeville sought to attract a "family" audience, while burlesque catered from its early years to a male audience, and increasingly its raison d'être became sex. Turn-of-the-century burlesque featured three main types of acts. The female body occupied center stage in musical numbers, featuring a cooch-dancing, shimmying woman principal who sang a suggestive song against a background of barely dressed chorus girls. There were also brief tableaux vivants in which groups of seminude women posed for several minutes, creating "living pictures" that supposedly recalled classical art. The comedic bits featured a male comedian, whose character was often structured around ethnic stereotypes, and a straight man who fed the comedian lines. The actors' sexual innuendo often concerned a female performer; sometimes she bantered with them, but she might also stand silent on the stage as the men discussed her physical characteristics.[10]

As the twentieth century advanced, the evolving structure of the burlesque industry and developments in the legitimate theater resulted in an even greater role for female sexual display within burlesque performances. Early in the century burlesque entrepreneurs sought to standardize the industry by creating two national "wheels," or circuits, each of which provided a succession of traveling shows to the theaters with which it contracted. Beginning in the late 1910s and into the 1920s, however, the wheel shows in New York and throughout the

United States began to suffer from competition with locally produced "stock" shows. These had always been somewhat more risqué, especially as compared to the national circuit known as the Columbia wheel. The Columbia circuit built its reputation on offering "clean" shows: its comics were prohibited from using words such as *hell* and *damn,* chorus girls were not allowed to dance with or sit on the laps of male patrons, and men in the audience were asked to refrain from smoking. But when in New York higher-priced Broadway revues such as Flo Ziegfeld's *Follies*, George White's *Scandals*, and Earl Carroll's *Vanities* began competing successfully for this audience, the Columbia circuit turned to more explicit shows in hopes of reviving its profits.[11] Rather than having some burlesque shows that used "cleanness" as a strategy to attract consumers and some that proclaimed the "hotness" of their shows, all sought to outdo each other as well as the Broadway revues in their daring.

As a result, innovations in burlesque performance focused the audience's attention ever more closely on the female performer's body. During the 1910s producers constructed runways that allowed chorus girls and principals to perform among the audience, not just on a distant stage. A decade later, burlesque women abandoned flesh-colored body tights in favor of bare legs in the chorus numbers and bare breasts in the tableaux. Also during these years, producers inserted more skits in which women undressed under a pretext such as getting ready for bed or putting on a bathing suit (although always in silhouette behind a curtain).[12] During the 1920s such skits gave way to what would become the most well-known feature of burlesque shows, the striptease.

Much like the stripper's body itself, the origins of the striptease are shrouded in mystery. It seems that women may have been undressing to music on stage through the first decades of the twentieth century. But the striptease — in which the teasing played as important a role as the stripping — probably did not make its debut until the late 1920s. Morton Minsky, whose family managed a number of burlesque theaters in New York, observed that before this time stripping was "done as much for comedy as for titillation and [was] not the highly glamourized display of nudity that [it] later became."[13] Minsky claimed that a performer in one of his family's theaters, Mae Dix, "accidentally" invented the striptease in 1916 when she tried to save on laundry costs by removing her detachable collar and cuffs as she left the stage, and was lured to take off more by the ensuing applause. Other writers name 1928 as the year of its birth, attributing the innovation of the striptease to either Hinda Wassau or Carrie Finnell (the latter is also considered the inventor of tassel-twirling).[14] All agree, however, that by 1930 the striptease was an increasingly important feature of the burlesque show.

In general, a striptease took one of two forms. In its earliest incarnation a fe-male performer sang a song fully dressed. At the conclusion of the song she left the stage, perhaps slipping off a shoulder strap or toying with her buttons. In response to audience applause, she returned minus one article of clothing. She sang another chorus, left the stage once more, and returned for another encore, again wearing less, and so on, for up to six or seven encores. By 1932, although this type of strip was still being performed, stripteasers had developed a new style that would be the hallmark of 1930s burlesque. Now a stripper took off her clothing while she was on stage. She might or might not sing to the accompa-nying music, but like earlier strippers she too responded to audience applause by undressing further. A performer would never remove all of her clothing. While strippers and performances varied,[15] during the 1930s at the end of a striptease the performer's breasts were usually covered, either by pasties, a brassiere, or some artfully concealing prop, and she always wore at least a G-string and sometimes panties or a flesh-colored leotard.[16]

The fact that, by the 1930s, the striptease was the "feature[d] class of enter-tainment" in burlesque shows confirms the increasing importance of sexual display as a marketing strategy; nonetheless, burlesque shows' defining attrib-ute was not exhibitionism per se but sexual suggestiveness.[17] Burlesque perfor-mance worked as entertainment because it invited the spectator to imagine that which was not shown or not said. The key to a striptease's success, for example, was not how much of her body a woman revealed but how much the people in the audience thought she revealed and how well she encouraged their desire that she reveal more. Thus, strippers wore net or flesh-colored brassieres and panties to give the impression of nudity. They used body makeup and even stage lighting alternatively to hide clothing or to hide potentially unlawful nakedness.[18] The central role of illusion in the striptease made it possible for performers simultaneously to satisfy their customers and, usually, protect themselves legally.

The technique of one popular stripper who often performed in New York City may serve to demonstrate the importance of suggestiveness to the striptease of the Depression years. Margie Hart was rumored to "show more" than other principals. Yet she never removed her full-length panel skirt (a gar-ment with two separate panels, one in front and one in back, hung low on the hips). Instead, as she strutted back and forth on the stage she used her fingers to flick the panels, offering spectators quick glimpses of what was concealed be-neath. Hart's reputation as an especially daring performer resulted from ru-mors that she sometimes did not wear a G-string under her skirt. Those in the know suggest, however, that Hart built illusion upon illusion: industry gossip held that she wore a G-string that sported artificial pubic hair so that she could give the audience what she thought they wanted, while still obeying the law.[19]

Burlesque operators, performers, and even some fans agreed that suggestiveness and illusion were more important to 1930s striptease than was actual nudity. Ann Corio says of Margie Hart, whom she calls the "most daring" stripper, that "she gave the boys . . . flashes so brief that they didn't really reveal anything, but that suggested all."[20] Some members of the audience, at least, suspected that all was not as it seemed: one businessman who testified in favor of burlesque shows before New York's license commissioner stated that he couldn't tell if a stripper was actually nude or "something intended to appear as nude."[21] And burlesque producer Morton Minsky, meditating on the nature of the industry, observed that "we're dealing in a world of illusion, and if the customers . . . *thought* they were seeing actual nude flesh, then what's the difference?"[22]

Burlesque comics depended upon teasing and suggestion as much as did the strippers. Burlesque bits featured stock characters: the comic, whose naïveté could sometimes win him and sometimes cost him the girl, the suave, smooth-talking straight man, the juvenile, who might also portray a nance (homosexual) character. The female performers who appeared in the bits also played stereotyped roles as the shrewish or cuckolding wife, naive virgin, or sexually insatiable woman. The comedic quality of burlesque skits derived from the juxtaposition of formulaic characters and plots with a series of double entendre jokes that acknowledged, validated, and satirized sexual desire, all at the same time. The formulaic character of the comedy — it has been said that by the 1930s no new burlesque skits had been written in twenty years — together with its multivalent nature, called upon spectators to interpret the performance in the light of their own preexisting knowledge of sex — indeed, their knowledge of burlesque itself.

This particular brand of knowledge found few other sites for public articulation. Burlesque humor encompassed a variety of desires, some more unconventional than others. Heterosexual lust was a common theme. In one typical scene performed in a Times Square burlesque theater in the early 1930s, for example, a married couple visited a lawyer seeking a divorce. As one burlesque opponent described it, the attorney successfully urged them to reconcile: "Finally, both agree[d] to let bygones be bygones. The husband said, 'All right, I'll forget if she will give me a little peace when we get home.' The wife said, 'Yes, I'll give you a little peace as often as you want, providing I can have some, too, whenever I want it."[23] More unusual was the "Beautiful Fairy" skit, in which the straight man told the comic and another man that he had stolen a chemical that "would bring a beautiful Fairy to every man who possessed it. A Fairy that would guide man to his port of happiness." The straight man then rubbed a drop of the liquid on his leg. After a blackout, a young woman "dressed very sexy" appeared and told him, "I am your beautiful fairy come to guide you to your port of happiness." The straight man and young woman exited. Then the second man rubbed a drop of liquid on his leg, another woman appeared, repeated the speech and they left the stage together. Finally it was the comic's turn. However, he rubbed the liquid on the seat of his pants. When the lights came back up, a young man was standing on the stage, "posing very nancy."

COMIC: Who the Devil are you?
JUVENILE (*VERY NANCY*): I am a beautiful fairy come to guide you to your port of happiness.
COMIC (*TAKES HIM BY THE ARM*): Well, any old port in a storm.[24]

The comedy in these bits arose from the audience's ability to identify the sexual meanings of common words such as *piece* (*peace*), *fairy*, and *port*; in the latter scene it played on their presumptions about the nature of homosexual pleasures as well.[25] The joke's sly familiarity was what made it "sexy."

In the average burlesque show, according to one observer, there were "situations which would appeal to the homosexual, the pederast, the sodomist, the fetishist, the sadist, the masochist, [and] the necrophiliac," but it was up to the viewers to tease out the meanings of these situations.[26] For example, "The Bull Fight" incorporated the "machuka" gag into a skit with intimations of bestiality and homosexuality. In this skit the straight man reveals that the bullfighters are on strike, so the comic will have to fight the bull. He tries to explain how to do so to the comic:

STRAIGHT MAN: He pulls out his machuka.
COMIC: The dirty thing, and there are women there.
STRAIGHT: Now you'll have to have one.
COMIC: Oh, I've got one.
    . . .
STRAIGHT: Is it a long one?
COMIC: Oh, it's about that . . . (*gestures showing its great length*)
STRAIGHT: I must examine your machuka . . .
COMIC: I don't know you well enough.

STRAIGHT: Come on, just lay it in my hand. I won't drop it.

COMIC: But if you do, don't drop it in the mud.

The comic leaves the stage to enter the arena, and the straight man describes the bullfight to the audience: "He stuck the bull in the rear with his machuka. . . . The bull is down, he's up, he's down, he's up."[27] There are a number of versions of this skit, all of which focus on the comic's misunderstanding of the meaning of *machuka*, or a similar word. The skit was amusing only because the audience, invested with sexual knowledge, simultaneously understood the misunderstanding, collaborated in it, and mocked it.

Sex and suggestiveness were not unique to burlesque. It was during the first years of the Depression that Mae West, for example, transferred her own rendition of the double entendre from the Broadway stage to Hollywood. Burlesque's nearly nude women had their counterpart in Broadway revues and, especially after Prohibition repeal, nightclubs.[28] But sexual suggestiveness constituted the essence of burlesque in a way that it did not for these other entertainment forms. The centrality of suggestiveness may have been part of what made burlesque a growth industry in the 1930s. Burlesque built upon the increasing sexualization of commercial culture in its own way, treating sex in its various forms as a welcome diversion from daily troubles. But burlesque's diversions were not simply an escape; simultaneously they invoked, echoed, and caricatured spectators' own experiences of sexual attraction and hostility, desire and frustration, fantasy and the often humdrum reality.[29]

Its suggestiveness may also have been what made burlesque so threatening to New York's vice reformers, clerics, and city officials. Especially in the striptease, suggestiveness operated as an incitement to desire. As such, it seemed to betoken that the changes in sexual ideology and practice that had occurred over the past several decades were spiraling out of control. As Estelle Freedman has pointed out, it was during the interwar years that "female purity lost its symbolic power to regulate sexual behavior."[30] How much greater this loss must have seemed to some in the shadow of the stripper's body as she strutted across the stage. And how much greater it must have seemed within the disordered world that was the early Depression.

Paradoxically, its suggestiveness contributed to the difficulty of controlling burlesque, since it could be nearly impossible to convey the sexiness of the performance in courtroom testimony, as numerous reformers lamented. At the same time, burlesque's ambiguities shaped the confrontations over how the genre would be regulated.[31] The fact that burlesque was structured so as to encourage several interpretations increased the opportunities for contestation. Respectable citizens easily could — and, in 1932, did — argue over the sexual content and meanings of a striptease or comedy act. Any interpretation might be dismissed as just one person's view. As we shall see, however, over the course of a decade one interpretation prevailed — that linking burlesque with deviant and dangerous male sexuality. The process by which burlesque's meanings were circumscribed occurred within, and simultaneously expedited, an expansion of state regulatory authority.

"A CLASS OF DISORDERLY PERSONS": MUNICIPAL AUTHORITY AND THE LICENSING OF BURLESQUE

Burlesque flourished under economic conditions that were deadly for some other sectors of New York's entertainment industry, especially the legitimate theater.[32] In the wake of the stock market crash New Yorkers abandoned Broadway shows, for which admission prices ranged up to five dollars and more. During the 1930–1931 season Broadway producers offered fifty fewer new shows than in the previous year, and the next season proved even more disastrous. As a result, many theaters remained dark, and rents plummeted.[33] Until this point burlesque had been confined to theaters outside of New York's entertainment district — on the Bowery or the Lower East Side, in Brooklyn and Harlem. Burlesque entrepreneurs, especially Billy Minsky and his brothers, moved into the newly affordable Broadway theaters. On February 12, 1931, the Minskys opened the Republic Theatre on West 42nd Street between Seventh and Eighth Avenues as a burlesque house. One month later Max Rudnick began offering burlesque at the Eltinge Theatre across the street. By the end of the year the Minskys had established two more burlesque theaters on Broadway. Burlesque had invaded Times Square.[34]

The burlesque theaters were profitable where legitimate theater was not because their overhead was so much lower. In 1931 burlesque performers had no union, and wages were substantially less than in any other branch of New York's entertainment industry. Chorus girls might earn as little as $15 for an eighty-two-hour work week.[35] Although the salaries of featured performers were higher — Phil Silvers earned $250 a week as a top comic for the Minskys later in the decade and a few of the best-known strippers were paid in excess of $1,000 weekly — many collected only $30 a week.[36] In addition, during the 1930s burlesque theaters adopted a "grind" policy under which they offered three, four, or even five

or more shows per day. Performers were required to work every show. Those theaters that offered only two shows daily, such as the New Gotham in Harlem, were
able to cut wages in exchange for the better working conditions.[37] Other production costs were also quite low. Sets and lighting design were simple and inexpensive. Little money was spent on chorus girls' costumes, and strippers were
responsible for furnishing their own outfits. As a result, tickets to a burlesque
show could be had for much less than the price of admission to a Broadway comedy or musical revue. At the Republic Theatre, whose owners sought a more
"high-class" audience, tickets ranged from 50¢ to $1.50. Across the street one
could gain admittance to the Eltinge for as little as 15¢. Broadway's burlesque theaters did a booming business from the start.[38]

Burlesque's prosperity did not go unnoticed. Burlesque shows had constituted a target for the wrath of reformers since the mid-nineteenth century.
From almost the moment of its arrival on the American stage, many commentators on burlesque performance identified it as "diseased," symbol as well as in-
strument of the degeneration of American society.[39] Such criticisms became the
basis for a largely ineffectual campaign by the staff of the New York Society for
the Suppression of Vice, which monitored burlesque shows and informed city
officials of especially racy performances. During the 1920s municipal authorities sporadically raided burlesque theaters at their behest, but the raids had little lasting effect.[40] When burlesque houses began opening in the theater district,
the antivice reformers who had traditionally opposed burlesque and their supporters among New York's clergy were forced to recognize that, far from driving burlesque from the stage, they were unable to contain its expansion.

This shift in geography made it possible for burlesque's customary foes to
join forces with a new ally — the 42nd Street Property Owners' Association.
This commercial organization counted among its members numerous Times
Square corporations and businessmen, including banks, hotels, and legitimate
theater producers. Members of the POA witnessed firsthand the Depression's
effect on Times Square, watching as storefronts were rented to proprietors who
catered to working-class and lower-middle-class customers. Many in the group
blamed the new burlesque theaters for this state of affairs, claiming that their
presence chased away more respectable merchants, drove down property values, and generally "cheapened" the street.[41] In partnership with the New York
Society for the Suppression of Vice, they tried to secure convictions for obscenity violations against the 42nd Street burlesque theaters. When municipal
judges refused to sustain the charges, POA members turned to a new strategy:
pressuring New York City's license commissioner not to renew the burlesque

theaters' annual licenses. Responding to their lobbying, as well as to that of the more traditional burlesque foes who joined them, Commissioner of Licenses James F. Geraghty opened hearings into the question of license renewal.[42]

Prior to these hearings New York City's license commissioners had rarely participated in efforts to regulate burlesque theaters because the extent of their power over theater licenses was unclear. In 1922 the New York Supreme Court had ruled in *A. H. Woods Theatre Company v Gilchrist* that the New York City commissioner of licenses had no power to revoke a theater license because he believed a performance there "improper."[43] The court determined that only a judge could revoke a license after proper hearing. In 1927 the license commissioner's authority was somewhat enhanced with the enactment of a state law empowering him to revoke a theater license if a play it housed was found obscene in a criminal court.[44] But the question of whether a license commissioner had the power to refuse to *renew* a theater license without court proceedings — that is, whether a refusal to renew was tantamount to a revocation — remained unsettled. It was this ambiguity in the law that permitted Commissioner Geraghty to respond to the proddings of the POA and convene hearings on license renewal.

This uncertain legal regime shaped an ensuing public debate that focused upon the relationship between burlesque performance and its audience. Despite his assertion that nonrenewal was not revocation, Commissioner Geraghty felt himself bound by the court's ruling in the *Woods* case that he had "no right of censorship of any play." He announced that he could not base a decision against license renewal upon his assessment of the nature of the performances inside the theaters. Nor, he asserted, could his ruling rest upon an economic rationale such as falling property values, which was outside the purview of his office. The most articulate critics of the Times Square burlesque houses, however, acted out of just such considerations: clergy and vice reformers lamented the immoral and indecent performances, while the POA and allied commercial interests blamed the burlesque theaters for "cheapening" the street. As a result, whereas much of the testimony offered at the 1932 hearings concerned the content of burlesque shows and analyses of Times Square's economic health, the commissioner asserted that he received this testimony only for the light it shed on the character of the burlesque *audience*. Drawing upon statutory language governing general licensing powers, Geraghty contended that he had a right to withhold licenses only if, in his words, "it could be proved that a theatre attracted a class of disorderly persons."[45] In response, burlesque opponents set out to demonstrate that the Times Square theaters catered to poor men, whose class and gender marked them as disorderly even before they stepped into the theater.

Legal considerations may have placed the burlesque audience at the center of this controversy, but contests over audience also played an important role in earlier debates about regulating burlesque. Indeed, almost at the very moment of its emergence the potential of nineteenth-century burlesque to subvert middle-class gender relations had been contained by the successful confinement of burlesque to predominantly working-class male audiences.[46] By the twentieth century this mostly working-class audience was supplemented by middle-class men out for a night on the town.[47] With burlesque's migration to the theater district in 1931, its producers set out to expand their audience in a new way, by capturing the mixed-gender, middle-class audience that had previously supported the legitimate theater. No longer, they hoped, would middle-class men come to burlesque theaters on the sly. Rather, they would bring their wives and their neighbors, and they would do so as a mark of their sophistication and worldliness, their modernity. The popularity of the Times Square theaters suggests that this strategy met with some success. Certainly the presence of women and men in formal attire on opening night at 42nd Street's Republic Theatre intimated a potential shift in burlesque's audience.[48]

Other reports also suggest a measure of diversity in the audience. While most burlesque patrons of the 1930s were men, in some neighborhoods a substantial minority of attendees were women, sometimes in the company of men, at other times alone or with children in tow.[49] A description of a mid-1930s burlesque audience that appeared in *Fortune Magazine* inadvertently demonstrates the difficulties of definitively characterizing its social class as well:

> Weed out the regular patrons of long-established houses, weed out slumming socialites, rowdy collegians, and honest seamen ashore, and where once the blood of the town sat now sit the backwash of a depressed industrial civilization, their eyes alight and most of their mouths open. It is not a pretty sight.

A good deal of weeding must be done to contend that poor men alone populated burlesque theaters.[50] This impression of diversity, however limited, was confirmed by the admittedly inconclusive but nonetheless suggestive research undertaken by one student of New York's burlesque industry. In a survey of over one thousand city residents, he found that almost 19 percent of "white-collar" men and 31 percent of "non-white-collar" men attended burlesque shows "often" or "occasionally." Further, only 40 percent of the first group, but almost 49 percent of the second, claimed to have never seen a burlesque performance.

While his results confirm the predominantly working-class nature of the audience, they also provide evidence that men of a variety of occupational categories visited burlesque theaters, leading to his conclusion that there was no "typical" burlesque patron.[51] In sum, there was just enough variation to permit those debating burlesque's future to emphasize certain of its audience's components as a way of accomplishing their goals.

Burlesque opponents who sought, at the very moment the audience was becoming more diverse, to portray it as exclusively male and poor played upon fears exacerbated by the Depression. The presence of large numbers of unemployed men on the streets during the day — perhaps hanging out in front of burlesque theaters, gazing at the larger-than-life posters of female performers — served as an unwelcome reminder of the challenge to masculinity occasioned by many men's inability to provide for their families.[52] Such "marginal men" were apparently beyond the reach of the institutions — family, employment, or church — that provided the bedrock of the social order.[53] When burlesque opponents described those men as sitting in burlesque theaters for the purpose of indulging their sexual appetites, or as "crowding" the streets outside the theaters, making it impossible for women to pass, they translated anxieties about economic crisis and social control into gendered discourses about sexual control, providing a common language with which the Times Square businessmen, clergy, and reformers could voice their concerns.

At the license renewal hearings, therefore, lawyers hired by the POA mustered a parade of witnesses who testified to the burlesque audience's disorderliness. Much of this testimony concerned not disorderly behavior but a kind of disorderly status, as opponents of renewal sought to demonstrate that the burlesque audience remained one of poor men. When offered with the intention of damning the theaters, statements that burlesque patrons were lower-class men, unclean and poorly dressed, and that they were not "the highest type of American citizenship," carried the insinuation that economic poverty meant spiritual and moral poverty as well. The additional observation that one would not want one's children or wife to come into contact with such men suggested that they were somehow menacing, even in the absence of any disorderly behavior.[54] Their disorderly character was proven by their very presence within the theater, for burlesque "pander[ed] to the lower instincts" and attracted only "lewd and dissolute" men. When POA lawyers snidely questioned witnesses for the burlesque theaters about their frequent attendance at the shows, implying that they could not control their responses to the performances, or their need for arousal, they made going to a burlesque theater itself a disorderly act.[55]

Burlesque patrons allegedly took their disorderliness into the streets as well.

Police officers and a neighborhood priest testified that since the theaters had opened "steerers" (who directed men to speakeasies) and streetwalkers had proliferated in the Times Square area, drawn by the type of man who attended a burlesque show.[56] Other witnesses complained that such men's presence in Times Square disrupted area commerce and, those hearing their testimony might imagine, undermined the nation's economic recovery. One restaurateur, testifying that his business had been hurt since the burlesque theaters opened, stated that as opposed to devotees of "high class" theaters, those who went to burlesque shows "patronize[d] them for the purpose of deriving a depraved satisfaction rather than coming out and getting something to eat when it is over."[57] Similarly, a real estate broker voiced his opinion that the people drawn to Times Square by the burlesque shows would not visit a department store. Invoking an earlier symbol of New York's commercial and moral degeneration, he suggested that if the theater licenses were renewed "we will have a regular Bowery of Burlesque theaters in 42nd Street."[58] Several merchants testified that their customers had deserted them because they did not want to walk past the crowds of men before the theaters.[59] The complaints of these men suggested that sexual debauchery within the theater also caused economic decline outside it.

The frequency with which burlesque opponents described "crowds" of men and boys attending burlesque shows and congregating on the streets is striking.[60] These crowds were not merely a nuisance; they were also a threat. A lawyer for the POA opened his attack on the burlesque theaters by charging that the "undesirable elements" who attended the performances "have made it unsafe for young women having business in that block, working in business buildings abutting on that thoroughfare, to pass through the street." One man who worked at a publishing house on 42nd Street testified that his secretary returned to the office one day complaining of a man who called out to her, "Hello, baby, can I take you out for lunch." Similarly, a realtor told the license commissioner that he had seen both sides of 42nd Street "lined by young men and old men of every kind of character, almost blocking passage at some times, and calling forth remarks to girls and ladies who happened to be passing on the street."[61] It is not necessary to dismiss these allegations of harassment of female pedestrians to recognize the ways in which, by offering testimony about such behavior, foes of the Times Square burlesque theaters linked fears of economic nonproductivity and sexual disorder, marshaling images of unruly, idle, even dangerous, men and innocent industrious women to support their objections to the renewal of licenses. Such arguments would become much more explicit later in the decade.

Commissioner Geraghty's assertion that his findings about the nature of the audience would provide the basis for his decision shaped the testimony presented by burlesque defenders as well. Those who testified on behalf of the theaters — including burlesque producers, employees, and patrons as well as theater critics and members of the recently formed New York-based National Council on Freedom from Censorship — had varying motives for desiring the renewal of the theater licenses.[62] Some acted from financial interests; others sought to preserve their access to burlesque shows; a few intended to protect an abstract conception of freedom of speech; several likely were driven by a combination of these factors. It was not so much these divergent motives as the regulatory context in which they operated that gave rise to an inherently contradictory strategy for defending burlesque.

In one respect, advocates of license renewal capitulated to the logic if not the facts asserted by their adversaries, countering the image of the poor male audience with a vision of burlesque theaters filled with women and men of all classes. Supporters of burlesque attached great importance to women's presence in the audience as a signifier of morality, emphasizing that women as well as men attended and enjoyed burlesque shows. Several women testified that they found the shows entertaining, including ninety-three-year-old former burlesque dancer "Mother" Annie Elms, who told Commissioner Geraghty that "I think I am the best woman in America, and I see nothing wrong in a burlesque show."[63] Numerous men also attested that their wives, mothers, and other female relatives accompanied them to burlesque performances, and along with "usherettes" employed in the theaters they asserted that a sizable proportion of the audience — up to 20 percent — was composed of women.[64] In addition, the burlesque theaters' attorneys presented a parade of male witnesses who could claim professional status, including lawyers, architects, and realtors, in order to show that middle-class New Yorkers could be counted among burlesque fans. These men, all of whom themselves attended the shows, described a heterogenous audience containing "average" and "ordinary" citizens, plumbers and bricklayers, and "prominent" people.[65] The argument that middle-class as well as working-class people, women as well as men, enjoyed burlesque had the undoubtedly unintended effect of supporting burlesque opponents' contention that a predominantly male working-class audience was incapable of exercising self-control in the face of the sexual display on the stage.[66]

Defenders of burlesque did, however, argue vigorously against the allegation that burlesque "aroused" sexual passions and called forth uncontrollable responses from the men in the audience. For example, they went to great lengths to show that female patrons, employees, and pedestrians were not harassed by theater patrons.[67] They also shifted accusations of sexual abnormality from burlesque's patrons to its critics, postulating that smuttiness resided not in the burlesque show itself but in the mind of the person who perceived obscene meanings in the entertainment. Such a strategy was possible because it highlighted burlesque's definitive characteristic: its suggestiveness, through which the genre's practitioners refused to limit themselves to one meaning.

Yet this defense of burlesque also was laden with contradictions. Witnesses who advocated license renewal used burlesque's capacity for diverse meaning by denying this capacity, testifying that burlesque humor had no double (read sexual) meanings, or at least that they detected none. Numerous men told disbelieving attorneys for the POA that they liked burlesque not because it was sexual but because it was "good clean fun." Rejecting the idea that burlesque humor turned on double entendre, they contended that they laughed at burlesque because "there was no sense to it" or because it represented "good old slapstick." Just as their attempt to prove that the burlesque audience included others besides poor men could backfire, operating as a confirmation of the deviance of such men, when burlesque advocates denied that burlesque shows were "sexy" they seemed to be conceding the immorality of sexual humor and sexual display.[68]

Still, such testimony succeeded in problematizing the relationship between burlesque performance and its interpretation by audience members. When a POA attorney read aloud lengthy transcripts of burlesque skits in an effort to get stage designer and burlesque fan Cleon Throckmorton to admit their double meaning, Throckmorton's rejoinder that "these things must mean something to you. You must like reading them" suggested that depravity resided in middle-class critics more than theater patrons. Conversely, when lawyers representing the theater owners repeatedly asked opposing witnesses whether they had been "demoralized" or "depraved" by their investigations of burlesque shows, those witnesses' insistence that burlesque performance did not inflame their own sexual passions supported the theater advocates' contention that all audience members could control their responses to the striptease and comic bits.[69]

Embedded within this debate about the burlesque audience were contending beliefs about the nature of popular culture within a democracy, beliefs that took on exaggerated dimensions in the economic and political context of the 1930s. During this decade intellectuals developed a critique of "mass culture" that focused on the deadening conformist aspects of culture as a commodity under modern capitalism and argued that the consequences included the fostering of totalitarian and fascist tendencies. The outlines of these contests over burlesque suggest that this mass-culture critique was merely one manifestation of a more pervasive anxiety about the relationship between democratic culture — that is, culture that escaped the control of, and arose from a different sensibility than, the cultural elite — and the democratic citizen. Indeed, this leftist critique shared much with an older, more conservative tradition that imagined an entertainment consumer entrapped within and manipulated by low cultural forms that did not uplift but merely entertained and, all too often, corrupted. It was exactly such a vision of the relationship between audience and entertainment that underlay all demands for censorship in the late nineteenth and early twentieth centuries. It was captured neatly in the title of the 1933 bestseller, *Our Movie-Made Children*, a volume that gave "scientific" proof that America's future citizens were being mentally, morally, and ethically wrecked by the nation's vast mass culture industry.[70] And it was simultaneously articulated by those who, through their descriptions of hordes of poor men crowding the burlesque theaters, suggested that burlesque was a dangerous form of mass culture, one that threatened less to enforce conformity than to foster an infectious disorderliness — even, perhaps, a kind of sexual revolution. Those defending the burlesque industry from this attack sought to offset the critique of burlesque's lewd poor man by transforming him into an "average citizen" who brought his (or, occasionally, her) own meanings to culture and was capable of controlling his response to it. Thus, while foes of burlesque described the theaters as a magnet for "lewd and dissolute" lower-class men, a kind of *lumpenproletariat* whose presence posed a threat to the social order, advocates of license renewal contended that the average New Yorker was capable of attending a burlesque show and remaining a productive citizen, of participating in a form of mass culture and retaining his or her capacity for self-control and (democratic) self-governance. The fact that professional men, businessmen and women, journalists and legitimate theater people all were willing to testify in public to their liking for burlesque suggests that in 1932 this latter argument appeared a viable one.[71]

The lively debate about burlesque's morality in 1932 indicates that the genre's cultural meanings remained ambiguous, and as a result burlesque foes succeeded in closing down the Times Square theaters only temporarily. Indeed, despite the lengthy hearings the fate of New York City's burlesque industry seemed to depend as much upon the political fortunes of the city's mayor as upon whether antiburlesque activists were able to connect burlesque, poverty, and male sexual deviance. Mayor Jimmy Walker favored keeping the Times

Square burlesque theaters open (nicknamed "Playboy Jimmy," he had in fact been among those in attendance at opening night at the Republic Theatre), and perhaps as a consequence the hearings ended without a decision from the license commissioner. It was not until four months later, when Walker was forced from office in the wake of revelations of widespread corruption in his administration, that Acting Mayor Joseph McKee ordered Commissioner Geraghty to deny the license renewal applications.[72] Within weeks the license commissioner, less reform-minded than McKee, had agreed to reissue the theater licenses if the burlesque producers promised to subject their performances to internal censorship.[73]

While the 1932 hearings did not decisively resolve the fate of the Times Square burlesque theaters, they marked an important moment in the development of a new regulatory regime. In 1932 municipal officials and antiburlesque activists turned their attention from the criminal law to the licensing process as a means of controlling burlesque. Although they did not abandon attempts to prosecute burlesque performers and producers, beginning with the 1932 license renewal hearings they sought to circumvent the limitations of the criminal law and thereby to increase municipal regulatory authority over the theater. In the period between 1932 and 1935 the legal framework within which such licensing authority could operate was refined through the efforts of city officials to control burlesque performances and ensuing litigation over those efforts.

After the license renewal hearings a succession of New York City license commissioners repudiated the viewpoint that they had no jurisdiction over the *content* of burlesque shows. They embarked upon a series of attempts to control what was presented on the stage by issuing regulations that defined the boundaries of permissible performance and threatening to revoke the licenses of burlesque theaters in which performers transgressed those boundaries. In 1933 Commissioner Geraghty recanted his earlier assertion that he was "no censor," issuing rules forbidding female performers to remove any part of their costumes offstage or to touch them while onstage.[74] There is no evidence he tried to enforce these regulations, but subsequent license commissioners seemed more determined. Later the same year his successor required that all strippers and chorus girls be "decently clad" in "opaque" rather than "transparent" costumes.[75] When reform mayor Fiorello LaGuardia took office in 1934, he and his license commissioner, Paul Moss, launched a more concerted attack upon the content of burlesque shows. First they engineered the elimination of theater runways that had permitted female performers to parade out into the audience.[76] A few months later they issued a list of official regulations that prohibited women from appearing on the stage "with breasts or the lower part of the torso uncovered, or so thinly covered or draped as to appear uncovered" and enjoined language "offensive to decency or propriety" in the comic sketches.[77]

New York's license commissioners found support for this strategy of formulating regulations and threatening to revoke theater licenses for their violation in a court decision arising out of the 1932 license renewal hearings. In *In re Rudhlan Amusement Corporation* a New York Supreme Court justice ruled that Commissioner Geraghty's refusal to renew licenses could be predicated on a variety of factors beyond the character of the audience. While denying that the license commissioner was seeking to act as a censor, he contended that the general "conduct and operation of the theatre" provided grounds for withdrawal of its license:

> the type of production, with the lewd scenes that have been mentioned, the vulgar titles given to the plays and exhibited outside the theater, the character of the pictures reproduced in large numbers outside of the theater, the sale of lascivious literature in the theater — all these facts . . . were sufficient to justify his refusal to renew the license.[78]

Each of the conditions cited concerned not the presence of disorderly persons but the content of the show and its advertising. From 1932 to 1935 New York's license commissioners used the decision to justify their efforts to control burlesque by regulatory fiat, while ignoring its insistence that license renewal presented an entirely different situation than did license revocation.[79] But when, in 1935, Commissioner Moss revoked a burlesque theater's license for allegedly breaking his rules regulating performance, the state's highest court rebuked him, making it quite clear that a license commissioner could only revoke or suspend a theater license during its term if municipal officials had first obtained a conviction on obscenity charges. This ruling left open to city officials two options for controlling burlesque: suspending theater licenses at the end of the license term or criminal prosecutions.[80]

Yet New York officials seemed fundamentally dissatisfied with these options. Criminal prosecution was impractical because convictions of burlesque performers for violating obscenity statutes were notoriously difficult to obtain in New York City.[81] Perhaps most judges and juries would have agreed with one New York magistrate who in 1935 dismissed charges against two strippers performing at a nightclub on the ground that "nudity is no longer considered indecent in uptown nightclubs and theatres."[82] The difficulties with license

nonrenewal were more subtle, encompassing political as well as legal considerations. Having to wait until the end of the licensing year to put a burlesque show
out of business meant that government officials might be unable to respond in
a timely fashion to the demands of anti-obscenity activists. Official attempts to
"clean up" New York City often corresponded to the rhythms of elections and
to political imperatives more generally. As a result, politicians desired a regulatory mechanism that allowed them to act against burlesque shows quickly in
order to demonstrate their merit as guardians of the public interest.[83]

This was especially the case for Fiorello LaGuardia and his license commissioner, Paul Moss. LaGuardia's forceful personality and frequently autocratic
governing style, his commitment to political reform, and his ascension to the
mayoralty at a time when citizens expected and tolerated activist government
ensured that he would leave a long-lasting imprint on the city of New York. The
"Little Flower's" reform vision encompassed not just good government but also
good morals. LaGuardia proclaimed his "desire to be the Mayor of a clean
American city and protect its morals," and he pursued his role as protector very
visibly: publicly burning books and magazines adjudged obscene, ordering the
city's sanitation department to dispose of the "trash" being sold at local newsstands, or taking a sledgehammer to confiscated slot machines.[84] LaGuardia
was labeled "prudish" and a "puritan at heart" by his contemporaries and historians alike.[85] Whether this prudishness was a reflection of his personal views
on sexuality or merely the political strategy of a consummate politician has not
yet been a matter of historical inquiry. It is certain, however, that crusades on
behalf of social and sexual morality could be of immense political value in Depression-era New York. The anti-Tammany LaGuardia's election brought a significant diminution of the political power of Irish Americans in New York, and
in fact he never carried more than a third of the Irish vote. Nonetheless, as a Fu-
sion candidate, he was dependent on coalition building, and in the New York of
the 1930s, where Catholics of all ethnicities comprised almost half the population, his support for "morality" could provide one means of attracting at least a
portion of the substantial Irish Catholic vote. LaGuardia's political motives
were complemented by Paul Moss's special disdain for burlesque. Moss spent
much of his life in the theater: he was a vaudeville performer as a youth, and
later ventured into film, vaudeville, and legitimate theater production. Asserting that "real showmen do not go in for filth," he seemed to see New York's burlesque industry as an insult to the theatrical profession, and he pursued his
campaign against burlesque with vigor.[86]

Initially, LaGuardia's efforts to bring the reform agenda to the problem of the burlesque shows met with little success. Burlesque prospered in New York in spite of the promulgation of rules, threats to revoke licenses and occasional raids. Commissioner Moss despaired that, because of adverse court rulings, "we can do nothing regarding the indecent performances given at the burlesque theatres."[87] By 1937 the city was home to fourteen burlesque theaters, and applications for three more licenses were pending.

The unfettered growth of burlesque came to an abrupt halt in April 1937 when municipal officials finally succeeded in convicting two employees of Harlem's New Gotham Theatre on charges of offering an obscene performance. Seizing the moment, Commissioner Moss revoked the New Gotham's license. Then, at the urging of the New York City chapter of the Knights of Columbus, he launched another hearing to determine whether to renew the licenses of the city's other burlesque theaters, all of which were scheduled to expire in May.[88] After representatives of child welfare organizations and Catholic, Protestant, and Jewish clergy testified against burlesque, Moss denied applications to renew the licenses of every one of the city's burlesque theaters.[89] The contest over the survival of burlesque in New York City was renewed. This time theaters all over the city, not merely those in Times Square, were threatened.

"THE HABITATS OF SEX-CRAZED PERVERTS": BURLESQUE AND THE SEX CRIME WAVE

The New Gotham conviction may have provided municipal authorities with a new weapon for attacking burlesque, but the sex crime panic that erupted in New York City and across the nation in 1937 provided both the motivation and the justification for a renewed campaign. This panic resulted from sensationalized media coverage of violent sexual crimes against women and children.[90] In New York City a hint of things to come was offered in 1936 by the front-page stories detailing the rape and murder of Nancy Evans Titterton, a wealthy young writer. In March 1937 the sexual assaults and deaths of two young girls added fuel to the fire.[91] Under pressure to do something about the "wave" of sex crimes, beleaguered municipal officials began searching for a solution to the problem. Closing the theaters on the grounds that burlesque caused sex crimes became one of their most visible responses to the panic. Just as burlesque theaters had earlier served as a scapegoat for Times Square property owners' financial troubles, now they offered politicians a scapegoat for sex crimes. At the same time, the sex crime panic provided burlesque's traditional foes with new ammunition, echoing as it did the concerns about male sexual disorderliness that they had articulated in 1932.[92]

Neither the sex crime panic nor the assertion of a causal relationship between burlesque and the sexual psychopath was unrelated to the continuing Depression. The increased attention to violent sex crimes that exploded in the local and national media in 1937 was itself a manifestation of the anxiety about masculinity that the economic crisis fostered and that the 1932 antiburlesque campaign expressed.[93] The sexual psychopath was merely the newest incarnation of the "lewd and dissolute" poor man who frequented burlesque theaters, unable to control himself. Rather than rail against the presence in the neighborhood of vaguely undesirable male patrons, reformers and government officials now focused their attack on a more insidious, considerably more dangerous, and less geographically specific degeneracy. No longer did they argue that burlesque attracted sexual perverts; now they claimed that it created them and then unleashed them on the wider community.

Critics of burlesque had begun suggesting that the genre was linked to sex crimes in 1936, despite the lack of any indication that sex criminals visited burlesque performances. The president of the New York Society for the Suppression of Vice declared in that organization's annual report that burlesque shows were a "proximate cause" of sex crimes.[94] More often burlesque was blamed along with other corrupting influences. One commentator on Nancy Titterton's murder observed of the confessed killer that he

> was a highly imaginative young man who fed his imagination with the wrong food. . . . If we do not want any more Fiorenza cases let us close up the burlesque shows. Let us stop publication of filthy sex magazines. Let us stop making dirty motion pictures to be shown at private parties. Let us clamp down on insidious sex appeal advertising.

He called for a "return to the old tradition of self-control."[95] But until mid-1937 arguments that burlesque caused sex crimes were made infrequently.

In the wake of the New Gotham conviction increasing numbers of antiburlesque activists and municipal officials alleged such a causal relationship, refashioning traditional fears about sexual contagion into the specter of sexual psychopathy. Upon revoking the New Gotham license, Paul Moss announced his belief that burlesque shows contributed to the sex crime wave. New York's police commissioner chimed in, telling a group of Catholic policemen that he had been to a burlesque performance and observed "hundreds of boys and young men avidly absorbed in the immoral proceedings on the stage." The commissioner suggested that closing up the burlesque theaters was a better solution to the sex crime problem than another common proposal, sterilizing sex offenders. That burlesque shows provided an incentive to sex crimes went without saying: "We know what it leads to. I don't have to tell you."[96] Several days later, at the license renewal hearings conducted by Commissioner Moss, numerous witnesses took up this refrain, asserting that "absolute closing of the burlesque houses was the only way to deal with a situation that [is] breeding 'sex crime' in the city."[97]

Other municipal officials, relieved to find a scapegoat for the alleged increase in sex crimes, also turned on burlesque shows. Even while Commissioner Moss was deliberating whether to renew their licenses, police raided three Brooklyn burlesque theaters. The Kings County (Brooklyn) district attorney asserted that these theaters were "largely responsible for the sex degeneracy and the sex crimes."[98] Mayor LaGuardia also chimed in, requesting an investigation of the relation between burlesque and sex crimes against children. He learned that judges and probation officers knew of only two incidents: one in which a fifteen-year-old boy blamed burlesque shows for inciting him to attack his sister and another in which

> a girl was . . . found in company with a man at a hotel. Her explanation was that she had applied to the manager of a Burlesque show for a position; had been referred by some one there to an art place where models pose practically in the nude [and] had become interested in activities which finally led to her appearance in the Children's Court.[99]

Despite very scanty evidence that burlesque caused sex crimes, however, city officials persisted in connecting the two.

As the report to LaGuardia reveals, the charge that burlesque shows created sexual psychopaths often shaded into a looser connection between sex "crime" and burlesque's danger to youth. Women of the Catholic and Protestant Big Sisters organizations argued that burlesque corrupted young girls' morals, proclaiming that "burlesque shows are the first step on the down-grade for young girls. . . . From the confessions of young girls who have been placed in homes operated by our organization, it is evident that the down fall of many of them is due to burlesque." Other New Yorkers lamented burlesque's effect upon young boys. A female representative of the Hudson Avenue Boys' Club who testified before Commissioner Moss charged that burlesque shows "wrecked in a week all the churches could do in a year."[100] One father, offering a more personal testimonial, wrote to Mayor LaGuardia that his two high-school-age sons "began to go with prostitutes and bad company" after they started attending burlesque shows. When they became pale and thin and lost interest in their schoolwork, this parent moved away from New York City in order to protect his boys.[101] Brooklyn's district attorney, announcing his campaign against the borough's burlesque theaters, played upon fears for children's safety that had been fanned by the sex crime panic. Having asserted that burlesque caused sex crimes, he lamented that "the sad part about this situation is that young boys and girls are in these theatres. Most of them are school children, going into these places with their books under their arms."[102] He implied that burlesque shows endangered children in myriad ways, whether by placing them in close proximity to sex criminals or turning them into "bad girls" or even psychopaths.

The weakness of the counteroffensive mounted by burlesque entrepreneurs provides one measure of the success of a strategy that blamed burlesque for the creation of the sexual psychopath. A narrower range of people had the temerity to defend the burlesque theaters in 1937, and they offered very different arguments than had been tendered in 1932. No patrons were willing to express publicly that they enjoyed burlesque's humor and the striptease acts. At the hearings conducted by Moss the only speakers in favor of renewing the licenses were men who made their living from burlesque.[103] The testimony of middle-class burlesque consumers, who in 1932 had been happy to testify that they thought burlesque was "good clean fun," enjoyed by average citizens, remained noticeably absent.

Their inability to argue convincingly for the genre's morality required that the industry's proponents find new ways to resist the attack upon burlesque. Reflecting the growing burlesque industry's increased importance to New York's economy, they sought to emphasize the financial impact of Moss's action. Burlesque advocates recast the fears about economic crisis and lack of productivity that had played so important a role in the 1932 campaign, this time focusing upon the wage-earning women and men who would be put out of work if the theaters remained dark. Mayor LaGuardia received scores of letters and telegrams from chorus girls, musicians, cashiers, technicians, and other burlesque employees. Most echoed the themes raised by one such woman, who pleaded with the mayor to "realize what will happen to our families if you close up the burlesque theatres. I am the only one working and supporting my family. Jobs are so scarce in New York." Many correspondents invoked the specter of the dole, arguing that burlesque provided them with an honest living and complaining that they and their families would be forced to go on relief if the licenses were withheld.[104] In making such arguments they sought to supplant the connections that had earlier been alleged between burlesque and the marginal man, asserting instead that burlesque sustained economic prosperity and family life.

Between 1932 and 1937, then, the meanings of burlesque shifted. In both years burlesque opponents voiced concerns that audience members would be unable to control their reactions to the suggestive sexuality offered in burlesque theaters, but these fears had intensified by 1937. In the earlier campaign foes of burlesque contended merely that the performances aroused sexual passion. The worst consequences they envisioned were confined to a forward invitation to lunch. Just five years later the rather passive deviance of the men and boys who attended burlesque shows had been transformed into pathology. Boys who snuck into burlesque theaters, it was alleged, patronized prostitutes and attacked their sisters; men who watched strippers raped and murdered. Thus, the unemployed and dissolute man of the early Depression years had become the sexual psychopath.[105] Their ability to convince New Yorkers that burlesque caused sexual violence against women and children allowed antivice activists and city officials to argue that, as required by the Hicklin Rule and the obscenity regime it represented, burlesque did indeed corrupt its audience of adult men.

Everywhere they looked, burlesque producers saw signs that the attack upon their industry would succeed. The antiburlesque campaign prompted efforts in the state legislature to pass a law that would give New York City's license commissioner power to revoke theater licenses if he believed a performance was obscene. Legislators approved the so-called Dunnigan Bill in the space of merely two days. Governor Lehman vetoed the legislation, but only after intense lobbying by members of the legitimate theater industry, who were no friends of burlesque but had their own reasons to fear an expansion of licensing powers.[106] And while enactment of this legislation was averted, the fact remained that this time licensing authorities had operated within the bounds of their authority by suspending licenses either after a criminal conviction or at the end of their term. In the courts New York City's counsel successfully defended the refusal to renew the theater licenses by arguing that burlesque shows "are the cause of many of our sex crimes and the theatres which house them are the habitats of sex-crazed perverts."[107] As a consequence, burlesque producers were ready to agree to anything proposed by the city in order to protect their investments.

City officials had their own reasons for desiring a compromise. Fiorello LaGuardia's political career had been built in part upon his reputation as a friend of labor, and he was not eager to be blamed for creating additional unemployment in the midst of the Depression. At the same time, LaGuardia's reputation as a reform mayor owed as much to his frequent campaigns against gambling, obscenity, and other moral infractions as it did to his abhorrence of political corruption. LaGuardia personally intervened in the burlesque controversy, seeking to demonstrate both that he was doing something about sex crimes and that he cared about workers.[108] Ten weeks after the license commissioner banned burlesque, he granted seven theaters licenses to operate as "variety revue" theaters under the auspices of a new trade association known as the Variety Revue Theatre Association. Proclaiming that burlesque was "a thing of the past," LaGuardia declared that VRTA theaters would offer only "wholesome" attractions on a "high artistic plane."[109]

Mayor LaGuardia hailed the Variety Revue Theatre Association as a "completely voluntary" form of self-censorship, but it was in fact a compulsory mechanism that relied on licensing powers to institutionalize greater state authority not only over the content of theater productions but also over the organizational structure of the industry itself.[110] The bylaws of the association provided, among other things, that the words *burlesque* and *Minsky* could not be used in connection with the new theaters or their performances. A system of penalties, ranging from fines to expulsion from the association, was devised for violation of the rules promulgated by either the association or the license commissioner. The annual dues paid by association members provided the salary for one or more censors who would inspect each show weekly. LaGuardia personally selected the six men who sat on the association's Board of Governors, contrary to VRTA bylaws providing for election of governors by association members. All of them belonged to organizations that had been active in the antiburlesque campaign; the chairman was a member of the Knights of Columbus.[111] The voluntary nature of this economic restructuring was belied by the fact that only VRTA members in good standing would be granted licenses to operate the variety revue theaters.[112]

This transformation of the industry's corporate structure enhanced the license commissioner's power in other ways. Before the commissioner issued licenses to producers, he required them to agree in writing to exhibit only types of entertainment that he approved. This written agreement also stipulated that any deviation from its terms would result in the revocation of the license, and, significantly, the licensee was required to waive his or her rights to contest the revocation in court.[113] To further cement municipal authorities' control over the former burlesque operators, Commissioner Moss issued only three-month licenses to variety revue theaters. The shorter license period meant that city officials could act against the theaters more quickly than ever before, even if courts struck down the waiver of rights.

Municipal officials did not stop at these interventions in the industry's corporate structure but also used the 1937 burlesque closings to force a restructuring of labor relations within the industry. Since 1933 performers had been represented at all but one of New York's burlesque theaters by the Burlesque Artists' Association, led by performer Tom Phillips. Moss disliked Phillips and the BAA, believing that the union's members were "usually of the type that use the indecent sketches that are particularly offensive."[114] The leaders of a rival union, the American Federation of Actors, used the burlesque crisis to build their own membership. Perhaps they promised to control union members' performances more strictly in return for government support. In any case, in 1937 Moss and Mayor LaGuardia required members of the VRTA to sign a contract not with the BAA but with the AFA, arguing that they had banned the use of the word *burlesque,* and therefore the performers in variety revue theaters were not burlesque performers and ought not to be represented by the burlesque union.[115] The collective bargaining agreement signed by the theater operators and the AFA contained a morals clause that required the withdrawal of any material violating the rules established by the VRTA or New York's license commissioner. Municipal officials' foray into union jurisdiction occasioned a lengthy battle between the two labor organizations, and ultimately the parent union awarded the BAA jurisdiction over the former burlesque theaters. Even then, the intervention in labor relations did not end; the chairman of the Board of Governors of the VRTA ordered that the union change its name to the Brother Artists Association at the same time that he required the theaters to give musicians and chorus girls one day off a week.[116]

In the end, city officials did not abolish the burlesque industry, but they transformed it through their creative and assertive use of licensing powers that far exceeded anything earlier attempted to control the stage. Caught between the demands of labor and those of the city's moral guardians, they invented variety revue theaters that presented burlesque not only by another name but also of another nature. While above-the-waist nudity in the tableaux vivants remained, the teasing sexual style that had been the hallmark of burlesque was muted: the humor was toned down and the striptease ostensibly banned.[117] This reincarnation of the burlesque industry represented a significant expansion of state regulatory authority over commercial culture in New York City. The associations forged between burlesque, male disorderliness, and violence against women and children made this expansion possible.

"BUILDING A NATION OF MEN, NOT SUCKERS": WORLD WAR II AND BURLESQUE

Contrary to the assertion of several scholars and observers, burlesque did not vanish from New York City in 1937.[118] The number of theaters presenting burlesque declined drastically, however. Of the fourteen theaters that had been denied licenses in May, only nine ultimately reopened as variety revue theaters, and by November three more of the Times Square burlesque theaters had closed because of declining profits. By the end of 1938 only five theaters remained; in 1939 Manhattan had only three, including the Republic and the Eltinge on 42nd Street. The performances, which at least at first came under the strict observation of the Board of Governors of the VRTA, had become a mix of vaudeville and subdued burlesque. The theaters had lost their old audience and had little to offer a new one.[119]

Despite declining numbers of burlesque theaters and the imposition of greater restrictions on burlesque performance, clergy and religious groups continued to condemn burlesque in the years after 1937. Commissioner Moss dismissed most of these complaints, stating that the theater owners were doing their best and that the shows were being censored vigilantly by the VRTA Board of Governors.[120] In February 1942, however, the LaGuardia administration finally abandoned the attempt to regulate rather than abolish burlesque performance. Late in 1941 the delegates to the annual meeting of the Lord's Day Alliance, a national evangelical organization, petitioned Mayor LaGuardia to close the variety revue theaters on grounds that they were "obscene, vulgar and perniciously poisonous" as well as a threat to national defense. When in February 1942 the Catholic archbishop, Francis Spellman, and the Protestant Episcopal bishop, William Manning, added their protests as well, Commissioner Moss refused to renew the licenses of Manhattan's three remaining burlesque theaters. Burlesque had finally been banished from New York.[121]

Although the content of the shows had not changed all that much in the five years after the VRTA began censoring burlesque,[122] political conditions in 1942 facilitated this final state action against burlesque shows. A new campaign against the burlesque theaters fit with LaGuardia's political strategy of linking the defense of public morality with defense of the nation during wartime. Throughout World War II LaGuardia's popularity, which had been under severe strain by the end of the 1930s, was bolstered by his efforts to boost morale via morality.[123] Thus Paul Moss explained his decision to suspend the licenses with the observation that the mayor had "repeatedly stated that war conditions will not be permitted to lower the standards of morals and decency in this city."[124] A tradition of toleration for increased government regulatory powers during wartime abetted this strategy. In addition, the disadvantages to vigorous action against burlesque had evaporated. The high unemployment rate that made closing theaters unpopular in 1937 had dissipated with the wartime boom. Finally, the burlesque industry had been weakened by a decade of persecution. The remaining theaters, presenting a watered-down version of burlesque, were losing money and made an easy target.

In the context of wartime prosperity the debate over the closing of New York's last burlesque theaters articulated a different economy of sexuality, one that revived older concepts linking nonprocreative male sexual activity and profligacy.[125] In 1942 burlesque opponents inverted assumptions about the relationship between burlesque and male sexuality that had been offered by antiburlesque activists in the 1930s. Retreating from the notion that burlesque bred overly aggressive men — "sex-crazed perverts" — those who advocated the closing of the theaters alleged that burlesque *undermined* male virility. As a result, they suggested, the toleration of burlesque within American society threatened the war effort.

Burlesque now endangered democracy in a new way, by directly attacking the virtue of those charged with defending the nation. Young men in uniform were conspicuous among those who attended the burlesque shows, and activists framed much of their concern in relation to these men. For example, one out-of-town correspondent wrote to Mayor LaGuardia to praise his effort "to eradicate the filth in the form of the burlesque shows . . . to which so many thousands of our boys in the army and navy are being brought." Another man told LaGuardia of his experience at the Gaiety Theatre, where in the company of many young soldiers and sailors he witnessed "an exhibition that would, certainly, not uplift [their] morals."[126] These concerns were apparently shared by some military men themselves. "A Praying Soldier" linked the fate of burlesque with the fate of the nation. He declared to Mayor LaGuardia that "this is the greatest opportunity of our United States to build a nation of men, not suckers. If you can close up all the burlesque houses and such forms of depravity in all corners of the world we, as soldiers, sailors and marines would be much indebted to you."[127] For this soldier, and others who shared his view, burlesque shows imperiled normal masculine identity, sapped the virtue not only of soldiers but of all male citizens, and undermined the defense of the nation.

Such sentiments reflected concerns about the relation between war and male sexuality that Americans articulated most often in the context of debate about the military's venereal disease policy. Those who asserted that burlesque drained male virility echoed the fears of critics of the military's policy of preventing venereal disease by giving soldiers prophylactics. Like arguments that soldiers' extramarital sexual intercourse should be discouraged, the contention that burlesque threatened male potency (perhaps by inducing masturbation among soldiers in the audience) affirmed that state toleration of deviant sexual activity imperiled the war effort. When burlesque critics shifted their emphasis from masculine sexual aggressiveness to masculine debility, they altered the contours of the relationship between burlesque and sexual deviance they had crafted in the previous decade, but they maintained at the center of their critique the concern with burlesque's effect on its male audience and, implicitly, the women and children dependent on that audience.[128]

In the face of this renewed charge that burlesque eroded the social foundations of democracy, critics of the city's decision not to renew licenses asserted, as they had in 1932, that defending burlesque was akin to defending democratic culture.[129] To the traditional arguments — that burlesque was not immoral, that it offered the poor man entertainment, that it provided needed employment, or that New York was too cosmopolitan for the imposition of one moral standard[130] — they added a new, and increasingly prominent, emphasis upon city officials' "totalitarian" and "dictatorial" violation of democratic process. They asserted that Moss's decision to suspend the licenses was "un-American" and in contradiction to the values being fought for overseas.[131] Some used a slippery slope argument, cautioning that action against the burlesque theaters might endanger the legitimate theater as well.[132] Authors/producers Russel Crouse and Howard Lindsay were most histrionic. They proclaimed that "burlesque is the Czechoslovakia of the stage and the legitimate theater might soon be its Poland" and went on to warn that "we are at Munich. And complacency at this point, just because it involves burlesque, does not mean peace in our time."[133] Others attacked "one-man censorship" on the basis of its impact upon burlesque alone. They lamented that "in these days when we are making every effort to defend and preserve democratic institutions it is deplorable to see our own municipal officials adopting the methods of Hitler and Mussolini."[134]

In the short run, at least, antiburlesque activists had greater success than did foes of censorship in capturing the language of democracy for their own purposes, for municipal officials succeeded in countering accusations of totalitarianism and in keeping the burlesque theaters closed. Calling the charge of censorship a "red herring," the mayor proclaimed that he "challenge[d] any of the partisans of 'G-string' morality . . . to state publicly that the endless debauches in undressing which characterize the burlesque performances were not indecent and obscene." In arguing that "there is no constitutional right to be immoral[,] and filth, vulgarity and immorality do not come within the constitutional provisions for the freedom of speech," LaGuardia sought both to deny that democratic process was being subverted and to assure New Yorkers that the "abnormal and extraordinary conditions" of wartime would not be allowed to undermine America's moral strength.[135] Since city officials, despite numerous attempts, had succeeded in obtaining a conviction on obscenity charges related to a burlesque performance just once in a decade, his argument was convincing only because burlesque had been discursively linked to sexual depravity outside of the criminal law.

Although it is impossible to determine whether LaGuardia's explanations proved satisfactory to interested New York residents, they did convince Supreme Court Justice Levy, who dismissed the Gaiety Theatre operators' petition to force Paul Moss to renew their license.[136] With his decision, all hope for saving New York's burlesque theaters evaporated. The four theaters that had been able to hang on until 1942 — the Eltinge, Republic, and Gaiety in Manhattan and the Star in Brooklyn — never reopened their doors as burlesque houses. The display of women's bodies continued in New York's nightclubs and sometimes on the legitimate theater stage; in the postwar period stag movie houses and later adult bookstores and peepshows continued the tradition of commercialized sex entertainment on Times Square that was begun by the burlesque houses. However, the particular combination of sexual humor and sexual display that had been burlesque was to be no more.

In these contests over burlesque anti-obscenity activists compensated for the absence of a vulnerable audience in need of protection by imagining a new audience, one that posed a danger to the wider community. Whether that danger lay in the propensity to harass and rape or in abdicating the responsibility to preserve and protect, its most awful consequences could be felt not in the discomfort of female pedestrians or the violated bodies of children but in the frailty of democracy at which it hinted. Burlesque's suppression was demanded not least because, in these years, men's attendance at burlesque theaters suggested an out-of-control male citizenry and a democratic culture inadequate to the task of rebuilding and defending the nation. For anti-obscenity activists, democracy could be saved only if its culture was destroyed.

CHAPTER 3

"In the Clutches of Lesbians":
Legitimating Regulation on Broadway

In 1945 the Reverend John Sutherland Bonnell, pastor of New York City's Fifth Avenue Presbyterian Church, wrote to Mayor Fiorello LaGuardia to complain about *Trio*, a Broadway play portraying a young woman's encounter with, and escape from, lesbianism. Concerned that the play was "likely to spread the abnormal perversion with which it deals," Bonnell urged the mayor to use his powers to close the production. He confided to LaGuardia that his fears the play might harm New Yorkers had already been realized, as he knew of one young woman whose latent homosexuality had become active after she saw *Trio* three times.[1] Always the guardian of the young, the mayor sprang into action. Within four days his administration had used its licensing powers to coerce the owners of the theater housing the production to evict the play. Much to LaGuardia's surprise, however, New Yorkers greeted his action with outrage, condemning him for being prudish, short-sighted, even un-American.

In citing the harm to young women as justification for the suppression of a lesbian-themed play, LaGuardia honored a twenty-year-old tradition. Several similar plays had met with the same fate. Yet the widespread condemnation of the closing of *Trio* heralded changes in theater regulation.[2] Since the 1920s, government officials had used the production of plays about lesbians and gay men to expand their regulatory power over the legitimate theater. They found it necessary to do so because Broadway shows, playing to a middle-class and mixed gender audience that believed itself eminently capable of self-governance, had established something of a "right" to regulation in a democratic manner. When anti-obscenity activists and city officials adjudged such democratic regulation lacking, they focused attention on the proliferation of plays about homosexuality, which, like a few other especially racy productions, so violated notions of acceptable theatrical representation that they overwhelmed New Yorkers' wariness of theatrical "censorship." Shrewdly suggesting that the young women who were drawn to witness such productions might be seduced into lesbian relationships, as had been their sisters on the stage, they identified an audience in need of protection and legitimated their own regulatory efforts. By 1945, however, growing opposition to government power over the stage combined with new attitudes about how to prevent homosexuality to render campaigns against the "lesbian plot" on Broadway less useful as a means of controlling the legitimate theater.

CULTURAL HIERARCHY AND THEATRICAL REGULATION

If burlesque posed certain challenges to effective obscenity regulation because of its allegedly low, already corrupted audience, efforts to police Broadway faced a different set of difficulties, deriving from the presumption that, as high culture, the legitimate theater was entitled to artistic freedom. This claim to high cultural status had been made over the course of a century, and it was based as much on the character of the theatrical audience as on the productions offered. Early nineteenth century theaters accommodated both a "mass" and a "class" audience, although plebeian and elite patrons were seated separately. As the century progressed, segregated seating was replaced by segregated theaters, as theatrical entrepreneurs employed a variety of strategies to attract particular audiences to particular genres. Some mid-nineteenth-century theatrical producers welcomed middle-class women into their theaters by evicting prostitutes, banning alcohol, and establishing stricter controls over rowdy audiences, in the process distinguishing the "legitimate" theater from working-class concert saloons and variety shows. Later in the century vaudeville entrepreneurs undertook the same strategies to distinguish their art from low burlesque and thus to capture the so-called family audience. By appealing to an audience drawn from the upwardly mobile and middle classes, theater producers could at one and the same time improve their profitability and shield themselves from criticism for pandering to the lower instincts. By the early twentieth century Broadway's audience of relatively affluent adult women and men assured its place near the apex of a cultural hierarchy.[3]

This high culture status had important consequences for the regulation of the legitimate stage. Even in the early years of the century Broadway's producers and consumers had more success than did champions of motion pictures, for example, in invoking principles of artistic freedom against the specter of government regulation. By the 1920s the insistence that "the public is the best censor," and that official control of the theater violated the tenets of democracy and individual liberty, was commonplace.[4] The popularity of such beliefs was attributable as much to the nature of the theatrical audience as to the alleged seriousness of "drama." Within Broadway's auditoriums there were to be found few children in need of protection; nor were there the marginal men whose presence at burlesque shows would seem so threatening in the 1930s. Instead, there were middle-class adults — the nation's citizens — who were generally presumed to be capable of governing themselves. As a result, even the most militant of New York's anti-obscenity activists recognized that the options for regulating the legitimate stage were narrower than for other cultural forms. Setting up state censorship boards to oversee Broadway or aggressively using licensing powers to close theaters would be difficult, as Monsignor Lavelle of New York's Catholic hierarchy observed, for the term *censorship*, however defined,

> seems to have settled in the public mind as something of an abomination.
> . . . Freedom of speech, of the press, and of other things is so deep in the public mind that there is a general revulsion of feeling when anything appears that would seem to restrain liberty, even when liberty goes so far to be license [*sic*].[5]

Without a vulnerable viewer to protect or a dangerous spectator to control, advocates of strict regulation of the stage faced a good deal of opposition.

Nonetheless, Broadway's claim to cultural legitimacy became harder to sustain as its shows integrated more representations associated with low cultural forms. Contemporary observers and scholars alike have noted the proliferation of sexy costuming and sexual themes on Broadway stages during the 1920s.[6] While sex was not new to Broadway, certain types of representation of sexuality were. In the period after World War I, female performers in plays and musical revues appeared more frequently in less clothing. Chorus girls, for example, who earlier were arrayed seminude but motionless in tableaux vivants were transformed into "showgirls" who paraded about the stage wearing little besides a G-string and strategically placed beads, as the sumptuous but relatively sedate Ziegfeld Follies were eclipsed by more revealing revues.[7] Actresses in comedies and dramas might play a scene clad in lacy lingerie. In addition, the flappers and independent working women who had become a staple of motion pictures in the teens materialized on the stage as well. On Broadway the commodification of the New Woman proceeded apace as the revues offered scantily dressed women as objects of consumption, and the comedies featured characters whose flirtations, riotous living and sexual liaisons suggested that the modern girl was rapidly losing her respect for respectability.

The movement of such representations of sexuality onto the Broadway stage in revues and comedies coincided with an increasing realism in the legitimate drama. Realist playwrights sought to represent "truth" on the stage through the "close observation of existence."[8] Rejecting the Victorian notion that a playwright's goal should be to portray the ideal in order to uplift humanity, advocates of realism championed the dramatic representation of the negative as well as the positive aspects of contemporary life, often arguing that only this approach could reveal and solve societal ills. While some realist plays, concerning such issues as prostitution and venereal disease, were produced on the stage after the turn of the century, American realism did not begin to come into its own until the 1920s, heralded by the plays of Eugene O'Neill. O'Neill's plays demonstrate the extent to which questions of gender and sexuality were central to realist theater. *All God's Chillun Got Wings*, produced in New York City in 1924, portrayed the consequences of a marriage between an African American man and a white woman; *Desire Under the Elms*, staged a year later, concerned adultery and infanticide.[9] Each of these plays asserted the fact of female sexual desire and critiqued conventional morality for manufacturing human misery. While realism did not dominate the legitimate theater of the 1920s, its advent yielded a new rationale for consideration of sexual and gender issues in myriad theatrical productions, even those with only realist pretensions.

The foregoing suggests that in the early twentieth century there was a very complex relationship between Broadway's use of sex to draw an audience and its position within a cultural hierarchy. On the one hand, the legitimate theater's integration of "low" representations of female sexuality, particularly in the comedies and revues, posed a challenge to its reputation as highbrow culture. On the other hand, champions of realist theater heralded its portrayal of sexual problems as evidence of its highmindedness and seriousness; they believed the stage's treatment of sex could constitute *proof* of its high status. Since both the challenge to the stage's cultural legitimacy, and the defense of it, were elaborated in relation to its representations of sexuality, the battles over obscenity on Broadway intensified.

Anti-obscenity activists who sharpened their attack on Broadway in the 1920s resuscitated a critique of the theater's commerciality that dated to the colonial era. Many early Anglo-Americans saw the stage as a source of profligacy and a venue for decadence; the prostitutes and actors who were its habitués were deemed alike in their willingness to sell their selves in the marketplace. Such attitudes faded in the eighteenth and nineteenth centuries, but they did not completely disappear. When in the twentieth century financial success in the theater came to depend increasingly upon the commodification of sexuality, anti-obscenity activists countered the image of the theater as art by emphasizing its corruption by commerce, arguing that producers inserted "dirt" into plays for the sole reason that it increased their box office receipts.[10] To the assertion that the dramatist's quest for truth justified an increased frankness, these critics responded by pointing to a distinction between "liberty" and "license." Typical is a 1923 statement by one New York official that "cries of 'assaults upon personal liberty,' 'violations of the American spirit of freedom'" were in fact disingenuous protests by those "interested primarily in the theatre from a box-office standpoint [who were] really demanding that license shall be interpreted as liberty and the spirit of bawdry as the spirit of American freedom."[11] The use of the term *license* is especially telling, for it carries intimations not only of excess in general but of commercial excess in particular and, even more, of sexual excess ("licentiousness"). Sex onstage, anti-obscenity activists contended, was not about the search for truth; indeed the truth was, simply, that sex sells.[12]

This blurring of the lines between liberty and license, theater critics charged, was furthered by a modernist belief in moral relativity that erased the clear and fixed distinction between art and obscenity.[13] Only a reassertion of the immutability of moral standards could stop the proliferation of stage indecency. For example, one speaker warned a group of Catholic actors that the "sophisticated argument . . . that moral standards change" was itself "heretical [and] absolutely immoral." Episcopal Bishop William Manning made a comparable argument when he proclaimed that "the so-called 'new morality' which is a term brazenly used for the age-old immorality [is] a sin against God and a crime against the life of our land." As late as 1942, a city magistrate decided to hold for trial the producers of one allegedly obscene play because "moral standards were set by Moses in the Decalogue and have not been changed so far as I know."[14]

Such general criticisms, which were frequently leveled against culture in general, took on greater specificity when they were directed toward realist dramatists who self-consciously embraced a modernist outlook. Realism was dangerous, anti-obscenity activists believed, on two counts. Its emphasis on showing only "one side of life, its failures" constituted an insidious attack on the premises of social order and the belief in moral absolutes. Underlying the lament that "the stage of today wallows in indecency and holds the mirror not up to nature but only to its basest and most degrading weaknesses" was the fear that, in seeking to explore the baser aspects of human nature, realist playwrights legitimated them. Further, as one New York rabbi argued, even "an honestly intended work of 'realism' [could] be dangerous in its effect upon the public" because those who observed representations of immorality might themselves become immoral.[15] When the director of the Catholic Theatre Movement observed that it was impossible "for a person to witness an evil play and be unaffected by it, just as it is impossible for one to dig his arm into filth and not be contaminated," he revealed the bedrock assumption of opponents of realism: that, in its effect on the playgoer, realism would create a new reality, one marked by decadence, disorder, and sin.[16]

Nonetheless, it was difficult to reconcile the fear that those in the audience would leave the theater and act in real life what they saw on the stage with the presumption that Broadway's elite audience was relatively invulnerable to such influence. Father James Gillis, editor of the *Catholic World*, might well argue that "we are all children, and everything that we see or hear is put away by our intellect for further use. We are children with the passions of adults, and we better [*sic*] stop deceiving ourselves by saying 'smutty' plays do us no harm."[17] But the reality was that Broadway's patrons were middle-class adult women and men, not children. In the 1920s, even as Broadway producers and realist playwrights made sex central to their craft, and antivice activists directed greater attention to the legitimate stage, resistance to the idea of censorship of the stage was widespread. A legitimate strategy for regulating the legitimate stage had to be found.

"A COMMITTEE OF REPRESENTATIVE CITIZENS": THE PLAY JURY AS DEMOCRATIC ALTERNATIVE

Before the 1920s there was sporadic agitation against the Broadway stage. In 1912 the founding of the Catholic Theatre Movement heralded increased concern about the alleged immorality of the theater. New York's Cardinal Farley announced that a committee of Catholic women, laymen, and clergy would conduct a "war against infamy" on the stage by drawing up lists of plays that were approved by the Church.[18] By 1916 the *New York Catholic News* was giving much publicity to the "white list" of plays and editorializing that Catholics were "under grave obligation" to forswear plays absent from the list.[19] Catholic Theatre Movement personnel also requested that offensive dialogue be removed from otherwise satisfactory plays, and they claimed that producers often complied with these requests.[20]

Behind-the-scenes pressure was frequently more effective than criminal prosecution, for city officials had no success in obtaining convictions in the case of plays alleged to be obscene. They encountered failure when prosecuting several plays about prostitution in the first decade of the century, including *Sapho* in 1900 and the 1905 production of George Bernard Shaw's drama, *Mrs. Warren's Profession*. Even if conviction was impossible, however, the threat of prosecution could be a useful regulatory tool.[21] For example, in 1913 the mere threat of filing charges against the producers of two "white slavery" dramas, *The Fight* and *The Lure*, resulted in substantial editing of the productions.[22] And in 1919 municipal authorities forced changes in *Aphrodite* when the Hearst newspapers, the New York Society for the Suppression of Vice, and fundamentalist Baptist leader John Roach Straton condemned its intimations of interracial sexuality.[23] The play was set in ancient Greece, and the complaints focused not only on its orgy scene, which, in Reverend Straton's words, featured "barelegged negro men . . . squirming in and out and rubbing against the practically naked white girls," but also on an allegedly nude "living statue" scene.[24] A subsequent police investigation of the play persuaded the producers to make several changes, including firing the eight African American men who appeared in the orgy. Nonetheless, government action against stage productions was only sometimes effective and often unpopular, and it could provide publicity for the offending plays. In the case of *Aphrodite*, for example, alterations in the production did little to appease the play's critics, and once it was known that city officials were investigating the play attendance skyrocketed.[25]

Aphrodite was the most notorious of a series of plays in 1919 and 1920 that gave antivice activists cause for alarm, and the play's success underscored their concerns about the lack of effective regulation for Broadway. During those years John Sumner of the New York Society for the Suppression of Vice found himself appealing to one city official after another to suppress plays of "questionable character," but the mayor, police officials, and the license commissioner all declined to take action, either pleading a lack of authority or contending that the productions were not sufficiently bad to obtain convictions. In response, Sumner gathered other concerned New Yorkers, among them the clergy of the Presbyterian Ministers Association and laymen affiliated with the Catholic Theatre Movement, into the Better Public Shows Movement. Under Sumner's direction those affiliated with this group lobbied for greater official attention to the problem of the modern stage. Arguing that "whether or not the criminal law has been violated in such a way that a conviction may be had, the theatrical situation in New York is one which certainly requires regulatory attention," they advocated a new solution. If neither the police nor the licensing authorities could act effectively against Broadway, then it was up to "representative citizens" to devise a regulatory mechanism that would work. To this end, Sumner proposed that New York's mayor create two committees, one composed of citizens and one of theater managers, that would cooperatively resolve complaints about objectionable plays, with the mayor himself arbitrating in controversial cases. Sumner responded to the mayor's rejection of his proposal by initiating discussions with representatives of the theater industry to explore whether they could come to some agreement on their own.[26]

City officials took another look at Sumner's plan after they found themselves completely unable to do anything about the production of *The Demi-Virgin*, a play that made sexual intercourse, divorce, and marital rape the subjects of comedy.[27] Sumner and his allies in the Better Public Shows Movement attended opening night, alerted to the nature of the play by a *Billboard* review of out-of-town tryouts that scored its "raw lines," "brazen and suggestive situations," and "immoral tone." They took their complaints to the chief city magistrate, but almost a month elapsed before he conducted a hearing at which he decided there was sufficient evidence to hold its producer, A. H. Woods, for trial in the city's Court of Special Sessions. During this time, the theater was crowded with standing-room-only audiences whose curiosity about the play's lewdness outweighed its mixed reviews, and even after he was held for trial Woods refused to close the production. When, at the urging of representatives of the Better Public Shows Movement, the city's license commissioner threatened to revoke the license of the theater at which *The Demi-Virgin* was playing, Woods continued his defiance, challenging the commissioner in court. At the same time, he moved successfully to have the criminal case transferred to the Court of General Sessions, which required a grand jury indictment before trial could be had. When all was said and done, the grand jury failed to indict, the New York Court of Appeals ruled that the city's license commissioner had no power to revoke a theatrical license, and *The Demi-Virgin*, aided by the publicity, had become one of the most successful productions of the season, playing to more than two hundred thousand patrons.[28]

The *Demi-Virgin* fiasco refocused attention upon Sumner's proposal for a new departure in theater regulation, and by early 1922 plans were underway to create a "citizens' play jury." The scheme appealed not only to antivice activists and municipal officials, who were frustrated by their inability to close offending plays, but also to people involved in the theater industry. For the very reason that municipal authorities seemed unable to employ available remedies to control the portrayal of sexuality on the stage, rumors surfaced that a statewide censorship law akin to that recently imposed upon motion pictures would be passed for the legitimate theater. For the first time, it seemed that government censorship might be a real possibility, as the perception of Broadway as out-of-control commercial culture threatened to overwhelm its definition as high art.[29] To avoid this possibility, members of the theater industry cooperated with anti-obscenity activists to create the play jury. Municipal authorities endorsed the plan.[30]

The play jury was a remarkable innovation, bringing together long-standing foes in an effort to create what they believed was a democratic alternative to government regulation of the theater, stemming Broadway's commercial corruption while giving free rein to its art. Its statement of purpose, agreed to by groups as diverse as the Authors' League of America, Actors' Equity, and the Better Public Shows Movement, opined that

> it is high time some effective method should be devised to eliminate, for example, contemptible, salacious plays, written from the catch-penny motive of appealing to the taste of a Peeping Tom. It is not less important, both for the Public and for the art of the American Stage, that the Drama should be assured of protection from fanatical interpretations of Blue Laws.[31]

The groups formulating the play jury scheme expressed the hope that a panel composed of New Yorkers of "the highest type of good citizenship" could reconcile in a democratic manner the conflicting calls for control and freedom. No less remarkable is the fact that the scheme depended upon the willingness of all involved — antivice activists, theater people, and city officials — to abide by the decisions of private citizens regarding the morality of plays. The plan provided that three hundred prospective jurors would be selected from two lists, one offered by theater groups, the other by city officials and anti-obscenity activists. When government authorities received a complaint against a legitimate theater production, a jury of twelve men and women would be impaneled to see the play. If nine or more jurors agreed that a play ought to be closed, or that portions of it should be changed, the producers promised to abide by their decision. City officials, for their part, refused to completely waive their rights to move against potentially obscene plays, but they agreed to be guided by the decisions of the play jury.[32]

Despite their agreement to the plan, municipal officials remained somewhat skeptical of its circumvention of their authority, and as a consequence the citizens' play jury was not tested until 1925. Its tenure was brief, for the jurors' "unexpected liberality" in a series of cases ensured its demise by 1927.[33] This liberality became apparent the first time the system was put into use. In the spring of 1925 New York district attorney Joab Banton activated the jury system in response to a rash of complaints about profanity and sexual themes on the stage.[34] However, when volunteer jurors considered three plays — Eugene O'Neill's *Desire Under the Elms*, *They Knew What They Wanted* by Sidney Howard, and *The Firebrand* by Edwin Justin Mayer — they unanimously approved the first two productions and ordered only that the length of a kiss in the third be shortened, to which the play's manager immediately agreed.[35]

A brief summary of these plays reveals the breadth of themes and portrayals that aroused the ire of critics of the stage in the mid-1920s. *The Firebrand*, a romantic comedy set in the sixteenth century, detailed the many loves of Benvenuto Cellini, sculptor to the aristocracy and ladies' man. The production featured court intrigue, several sword fights, adulterous flirtations, and a number of kisses that leading man Joseph Schildkraut described as "serious, rapturous and important."[36] *They Knew What They Wanted*, described by one reviewer as "a winning little idyll of the California vineyards, none the less fond and sunny for the thumbprint of reality that is on it," concerned the trials of Tony, a middle-aged Italian orchard owner and Amy, his young mail-order bride.[37] Tony's bad luck lands him with two broken legs on his wedding night, and Amy, somewhat bewildered to find herself married to a homely older man, takes comfort in the arms of his handyman, Joe. Three months later she realizes she is pregnant. Amy refuses Joe's offer to pay for an abortion and confides in Tony, whom she has come to love. They agree to raise the child as their own as Joe, never very settled, goes off to join the Wobblies. Despite this happy ending, those opposed to the play probably objected not merely to its theme of adultery but also to the "goddams" and "sonuvabitchs" that were sprinkled liberally throughout the script.[38] The play won the Pulitzer Prize on the same day that it was acquitted by the play jury.[39]

O'Neill's *Desire Under the Elms* had nothing of the "sunniness" of Howard's play, but shared with it the theme of adultery. Like *They Knew What They Wanted*, *Desire* tells the story of a young woman married to an older man, this time living on a nineteenth-century New England farm. Abbie falls in love with her husband's son, Eben, and seduces him. She kills the baby she bears as a result of their affair because the child would replace her lover as heir to the family farm. The play ends with Abbie and Eben's arrest for infanticide. *Desire* was praised by many, but it also prompted harsh criticism, including condemnation by District Attorney Banton, who initially refused to present the play to a volunteer jury because the production was "so bad that it must be summarily executed without trial."[40] Ultimately he acceded to pressure, and it, too, was evaluated by the citizen jurors.

Although municipal officials and anti-obscenity activists had believed each of these plays sufficiently indecent to instigate its review by a play jury, many of the individuals who served on the juries praised the productions as highly moral. One reason that the play jury "functioned with unexpected liberality" may have been its composition. A substantial proportion of the jurors belonged to occupational groups — artists, writers, journalists — whose members were especially likely to value ideas such as artistic freedom. For example, of five female and five male play jurors interviewed in the newspaper in 1925, one was an English professor at Columbia University, five were involved in journalism or the arts, and the others identified themselves as an educator, an architect, an economist and a clubwoman.[41] Other reports make it clear that the play jurors were selected primarily from the so-called intelligent classes.[42] Despite the proclaimed intention to make the play jury the voice of "representative citizens," the panels were far from representative of New York City's population, and the preponderance of wealthy and highly educated city residents reflected the elite assumption that only such persons were "qualified to judge in questions of art and ethics."[43] At the same time, municipal officials' typical inability to obtain convictions against legitimate theater productions for obscenity violations suggests that the standards and attitudes of the play jurors may have been similar to those of New Yorkers in general.

When the play jurors reprised their liberality in 1926, city officials and antivice activists abandoned the plan. That year, jurors considered five plays. As a result of their deliberations, one scene was excised from one musical revue. Another revue was ordered closed, but its producers (who did not belong to the producers' organization that had helped create the play jury) refused to abide by the jurors' verdict.[44] Play jurors exonerated the three other plays they had considered: *The Shanghai Gesture*, a sordid story of prostitution and miscegenation, betrayal and revenge involving a British businessman and a Chinese madame, *Sex*, a comedy about a prostitute with a heart of gold that was authored by and starred Mae West, and *The Captive*, a French import about a lesbian relationship.[45] Vindication of *The Captive* particularly infuriated anti-obscenity activists. When, at the same moment, rumors surfaced that yet another play about homosexuality would be produced on Broadway, government authorities took matters into their own hands. The play jury faded into posterity as municipal and state officials manipulated anxiety about theatrical portrayals of homosexuality to reject censorship by representative citizens and return to government regulation of the stage.

"A QUEER CONCEPT OF MORALITY":
THE LESBIAN PLOT ON BROADWAY

The Captive was the second of several plays about lesbianism that debuted on Broadway during the 1920s. Producers and authors may have been willing to begin explorations of this topic because they believed that any treatment of sex would draw in the crowds. As much as it was part of a general commodification of sexuality, however, Broadway's tentative embrace of the lesbian (or, as we shall see, of her prey) was specifically related to the realist focus of the legitimate theater during this decade. On Broadway lesbianism was portrayed almost exclusively in tragic terms (unlike male homosexuality, which was sometimes the object of comedy), and plays about the subject articulated popular consternation over the erotic potential of relationships between women. Theatrical treatments of lesbianism seemed revolutionary to antivice activists, broaching a subject they deemed unfit for public discussion. But, in fact, the lesbian character on Broadway was a conservative one, a grotesque representation of concerns arising from the acknowledgment of women's sexual desire and the prospect of their independence from men and marriage. Broadway's lesbian embodied the worst of modernism's transformation of gender roles and gender relations to antivice activists, at the same time that she was meant by playwrights and producers as a demonstration of the seriousness and the truthful nature of modern theater.[46]

The appearance of this character on Broadway facilitated the exercise and expansion of government authority over the legitimate theater from the early 1920s through the war years. Yet not all plays with lesbian characters were treated as obscene. Those productions that were closed by municipal officials combined several elements in a tradition of representing women's erotic relationships that we might call the lesbian plot. First, these plays each featured an innocent but confused young heroine who was stalked by a predacious lesbian. Second, the women experienced mutual sexual desire, and in each play there was at least the suggestion that the sexual relationship was or would be consummated. Finally, the young innocent's relationship with a lesbian prevented her from making a successful marriage. Over the course of two decades the outlines of this plot were clarified in three succeeding productions: *The God of Vengeance* (1922–1923), *The Captive* (1926–1927), and *Trio* (1944–1945).

The God of Vengeance was the first Broadway play to raise the suggestion of lesbianism. Authored by Yiddish-language playwright Sholem Asch, the play tells the story of a Polish brothel-keeper (Yekel) whose efforts to keep his young daughter Rifkele pure are destroyed when the girl spends the night in the company of Manke, one of the prostitutes who works for him.[47] Rifkele clearly is enamored of Manke, to whom, she admits, she is drawn "so irresistibly." The play features scenes in which the girls kiss passionately, caress each other, and play at being bride and bridegroom. When Manke asks Rifkele, "Do you want to sleep with me tonight?" the two women escape, apparently to another brothel.[48] Rifkele's attempt to run away with Manke is foiled after one night, yet her destiny is sealed. Yekel denounces his dishonored daughter before the man who has arrived to arrange a marriage between Rifkele and his son. The marriage is aborted and Rifkele and her ex-prostitute mother are cast out into the world to live as harlots.[49]

The God of Vengeance contained all the elements of the lesbian plot, but their presentation was so ambiguous that audiences and critics disagreed about whether or not the play was even about lesbianism. The playwright himself insisted that the relationship between Rifkele and Manke did not represent "the sensuous, inverted love of one woman for another," claiming that their relationship was one of the "woman-mother . . . for the woman-child."[50] Some reviewers of the play agreed that the relationship between the two young women was not erotic. Others hinted that it was suspect, while still others named it lesbian. Included among the latter was *Theatre Magazine* reviewer Arthur Hornblow, who indignantly sputtered that Rifkele

> fall[s] into the clutches of Lesbians and the audience is treated to a nightgown scene in which the women make overtures to each other which go so far beyond the pale of what is permissable that I can only voice my astonishment at the authorities allowing a thing of this sort to be continued before heterogeneous audiences, comprised of individuals young and old who go to the theatre to be entertained and without any conception of what they may be asked to witness.[51]

Hornblow's concern that such a portrayal might corrupt the "immature, easily influenced individuals" in the audience was echoed by others.[52]

Several factors account for this debate over the meaning of the women's relationship. In this play women's eroticism is scripted as degraded in two ways — as lesbianism and as prostitution — and these are not clearly distinguished.

Indeed, Manke schemes to use Rifkele's affection for her as a means of leading the pure young girl into prostitution. Another prostitute and her procurer boyfriend are trying to convince Manke to join them in establishing a brothel, and she tells them that she wants to bring a "chum" with her to her new job. After spending the night with Manke, Rifkele herself seems to understand that she is being courted for prostitution. When her father asks if she is still chaste, Rifkele, referring to her parents' profession, answers, "It was all right for mamma, wasn't it? and it was all right for you, wasn't it?"[53] The clear implication of the play is that the vengeance exacted by God for the father's sin in being a whoremonger is Rifkele's fall from purity into prostitution; Manke's seduction of her is only a means to this end.

This ambiguity in the plot was compounded by the play's origins in Yiddish culture and its translation to the English-language stage. *The God of Vengeance* had several Yiddish-language productions in New York City before its 1923 premiere in English, yet these prompted no protest. The earlier lack of complaint about the play may have reflected Yiddish theater audiences' more tolerant attitude toward portrayals of sexuality in general,[54] but perhaps it also indicates the salience of distinct cultural attitudes toward "lesbianism." It may be that many in the New York audience for the Yiddish theater abided by a tradition of female sexuality in which women's physical affection for each other was not considered deviant. The English-language production attracted a different audience, one that might be more cognizant of the process of stigmatizing female same-sex relationships that had been ongoing in American medical and scientific discourse for forty years.[55] While some members of this audience may have interpreted the play within the context of its origins in Yiddish culture, others likely understood it within the framework of current medical discourses about homosexuality. The debate over the nature of the intimate relationship between Rifkele and Manke demonstrates that "the morbidification of love between women," to use scholar Lillian Faderman's phrase, remained incomplete even at the beginning of the 1920s.[56]

Despite this ambiguity, *The God of Vengeance* became the first play ever to be found obscene under New York criminal statutes.[57] Although several antivice groups urged the license commissioner to make the production the first test of the new play jury plan, city officials bypassed that experiment in regulation, after some of New York's Jewish leaders, believing that the play "put the Jews in a bad light," took their complaints directly to the grand jury.[58] That body, after hearing testimony from a prominent New York rabbi, indicted the producer, theater manager, and the twelve cast members for participating in an obscene production.[59] The lesbian seduction scene figured prominently in the prosecution of the case. At trial the district attorney presented witnesses who recounted the physical affection between the two young women, describing their caresses of each other and a scene in which Manke runs her fingers through Rifkele's hair and "washes her face" in it. While erotic relationships between women may have retained a measure of cultural ambiguity for the audiences who witnessed *The God of Vengeance*, government officials succeeded in convincing a jury of twelve New York men that the theatrical portrayal of such a relationship was obscene, and all the defendants were convicted.[60]

The 1923 production of *The God of Vengeance* set a pattern that would be repeated over the next two decades. Because it presented a conventional plot about a female sexual predator who seduced a young woman away from heterosexual marriage, it was suppressed by government authorities. Fears that such a portrayal would corrupt its audience overwhelmed the claims to artistic freedom that had heretofore made the use of obscenity statutes against the legitimate stage almost impossible. Like other plays featuring the lesbian plot, *The God of Vengeance* seemed so threatening that government officials responded to it by expanding their supervision of the theater.

When Edouard Bourdet's *The Captive* was staged in New York City in 1926, the ambiguity of three years previous had vanished. The play depicts the fall of a young woman, Irene de Montcel, into a lesbian relationship. Irene is "fascinated" with a married woman named Madame d'Aiguines. Although Madame d'Aiguines herself never appears on stage, she is described by others in terms that make it clear she is a lover of women.[61] Irene vividly tells of the lesbian's effect on her: "You see, there are times in which I can see clearly, such as now, when I am sane and free to use my own mind. . . . But there are other times when I can't, when I don't know what I'm doing. It's like — a prison to which I must return captive, despite myself."[62] Irene seeks to escape her captivity by marrying her old friend Jacques, who is in love with her. But when Irene once again encounters Madame d'Aiguines, she is so shaken that she implores Jacques to save her by taking her away, for she does not know how long she can resist. Jacques refuses: he does not want a wife who submits to his sexual attentions without sharing his passion. The play closes as Irene, left without her husband's protection, departs to be reunited with the woman she desires.

Here the outlines of the lesbian plot are unmistakable. Despite the fact that the seductress never appears onstage, her predatory nature is clearly conveyed by the effect she has on others — both her own husband, who has aged beyond his years, and Irene, who describes herself as made "sick" and "crazy" by the woman.[63] The play's dramatic tension derives from its treatment of the risk posed by lesbianism to marriage. Not only does Irene's marriage crumble because she cannot resist Madame d'Aiguines's attractions, the seductress's husband explicitly warns Jacques of lesbians' threat to heterosexual marriage and to heterosexual men:

> A woman can enter any household. . . . She can poison and pillage everything before the man whose home she destroys is even aware of what's happening to him. . . . If a *man* tries to steal your woman you can defend yourself, you can fight him on even terms, you can smash his face in. But in this case — there's nothing to be done — but *get out* while you still have strength to do it![64]

The lesbian in this play destroys not only Irene's chances for true happiness in heterosexual marriage but those of Jacques and Monsieur d'Aiguines as well. Each of them is, in a sense, her captive.

Despite the fact that *The Captive* was intended as a warning against the lesbian threat, a number of New Yorkers contended that the play was dangerous because it would start suggestible young women to thinking about homosexuality.[65] Theater critic George Jean Nathan articulated this position most strongly. Although he claimed not to advocate censorship himself, Nathan penned a column in *Theatre Magazine* that strengthened the position of proponents of the play's suppression. Nathan objected to *The Captive* because he believed that its message was that "a degenerate physical love between women is superior to the normal physical love of the opposite sexes." Alleging that, far from fleeing her captivity to the unseen Madame d'Aiguines, the heroine welcomes it, Nathan contended that

> we have . . . a character who deliberately, despite a few arbitrary, preliminary, moral but entirely undeceptive theatrical shudders, enters upon perversion and intimates her enjoyment of it. This enjoyment is made perfectly plain to the women in the audience. . . . The heroine is definitely and ecstatically devoted to her abnormal practice which, in turn, is held out as an adventure of high excitement.[66]

Having eavesdropped on several conversations among the "susceptible young women" attending the play, Nathan asserted that the performance had indeed persuaded them of the superiority of lesbian to heterosexual love.[67]

It was the production's potential effect on its audience that mobilized antivice activists and city officials as well. John Sumner reported that when he attended a performance it was "crowded from orchestra to second balcony with women and girls." Municipal authorities explained their decision to suppress the play with the observation that women, especially "unescorted" young girls in groups of two and three, predominated among audience members. Defenders of the play sought to assuage the fear that it made lesbian sex seem "an adventure of high excitement" by arguing that portrayal of the tragedy of homosexuality would protect unsuspecting young women from falling into its trap. The play's stage manager, for example, reported that women boarding school directors and college deans had written the actress who played Irene thanking her for helping them in their attempts to prevent such relationships among their students.[68] But this defense came to naught, for city officials were convinced that in a place like New York "many people must be protected from their very selves," especially when those people were young women in danger of succumbing to the temptations of "Lesbian Love."[69]

The failure of play jurors to condemn *The Captive* despite these concerns convinced John Sumner, among others, that "there is the absolute need of outside, official, enforceable, pre-production control."[70] But municipal officials did not move against *The Captive* until several months later, when rumors surfaced that Broadway would soon see another play portraying homosexuality's disruption of heterosexual marriage. This was *The Drag*, authored by Mae West. Very different in tone, but somewhat similar in plot to *The Captive*, *The Drag* portrays the tragedy that occurs when a young man enters into a sham marriage to conceal his own preference for men. In the end, the erstwhile husband is murdered by his jilted lover, described as a drug addict and madman. The play's title highlighted its depiction of a drag party that was attended by "queens" and "fairies" who engaged in sexual banter, flirted with other men, and exclaimed over each other's outfits. It was this scene in particular that incited reformers' ire, not least because the actors who appeared in it were rumored to be themselves gay.[71] Although gay male characters had appeared previously on the Broadway stage, this would mark the first time that a production made male homosexuality its central theme.[72]

When it seemed that *The Drag* might open on Broadway while *The Captive* was still enjoying a successful run, municipal officials were forced to act. In February 1927 they raided *The Captive* and two other plays: Mae West's *Sex*, which had also been approved by the play jury, and *The Virgin Man*, a comedy about the efforts of three women to seduce an innocent Yale undergraduate.[73] West's play was targeted not only because it was the most "flaming, palpitating play seen hereabouts for some time"[74] but, more important, to pressure her to drop plans to produce *The Drag*. The producers of *The Captive* escaped prosecution in return for canceling the show within a week of the raid. The other two plays continued their runs for another month, and shortly thereafter their producers were convicted on obscenity charges.[75] Mae West was sent to jail for ten days, an opportunity for publicity that she exploited in her inimitable way. In the wake of her incarceration, and unable to find a theater in which to house *The Drag*, West abandoned her plans to bring her "homosexual comedy-drama" to Broadway.[76] But despite their success in driving dirt from Broadway, government authorities were not satisfied. At the behest of New York's District Attorney Joab Banton, they engineered a substantial broadening of their power to proceed against allegedly obscene productions, in the form of a law known as the Wales Padlock Act.

Both the police raids and passage of the Wales Act in early 1927 were a result, in part, of state and national politics. The local politicians who arranged the raids against *The Captive* and other plays were seeking to defend Democratic governor Alfred Smith against publisher William Randolph Hearst's attempts to foil his bid for the presidency. Hearst had launched a campaign for passage of a state law subjecting plays to the same preexhibition censorship that already applied to motion pictures. He intended to force Governor Smith either to sign censorship legislation, the idea of which he had consistently opposed, or to veto such legislation and hence place himself in the position of supporting obscenity.[77] The Broadway arrests were an attempt to avoid this dilemma, but they were not enough. While the charge of tolerating obscenity could perhaps be withstood when the allegedly obscene material portrayed marital infidelity or promiscuous heterosexuality, the burgeoning portrayal of homosexuality on stage proved so far beyond the bounds of acceptable theatrical representation that it necessitated drastic action.

Thus, the specter of gay men and lesbians on the stage smoothed the way to enactment of the Wales Law, which amended New York state's obscenity statute. Meant to undermine support for Hearst's proposal, the law expanded government authority over the legitimate stage at the same time that, in its rejection of preexhibition censorship, it seemed to defer to beliefs about theatrical entitlement to free speech. The Wales Law achieved this balancing act through three major provisions. First, it made prosecution of allegedly obscene plays easier by permitting a conviction if any part of a play — even one line or one word — could be deemed obscene, rather than requiring that the work be considered as a whole. This clause placed theatrical productions in a different category than books, which New York courts had ruled "must be considered broadly as a whole" before they could be adjudged obscene.[78] Second, the act increased the authority of municipal licensing authorities by permitting them to revoke the license of a theater in which a play was produced (or to "padlock" the theater) for up to one year after a conviction on obscenity charges; previously, only a judge was empowered to revoke a theatrical license. Significantly, this provision made theater *owners*, as well as actors, playwrights, and theater managers, liable under obscenity laws. It also increased the financial stakes involved in leasing a theater for a potentially objectionable play; in the case of a conviction, not only might the anticipated rent from a particular production be lost but theater owners risked losing all income from a theater for an entire year. Those opposing the provision feared, correctly, that it would stifle production of controversial plays because theater owners would be unwilling to take such risks.[79]

Finally, the Wales Law banned "sex degeneracy or perversion" themes in theatrical productions, language that was universally understood to denote homosexuality. New York's district attorney contended that this clause did not really constitute a change in the law, as "a proper interpretation of the old law would have had the same result."[80] Nevertheless, this provision injected into New York law, for the first time, an absolute ban on a specified type of sexual speech, defining the discussion or portrayal of homosexuality on stage as inherently obscene.[81] Although government officials declared that the Wales Law was an alternative to preexhibition censorship, plays about lesbians and gay men were, apparently, not entitled to the same freedoms as more "legitimate" productions.

The Wales Law was not an unmitigated success. Indeed, the first prosecution on obscenity charges after the law's amendment was something of a failure. In 1928 New York police raided yet another play authored by Mae West, *The Pleasure Man*. The play is about a philanderer who is castrated and killed by the brother of a young woman whom he has seduced. Once again, however, it was the perception that some of the play's characters were homosexual that prompted government action against it. The prosecution highlighted *The Pleasure Man*'s alleged violation of the sex degeneracy and perversion provision of the Wales Law, arguing that the presence of five campy "female impersonators" among the production's cast made the play obscene.[82] Indeed, the evidence submitted by the district attorney's office was meant in part to prove that the actors portraying the female impersonators were themselves homosexuals. For example, one police officer testified that these actors refused to change into men's clothing after the raid. The defense sought to counter such testimony by proving that each of the actors was "a very mannish man": one actor testified that "he heard no feminine shrieks, saw no hands on hips or under chins, and no kimonos" worn by the cast members. The prosecution also introduced what it called expert testimony on the behavior of homosexual men, asking Vice Squad detective Terence Harvey to describe the men whom he had arrested over the past sixteen years, in an effort to prove the female impersonator characters engaged in similar behavior.[83] Despite such testimony, the jury was unable to agree upon a verdict, and the charges were dropped.[84]

Although it was not until 1943 that New York officials translated their enhanced power under the Wales Act into a criminal conviction and license revocation, the law had far-ranging effects. The same year they failed in prosecuting the cast and producer of *The Pleasure Man*, they were able to suppress *Maya*, even though it did not treat the "sex perversion" theme. This play depicted nine episodes in the life of a French prostitute named Bella. In one scene, Bella chats with other prostitutes about the difficulties of getting out of the business; in another, she fails in her efforts to go to the funeral of her three-year-old daughter, whom she had been forced to put out with a rural woman after her birth.[85] In its portrayal of the everyday conditions of prostitutes' lives and of the exploitative nature of the relationship between pimp and prostitute, *Maya* was, if not a feminist play, one that explored sex and gender relationships from a woman's perspective; at the same time it provided a reenactment of the familiar story about the prostitute with a heart of gold.

City authorities did not have to invoke the Wales Law formally to close *Maya* with little effort. Soon after the play opened, New York City police warned the owners of the theater at which it was showing that if the production was not closed within ten days they would prosecute and padlock the theater. As several journalists noted, because the financial risk was so great, the warning issued by city officials was "almost equivalent to a command," and the theater owners evicted the play.[86] The increased financial risk and lower standard of proof required for conviction afforded an effective enforcement tool and facilitated government control over theater productions, even though no "official" censorship occurred. Similar tactics were used frequently in the late 1920s and early 1930s, as municipal authorities kept up a continual, and successful, harassment of Broadway productions.[87]

The threat implicit in the Wales Law was almost sufficient to keep *Trio*, the third production featuring the lesbian plot, off New York's stage in 1944. The year before, city officials had obtained their first conviction under the law against the producers of *Wine, Women and Song*, a Broadway revue that was in fact a thinly veiled effort to revive burlesque. Licensing authorities subsequently revoked the license of the Shubert-owned theater where the production had been housed. The repercussions of this successful prosecution became apparent when Lee Shubert, who controlled the vast majority of Broadway playhouses, refused to lease a theater to the producer of *Trio*. Shubert feared that permitting production of a play about lesbianism might result in conviction under the Wales Law and another costly license revocation.[88] Finally, the management of the independent Belasco Theatre agreed to take in the production, and the play opened in late December 1944.

Several plays that discussed or hinted at the theme of lesbianism appeared on Broadway after *The Captive* was suppressed, but *Trio* was the first to offer the combination of predacious lesbian and innocent young girl that so raised the ire of anti-obscenity activists and municipal officials.[89] This time the evil lesbian is a university professor and literary critic (Pauline Maury) who has seduced and now lives with Janet Logan, her graduate student and protégée. We learn that a year before the opening of the play Janet had a nervous breakdown as a result of this relationship and was secretly placed in a mental institution by Pauline. Although she has since recovered, Pauline uses her knowledge of Janet's breakdown to keep the young woman under her power. Pauline's vileness knows no bounds: from attempting to prevent the tenuring of a male colleague (who, having recently become a father, possesses the family that Pauline apparently wanted but could never have), to plagiarizing her dead lover's research in her own widely acclaimed book, she preys on everyone who crosses her path. Janet's worship of Pauline has turned to hate, but she declares that she cannot leave her: "I pray for her to die, because I haven't got the nerve to kill her," she says. "She won't die, of course. . . . But if she doesn't die, I can't live."[90]

When a young man named Ray arrives on the scene, he provides the opportunity for Janet to escape Pauline's clutches. Although they fall in love, Janet's relationship with Pauline remains an obstacle to their marriage: she is afraid to tell Ray about its sexual nature, and when she finally does he is so repulsed that he leaves her. Still, true (heterosexual) love wins in the end; Pauline conveniently commits suicide and Janet falls into Ray's sheltering arms. As Janet has predicted, it is only with the lesbian's death that the heterosexual marriage both she and Ray desire becomes possible.

Although city officials knew about the play's theme, they took no action against *Trio* until two months after its premiere, when the Reverend John Sutherland Bonnell complained to Mayor LaGuardia about the play. Bonnell's renown reached beyond New York City to the nation. He broadcast weekly sermons on the ABC radio network, reaching three million listeners. An advocate of the use of modern psychology by clergy, Bonnell established a clinic for pastoral counseling at his church.[91] It may be that his prominence, as well as his credentials as a proponent of psychology, gave his words more weight with municipal authorities, especially on the issue of "latent female homosexuality." In any case, as a reform mayor, LaGuardia had a long history of responsiveness to complaints from clergy about obscenity in the theater. Yet rather than seeking conviction under the Wales Law, which forbade plays with *Trio*'s theme, Mayor LaGuardia and his license commissioner, Paul Moss, elected to circumvent the criminal law and use their licensing powers to force the production off the stage. While superficially their decision seems a break with the tradition of prosecuting plays with the lesbian plot, in fact it represents another attempt to broaden the regulatory regime when faced with lesbian representation on Broadway.

New York City officials drew upon a decade of experience in defining, refining, and enlarging the boundaries of licensing authority in their action against *Trio*. In the antiburlesque campaign of the 1930s and early 1940s, members of the Department of Licenses had obtained judicial affirmation of their right to refuse to renew theatrical licenses on the basis of the content of plays produced in a theater.[92] They had employed that right aggressively in 1937 and 1942 to wipe out New York's burlesque industry. Now they set out to use that power against a legitimate theater production about lesbianism. By coincidence, the owners of the Belasco Theatre had recently applied for a license transfer. When Bonnell complained about *Trio* to city officials, the transfer had not yet been officially granted. Three days after Bonnell wrote to LaGuardia, Moss denied the transfer on the grounds that "the licensee intends to use this theater for the production of a lewd, lascivious and immoral play."[93] Without a license, the Belasco Theatre would be forced to close. The Belasco owners evicted *Trio*, on Moss's instructions, and were granted their license in return.[94]

LaGuardia and Moss had miscalculated. In the past a few defenders of lesbian-themed plays had surfaced, but there was a great deal of public support for official suppression of such plays. This time such conduct provoked a storm of criticism. In part, that criticism reflected a shift in sentiment about the relationship between theatrical representations of homosexuality and the social problem of homosexuality. Dozens of New Yorkers lectured Mayor LaGuardia that, far from inducing young women to act on their latent homosexuality, the production presented "a most potent sermon against sex perversion."[95] For example, in what must have been a purposeful play on words, one man admonished the mayor that the clergy who condemned *Trio*

> have a strangely perverted sense of morality. Speaking purely from the standpoint of accepted mores, the play is one million per cent moral! Doesn't the boy destroy the Lesbian hold on the girl he loves, thus winning her over to an orthodox relationship? And doesn't the girl herself, through exercise of free will, victoriously fight against the other woman's control?
>
> Immoral, indecent indeed! [These clergy have] a queer concept of morality.

His argument that a play that condemned homosexuality could not be considered obscene was a popular one among New Yorkers who complained to the mayor.[96]

In addition, opponents of the suppression of *Trio* contended that the dilemma of homosexuality could be solved through just the kind of speech represented by the play. They argued that only frank and sincere discussion would permit the development of solutions to sexual problems and that prohibiting such discussion would make the problems worse. One man told LaGuardia that

> by making Lesbianism a thing to be whispered about . . . you are merely making the public more curious about it. I believe it is a problem that should be understood and openly discussed. . . . Prostitution, abnormal love and immorality will not be cured by raids and puritanical censorship. Understanding and education will, I believe, be a far more effective treatment.[97]

Similarly, a New York woman informed the mayor that *Trio*'s portrayal of the evils of lesbianism would prevent similar real-life tragedies from occurring:

> If knowledge of the menace of this insidious ill which exists in most colleges — where young girls of the most susceptible age, have crushes on older girls, would seem far fetched, I as the mother of married daughters, and myself a college woman — know how dangerous it can be!!
>
> [*Trio* is] an excellent eye opener to the naive and unsuspecting mother. It is most timely because of the Waves, Wacs & Spars now congregated, and far from home influence. . . .
>
> A play that offers so much, and above all, could serve a good purpose is not immoral, and closing it is an injustice to all concerned, but especially those

adolescents, who without this lesson so charmingly given, might fall victim unwittingly.[98]

These correspondents condemned the "ostrich-like" attitude of those who sought to prohibit the play. Avoiding public discussion of sexual problems like lesbianism, they contended, would only exacerbate them.[99]

These pleas for unrestrained debate about sexuality did not go unchallenged. Those who favored closing the play, including Mayor LaGuardia himself, continued to cite the danger of permitting the public portrayal of lesbianism, arguing like Reverend Bonnell that plays such as *Trio* increased the likelihood of homosexual behavior among young women. LaGuardia claimed that as mayor he had special knowledge about the effect of such productions. In response to one complaint about the closing, LaGuardia wrote:

> To you this unfortunate kind of degeneracy may seem interesting or perhaps an amusing incident. To me, as head of the City government, it is a heart breaking, difficult problem. . . . You have not seen the complaints. You do not know of the many borderline cases and how a play of this kind may cause irreparable damage.[100]

Several Protestant, Catholic, and Jewish clergymen, as well as a few other New Yorkers, expressed their agreement with this view.[101] In contrast to earlier controversies, however, they constituted a distinct minority.

The popularity of the position that *Trio* could warn against the seductions of lesbian love suggests an important shift in New Yorkers' attitudes toward the public discussion of sexual problems, including homosexuality. One source of this shift was the popularization of medical, and especially psychoanalytic, explanations of the causes of and cures for homosexuality. Greater tolerance for the portrayal of sexual problems on the stage reveals growing acceptance of the idea that homosexuality posed a social problem that could be solved through speech — whether that speech occurred on the psychoanalyst's couch or in a Broadway theater. Furthermore, when New Yorkers offered vociferous protests to government suppression of plays about lesbians, they endorsed the view that "repression" of sexual deviance, whether in an individual or in the social body, merely contributed to the creation of greater sexual problems.[102] At the same time, because the popularization of such discourses meant that *Trio* could present a more detailed elaboration of the alleged perversity of homosexuality, the specificity and vehemence of its portrayal of the lesbian menace likely fostered support for the production.

Other social trends also shaped the response to *Trio*. Between the 1920s and the 1940s the contours of anxiety over gender and sexual roles changed. American entry into World War II provoked a range of concerns about women's conduct, including their sexual behavior. As young women flocked to urban areas to work in war factories or joined the military, fears about their susceptibility to lesbian relationships grew. In this context the strategy of maintaining silence about lesbianism to prevent its growth may have appeared obsolete.[103] Conversely, the expansion and consolidation of lesbian and gay communities within much of urban America during this period may have played a different role in mustering support for *Trio*. It is probable that at least some of those who wrote to Mayor LaGuardia protesting the play's closing were members of those communities who were interested in protecting one of the few cultural forms that spoke to, although it did not represent, their own sexuality.[104]

Criticism of city officials for suppressing *Trio* was related as well to the strategy they elected to use. Substantial numbers of New Yorkers viewed their recourse to licensing powers as an illegitimate strategy for regulating the legitimate theater. While most New Yorkers seemed to believe that such tactics might be an appropriate way to police low-culture burlesque, high-culture Broadway deserved protection from the prior restraint imposed by license suspension. A number of citizens protested to Mayor LaGuardia that his license commissioner's action was "undemocratic" and "unamerican" because it denied those involved with the play the right to a fair trial.[105] Many echoed the sentiments of a U.S. Army sergeant who observed that "it is quite frightening being a member of the Army of the United States, fighting supposedly for the freedoms and unconditional defeat of all forms of dictatorship; realizing meanwhile that such flagrant and outrageous misuse of authority is taking place in New York City." Or, as another man reminded LaGuardia, "Democracy should be fought for at home as well as on the battlefield."[106]

As these sentiments suggest, the accessibility of a particular patriotic language during World War II, and the wartime experiences of Americans, structured individual understandings of free speech protections' applicability to entertainment media. The belief that the U.S. was fighting a war against intolerance and for freedom, the ever present oppositions between "democracy" and "dictatorship," increased the likelihood that New York citizens would perceive the use of licensing laws against *Trio* as improper. In this context few were persuaded by LaGuardia's protestations that the closing of *Trio* did not constitute "censorship" because it was the theater owners, rather than government officials, who actually evicted the play. Ultimately, the outcry against the license commissioner's "dictatorial" behavior forced LaGuardia to promise that members of his administration would refrain from using licensing powers to force a play to close until after they obtained a conviction under obscenity statutes, as the Wales Law provided.[107] While *Trio* never reopened, LaGuardia's reluctant abdication of this strategy indicates that new limits on state power over stage obscenity were being established.

Yet, as we have already seen, shifts in New Yorkers' perspectives about homosexuality also facilitated these emerging limitations. In past years municipal officials had been able to enlarge the regulatory regime for the legitimate theater through action against plays about lesbians because many New Yorkers believed that even negative portrayals of women's erotic relationships could ruin young women in the audience. By 1945 this belief had been supplanted by the attitude that theatrical representations of the perversity of lesbianism were effective in protecting the same innocent young women. It was this understanding of the relationship between theatrical representation and reality that made it possible for large numbers of New Yorkers to assert that even plays about lesbians were entitled to guarantees of due process and artistic freedom.

∼

The controversy over *Trio* aroused the passions of a great number of New Yorkers, including Long Island resident Mary Nolan Bonbrake. Mrs. Bonbrake sent the mayor and Commissioner Moss a steady stream of letters offering praise for their forthright action against the play and moral support in the face of widespread condemnation. She agreed with them that the portrayal of homosexuality on the stage could have the same result as seduction by a homosexual, ending in a girl's ruin:

> These abnormal people work on normal young people. I know, in my own actual experience, a man teacher who in my home-town in Wisconsin, involved most of the boys in his grade in perversion, but *only one* was ruined for life — one too many. I knew of a young girl just home from a girls' college, who involved large groups of high school girls, who fortunately went to their parents. But when the young woman left town, one of the girls went with her — one too many.

Arguing that "the thought is father to the deed," Mary Bonbrake worried that plays such as *Trio* might give young people the idea that homosexuality was "an accepted thing."[108]

However, after several weeks during which she read numerous condemnations of Moss and LaGuardia in the New York newspapers, even Mary Bonbrake had become confused about the right thing to do in such cases. While she still believed that such themes had no place on the stage, she urged the mayor to clarify his stand, asking why such a "roundabout" way of closing the play was necessary in view of the Wales Law's ban on the theme of sex perversion. Responding to LaGuardia's agreement to limit the use of licensing powers, she wrote:

> I understand that in the future the license commissioner will not censor. It will be done by trial. I can understand why a trial should be necessary to decide the obscenity of some plays — it might be a matter of opinion. But in the matter of perversion, why a trial, that is if the Wales act [sic] still is in force. Do you need a trial to decide if Lesbianism is perversion? Everyone knows it is and therefore forbidden by the Wales Act. Or is it? I'm not sure now.[109]

Mrs. Bonbrake had an inaccurate understanding of how the Wales Law worked. Yet, it is clear from her letters that as debate over *Trio* went on, she felt increasingly unable to defend the actions of city authorities. The moral certainty with which she had initially viewed the closing of the play seemed to be crumbling.

Mrs. Bonbrake's dilemma must have been shared by other New Yorkers who had approved city officials' efforts over the course of two decades to prevent portrayals of lesbian seduction on Broadway.[110] For years anti-obscenity activists and municipal authorities had decried the danger to young women allegedly posed by theatrical representations of lesbianism in order to circumvent the obstacles to government regulation posed by the legitimate theater's high position in New York's cultural hierarchy. The production of plays with the lesbian plot proved especially useful to their endeavors, as advocates of government regulation implicitly suggested a connection between the innocent young woman being pursued on the stage by the lesbian predator and the innocent young women seated in the audience. In so doing, they invented a legitimate theater audience that provided a rationale for controlling the content of commercial culture, much as they had for motion pictures and burlesque shows. And they used opposition to homosexuality to overwhelm the presumptions of entitlement to "liberty" and "democracy" from which Broadway had benefited.

Yet, as attitudes about how to prevent homosexuality changed, this strategy became less useful for increasing authority over the stage. Indeed, when Paul Moss engineered the eviction of *Trio* in 1945, he became the last New York official to close, or even attempt to close, a Broadway play that treated themes of homosexuality.[111] Municipal authorities' final attempt to expand their regulatory power over representations of sex on the stage foundered in the face of the ascension of new ideas about sexuality and the growing prominence of ideas about freedom of speech. In the years after 1945 a new regulatory regime for the theater and for commercial culture in general would be established, one that confirmed these limitations on government power.

PART II

Moral Authorities

CHAPTER 4

The Shifting Contours of Anti-obscenity Activism

A t the end of World War II denunciations of obscenity sounded, superficially, much as they had at century's turn: warnings about the effect of lewd movies, plays, and magazines on children and young people predominated, as did demands that municipal authorities do something about the "flood" of immorality. But these similarities obscured significant changes in the leadership of anti-obscenity activism, in the ways that activism was justified, and in the solutions offered. By mid-century there had occurred a de facto masculinization of campaigns against obscenity, for the white middle-class clubwomen who had been active in campaigns for motion picture censorship were marginalized in debates about Broadway and burlesque. Not all men were able to retain their leadership of these campaigns, either; the staff of the New York Society for the Suppression of Vice, who had long reprimanded New Yorkers for their moral laxity and prodded government officials to strengthen their control over obscenity, struggled to maintain a minor role for themselves in these debates. Because religious leaders alone among anti-obscenity activists effectively portrayed themselves as representatives of the broader community of New York residents, they rose to prominence as critics of sex in commercial culture. Building an interfaith movement for the suppression of obscenity, they offered both justifications for their activism and a range of strategies that, they hoped, accorded more fully with the traditions of a democratic culture.

"NATURAL GUARDIANS OF THE YOUNG": WOMANLINESS AND OPPOSITION TO OBSCENITY

Early twentieth-century anti-obscenity activists inherited from their nineteenth-century forebears a belief in moral absolutes that pervaded their understanding of moral authority and its relation to social order. Their belief in an eternal, divinely ordained morality to be enforced by those positioned atop a social hierarchy made comprehensible the endeavors of the New York Society for the Suppression of Vice, a private organization, to enforce federal and state laws against obscenity. It also provided the justification for clerics' pulpit condemnations of the "cesspools" that masqueraded as the city's theaters and newsstands. And the constellation of beliefs that was moral absolutism underlay the anti-obscenity activism of white middle-class women, whose foray into the making of public policy depended upon their ability to claim moral authority even before they had secured their claim to political authority.

A wide range of middle-class women's activism in the nineteenth century was premised in the concept of female moral authority — the idea that white middle-class women's nature and experience accorded them a measure of piety and purity that fitted them to guide and regulate the behavior of others. Female moral authority legitimated their efforts to establish institutions and lobby for legislation they believed would protect other women and children from the depredations of abusive, lustful, and dissipated men. It authorized women, in organizations such as the Woman's Christian Temperance Union, to try to limit the consumption of alcohol, to establish rescue homes for prostitutes, to strengthen age of consent laws, and to campaign against impure literature, immoral dancing, and indecent art.[1]

Yet while nineteenth-century women active in the social purity movement did not hesitate to invoke the existence of a distinctly womanly sexual morality as justification for their efforts, in twentieth-century New York City female anti-obscenity activists were strikingly silent on the topic. Certainly their very critique of the willingness of purveyors of commercial culture to disregard the well-being of the community for their own monetary benefit, or of the failure of public officials appropriately to regulate obscenity, sometimes carried with it the implication that women had distinct sexual standards and a more fitting sense of morality than the men who conducted commerce and government. Nonetheless, most New York women who advocated stricter control of cultural representations of sex articulated their claim to female moral authority through children. They used the language of maternalism, rather than that of piety or purity, to legitimate their position as activists.[2]

Maternalism became the sole justification women anti-obscenity activists offered for their efforts in part because the other props of female moral authority were less persuasive by the early twentieth century. As white middle-class women, in particular the Protestant women who were the mainstay of the club movement, moved from Christian-identified to secular women's organizations, religiousness became somewhat less useful both as a means of cementing group unity and as an explanation for activism. And by the first years of the twentieth century the idea that women were sexually purer than men (or that, if true, this was a good thing) was increasingly contested. The decline of the ideology of purity can be traced to a number of forces, including new scientific theories of sexuality, urbanization and its effects upon reproductive patterns, an increasingly heterogeneous population, and commercial culture itself. An accelerating shift toward the celebration of heterosexual intimacy and heterosocial life in general also countered the idealization of female purity, as did the demands of a young generation of feminists for "sex rights." Furthermore, it is very likely that in New York City, where the feminist movement was at its strongest and moral standards generally were more relaxed than in the hinterlands, arguments from purity were abandoned by women activists more quickly than elsewhere in the nation.[3]

References to female purity did not completely disappear from the repertoire of arguments for enhanced government regulation of obscenity, but they were voiced almost exclusively by men.[4] Christian clergy and laymen wielded the idea of female sexual purity as a weapon in their battle against immorality in popular entertainments well into the twentieth century. Clerics tried to mobilize their female parishioners, for example, by arguing that women's purity mandated a heightened responsibility for fighting indecency in the entertainment industry. Much of this work could be done within the family, and wives were entreated to prevent their husbands from attending "off-color" performances and to persuade them to stay away from bad plays and burlesque productions. Similarly, the president of the Holy Name Society of New York urged the women attending a local meeting of the Catholic Daughters of America to "bring about a sane censorship of stage and screen" by using their "feminine influence over men to bring them to the feet of Christ."[5]

Male campaigners against obscenity also suggested that women's responses to amusements could serve as a barometer for reading the moral condition of New York's entertainment. So, a Protestant minister demanded that the commissioner of licenses, Paul Moss, close the city's burlesque theaters because a member of the Woman's Christian Temperance Union "could not tell me the things she had seen" there. The presumption that if a white middle-class woman was offended by a theatrical production it was prima facie evidence of its obscenity is to be found as well in a police officer's testimony that a woman attending an allegedly immoral Broadway play was observed to flush.[6] Conversely, if entertainment could be considered obscene because it embarrassed women in the audience, so too the fact that women were *not* outraged gave anti-obscenity activists cause for alarm. Tourists and city residents alike commented on women's acceptance of immorality on Broadway. In 1925 one man wrote that "I have heard such language as the stage of today exploits, but never before in the presence of decent women. . . . Yet the women in the audiences applauded these filthy shows. . . . Where are we heading?" Almost twenty years later, Archbishop Spellman related a similar story. An acquaintance had told him that "he had been obliged to get up and leave in horror and shame at some of the performances. . . . And what is worse, he said . . . there were girls of eighteen and nineteen years of age, some of them apparently with their mothers, who were not shocked into leaving the theatre."[7] Other opponents of obscenity pointed to the willingness of actresses to perform in immoral plays as an indicator of the seriousness of the problem.[8]

In marshaling arguments about women's purity to attack obscenity, men such as these pursued two distinct rhetorical strategies. When they urged women to influence their husbands' choice of entertainment, they offered a justification for women's activism, but activism that was by and large restricted to their own families and their own homes. References to blushing, speechless, or debased women, on the other hand, used women as a touchstone for obscenity without specifically legitimating their efforts to combat it. When male anti-obscenity activists charged that burlesque performances "degrade the dignity of women" or that "the stage today has dragged [woman] down from her high estate and hauls her pitilessly before the ribold [sic] mobs in the market place" they spoke for women, advocated on their behalf, and sought to protect them.[9] Female anti-obscenity activists, on the other hand, sought to assert their own proficiency for guarding morality, not only within their families but in the local, state, and national communities in which they lived. It might be that by the early twentieth century allusions to female purity seemed to women activists to contain them as objects of male guardianship more than to empower them as guardians of others or even keepers of themselves.

Or it might be merely that female opponents of obscenity had another, more compelling, justification for their efforts. The language used by most of these women suggests that they preferred to legitimate their social activism from the "high estate" of motherhood rather than the pedestal of purity. Maternalist arguments avoided the pitfalls of purity — its susceptibility to accusations of "prudery" as well as the opportunities it afforded for justifying women's protection by men — while fitting neatly within the existing legal discourses about obscenity, which emphasized the harm done children by portrayals of sexuality. Further, by the early twentieth century women reformers throughout the nation used the language of motherhood to influence the framing of public policy about an array of social problems, including child welfare, labor relations, housing reform, pure food and drug laws, and a host of others. The resolve to "mother the world" that moved so many women to activism during the Gilded Age and Progressive era was expressed in women's anti-obscenity activism as well.[10]

To a degree, maternalism was so taken for granted as the basis of women's anti-obscenity activism that it remained partly unarticulated: their demands for the "moral protection of youth and children" differed little from those of other anti-obscenity activists, and so the fact that they were speaking particularly as mother figures was obscured.[11] On occasion, however, specific proposals revealed that the presumption of women's motherliness — a capacity to be the best possible protectors of children — was behind these efforts to shape public policy. Both women and men anti-obscenity activists, for example, argued that mothers would make the best censors, whether on voluntary boards or as government officials. When the citizens' play jury was being considered as a method of regulating Broadway, some supporters suggested juries dominated by "wives and mothers"; others wanted woman-only boards.[12] A similar premise shaped the composition of the New York State Motion Picture Censorship Commission created in 1921: upon the urging of Brooklyn clubwoman Mrs. Clarence Waterman, Governor Nathan Miller agreed to reserve one of three positions for a woman. At least into the 1930s there was always one woman on the commission.[13] The female commissioner served as an example and a representative to the women of New York state, as the chairwoman of the Motion Picture Committee of the New York State Federation of Women's Clubs exhorted Federation members:

> On our State Censorship Commission is a woman, Mrs. Eli Hosmer of Buffalo, appointed to hear the woman's point of view. In order to make her work effective she must have the written word from the women of our state. If you see or hear of an objectionable picture, it is your duty, as the guardians of the morals of youth, to write your protest to Mrs. Hosmer.

While the allocation to a woman of one slot on the three-person commission signifies women's political marginalization as much as their empowerment, it nonetheless reflects the influence of maternalist rhetoric in shaping regulatory strategies for motion pictures. Insisting that women should be represented in government censorship boards and voluntary juries was merely the most concrete of the many ways in which anti-obscenity activists contended that as the "natural guardians of the young" women had a special role to play in ensuring that commercial culture was adequately regulated.[14]

Their use of maternalist rhetoric had ironic consequences for women involved in campaigns against obscenity, ultimately contributing to their displacement from the forefront of those campaigns.[15] By choosing to argue that obscenity regulation was necessary for the protection of childhood innocence, women made claims on the state on the basis of their unique knowledge of children's needs. The position of protecting others that they secured to themselves by such rhetoric harmonized with the logic of early twentieth-century censorship discourse and the culture of moral absolutism out of which it grew. But in professing to represent not their own interests but the interests of others, these women adopted a stance that was essentially antidemocratic. When during the interwar years discourses of democracy became increasingly more compelling as arguments against regulation of speech of all sorts,[16] the forces of organized womanhood moved to the sidelines of anti-obscenity activism.

Indeed, the possibilities for carving out a "women's position" on the issue of obscenity were severely limited. Maternalism had its drawbacks as a justification for women's leadership of the battle against immoral culture, but purity was even less attractive: as the cultural ideal of female purity eroded, it became far less likely that many women would want to stake a claim to activism on that terrain, even among those whose class and race privilege made it possible to do so. However, it was not easy for such women to justify their anti-obscenity work on the grounds that they spoke for the community as a whole, since elite women's "purity" was now reinterpreted as their "prudery." As female continence was degraded from cultural ideal to a deviation from the male norm, women's perceived difference from men excluded them from the community of those whose opinions counted when it came to regulating obscenity, especially that aimed at adults.[17]

"COMPLAINING WITNESS FOR THE PEOPLE": MODERNIZING THE NEW YORK SOCIETY FOR THE SUPPRESSION OF VICE

A similar fate awaited the men affiliated with the New York Society for the Suppression of Vice, whose effectiveness as anti-obscenity campaigners faded after World War I, even as they shifted their attention from "dirty books" to New

York's legitimate and burlesque theaters. In the early years of the twentieth century the vice society was simultaneously feared and ridiculed, identified as it was with its pugnacious, single-minded, often myopic secretary, Anthony Comstock. When Comstock died in 1915, his successor, John S. Sumner, made it known that he intended to bring a different sort of leadership to the NYSSV. Sumner, who worked as a banker and a lawyer in his early career, came to the vice society in 1913 as Comstock's assistant, hired by a board of directors that was concerned about the aging secretary's increasingly erratic behavior. He stayed until his retirement in 1950.[18] During those years he tried to recast the vice society as less old-fashioned while continuing its commitment to uphold "fundamental principles of morality and decency that are eternal," a paradoxical task.[19]

Sumner had reason for optimism about his efforts to repair the society's reputation after Comstock's death, for there is evidence that many New Yorkers shared its goal of suppressing vice. Absent from the society's annual reports but noted in its internal documents are accounts of an enormous amount of sexual surveillance by the vice society's agents, a good deal of which was invited by ordinary citizens. In May 1916, for example, the NYSSV caused sixteen arrests for selling obscene magazines, but its agents also investigated an anonymous report of a child who was "the victim of vicious home surroundings," referred to the Brooklyn police a letter from a New Jersey woman accusing a man of deserting his family and living in adultery, looked into another man's allegations that his daughter was living with a married man, and informed the Children's Aid Society about two teenage girls who had used "vile and indecent" language to a janitor who reprimanded them for being on the streets at night.[20] During that year, Sumner reported, they also viewed objectionable motion pictures at the request of New York's license commissioner, cooperated with him in court proceedings to prohibit sex problem films, forced producers to eliminate scenes in burlesque shows and a ballet, and had offending theater posters removed. Despite the fact that the society failed to achieve any convictions in its 1916 campaign against immoral magazines, the readiness of New York citizens and public officials to appeal to vice agents for assistance suggests that the group retained legitimacy for many New Yorkers.[21]

Sumner expended a good deal of energy trying to build popular support for his agency's activities. One of his first projects was to strengthen the NYSSV's connections with New Yorkers other than the Protestant elite that had constituted its main supporters during Comstock's reign. He recruited prominent Catholics to join its Board of Managers, in an effort to make the board more representative, and also solicited a wide range of child-saving organizations "to accept the public duty of directorship in this Society." A good many of the city's community groups heard addresses by Sumner, including (according to his estimate) five or six hundred members of Brooklyn's Jewish Community Center to whom he spoke in December 1921. This crowd, he reported to the Board of Managers, was "very attentive and apparently friendly to a very large extent. This is said to be one of the wealthiest and most important Jewish communities in the city. They occupy a million-dollar building, just completed, carrying on all forms of community activities [sic]." Meetings like this one could help broadcast the vice society's message to New Yorkers who might not be familiar with it and offered the potential for additional financial support.[22]

Sumner sought to update the society's message as well, especially after the NYSSV had come under increasing attack in the early 1920s from individuals within the publishing industry in the wake of a campaign against "dirty" books.[23] In 1923, for example, the vice society launched a fundraising campaign on the occasion of its fiftieth anniversary. A brochure announcing the campaign featured prominently a statement of "what [the society] is" and "what it is not." The NYSSV was not, it stressed, "narrow, prudish, nor 'puritanical.'" It did not seek the right to censor, nor had it any "rights or powers of oppression." Rather, the society exercised "the right of the individual citizen to appeal to the law to restrain and punish the criminal." Acting "instead of the citizen, but in about 80 per cent of its cases on complaint of a citizen," the vice agents sought to uphold "American ideals of decency and morality." Descriptions such as these proliferated in the public pronouncements of the NYSSV through the 1930s.[24]

Through the use of such rhetoric, Sumner and his colleagues sought to counter efforts to portray their agency as priggish and intolerant. They did so by interpreting their society's activities to the public as consistent with the principles of a democratic nation. Acting as "complaining witness for the people at large," the logic went, vice agents represented the public's wishes, exercising a citizen's right to demand that the law be enforced. They were less protectors of others than they were delegates who executed the popular will.[25]

Unfortunately for Sumner, such arguments were extraordinarily difficult to sustain in the face of the society's history, the scope of its activities, and much of its own rhetoric. The New York Society for the Suppression of Vice was founded precisely on the notion that it was responsible for protecting others who had neither the means nor the desire to protect themselves. Children and adolescents were usually identified as the beneficiaries of this protection, which was needed, NYSSV officials sometimes implied, because their own parents did not provide it. In 1926, for example, the society's annual report reminded readers that

> obscenity is dangerous in proportion to the lack of preparation to withstand it. . . . It is obvious that the period of "youth's awakening" is the period most necessary to be guarded against this danger. It is obvious too that in no period of our country's history has youth received so little preparation to withstand the demoralizing inroads of indecency as at the present time.[26]

But too often the vice agents betrayed a concern with the protection of a far greater population. In 1923 they voiced an opinion common to many anti-obscenity activists, noting that greater New York was home to more than one and a half million children

> between the ages of five and nineteen. . . . If we add to these the adults who have the mental capacity of a twelve or thirteen year old child — discounting by 50 per cent the startling facts revealed by recent intelligence tests — *then*, a full half of our population needs special protection from the vicious and the venal.

Several years earlier they had explained that

> the whole theory upon which the work of this Society is based [is] that while there is a minority of persons equipped with unusual mental faculties, the minds of the great majority of people are not given to analysis of art, literature or abstruse moral propositions; but . . . they see what is to be seen and hear what is to be heard and are impressed and act accordingly.[27]

Such characterizations of the work of the society became much rarer after the mid-1920s, as Sumner sought to recast it as more democratic. Yet their memory shadowed the organization, and the increasingly frequent reminders by anti-censorship activists that the NYSSV abused its "exceptional powers" in pursuit of a "narrow conception of public morality" impeded Sumner's bid to act as representative of New Yorkers at large.[28]

In the end, this history, combined with the NYSSV's status as a private organization granted law-enforcement responsibilities, overwhelmed Sumner's efforts to accommodate an increasingly persuasive rhetoric about the need for democratic regulation of obscenity. The vice agents' very adeptness at justifying their activities by citing the need to protect others made it impossible for them to convince the public that the society existed to help citizens protect themselves. Through the 1930s public support for the group declined, and by the 1940s far fewer New Yorkers petitioned the NYSSV for assistance. When John Sumner, concerned about the proliferation of pornography, offered to come out of retirement in 1954, an officer of the vice society told him it would be of no use: "I do not think that any City official would have it known that he has any regard for us or for our work. It would be as unpopular as coming out in support of Senator McCarthy, in New York that is."[29] Haunted by its own history, by the 1930s the NYSSV had retreated to the shadows of anti-obscenity activism, providing support and technical assistance but rarely taking the lead.

"AROUSING PUBLIC OPINION": RELIGION AND DEMOCRACY IN ANTI-OBSCENITY CAMPAIGNS

More successfully than either the staff of the New York Society for the Suppression of Vice or the white middle-class women who had led the early movement to regulate motion pictures, New York City's male religious leaders maintained a role for themselves as moral spokesmen. This was accomplished, in part, through the democratization of anti-obscenity activism, as Catholic and Jewish clergy and laymen joined Protestant ministers in their condemnations of immoral entertainment. When the leadership of anti-obscenity campaigns could no longer be imputed to a Protestant elite who, in New York City, could hardly claim to speak for a majority of citizens, clerics found it possible to portray their activism as democratic participation in the political process.

The clergy's interest in anti-obscenity campaigns arose in part from the challenges posed to clerical influence by urban life and the growth of commercial culture. The ethnic and religious heterogeneity of the city's population tested the moral and cultural authority of clerics of all denominations. Further, the central role accorded sexual representation by the purveyors of urban commercial culture as a strategy for drawing audiences threatened clerical authority, which was itself founded, in part, upon the policing of morality. Clergy who had established their influence over their parishioners and within the larger community by seeking to define standards of sexual behavior and moral values feared, correctly, that the secular institutions of commercial culture were offering conflicting views of appropriate morality.[30] New York's religious leaders portrayed this battle to define moral standards in straightforward — sometimes almost apocalyptic — terms. Protestant ministers, for example, argued that children would flee Sunday schools for the movies and that young people influenced by stage immorality would defy "the pure teaching of home and Church." Cardinal Patrick Hayes, head of the Catholic Church in New York City, agreed, warning a gathering of young working women that "books and the stage and screen are now almost a diabolical influence, trying to lure you from your loyalty to the Church." Earlier in his career Cardinal Hayes had portrayed the struggle for authority between church and stage more nakedly, lamenting the fact that "our Catholic people, our Catholic young women, our Catholic ladies . . . will argue with us, sometimes contradict us, when we tell them that such and such a play is not fit for any woman to attend." It was because clerics perceived themselves in direct competition with the entertainment industry to define the city's sexual and moral values that they assumed the leadership of anti-obscenity campaigns. The ridicule clergy sometimes encountered when they spoke out against the lewdness of New York entertainments only served to reinforce their sense of the task's urgency.[31]

The clerics who participated in anti-obscenity campaigns did not always agree on what those sexual values should be. While Western religious authority has long been founded upon the interpretation and control of sexual behavior, Protestant, Catholic, and Jewish clerics operated within distinct sexual traditions that shaped their positions on obscenity.[32] By the early twentieth century Christians and Jews generally concurred in the celebration of procreative sexuality within marriage, but important denominational distinctions remained. Literary critic John Maynard has suggested that Christianity tended to treat sexual issues from a "master discourse of lust," that is, a concern with subduing humans' "uncontrolled drive for pleasure" by strictly disciplining it to marital procreative sexuality. On the other hand, Judaism did not merely sanction such sexuality but sought to maximize it by recognizing a right on the part of women and men not only to sexual relations but to sexual pleasure.[33] Further, these distinct approaches were complicated by doctrinal diversity within each denomination: Reform and Orthodox rabbis, mainstream and fundamentalist Protestant ministers were as likely to disagree as agree about the proper approach to sexual issues. These differences were frequently expressed in clerics' approach to commercial amusements. The Catholic hierarchy, for example, was certain to condemn plays or movies that portrayed birth control or divorce; Protestant ministers might also criticize such productions, but Jews almost never did.[34] Despite these differences, however, in the 1920s and 1930s clerics from all denominations became collaborators in anti-obscenity campaigns.

Strikingly, in the first two decades of the twentieth century clerical condemnations of immoral amusements were relatively muted. There were exceptions, of course: Protestant campaigns to outlaw Sunday theatrical productions sometimes called attention to the "vileness" of the theater, and Canon William S. Chase, claiming to speak for the Protestant Episcopal church in Brooklyn, waged a vigorous campaign for motion picture censorship on the local, state, and federal levels from 1911 through the 1930s. Indeed, church complaints were an important factor in Mayor McClellan's decision to shut down the city's nickelodeons in 1908. Compared to the years after World War I, however, local clubwomen and vice agents were much more active in anti-obscenity campaigns than were New York's clergy, who might occasionally fulminate from their pulpits but did little else to stem the tide of immoral amusements.[35]

The reasons for this lack of activity have much to do with unique conditions in New York City. Most important is the relative weakness of the Protestant church. Across the nation during the first two decades of the twentieth century there was an explosion of Protestant activism on moral issues, capped by the passage of the Volstead Act in 1919; but in New York, where by 1900 Protestants were a minority of city residents, the clergy may have been less willing to take up the mantle of moral guardianship so visibly. The presence of other influential groups concerned with the regulation of commercial culture, including the New York Society for the Suppression of Vice and the National Board of Censorship of Motion Pictures, both of which courted clerical support, may also have contributed to clergy's relaxed attitude toward obscenity; perhaps it seemed the necessary oversight was already in place. Furthermore, it was not until after World War I that Catholic and Jewish clerics began participating in debates about a range of moral issues that affected not only their followers but the urban population at large.

One exception to this general lack of clerical interest in obscenity was found in the Catholic Theatre Movement, established in 1912. From their "white list" of plays that Catholics could in good conscience attend, its personnel omitted plays that contained profanity or blasphemy, that dealt with issues of birth control, divorce, or infidelity, that featured scanty costumes, or that mocked religion. In 1930, for example, the list excluded a production of Aristophanes' *Lysistrata* because it was "unabashed pagan mockery." When in 1936 the staff of the CTM began to categorize all plays on Broadway as "acceptable," "objectionable in part," or "objectionable in whole" (that is, forbidden to Catholics), the latter category included *The Children's Hour* and *Tobacco Road*, which one Catholic activist noted was "unparalleled for obscenity, its insult to the Holy Name so sacred to all Christians, and its general immoral tone."[36] The New York-based Catholic Theatre Movement provided a model for later efforts, as the strategy of creating lists of acceptable entertainment and requiring boycotts of that considered unacceptable was extended to other media. Both locally and on the national level the Catholic hierarchy also employed this strategy to combat books, magazines, and films considered immoral. The Legion of Decency campaign, initiated in the 1930s against the American motion picture industry, is only the most famous and far-reaching of these efforts.[37]

The Catholic Theatre Movement's crusade against obscenity was one largely restricted to the community of Catholics.[38] The Catholic hierarchy justified the CTM as one expression of the Church's duty to protect the innocence of all of its followers, adults as well as children. Their readiness to make such arguments reflected Catholic conceptions of hierarchy and sin. As God's representative on earth, a priest had responsibility for interpreting God's will to his parishioners and ensuring their obedience to that will, thus preserving their souls. This responsibility was an especially weighty one when it came to immoral amusements, for disobedience of God's will in the arena of sexuality had serious consequences. Within Catholic theology sins of "impurity" were considered venial (that is, capable of forgiveness) only if they were indirect or involuntary. All other sins of impurity, whether in thought or in deed, constituted mortal sins that endangered the immortality of one's soul.[39] Because "bad thoughts" as well as "bad deeds" had such serious consequences, Catholics were urged to avoid opportunities for corruption by maintaining their sexual innocence. A 1927 papal pronouncement on immoral books described the Church's stance on plays and movies as well:

> So fragile and weak is corrupt nature, so strong is its tendency to lewdness, that neither eloquence of style . . . nor the intention of the writer whatever it be, can ever prevent the readers, fascinated by these unclean writings, from little by little having their souls perverted and their hearts depraved.[40]

According to such teachings, censorship was an important strategy for maintaining purity, because the only sure way to guard against sin was to shield Catholic women and men, boys and girls from exposure to treacherous plays, films, or books. Yet it was churchly, not government, censorship that was called for; the secular, Protestant-dominated state did not possess the moral authority requisite to such a task.[41]

Members of the Catholic hierarchy maintained, however, that their regulatory activities could hardly be called censorship. The Reverend Robert E. Woods, for example, argued that clerical supervision of the theater was necessitated by the fact that the Catholic Church had a "divine mandate to guide infallibly in matters of faith and morals" and that therefore censorship by the church "does not violate the right of free speech."[42] Similar explanations accompanied Catholic campaigns against other forms of entertainment, including books, magazines, and motion pictures. In 1929 Cardinal Hayes inaugurated a campaign against indecent literature by proclaiming that

> the reading of literature which is a proximate occasion of sin against faith or morals, is prohibited by the natural law. . . . Indulgence in such literature violates conscience — [it is] not a question of regulation or censorship on the part of the Church, but a matter of conscientious obedience to the law of God.

The cardinal further instructed New York Catholics that literature not included on his list of approved books could be read only if permission was granted by a bishop.[43]

Boycotts such as that organized by the Catholic Theatre Movement proved an effective strategy for a number of reasons. They harmonized with the growth of a consumer culture and its notion of consumption as a civic choice, a means of creating a better life. Catholic leaders exhorted their parishioners to consume only wholesome plays or books in the same way that Progressive-era agencies encouraged mothers to purchase only wholesome milk. In addition, however, the boycott was especially suited as a strategy for Catholic activism. Because it did not involve government coercion and therefore maintained clear lines of separation between church and state, emphasizing the boycott could allay Protestant fears about "romanizing" Catholics who allegedly desired to make the United States government an arm of the Vatican. As important, Catholic hierarchical structures facilitated its effectiveness. More than other religious leaders, the head of the archdiocese of New York had at his service an organizational structure that allowed him to publicize any boycott that he chose to implement and to encourage local Catholics to abide by it. Lists of approved plays, magazines, and movies were published in the diocesan newspaper; on occasion, the leader of the New York hierarchy issued letters condemning evil entertainment that were read in all of the city's Catholic churches; on a particular Sunday morning parish priests might sermonize about the dangers of immoral amusements, at the direction of Cardinal Hayes or his successor, Archbishop Spell-

man. These tactics were used more than once to implement the Catholic Theatre Movement boycott. More direct forms of pressure could be applied as well.
Around the nation, for example, one Sunday each year the Catholic hierarchy
urged churchgoers to reaffirm their Legion of Decency pledge to boycott immoral motion pictures. In at least one New York City church, worshippers were
asked to kneel and recite the pledge together, and it was broadened to include
the stage as well.[44]

That Catholic hierarchical structures allowed for the effective organizing of
boycotts does not mean that all Catholics were subservient to Church authority. Certainly not all New York Catholics abided by the CTM's white list, even if
they did see it in the diocesan weekly newspaper; not all Catholics attended
church each Sunday to hear the sermons warning them away from immoral entertainment; not all Catholics who knelt to recite the Legion of Decency pledge
stayed away from the films that the legion condemned. Although there is little
evidence for the middle years of the twentieth century, if earlier patterns held it
is likely that some Catholics — those of Irish descent, women, children, and the
upwardly mobile who yet remained within the "Catholic ghetto" that Church
leaders sought to create in urban areas — were more likely to attend Mass or to
belong to church-sponsored groups than were, for example, Italian Catholics;
the former were perhaps most likely to follow the Church's injunctions. Still,
Catholicism's centralized structure, combined with a theology emphasizing
obedience to the priest, bishop, pope, and God, made it possible for Catholic
leadership to trust in the effectiveness of nongovernment regulatory strategies
such as the boycott for molding Catholic consumption of commercial culture,
despite differences of ethnicity and class.[45]

Although the Catholic Theatre Movement was, by and large, restricted in its
scope to Catholics, it may have drawn other clerics' attention to the theater, or
this foray into supervising commercial culture may have whetted the appetite
of members of the Catholic hierarchy. Whatever the reasons (and changing
conditions on the stage and in publishing must also be numbered among
them), in the 1920s there erupted a vigorous clerical crusade against obscenity.
In this decade New York clergy of all denominations offered a chorus of denunciations of the stage. Catholic and Protestant clerics also consistently opposed the annual effort to repeal the state's movie censorship law and campaigned forcefully against "indecent" literature.[46]

This was an interfaith movement, but Catholic clergy and laymen were its
leaders. Their increasing visibility reflected a shift in the national Catholic
Church's social and cultural agenda, from adapting Catholicism to America (the

aim of the CTM) to transforming American culture in conformity with Catholic moral ideals.[47] Nonetheless, the Catholic effort to shape American culture must be understood as something more complex than an attempted conquest. It was quite unlike Protestant participation in anti-obscenity work across the nation, which was, to a degree, intended as a strategy for maintaining or defending Protestant domination of cultural affairs. For New York Catholics, participating side by side with Protestants in campaigns to impose a stricter morality upon the entertainment industry provided a means of proclaiming their respectability. The notion of moral respectability — marked by temperance, "genteel" conduct, and the accumulation of material goods — held great significance for Irish Catholic immigrants and their children striving to establish a place for themselves within American society. Anti-obscenity activism represented one means by which Catholics could proclaim their respectability and distance themselves from Protestant stereotypes of "sensual" Catholics — stereotypes that had never completely lost their salience, as was demonstrated by the particular forms taken by the anti-Catholicism of the 1920s.[48] Furthermore, it offered an opportunity for interfaith cooperation that Catholic positions on other sexual issues, such as contraception, prohibited. Thus anti-obscenity work served Catholic clergy and layworkers as a strategy for assimilation into the mainstream of American life.

The entry into anti-obscenity activism by the New York chapter of the Knights of Columbus beginning in the 1930s highlights the ways in which such activism could be an expression of class and national identity. The Knights' membership was composed primarily of Irish-American men who had moved, or were in the process of moving, into the middle class. Espousing "militant Catholicism [and] American superpatriotism," the organization's members declared their identity as middle-class Americans through Catholic activism. New York men affiliated with the Knights were adept at linking their traditional concern with patriotism to their newly minted crusade against obscenity. For example, the chairman of the New York chapter endorsed legislation to enhance the regulatory powers of the city's license commissioner on the grounds that "all good Americans will recognize and admit that indecency should not be tolerated." Crusading against obscenity offered the Knights an opportunity to shape New York's culture, to exercise political muscle, to demonstrate middle-class respectability, and to prove their Americanism.[49]

Some of New York's Jewish religious leaders also became more vocal in debates about obscenity during the 1920s and 1930s. To a greater degree than Protestants and Catholics, however, their participation came in response as much to the existence of anti-obscenity campaigns as to the existence of obscenity. Rabbis entered into anti-obscenity activism in the attempt to counter

Christians' perceptions of Jews as a different, alien, and more primitive people, by demonstrating that they shared the "Christian" morals of their Protestant and Catholic brethren and by trying to control the behavior of other Jews.[50] Prompted by the concern that Christian condemnations of obscenity might fuel antisemitism (and vice versa), they sometimes joined in such condemnations in self-defense. For Jews, anti-obscenity activism became a strategy for protecting the Jewish community by policing it.

Jewish fears that anti-obscenity activism could become antisemitic activism were founded in an amalgam of prejudice and fact regarding the place of Jews in the American entertainment industry. The important role of Jews in the development of Hollywood has been well documented. In New York City Jewish participation in the motion picture trade predated the rise of Jews as motion picture moguls in Hollywood, as many Jewish entrepreneurs opened nickelodeons in the city's ghettos. Jews were also well represented among New York's theatrical producers, and burlesque in particular was notable for the presence of Jews among producers, managers, and entertainers. While Christian contemporaries exaggerated the extent and effects of Jewish "domination" of American cultural industries, Jews did play a disproportionate role in moviemaking and the theater. Furthermore, Jewish participation as producers and performers of these types of entertainment occurred simultaneously with, and perhaps contributed to, the increasing portrayal of sexuality within them.[51]

The visibility of Jews in these industries nourished Christian fears that commercial culture in the metropolis would become even more corrupt and corrupting than it already was. Their association with an entertainment world built around the commodification of sexuality seemed to sustain a preexisting paradigm of antisemitism that fused prejudices regarding Jewish greed and sexual immorality in the conviction, as historian Edward Bristow has phrased it, that Jews "organized widespread conspiracies to corrupt and pollute the Christian world."[52] In the United States, as in Europe, many Christians subscribed to the view that Jews were so avaricious that they would permit neither legalities nor morals to stand in the way of their accumulation of wealth.[53] The belief that degradation and even bestiality characterized the sexual behavior of Jewish men likewise was a staple of antisemitic ideology. As a result, antisemitic thought linked gold lust with sex lust in the mind and body of the Jewish male.[54] Just as some New Yorkers blamed Jews for the existence of white slavery, a problem that symbolically united concerns about economic exploitation and sexual immorality, so some of them charged Jews with breeding immorality in the city's entertainment industry, which also blended commerce and sex.[55]

Those New York Protestant and Catholic clergy who offered condemnations of Jewish control of commercial culture usually tempered their remarks by declaring respect for "decent" Jews at the same time they singled out Jews for causing the growth of immorality. These charges encompassed both national entertainment media and local productions. For example, in 1921 the Lord's Day Alliance, headed by New York City minister and reformer Harry Bowlby, issued a statement contending that the American film industry was "largely controlled by a group of Jews, unfaithful to the religious traditions of their race . . . sordid, soulless, Godless worldlings."[56] New York Christians also could be influenced by similar statements offered by Americans elsewhere. When Bishop Joseph Schrembs of Cleveland spoke at the 1927 convention of the National Council of Catholic Women, the Manhattan diocesan newspaper reprinted his message. Discussing the role of Jews in the "amusement world," he declared that while he had much respect for the Jews as a race, he knew there was

> a large and influential group of Jews who are attempting to break down Christian morality. Let us go to the decent Jews — and thanks be to God there are decent Jews and lots of them — and ask them to join hands with us to solve the common problem of commercialized vice.

Such testimony clearly attributed America's moral decline to its Jewish residents at the same time that it created a distinction between "good" and "bad" Jews based upon the nexus of commerce and sexuality.[57]

Many New Yorkers shared attitudes like these, articulating them in ways that ranged from the blatant to the subtle. Few were so explicitly antisemitic as one former New Yorker who wrote Mayor LaGuardia that he had moved away from the city in order to rescue his sons from corrupting burlesque shows, which were owned by "Jews, all wealth, and all made their money on filth." More common were insinuations of the type found in an editorial cartoon published in a New York City newspaper in 1923, which showed a policeman evicting a distinctly Semitic-looking "money mad manager" from a theater, the front of which was emblazoned with a poster of a naked woman. Oft-repeated statements that anti-obscenity activists sought to defend "Christian morality" implied that non-Christian morality was inherently deficient. And it requires no great stretch of the imagination to discern antisemitic attitudes in the frequently voiced condemnations of theatrical producers "who would weaken our moral structure for the sake of the *shekels* they could pile into wide open purses." While certainly most New Yorkers concerned about obscenity did not mention Jews, the accumulation of such assertions, both those obvious and those less so, those clearly intentioned and those offhand, amounted to an indictment of New York's Jews for bringing the city's entertainment industry to the depths of degradation.[58]

Such proclamations provoked fears among Jews that anti-obscenity activism might fuel antisemitism, ironically leading many rabbis to participate in anti-obscenity campaigns. New York Jewish leaders articulated this fear when discussing the Catholic-led Legion of Decency, which in New York City targeted burlesque performances in addition to motion pictures. Rabbi Stephen Wise, for example, urged Jews to join in the boycott of indecent films but warned as well that the legion might become an antisemitic campaign that blamed Jews for motion picture immorality. Rabbis Sidney Goldstein and William Rosenblum joined Catholic and Protestant clergy to form an Interfaith Committee on Decency to support the legion's work in New York City. Rabbi Goldstein explained his participation on the committee by noting that

> as Jews, we are more interested than others in the endeavor to make sure that only wholesome pictures are shown in American theatres since, as is generally known, so large a part of the persons in the motion picture industry are Jewish. If motion pictures are not kept unobjectionable, it is a species of national disgrace for us, in so far as Jews are responsible.

Many of these clerical leaders believed that they could work behind the scenes, appealing to Jewish movie and theatrical producers to "clean up" in order to prevent the spread of antisemitism.[59]

Often, although perhaps inadvertently, through their anti-obscenity activism Jewish leaders reinforced the distinction between good Jews, who fought obscenity, and bad Jews, who created it. For example, during the 1932 hearings on license renewals for three Times Square burlesque theaters, lawyer Samuel Marcus testified that he, a rabbi, and another layman had visited one of the theaters in an attempt to induce the Minsky brothers, as fellow Jews, to cease "the commercializing of filth." Marcus was an attorney for the Society for the Prevention of Crime, an antivice organization, and he had been urged to investigate burlesque by his friends as well as by Christian ministers who asked him "if the Jews would stand for that sort of thing." Marcus and his colleagues never communicated their concerns to the Minskys, instead joining with Christian clergy and Times Square property owners in attempting to persuade government officials to put the Minskys out of business. When Samuel Marcus bolstered his testimony against Billy Minsky by casting aspersions against the "quality of [his] Judaism," noting that "he does not want filth in the house, but he serves filth to the public," he sought to avert antisemitism by demonstrating the distinctions between good and bad Jews.[60]

Similar concerns motivated Jewish clerical condemnations of *The God of Vengeance*. City officials instituted their prosecution of the play in 1923 at the behest of Jewish leaders, and Rabbi Joseph Silverman of the prestigious Temple Emanu-El appeared as the chief complainant before the grand jury that indicted those associated with the production. While there was by no means agreement among Jews about the effect of the play — Harry Weinberger, the producer, was a Jew, and Jewish leaders such as Rabbi Wise and Abraham Cahan defended it — those who opposed it feared that its portrayal of Jewish prostitution (and perhaps, perversion) would undermine their efforts toward assimilation by reinforcing ancient prejudices linking Jews and immorality. When the play was produced within the Yiddish theater for Jewish audiences, it presented no danger. However, its exhibition before gentiles who might see its discussion of immorality *among* Jews as evidence for the immorality *of* Jews led at least some Jews to combat it as obscenity.[61]

The Jewish debate over *The God of Vengeance* points to divisions within New York's Jewish community that made Reform rabbis, in particular, prominent within anti-obscenity campaigns but also contributed to a peculiar ambivalence about that activism. Before 1945 Reform rabbis remained more likely than other Jewish clerics in New York City to speak out on issues not narrowly defined as "Jewish" and to cooperate on social concerns with Christian clergy, reflecting their greater assimilation into municipal life. Orthodox and Conservative rabbis tended to be most concerned with the preservation of Jewish tradition and to devote their energies to activities that would advance that cause, and were less likely to participate in any type of interfaith efforts. Therefore, with few exceptions, those rabbis active in anti-obscenity campaigns were affiliated with Reform congregations.[62] Reform clergy's inclination to participate in anti-obscenity campaigns may also be related to the fact that these sectarian divisions frequently corresponded with differences of ethnicity and class. By the 1930s, when Jews became increasingly active in anti-obscenity campaigns, the distinctions between East European and German Jews that had divided the Jewish community were fading. Nonetheless, Reform rabbis continued to minister to congregations largely comprised of affluent German Jews whose families had long been in America and who had made their fortunes in (sexually) respectable ventures such as finance, retail, or real estate. Jewish entrepreneurs and workers within the entertainment industry, on the other hand, tended to be newer immigrants who sought upward mobility in the less respectable milieu of commercial culture. Thus the participation of Reform rabbis in anti-obscenity campaigns reflected, at least to a degree, the continuation of an older campaign by the Jewish community's elite to shape the behavior of Jews of Eastern European descent.[63]

Rabbinical participation in crusades against obscenity was complicated, however, by Reform's distinctive culture. These commercial amusements employed and were patronized by many Jews who undoubtedly resented rabbinical attacks upon their livelihoods and leisure activities, which they perceived as unwarranted intrusions into domains beyond the reach of a limited rabbinical authority. Rabbis' authority had traditionally been based on extensive knowledge of Jewish law, but Reform rabbis had relatively little authority, since the Reform movement "represented a revolt not only against the interpretation of the law but against the whole basis of its authority." As learned men, New York's Reform rabbis might provide guidance and inspiration, but their authority to tell Jews how to behave was minimal.[64] Further, Reform clergy tended to be the Jewish leaders most liberal on sexual issues, reflecting Reform's origins in a movement to adapt Judaism to the modern world. Their efforts to uphold traditional morality could come into conflict not only with the values of many in the broader Jewish community but also with Reform Judaism's self-definition as a modern religious movement, in an era when individual autonomy and relaxed sexual mores were two of the primary denoters of modernity.[65]

As a consequence, many Reform leaders communicated a profound ambivalence about their anti-obscenity activism. Rabbi Sidney Goldstein is a case in point. Rabbi Goldstein, who worked with Stephen Wise at New York's Free Synagogue, was decidedly liberal politically. He was an activist on social justice issues within rabbinical groups and belonged to secular organizations like the War Resisters League and the American Birth Control League. He was also an early member of the National Council on Freedom from Censorship, a group whose members defined censorship as "any power to suppress the expression of thought — either by preventing its expression in advance, or by prosecution under cover of vague definitions of law." Rabbi Goldstein, in accepting a position on the NCFC's Advisory Committee, advised the organizers that he opposed censorship, but "I must confess that I do believe in sanitation and wish that this committee . . . would consider in what way the city can be relieved of the cesspools that from time to time break out in the community." Despite his concern about the "filth" of obscenity, Goldstein apparently took an active role in the NCFC, visiting the New York City commissioner of licenses in January 1932 as part of a delegation that protested his threats to revoke the licenses of newsdealers who sold "objectionable" magazines.[66]

Yet Rabbi Goldstein's opposition to government censorship was not strong enough to survive the antiburlesque campaign that erupted merely three months later. Indeed, the rabbi testified at the burlesque license renewal hearings, this time telling Commissioner Geraghty that denying the renewal of licenses to the Times Square burlesque theaters "would be not an exercise of censorship . . . [but] an act in the direction of protecting the morality of the people of the City of New York, because I believe that these theatres constitute a grave danger to the moral life of our city." Perhaps Rabbi Goldstein's change of heart resulted from his belief that burlesque posed a more serious risk than magazines to New York's moral life, but the fact that the burlesque industry was so strongly identified with Jewish entrepreneurs likely affected his stance as well.[67] As a result of the conflict between his position and that of the other members of the NCFC, who supported the burlesque theaters, Rabbi Goldstein resigned from the organization. He went on to become an active opponent of obscenity, organizing protests against burlesque until 1942 and joining the Interfaith Committee on Decency to coordinate Jewish cooperation with the Legion of Decency as well.[68]

Still, when in 1955 Rabbi Goldstein offered an account of his activities he portrayed himself as a confirmed anticensorship advocate, reflecting the conflicts felt by Reform Jews on the question of government regulation. The rabbi disclosed that he had joined in campaigns to control burlesque and motion pictures out of his concern that the dominance of Jews in those industries might fuel antisemitism. As he remembered it, however, he never advocated any form of censorship, claiming (falsely) that he and other clergy insisted that the license commissioner pursue action against the burlesque theaters only through the courts, after obtaining criminal convictions. Rabbi Goldstein argued, in fact, that he participated in interfaith efforts to curb burlesque and the movies as a means of *preventing* government censorship. Indeed, he went on to issue a strong denunciation of censorship, one that mirrored the NCFC's position in the 1930s:

We must recognize that standards change from time to time and from culture to culture. What is regarded as obscene and indecent and immoral in one generation is not thought of in the same way in another. . . . In view of these facts it is perfectly evident that we cannot entrust censorship, local, state, or federal, to an individual, whether he be a Commissioner of Licenses, a member of the State Department of Education, or an officer of the Federal Government. Such authority should not be placed in the hands of any one man or any one group.[69]

Rabbi Goldstein's telling of his story suggests some of the complexities of historical memory, but it also reveals the difficulties posed by trying to combat antisemitic beliefs that Jews corrupted Christian morality through methods that often contradicted Reform Judaism's commitment to modernity.

Despite Reform rabbis' ambivalence, in the interwar years an interfaith movement for the suppression of obscenity coalesced. The city's clergy stepped into the breach created as the vice society's legitimacy eroded and New York clubwomen largely confined themselves to concern about a motion picture industry already under the supervision of state censors. In order to fend off accusations that they were "sin-sniffing" prudes, New York's clerics tried to frame their critique of obscenity in new ways.[70] Aided by the fact that the clerical assault on obscenity was an interfaith one, religious leaders found ways convincingly to present themselves as representatives of the people in their war on immoral entertainment.

Arguments that crusades against obscenity were necessary for the protection of the vulnerable began to give way, therefore, to the claim that clerics sought only to "arouse public opinion" against immoral entertainments. This justification, which portrayed anti-obscenity activism as consonant with democratic forms of government, was made necessary by a number of factors, including the backlash against interference with individual freedoms that constituted the major cultural response to Prohibition and the beginnings of a movement to extend free speech protection to cultural productions. Further, it had special attractions for clergy of each denomination. A rising tide of religious doubt among many Protestants as well as the bedrock Protestant affirmation of an individual's personal relationship with God, which gave Protestant ministers less authority than Catholic priests to dictate to their congregants what they could look at or read, made the emphasis on public opinion attractive to mainstream Protestant clergy. It was also essential to a Catholic hierarchy seeking to broaden its activism beyond the Catholic community while wishing to allay Protestant anxiety about an autocratic and romanizing church. And it was attuned to the limited authority accorded to Reform rabbis. Indeed, only when clerics began framing their activism in terms of their responsibility to help citizens control the culture around them could an interfaith anti-obscenity movement succeed.

Clerics had long claimed that their role in crusades against immoral entertainment included the responsibility to educate the public: by improving public taste through education and exhortation, they could eliminate the audience for bad plays and movies. Now, however, their informational role took on a more democratic cast. Seeking to counter the accusation that they were prudish and old-fashioned, New York's ministers, rabbis, and priests claimed that they simply attempted to inform city residents that entertainment purveyors were failing to meet the inhabitants' own moral standards.[71] Increasingly, they identified themselves as merely the spokesmen for what later in the century would be called the moral majority of citizens. By the 1930s the contention that clerics endeavored to help "normal, right-thinking, moral" New Yorkers to act against the "anti-moral . . . minority" who were corrupting their children and sullying their city had become commonplace in campaigns against obscenity.[72] Only if clergy warned New Yorkers that the commercial culture of their city was out of control, the argument went, could urban residents exercise their democratic rights to do something about it.

By the late 1930s and early 1940s this emphasis on facilitating public action evolved into the claim that, through anti-obscenity campaigns, religious activists represented the interests of both the local community and the larger nation. Catholic activists articulated this vision most forcefully, and in doing so they transformed in important ways a Protestant tradition of linking the fight against obscenity to the struggle to define national identity. In the early twentieth century Protestant ministers described this relationship rather narrowly, usually centering upon the defense of a Christian nation that was both Anglo-Saxon and Protestant in heritage. Some cast obscenity as a symbol of the threat that foreigners posed to a pure nation, using ethnicity as a proxy for religion. Such arguments were especially common during the 1920s, when nativist sentiments were on the rise. In 1927, for example, the Reverend Dr. Karl Reiland of St. George's Episcopal Church blamed stage immorality upon the "ethnic problem," warning that "we are being politically, artistically and culturally choked to death by . . . foreign influx." Similarly, the editors of the newsletter of the conservative Methodist Episcopal Board of Temperance, Prohibition and Public Morals supported the anti-obscenity activities of New York City Methodists by publishing several articles about the state of the theater. They warned that "the New York theater has sunk to depths of indecency which must be characterized alien," further charging that some theatrical producers believed that

> the old American sense of decency has been submerged and that today appeal must be made to the sensuality of the slums and of those slum children who have attained to fortune but not to Americanism. Our grasp on America is slipping. It is time to tighten the grip if it can be done.

While these accusations did not overtly summon Protestant New Yorkers to the defense of Christianity, they conveyed quite clearly the sense that the immorality of Catholic and especially Jewish "children of the slums" posed a threat to Protestant ministers' vision of what the nation should be.[73]

Catholic leaders also appealed to "American" decency, but they transformed it to support a more inclusive sense of nationhood, one based on the notion that all Americans — or, at least, all loyal Americans — shared common moral principles, regardless of ethnicity or religion. This theme became more central to anti-obscenity thought once the superpatriotic Knights of Columbus embarked on their campaign against burlesque shows and sexy magazines in the mid-1930s. And when Francis Spellman ascended to the post of New York archbishop in 1939, he took up this theme with a vengeance.

Spellman quickly became the city's most vocal and effective opponent of obscenity. He was a fervent anticommunist, with close connections to both the Vatican and President Franklin Roosevelt. The archbishop played an important role as informal emissary for Roosevelt during World War II, visiting troops as well as conferring with Pope Pius XII and other foreign religious and political leaders. Sexual immorality in commercial culture was a special concern of his.[74] He frequently intoned against the threat that obscenity posed to the nation's moral strength, joining fears about out-of-control commercial culture to war-related concerns with great skill. In March 1942, for example, Spellman used a nationwide radio broadcast to praise the LaGuardia administration's decision to close the last of the city's burlesque houses. He condemned the "Filth Column . . . who piously shout 'censorship' " if they are not permitted "to exercise their venal, venomous, diabolical debauching of the minds of our boys and girls." Warning that their "treachery from within" might destroy Americans' "God-given rights," he complained that opponents of censorship wanted "the freedom to kill the bodies and souls of their fellow Americans . . . the freedom to be obscene." In November of the same year, the archbishop delivered a similar speech to an organization of Catholic police officers. He warned that even mothers and daughters were enjoying obscene theatrical productions and asked,

> What would happen if we tried to do something about it? We would be accused of censorship — accused by a people hiding behind a smoke-screen of their own depravity, their own lust, their own smugness, their own treason!
>
> Censorship, which they define while giving themselves the right to drag souls down to hell while the fathers of these girls and the husbands of those women are fighting and dying for freedom.[75]

Among the riot of images presented in such speeches, a few stand out: the cleric as father-protector of the city's women and children, left unprotected in wartime, the invidiousness of obscenity that, like the enemy without, seeks to kill Americans and, like the enemy within, threatens treachery and treason, and the contrast between the false freedom desired by anticensorship activists and the true freedom championed by men such as himself. In battling obscenity, Spellman proclaimed, he was struggling for the soul of the nation.

By the 1940s, anti-obscenity activists thus identified their crusade with the protection of an America defined by its moral strength. The shift from the vision of a Christian or Anglo-Saxon nation to the vision of a morally strong America accelerated as Catholics became ever more prominent in anti-obscenity campaigns, but the participation of Jews contributed as well. As Jewish leaders joined in condemning obscenity, if not with equal fervor, at least visibly and dependably, it became more difficult for Catholic and Protestant clergy to frame their own endeavors as part of the attempt to defend a Christian nation. The protection of a moral community, united in the commitment of its Protestant, Catholic, and Jewish citizens to upholding a common sense of decency, accorded much better with the democratic culture of the mid-twentieth-century United States.

As religious leaders reframed their critique of obscenity, they also began to advocate different sorts of regulatory strategies. Clerics continued to champion government censorship of motion pictures; despite the efforts of the National Board of Censorship of Motion Pictures, the presumption that the audience for movies was composed of children who needed special protection was widely accepted. But, increasingly, they condemned "censorship" as an unwelcome encroachment on the personal liberty of adults. In its stead they advocated a wide variety of forms of regulation, both voluntary and government, which they carefully defined as not-censorship. Indeed, as *censorship* became a word denoting ineffective and improper control, anti-obscenity activists tried to expand the regulatory regime governing the entertainment industry. This expansion was not, however, just a response to the success of their foes in making *censorship* itself a dirty word. It also was an expression of the fact that some anti-obscenity activists, particularly Jews and, in certain cases, Catholics, themselves distrusted formal preexhibition censorship by government officials.

Clerics offered an array of reasons for rejecting censorship as a strategy for controlling commercial culture. Vague denunciations of censorship as "dangerous" or "evil" were accompanied by detailed descriptions of the problems that censorship brought in its wake. Government censorship undermined individual responsibility and interfered with parental duties.[76] It was ineffective because it did nothing to uplift public morals and too frequently was used against only the most "openly indecent" publications and plays, while "subversive morality [is] allowed to prosper provided its language is polite."[77] Some religious leaders complained that censorship violated the nation's democratic traditions, or was a despotic limitation of individual freedoms, while others merely affirmed that other strategies, such as boycotts or education of the popular taste, were more effective.[78] In their pronouncements on the hazards of censorship, clerics sounded remarkably like the civil libertarians, publishers, and entertainers who after 1920 joined together to limit the regulation of sexually explicit cultural materials.

The difference, of course, is that religious leaders always coupled their condemnations of censorship with assertions that commercial culture itself was dangerous and desperately in need of regulation. Episcopal Bishop Manning's 1930 warning to Broadway was typical: "We do not want censorship. We know well its defects and dangers, but unless something is done censorship in some form will be forced upon us." Priests, ministers, rabbis, and laymen all agreed that censorship had its risks, but the degraded state of commercial culture made it inevitable despite their opposition to it.[79] Unless, that is, a more effective and appropriate form of regulation could be substituted. Thus, instead of the "intolerable interference" of censorship, religious leaders promoted the citizens' play jury, advocated boycotts of immoral amusements, exhorted producers and publishers to institute self-censorship, and argued for police raids and criminal prosecution. As this list of remedies suggests, many clerics were careful to emphasize that opposition to censorship did not mean opposition to control, including government control. And some tried to establish the doctrine that obscenity, by its very definition, could not be censored, that "censorship of obscenity" was an oxymoron. A representative of the Knights of Columbus used this argument to refute the allegation that license commissioner Paul Moss had censored the 1945 production of *Trio*:

> Censorship, in any form, is abhorrent to us, if by the term is meant the arbitrary and capricious interference with one's right to speak or write as he sees fit on any topic. People forget, however, that no one has the right to publicly speak or write in a manner or on a subject that violates all accepted standards of morals and decency.[80]

In offering arguments such as these, religious activists were able to demonstrate their commitment to democratic ideals at the same time that they could demand that the entertainment industry submit to external control.

The opposition to censorship these activists articulated was sometimes merely a concession to "the times," which, clerics perceived, were less tolerant of limits on individualism, but it could also be deeply felt. A number of Protestant clerics, including S. Parkes Cadman of the New York Federation of Churches and George Reid Andrews of the Church and Drama Association, were especially consistent in their denunciations of censorship and dedicated themselves to creating voluntary strategies for cleaning up Broadway. As important, Catholics and Jews brought to their anti-obscenity activism distinctive attitudes toward censorship, attitudes shaped by their experience as religious minorities in the United States. Nationally, leaders in the Catholic Church frequently opposed Protestant-supported efforts to establish federal control over commercial culture, because they feared such proposals (such as that for a federal censorship of the movies) would advance Protestant influence within government. Indeed, despite the long-standing suspicion, voiced by many Protestants, that Catholics sought to "romanize" the United States and establish Catholicism as a state religion, American Catholics tended to favor the separation of church and state. They viewed with distrust Protestant attempts to pass blue laws and other moral legislation because their vision of a Christian nation often did not correspond with that of Protestants.[81] This distrust was somewhat muted in the New York context, where Catholics had an unusually prominent role in the municipal political system and were relatively powerful in state government as well.[82] Still, it shaped the arguments made and proposals advanced by local Catholic anti-obscenity activists, fostering Catholic support for strategies that could be fully directed by Church authorities (such as the boycott), or for those that left room for the levying of local political influence (such as licensing, which was implemented by a political appointee).[83] Jewish clergy were even more forthright in their denunciations of censorship. Drawn to anti-obscenity activism partly to defuse its perceived antisemitism, they also felt the need to defend themselves against a state that might express the prejudices of Christians.[84] Although it is difficult to gauge the influence that rabbis had upon their Christian colleagues, the emphasis of most Jewish clerics upon persuasion rather than regulation may have curbed efforts to increase government control over commercial culture. At the very least, Jewish caution regarding official regulation probably meshed well with Catholic amenability to such strategies as the boycott, perhaps increasing the willingness of anti-obscenity activists to first try voluntary measures under some circumstances.[85]

It is important not to confuse the rejection of a narrowly defined censorship with rejection of state authority over commercial culture, however. Indeed, in taking up the leadership of anti-obscenity campaigns, clerics implicitly constructed a partnership between church and government officials for the control of obscenity, for the shadow of state power lurked behind clerical condemnations of immoral entertainments. The full impact of their words and actions was to create a system of moral regulation in which the church's role was to arouse public opinion and the state's role was to respond to the democratic forces represented by that public opinion. By symbolically linking their own moral authority and that of the government through the trope of "public opinion," clerics and laymen hoped to reject attacks upon their leadership of anti-obscenity campaigns.

Indeed, despite some differences, clergy of all religions who led campaigns to combat obscenity in the 1930s and 1940s offered a more or less common vision of the relationship between morality, nationhood, the church, and the state. Within this vision America's strength, indeed perhaps the nation's exceptionalism, depended upon the maintenance of standards of morality. Religious leaders, in partnership with the state, had as their responsibility the protection of those standards. Clerics were to warn of impending dangers, inciting "good Americans" and, when necessary, government officials to action. State authorities had the responsibility of protecting citizens' "rights" to a moral community against what anti-obscenity activists saw as unbridled individual license, providing a last bulwark against the flood of immorality threatening to engulf America.[86] In forging a more modern link between the battle against immorality and the democratic defense of the nation, New York's clergy anticipated arguments that would characterize much anti-obscenity campaigning for the remainder of the century.

Among the three groups who were active in New York's anti-obscenity drives during the first half of the twentieth century, religious leaders were best able to shift from a position of claiming to protect others to one of claiming to represent the public opinion of the broader community. As a consequence, they moved into the leadership of crusades to control urban culture. Their ability to make these claims rested firmly on the development of an interfaith coalition to combat immoral sexual portrayals. Ironically, the democratization of anti-obscenity activism that occurred as Catholic and Jewish religious leaders joined Protestant ministers to supervise city residents' access to commercial culture was accompanied by the exclusion of women activists from the community of those willing or able to represent themselves. Their marginalization within anti-obscenity campaigns was, to an extent, their own doing, for maternalism provided only a narrow platform from which to advocate control over commercial culture — and a platform that, we shall see, was becoming narrower all the time. It also reflected the double bind that confronted women who sought to reform sexual behavior during a time that a male sexual norm was being reestablished. Whatever the cause, their marginalization signaled a masculin- ization of anti-obscenity activism. As religious leaders claimed to articulate public opinion, while women activists claimed only to protect vulnerable chil- dren, it was clergymen and laymen who could represent themselves as *citizens*, as those with the right to represent and govern themselves and the community in which they lived. The evolution of an anti-obscenity movement with an overwhelmingly male leadership helped cement more securely the identifica- tion of democracy with the male citizen. So, too, did the endeavors of anticen- sorship activists.

CHAPTER 5

Doing Things the American Way:
Gendering Democratic Moral Authority

The religious leaders who legitimated their anti-obscenity activism by professing to represent public opinion were seeking to turn to their own ends a democratic vocabulary that opponents of censorship had pioneered over the first half of the twentieth century. The vision of a democratic moral authority that would lessen the cultural influence of anti-obscenity activists and derail efforts to expand the regulatory apparatus for commercial culture emerged in fits and starts. Early in the century women's rights activists in New York declared their right to see plays and movies that critiqued male supremacy and women's exploitation. Just a few years later the staff of the National Board of Censorship of Motion Pictures coupled their own claims to represent public opinion with a campaign to steer clubwomen away from advocating government film regulation, trying to persuade them that female empowerment and effective child protection were to be found along a different path. In the interwar years a new anticensorship coalition made the state the guardian of a commercial culture embodying democratic standards and procedures. These efforts, disparate as they were, sought to dislodge the vulnerable viewer from a privileged position as the subject of government protection and to substitute adult rights in her or his stead. By the 1940s anticensorship activists in New York City enjoyed wide success in popularizing the concept of democratic moral authority, and it was well on its way to becoming the nation's dominant paradigm for the regulation of obscenity.

This conceptualization of the relationship between morality and authority was not without its contradictions. The particular forms taken by democratic moral authority — specifically, the emphasis upon the average person as both standard for defining and mechanism for regulating obscenity and the related assault upon child protection as a valid principle of an obscenity regime — especially undermined the legitimacy of female anti-obscenity activists. Sometimes, in fact, opponents of government regulation purposefully set out to accomplish this goal. As a consequence, this anticensorship discourse, like developments within anti-obscenity activism, contributed to the masculinization of debates about obscenity. The language of democracy could conceal consequences that were anything but democratic.

"GIRLS GO TO SEE IT": NEW YORK WOMEN AND OPPOSITION TO GOVERNMENT REGULATION

Throughout the first half of the twentieth century, groups that actively opposed government regulation were decidedly in the minority of women's organizations, but they were probably more prominent in New York City than elsewhere in the nation. Especially during the Progressive era, female opponents of government censorship were closely connected to the city's settlement and social work communities and thus were likely to advocate an approach to the regulation of leisure that emphasized the "positive" and "constructive" development of alternative forms of leisure rather than the suppression of leisure activities.[1] For these women opposition to government censorship was founded in the belief that repressive regulation was misguided and likely to be ineffective. Groups that occasionally took a stance against government censorship included the League for Political Education, which sponsored lectures and debates about municipal issues and whose members were connected to New York's Progressive reform community, and the Women's Conference of the Society for Ethical Culture, an organization that provided a secular alternative to religion and also had ties to liberal Progressive activists. In addition, the New York City Federation of Women's Clubs sometimes opposed government regulation, suggesting the singularity of the club movement in New York, but its members devised no uniform policy on the question.[2]

Many suffragists and feminists were also outspoken critics of government regulation of sex in commercial culture. The Women's City Club, for example, took a firm stand against censorship from the Progressive era through the interwar years. This association was founded in 1915 by New York suffragists who, anticipating the 1917 extension of the vote to women in New York state, created a civic organization that would give them a base for political education and lobbying. Among its members were many of New York's politically prominent women such as settlement worker Lillian Wald, reformer Belle Moskowitz, future Secretary of Labor Frances Perkins, and a host of others including, during the 1920s, Eleanor Roosevelt. At various times the group's members denounced the proposed clean books bill, condemned the revocation of burlesque licenses, and, alone among women's organizations, called for the repeal of state movie censorship. Not only did the City Club as an entity take such stands, but its members worked independently to oppose government regulation of commercial culture. For example, Belle Moskowitz, nationally known as an advocate of dance hall reform and an intimate of soon-to-be-governor Al Smith, campaigned against state censorship of motion pictures. She argued that sufficient laws for the protection of the public already existed, and that in any case films were not a threat to children's welfare. Lawyer Dorothy Kenyon, who was appointed a deputy commissioner of licenses by Fiorello LaGuardia, was a founding member of the National Council on Freedom from Censorship and became a voice against censorship within LaGuardia's administration.[3]

The prominence of suffragists and feminists among female opponents of cultural regulation reflected the fact that government officials often targeted movies and plays that offered a critique of male sexual behavior. We have already seen that in 1913, when city officials sought to prohibit the motion picture *The Inside of the White Slave Traffic*, suffragists testified in defense of the film, and feminist lawyer Inez Milholland Boissevain defended the picture's producer against criminal charges.[4] Just four months before they came to the defense of *The Inside of the White Slave Traffic*, New York's women's rights activists mounted a vociferous protest when New York City police tried to close two plays about white slavery, *The Fight* and *The Lure*. Eight hundred women attended one mass meeting condemning the city's attempt to close the plays, and almost a thousand New Yorkers attended a special performance of *The Fight* under the auspices of the Woman Suffrage Party. Included among their numbers were feminists Crystal Eastman and Harriet Stanton Blatch, suffragists Anna Howard Shaw and Carrie Chapman Catt, settlement worker Mary Simkhovitch, and Marie Jenney Howe and her husband, Frederic Howe; she was the founder of the feminist group Heterodoxy, and he was chairman of the National Board of Censorship of Motion Pictures. A number of these women went on to create the Women's City Club just two years later, from which they would carry on the fight against official censorship. In this case, however, they gained only a pyrrhic victory. While the plays did not close, their producers made substantial changes in order to avoid prosecution; indeed, in *The Fight* the entire plotline about prostitution was deleted.[5]

That so many New York City women joined together in these protests does not mean that they agreed completely on the reasons for doing so. Crystal Eastman, Inez Boissevain, and others of their generation were self-proclaimed feminists who sought social recognition of women's right to sexual expression as well as economic independence and political rights. They championed access to birth control, condemned the conspiracy of silence, and in general "urged a single [sexual] standard balanced in the direction of heterosexual freedom for women."[6] Their defense of sex problem plays and movies likely had as much to do with their belief in "frank, scientific discussion and presentation of all subjects pertaining to sex," as Boissevain put it, as with their hope that white slave productions could help women escape the exploitation of prostitution. Others, such as Alva Belmont and Carrie Chapman Catt, were advocates of women's political and economic rights but did not share feminists' views on sex; Belmont has been described by one historian as "a woman who had little use for the sexual revolution," and Catt argued for sexual continence "in the interest of common decency." Their opposition to government censorship probably grew out of their commitment to protecting young innocent women from predacious men; there is no evidence that it extended to portrayals unrelated to this issue.[7] Still, feminists and more mainstream suffragists were linked through an extensive network of women's organizations and professional and personal relationships. When the specter of government suppression threatened plays and films that critiqued male supremacy, they quickly came together to oppose it.[8]

Their arguments for defending these productions therefore tended to emphasize their practical effect on the problem of prostitution rather than abstract concepts such as free speech. One woman, identified in the newspaper only as "a woman of unblemished repute who exerts much influence in this community," combined a defense of the importance of public speech about sexual problems with a biting critique of New York officials' apathy about prostitution itself; she observed, "It would be better to suppress the real thing which it imitated than to war against the imitation." Nora Blatch DeForest, daughter of militant suffragist Harriet Stanton Blatch and, like her mother, an officer of the Women's Political Union, suggested that sex problem plays had an important role to play in the fight against oppression, writing that "*The Lure* would have done to white slavery what *Uncle Tom's Cabin* did to black." In contrast to those who condemned the plays as "vile and degrading," "crude" and "indecent," Mary Garrett Hay, president of the Woman Suffrage Party, recommended *The Lure* for its educational value: "Girls go to see it and see it with wide open eyes."[9] Her counsel that "girls" go to see this play was a pointed renunciation of the contemporary obscenity regime, which insisted that young people must be protected from exposure to cultural portrayals of sex. In contrast, Hay believed that girls would be empowered by their attendance upon at least some of those portrayals.

Feminists and suffragists objected to suppression of sex problem plays and films because they believed that accusations that the productions were immoral cloaked an attempt to protect male power and prerogatives. Although they did not frame their critique precisely in these terms, their protests asserted the principle that speech ought not to be curtailed in the interests or at the behest of the few. The women's movement was one to enlarge democracy, and female activists' critique of censorship begins to suggest the uses that a discourse professing the primacy of democracy might have for campaigns against government regulation of commercial culture. Their arguments at the same time reflected and advanced the deepening influence of assertions of democratic interests against government suppression of commercial culture. These assertions were soon to take a different turn under the direction of the National Board of Censorship of Motion Pictures.

"EMASCULATED CLUB WOMEN": DEMOCRATIC MORAL AUTHORITY AND THE ASSAULT ON MATERNALISM

While some New York City women might be speaking out against regulation of certain plays and films, the fact remained that throughout the nation sentiment for government censorship of motion pictures was building, especially among women's groups. The National Board of Censorship of Motion Pictures continued to be subject to criticism for lax standards, and its critics increasingly demanded the enactment of municipal and, more frequently, state and federal control of the content of the movies. By the mid-teens their demands were gaining a hearing. In 1914 the first bill to enact federal regulation of the motion picture industry was introduced in Congress. The following year, the U.S. Supreme Court ruled that preexhibition censorship of motion pictures by state boards was constitutional. In New York state legislators began considering a series of proposals to create statewide film censorship. In the wake of these developments the National Board moved to defuse the movement for official censorship.[10] In 1916 its members devised a new strategy for preventing legal censorship: the better films movement.

The better films movement had antecedents in earlier activities on the part of the board as well as other organizations like the National Juvenile Motion Picture Board.[11] By 1915 such groups had begun directing their efforts toward the "education" of the moviegoing public by issuing lists of recommended films, especially films for children. In May 1916 the National Board expanded its work in this area by forming the National Committee on Films for Young People, which became known as the National Committee for Better Films the following year.[12] This committee began an intensive campaign to organize mothers to persuade local exhibitors to sponsor special performances of movies that it had identified as suitable for children. The leaders of the NCBF included a number of longstanding board activists, among them women and men affiliated with noted Progressive organizations such as the Federation for Child Study, the Russell Sage Foundation, and the Public Education Association. Although better films work was not new, the board repackaged it as a movement, devoted greatly increased resources to this work, and sought to steer it in a different direction.[13] That direction is indicated by its slogan: "Selection — not Censorship — the Solution." Under the supervision of National Board members, the better films movement became not one strategy among many for those women concerned about the effect of motion pictures on children, but a *substitute* for censorship.

Much of the impetus for the better films movement came from New York area clubwomen who were active within the National Board, and they envisioned this work as a way to blunt growing support within the General Federation of Women's Clubs for government regulation of films. The General Federation was the largest women's organization of the Progressive era. In 1910 it claimed eight hundred thousand members, most of them middle class, and almost all of them white, since the organization effectively excluded African American women's clubs. The women's club network provided the most important institutional base for women's advocacy of the ideology of maternalism and for their participation in debates about public policy.[14] It also accommodated some of the most vocal and best-organized advocates of government censorship. This was the case not only in states like Illinois, where in 1915 a Chicago women's club launched a campaign for state censorship and began agitating within the GFWC for a nationwide clubwomen's campaign, but also in New York City, where the Women's Municipal League advocated strict municipal censorship throughout the 1910s. Clubwomen objected to motion pictures on the basis of their violent content, their seeming lack of respect for traditional authorities (including parents, police, and clergy), and, most frequently, their sexual themes. For example, when Illinois clubwomen surveyed almost 2,800 motion pictures in 1915, they found, among other problems, "prolonged objectionable love scenes" in 192 films, "infidelity or disregard of marriage vows" in 408, and "obscenity, immorality or vulgarity" in 338 of the motion pictures exhibited in their state.[15] These numbers gave them cause for alarm about the fate of American children.

During this decade the meanings of clubwomen's participation in moral reform efforts changed, making their demands for government regulation of motion pictures appear more threatening to anticensorship forces. Clubwomen
were unequivocally demanding their right to full participation in the nation's
political life. In 1912 the New York State Federation of Women's Clubs endorsed
women's suffrage; two years later the General Federation followed its lead. Although women were effective participants in the nation's politics even before
passage of the Nineteenth Amendment, as the symbol of women's formal entry
into political life — and as a mechanism for real access to new modes of political power, such as the referendum — the vote had much significance. Further,
women were being granted state suffrage at an accelerating pace. In New York
they finally acquired the right to vote in 1917. Some National Board staff discerned in that accomplishment potential consequences that were not wholly
positive, noting that "it must be remembered that the women in New York have
the vote and that in the past they have been easily swayed by excitable persons
who have dwelt upon the few objectionable pictures."[16] As the likelihood grew
that national female suffrage would be enacted, the possibility that clubwomen
would advocate government censorship appeared ever more alarming.[17]

Yet clubwomen remained divided over the desirability of official censorship,
as their presence among the founding members of the National Committee for
Better Films demonstrates. Women's clubs may have criticized the National
Board, but they also provided many of its volunteer censors.[18] And while members of the Illinois Federation of Women's Clubs may have called on their sister
clubwomen to enter the battle for government censorship, there were a number
of state federations that declined to follow their lead. Both because the voice of
those clubwomen who advocated official censorship was growing louder and
because there was evidence that many clubwomen were not yet convinced of
the wisdom of such a route, National Board members understood the better
films movement as a critical intervention.[19]

As a result, the National Committee for Better Films, which included a number of women active in the GFWC, ranked cooperation with the General Federation high on its list of priorities. Better films workers used the club network
to get their message out. They coordinated a wide range of efforts to recruit
clubwomen, including supplying articles for publication in magazines catering
to them, sending speakers to women's club and PTA meetings, and mailing information about the better films movement to club leaders across the nation.[20]
They also sponsored, with the General Federation's cooperation, organizing
tours that targeted women's clubs. One such tour was undertaken by Mary Gray
Peck, a former English instructor at the University of Minnesota, suffragist, and

chairman of the GFWC's Drama Committee. In 1916 and 1917 the National Committee for Better Films hired her to organize local better films committees in twenty eastern, southern, and midwestern states. Peck's job, as she understood it, was to convince clubwomen that "all the censoring necessary was being done, and that we had a job to do which would take all our spare time and energy in getting children's programs."[21]

As this suggests, the ultimate aim of the better films movement was to quash clubwomen's drive for legal censorship. Fund-raising letters for Peck's tour, sent to representatives of the motion picture industry, explained the importance of this work:

> Our experience in both Pennsylvania and Ohio indicated that in these two states the women's clubs were actively engaged in furthering the censorship movement; so that we feel very confidently that if the attitude of the women's clubs in the other states becomes one of opposition to legal censorship, much will be gained.

A press release announcing that Peck had been hired was only slightly less direct in its characterization of her intentions. Inferring that clubwomen were well-intentioned but naive, the statement commented that "many women's clubs, in seeking to meet the problem presented by the interest of children in motion pictures, have been responsible for censorship methods which have not proved successful from any point of view." It concluded that "Miss Peck will seek to aid them by showing how they can be constructive rather than destructive in their methods."[22]

Despite their frankness here about Peck's anticensorship agenda, board members were not completely candid about their role or that of the motion picture industry in sponsoring her talks. Attempting to emphasize Peck's affiliation as a clubwoman and to minimize her connection to their organization, board members arranging her tour recommended that filmmaker D. W. Griffith's monthly contribution of $400 toward her expenses be kept secret. They suggested that "as much should be charged [for Peck's lectures] as possible so that there would be little feeling that Miss Peck was being subsidized" by either the film industry or the National Board.[23] The fact that the GFWC agreed to cosponsor the lectures but National Board members were concerned that their own participation might offend local groups suggests the degree to which clubwomen across the country disagreed about how to solve the motion picture "problem." Indeed, Peck sometimes found herself in very uncomfortable situations. After a trip to Missouri, for example, she requested that she not be asked to lecture in states where the state Federation of Women's Clubs was backing censorship legislation, noting that such meetings were embarrassing to her, created dissension within the GFWC, and hurt the cause of the better films movement.[24]

This discord exploded at the General Federation's national meetings in 1916, 1917, and 1918, as Peck and other GFWC members who were allied with the National Board battled to prevent the women's organization from endorsing legal censorship.[25] At the 1916 convention motion pictures were a matter of hot debate. National Board president Cranston Brenton spoke to the delegates, and their response shook him deeply. He reported that when the clubwomen "registered objection after objection to the pictures we had passed, I realized that if we were to approximate public opinion we had failed, because that audience represents public opinion from all over the United States which is clamoring for legalized censorship."[26] At the behest of Illinois clubwomen, the delegates to the convention voted to establish a panel to investigate the problem of motion pictures, at the same time encouraging local clubs to create censorship committees of their own. Yet, perhaps because the convention was held in New York City, women affiliated with the National Board were able to secure positions on the General Federation's Special Motion Picture Committee.[27] When committee members delivered their report at a 1917 meeting, bedlam ensued. The committee was chaired by Helen Varick Boswell, a member of the National Committee for Better Films, and its members declared that

> too much emphasis has been placed upon the evil side of motion pictures and demonstrated [sic] the necessity for a positive, constructive policy to minimize the harm and emphasize the good. . . . A workable plan of procedure now in operation in many communities involves a special program for boys and girls. . . . This plan now operates through local groups working with their local exhibitors and exchanges involving the individual support of every club woman in the community.

This endorsement of the better films movement led to a bitter attack upon the committee members, and the motion picture committee was dissolved.[28] Despite the attempt of both the National Board and the NCBF to redouble their efforts to sway clubwomen against legalized censorship, at its 1918 convention the General Federation of Women's Clubs passed a resolution calling on clubwomen to work for the passage of state motion picture censorship laws. Reject-

ing better films work and voluntary censorship on the grounds that it was neither "the province, the duty nor the desire of women to review films each day,"
the majority of women at the convention agreed that cooperation with the industry was not enough; they needed the "authority . . . to cope with an evil
which so seriously threatens the proper foundations of society."[29]

Clubwomen's struggle over whether to endorse legalized censorship or embrace better films work did not completely subside after 1918. The pages of the
General Federation Magazine were filled with debate over the issue in the six
months following the convention. In the end, many clubwomen rewrote the
National Committee for Better Film's slogan, espousing both selection *and* censorship. While some women continued to work with the NCBF in its better
films movement, most national women's groups ultimately denounced the National Board for trying to thwart their efforts. Bessie Leach Priddy, head of the
General Federation's Civics Department, captured their sentiments well:

> The camouflage of the National Board of Review, of the National Committee
> on Films for Young People, of the Affiliated Committees for Better Films has
> become so nauseating that a person of average intelligence must protest at
> such attempts to dupe and delay. Their stream of literature and bulletins
> pouring into every corner of our land . . . is the Motion Picture Industry's
> attempt to furnish well-intentioned, reform-bent ladies with 'harmless busy
> work.' . . . They have persistently captured local movements for better mo-
> tion pictures. They have sent their speakers out over the country using the let-
> terheads and prestige of our own and other kindred organizations. By devi-
> ous and misleading propositions they have befogged the thinking; [*sic*]
> befuddled, delayed, diverted, emasculated and perverted the activities of
> many club women honestly interested in a crusade for better motion pic-
> tures. . . . Meanwhile the stream of filthy film flows on for him to see who
> may or will.[30]

Other clubwomen accused the National Board of betraying its own commitment to democracy. One West Virginia woman asked,

> Why does that particular group of persons whom we are told are "animated
> only by the ever present desire to register fairly and impartially the opinions
> of the American people," and are working only "for the good they feel they can
> do," why do these persons so persistently work against all the efforts of the club
> women who want to try State censorship? . . . Why are we called "narrow-

minded moralists" because we claim the right to form our opinions as to what we consider good and wholesome and what we consider bad or harmful?

She concluded that "it is because we do not believe that a single group of persons can correctly censor the pictures for the whole United States that we want the pictures that are to be shown in a particular State, judged by a group of persons residing within that State and responsible to the people of the State."[31] In the years to follow other national women's organizations would continue to advocate government censorship of the movies. These groups — the National Congress of Parent-Teacher Associations and the WCTU among them — withdrew from affiliation with the National Board and the NCBF, declaring that "we have resolved not to cooperate with the industry in making the wolf look and talk like Red Riding Hood's grandmother."[32]

Other scholars have seen the better films movement as a departure from the National Board of Censorship's early activities, but in fact better films work was an essential prop in the organization's crusade to offer so-called democratic alternatives to legalized censorship.[33] When clubwomen began lending their support to the gathering movement for state and federal censorship, it became clear the insistence that "it is impossible to reduce the film [sic] to the intelligence of young people" was not enough to protect the industry from government regulation.[34] Recognizing that these women viewed their censorship activism as part of their responsibility to guard children from the dangers of the world, National Board members sought to convince them that they could best fulfill that responsibility in voluntary action. They understood that "the questions of legal censorship and of better films . . . are the negative and positive plans. . . . The National Board can attack legal censorship in the interests of better films while the National Committee [for Better Films] is promoting the constructive movement."[35]

Those affiliated with the National Board launched the better films movement because they realized that their previous arguments against government censorship did not reckon with the continuing appeal of the language of maternalism or the potential that it might be translated into government power. They set out to convince clubwomen not only that they could protect children from within the traditional sites of maternal influence — the family and voluntary organizations — but also that a turn to the state would actually *lessen* their authority. For example William D. McGuire, executive secretary of the National Board, lectured New York City clubwoman Helen Varick Boswell that "a movement to create a federal censorship will tend to remove the influence of women from the motion pictures, placing it in the hands of appointees who will not be responsible to the sentiment of the country."[36] National Board members further insisted that government censorship lulled mothers into a false sense of security. Official oversight could not make all films safe for all children, and parents who relied on the state to protect their children tended to neglect their own responsibilities. By participating in the better films movement, on the other hand, women could supervise their children's recreation and at the same time buttress maternal authority and the family itself. As an article in a newsletter sent to members of better films committees observed, "the family group picture is the true aim of the Better Films Movement. Everything should be done to strengthen family ties. Civilization is built upon the family as a unit. . . . The motion picture can share in the preservation of civilization."[37] Through such arguments, better films workers sought to divest maternalism of its potential to shape public policy by denying that it was the route toward democratic empowerment that clubwomen believed it to be.

While some clubwomen shared the National Board's definition of democratic regulation as voluntary regulation, others most certainly did not. They believed they could maintain their authority within their own families as well as expand it beyond the home by embracing a variety of regulatory strategies. Rejecting the contention that government censors would "remove the influence of women from the motion pictures," Florence Blanchard, who chaired the General Federation's motion picture subcommittee after 1918, asked the clubwomen of America:

> What kind of censorship will serve the people of your State best? The voluntary reviewers, acting in conjunction with a paid office force, answerable to no one but themselves and those who supply the means to keep up their offices . . . or a State Board appointed by the Governor whom you elect? . . . This board would be *your* board and answerable to you as a citizen of the state.

Indeed, she argued, censorship was necessary if women were to do their job in the home: "Censorship we must and will have; the flood is too vast for us to cope with. If we are to have any time or strength left with which to educate and build, we must have relief from the undermining bad films that sweep away our work before our eyes."[38] Doubtful of their ability to affect an industry from which they were almost totally excluded, and operating within a political context that promised a greater role to women in appropriating state power, many of these women were willing to take their chances with the state, despite National Board members' warnings of the dangers of government regulation.

The debates over better films work and censorship provide insight into the relationship between moral authority and state power, and into how New Yorkers and other Americans tried to shape that relationship. Clubwomen who advocated legal censorship expected government officials to be their representatives and their partners in making the state a repository of maternal authority. Opposing them, members of the National Board tried to limit the power of this version of female moral authority not by strictly confining it to the home (which would be anachronistic) but by locating it in a particular public domain: voluntary efforts to provide appropriate recreational opportunities for children. In trying to dissuade clubwomen from making claims on the state, these anticensorship activists sought to contain some middle-class women's redefinition of the relationship between public and private at the very moment when American women's access to the public sphere was consummated in the winning of female suffrage. They did not oppose female empowerment, it must be emphasized; they did, however, seek to shape it in ways that they believed would attenuate the drive for government censorship.

If the response of the women's club network is taken as a measure, the National Board of Censorship's attempt to reconstruct the gendered meanings of moral authority failed. While federal censorship never became a reality, members of the National Board could not prevent the passage of a state censorship law in New York, a law that some local clubwomen championed. Indeed, it was this failure, combined with a series of Hollywood scandals in the early 1920s, that prompted the nation's motion picture producers to abandon the National Board as their primary strategy for staving off censorship and to establish the Motion Picture Producers and Distributors of America. When Will Hayes was installed as head of the MPPDA's Public Relations Office, he began anew the chore of channeling women's activism into "harmless busy work," inviting the leaders of women's organizations, along with clergy and other reformers, to serve on his advisory Committee on Public Relations.[39]

In the long run, however, the National Board's vision of democratic moral authority may have limited organized womanhood's influence in debates over censorship. Although some women's organizations continued to press for government censorship through the 1920s, they experienced little success, suggesting that the definition of government regulation as antidemocratic was becoming more widely accepted. As a result, in the later 1920s and early 1930s the battle for control over movie content shifted once more toward extralegal strategies. Yet when in 1934 the motion picture industry was compelled to establish a censorship regime in the guise of an enforceable Motion Picture Production Code, it was at the behest of the hierarchy of the Catholic Church. Clubwomen who remained interested in motion pictures, on the other hand, increasingly turned their efforts toward exactly the kind of better films work that the National Committee for Better Films had advocated, organizing children's matinees and publishing better films lists. Thus, even if clubwomen rebuffed the National Board in the early 1920s, a scant decade later they were mostly confining their maternalism to the voluntary sphere, where they eschewed pressure politics for cooperation.[40]

DEMOCRATIC MORAL AUTHORITY IN THE INTERWAR YEARS

In the Progressive era the pressures for government film censorship had given rise to the National Board of Censorship and its particular version of democratic moral authority; in the interwar years demands for theatrical regulation led to the development of a new anticensorship coalition that offered its own interpretation of the concept. This coalition, composed mainly of theatrical workers and civil libertarians, owed its particular contours not only to New York anti-obscenity activists' emphasis upon the theater in the wake of passing a state movie censorship law but also to the development of new legal understandings of freedom of speech. Its members sought to obviate most forms of regulation — both voluntary and government — by defining state officials as the primary guardians of a democratic moral authority, while retaining earlier reformers' focus on the average person. Their particular articulation of democratic moral authority became the dominant paradigm for obscenity regulation in the postwar United States.

The development of democratic moral authority during this period did not embody a wholly new attitude toward free speech but it did signal increasing acceptance by New Yorkers of the idea, articulated by only a few mavericks in the years before World War I, that so-called obscenity deserved a measure of protection from government regulation. Since the passage of the Comstock Act in 1873, some Americans had objected to criminalizing the dissemination of birth control information (which was defined as obscene by that act), and a few individuals had condemned any laws against obscenity. Nonetheless, U.S. law treated obscenity as an exceptional category of speech, not entitled to constitutional protection.[41] Furthermore, in the early twentieth century American courts distinguished as outside constitutional protection even some cultural representations of sexuality that fell short of the test for obscenity, defining them not as speech but as commerce. In 1915 the U.S. Supreme Court endorsed this interpretation in its decision to uphold state film censorship in *Mutual Film Corporation v Industrial Commission of Ohio*. The Court's ruling that movies were primarily commercial enterprises, and therefore not encompassed within Ohio's constitutional protections of a free press and free speech, broadened the distinction between sexual representations within commercial culture and other forms of speech. While the Court never ruled explicitly on whether other forms of entertainment similarly constituted commerce rather than speech, it suggested in *Mutual* that preexhibition government censorship might be permissible for other "spectacles" such as the theater, the circus, or other "business[es] pure and simple, originated and conducted for profit."[42]

However, despite jurists' agreement that speech about sex, especially within commercial culture, remained outside the purview of the First Amendment, anticensorship activists pressed their claims to the contrary. They were emboldened by the World War I-era development of what scholars have called a "mature free-speech theory" that established stricter limitations on government's ability to restrict political speech and exalted First Amendment protections of speech as one of the defining characteristics — perhaps *the* defining characteristic — of a democratic nation.[43] Although its proponents did not contend initially that this new formulation of free speech theory encompassed obscenity, the increased focus upon the First Amendment had important consequences for those concerned with government regulation of commercial culture. The beginnings of success in convincing some jurists to limit government suppression and punishment of other forms of speech highlighted the unprotected status of obscenity. Simultaneously, the arguments for expanding free speech protections to "political" speech became available for use by proponents of increased freedom within commercial culture as well. By the late 1920s the civil libertarians who were developing this expansive interpretation of constitutional protections for political speech began to turn their attention to censorship of commercial culture, and they brought many of the assumptions of this free speech theory to the debates about obscenity regulation.[44]

Because New York City was the nation's entertainment capital, it is not surprising that advocates of freedom for motion pictures, the stage, and the publishing industry were best organized there. When the motion picture industry established the Hollywood-based Hays Office as a strategy for assuaging public fears about immorality in the movies, the National Board of Censorship lost its prominence in leading this fight and a new anticensorship coalition emerged in New York. This coalition linked two groups. The first was composed of women and men involved in the entertainment industry. During the 1920s, theater-affiliated organizations created a series of committees intended to oppose government regulation of the stage, and they soon broadened the scope of their activities. Members of groups such as the Authors' League, the Dramatists' Guild, the Guild of Free Lance Artists, the Society of Dramatists and Composers, Actors' Equity, and the League of New York Theatres (a theater managers and owners organization) cooperated in attempts to prevent government censorship of the theater, to repeal the motion picture censorship law, and to oppose official suppression of printed materials.[45]

In the early 1930s these groups found an ally among lawyers and laypeople affiliated with the American Civil Liberties Union. In 1930 the ACLU launched several anticensorship initiatives in New York, seeking to repeal the Wales Padlock Law and surveying candidates for governor about their positions on "statutory interferences with freedom of expression," including movie and book censorship, obscenity statutes, and birth control laws.[46] Early the next year ACLU representatives announced the formation of a Committee Against Stage Censorship to oppose a legislative proposal to establish a statewide theatrical censorship board in New York. Included among its members were a number of New Yorkers involved in the entertainment industry who had led local anticensorship fights during the previous decade, including Dramatists' Guild leader Elmer Rice and producer Helen Arthur, whose play *Maya* municipal officials had closed in 1928.[47] When the agitation for censorship legislation died down, those on the temporary committee resolved to establish a permanent organization that would "take up the fight on any front where unreasonable censorship appears." The formation of the National Council on Freedom from Censorship signaled the ACLU's decision to expand its work from defending narrowly defined political speech against government suppression to opposing censorship more generally.[48] Members of the NCFC developed a national reform program and, beginning in the 1940s, concerned themselves with such issues as radio and postal censorship by federal authorities. However, during the 1930s the organization, the active members of which were all New York City residents, focused much of its attention on censorship efforts in New York.[49] Upon its formation, the NCFC became the leading proponent of the argument that the purveyors of commercial culture had at least some speech rights that should be strictly guarded.

This anticensorship coalition took up the crusade for a democratic moral authority, but its vision of this concept differed substantially from that of the National Board of Censorship. By the beginning of the 1930s, anticensorship activists by and large rejected *any* voluntary regulation of commercial culture. Recognizing the contradiction that had plagued the National Board of Censorship — that despite its intentions, enacting "voluntary" censorship supported the general idea that culture ought to be censored — they sought instead to combat government censorship by reconstituting the state as the repository and guardian of democratic moral authority.

This shift came on the heels of several years of theatrical endorsement of the ideal of voluntary regulation, in the guise of the citizens' play jury. The play jury was similar in many respects to the voluntary censorship of the National Board, fitting neatly within its version of democratic moral authority. In its assertion that judgments about morality ought to be the province not of state officials but of a group of average citizens, the play jury offered a mechanism for identifying public opinion, articulating it and making it the basis of public policy concerning the obscene. With few exceptions, throughout the 1920s the theatrical organizations that made up the anticensorship coalition lauded the play jury as an alternative to censorship.

By the end of the decade, however, members of this coalition began disagreeing publicly about what exactly constituted "censorship," and the consensus about the legitimacy of the play jury collapsed. In December 1930 Actors' Equity proposed a new play jury scheme in response to a renewed attack on the stage by New York clergy, but under the leadership of playwright Elmer Rice Dramatists' Guild members refused to participate. They argued that even if the play jury was not "government" it was still "censorship." Striking a far more militant tone than in years past, the playwrights condemned the new plan as self-censorship, proclaiming,

> The dramatists of America insist that the development of an adult theater in an adult civilization is dependent upon the free discussion of any and all subjects, whether in the field of religion, economics, politics or morals and announce their intention of resisting to the limit the forces of repression and intolerance which, under the pretence of fighting obscenity, may seek to strike another blow at American freedom.

They asserted that the time had come "to take a determined stand." When at this juncture the ACLU created its Committee Against Stage Censorship and announced its opposition to "voluntary self-censorship," the majority of anticensorship activists repudiated voluntarism as the foundation of a democratic moral authority.[50]

At the same time, they mounted a heightened attack upon almost all the approaches advocated by anti-obscenity activists in the past, labeling a wide array of regulatory strategies "censorship." Although preexhibition and predistribution scrutiny and suppression of plays, movies, books, and magazines topped their list of regulatory evils, they condemned as well most forms of content-based limitations on the stage. During the 1930s, members of the anticensorship coalition advocated repeal of the Wales Law and successfully lobbied against a municipal ordinance that would have prohibited profanity in plays. They also campaigned to revoke the charter of the New York Society for the Suppression of Vice and called for stricter controls on the ability of authorities to revoke theatrical licenses. Reflecting their broad definition of censorship as "any power to suppress the expression of thought" members of the NCFC opposed self-censorship schemes and censured the Legion of Decency movie boycott. They advanced the position that the only restrictions on commercial culture should be those imposed by "the good taste of dramatists, producers, artists, and the audience."[51]

Having construed such a wide variety of regulatory structures as illegitimate, anticensorship activists sought to create a narrow regime for controlling what they referred to as "commercialized pornography."[52] That regime retained the fundamental principles of democratic moral authority even as it reformulated some of them. The concern with judging obscenity from the standpoint of public opinion remained central, and throughout the 1930s and 1940s these New Yorkers maintained that it was the effect of commercial culture upon "reasonable" adults that should determine what was obscene: any other system would "establish the nursery and the Sunday school as the standard" for adult entertainment.[53] Anticensorship activists were not content merely to proclaim these sentiments, and they dedicated themselves to making this standard official. In a series of court cases, NCFC lawyers launched a frontal assault on the Hicklin Rule, arguing that the test for obscenity ought to be the effect of a work upon the "average person." When in 1934 they convinced a panel of federal judges that James Joyce's *Ulysses* ought to be judged according to this standard, they not only created a new rule for New York cases but also achieved a milestone in the propagation of a theory of democratic moral authority.[54] Just as important, anticensorship activists coupled their emphasis upon the average person test with the insistence that the *only* sufficiently democratic mechanism for judging and regulating obscenity was trial by jury on criminal charges of violating obscenity statutes.[55] By substituting one "people's forum" (the *petit jury*) for another (the play jury or other form of voluntary regulation), they placed the state at the center of a democratic system of obscenity regulation.

This new emphasis upon criminal law and jury adjudication satisfied practical concerns. Members of the NCFC recognized that most New Yorkers endorsed the idea of some form of regulation for obscenity. Asserting the legitimacy of criminal prosecution allowed them to circumvent partly the lack of First Amendment protection for obscenity by at least requiring due process guarantees for those accused of purveying it. Further, constituting criminal prosecution as the sole legitimate regulatory strategy would ensure that New York's new average person standard for judging obscenity would be applied in all cases. The emphasis upon trial by jury provided additional safeguards, as the right to jury trial was not secured to those accused of obscenity violations in New York City at this time, although a judge could grant one at his or her discretion.[56] In a jury trial all twelve jurors had to agree on conviction, and especially in a heterogeneous city like New York, where jurors were likely to differ in ethnicity, religion, class, and other social characteristics, this was a rare occurrence in obscenity trials. As anticensorship activists put it, obscenity posed "a question of general morals, the standard of decency of a particular time. [Therefore] the only tribunal which, with any degree of safety can be entrusted with the decision of such a question is a jury because there you do, at least, get people from varied walks of life." Judges, on the other hand, could be "possibly hand-picked and often bigoted."[57]

But in addition, the demand for trial by jury advanced the principles of democratic moral authority, for juries provided an opportunity for average citizens to deliberate about whether a representation is obscene and what to do about it. Juries, it was asserted, "reflect public sentiment" and their adjudication of obscenity cases embodied the "best of democratic practices." Conversely, the decision of one individual, whether it be mayor, license commissioner, or even a single judge, represented the "autocratic hand of dictatorship." The insistence upon a jury trial was merely the newest incarnation of the National Board of Censorship's public opinion: the jury was the place where public opinion could be formulated and the voice of the people heard.[58]

By identifying the jury trial as the legitimate arena for the exercise of democratic moral authority, anticensorship activists recast the state as the guardian of this authority. Municipal authorities who had been told by anti-obscenity activists that their role was to protect the city's children from the dangers of obscenity now were lectured that their duty was to defend American citizens' rights to speak — even about sex — as they wished. Anticensorship activists contended that the United States was a strong and enduring nation precisely because its legal system provided a guarantee of individual freedom through democratic processes. Regulation of obscenity by any means other than jury trial was "unamerican," they argued, because it violated both these precepts, subordinating individuals' freedom of speech to an imposed moral standard and abrogating democratic processes by entrusting power to a minority. Municipal authorities' responsibility became to ensure that any limitation upon individual liberty occurred only through the democratic mechanism of trial by jury on criminal obscenity charges.[59]

By the 1940s growing numbers of New Yorkers embraced this rendition of democratic moral authority. They were drawn into the debates about obscenity during the war years, when municipal authorities aggressively extended their control over New York's entertainment industry. In the years between 1942 and 1945 Mayor LaGuardia and License Commissioner Paul Moss shut down forever the last of the city's burlesque theaters, for the first time applied the padlock clause of the Wales Act, and used their licensing powers to force the closure of the lesbian-themed play *Trio*. They justified much of their behavior as crucial to the war effort: burlesque, they said, constituted a menace to the virility of the nation's armed forces; immoral Broadway productions threatened the morale of civilians.[60] But for many New Yorkers these concerns paled when compared to the importance of defending democracy. In the early 1940s those already involved in the anticensorship coalition responded to these incidents with the accusation that municipal officials were forfeiting their responsibility to guard cherished freedoms threatened by a world at war. Representatives of the Authors' League, for example, complained to LaGuardia:

> The question before the citizens of New York is not whether the burlesque theatres should be closed, but . . . whether or not they are to be closed by methods which are clearly dictatorial and in violation of democratic procedure. In these days when we are making every effort to defend and preserve democratic institutions it is deplorable to see our own municipal officials adopting the methods of Hitler and Mussolini. We are interested in knowing whether or not you believe in supporting and upholding the Bill of Rights, one of whose basic provisions is for trial by jury.[61]

As this suggests, the moral crisis posed by World War II could be profitably invoked by either side of these debates. The ranks of those voicing opposition to "censorship" grew not least because the language of democratic moral authority that had been put before the public during the 1920s and 1930s fit so well with the symbols and language of patriotism associated with World War II.

Similar sentiments were voiced when, three years later, hundreds of citizens criticized the government's actions against *Trio*. While some New Yorkers opposed closure of the play on grounds that public discussion would help solve the problem of homosexuality, more complained that municipal authorities ignored democratic process. Comparisons to Hitler again abounded; Paul Moss was labeled a "petty imitator of Hitler" and a "second Hitler on the Rialto."[62] Furthermore, individuals wrote to LaGuardia that Moss's "one-man censorship" was dictatorial, un-American, and undemocratic. One man, for example, lectured the mayor, "In a democracy, the people make the decisions and not one man, whether he is top man or one of top subordinates [*sic*]. . . . If *Trio* is so bad, why not let the people decide or at least a Court?" Another asked, "who is *HE* [Moss] to decide for the public?" Still another citizen demanded that LaGuardia "give the people involved a fair trial. Do things the American way."[63] Each of these New Yorkers brought their own understandings of democratic moral authority to this public debate. By their estimate, city officials' use of their licensing powers violated their responsibilities as the stewards of a democratic system for regulating obscenity.

In the crisis atmosphere of World War II the symbols by which New Yorkers interpreted their nation's involvement in warmaking also sustained a particular discussion of domestic politics. Yet this public outcry against "dictatorial censorship" was not merely an artifact of the war years. By the 1940s the discourse of obscenity regulation had changed substantially. The quickness of individual citizens to take up the language of democracy represents the culmination of a decades-long process by which anticensorship activists sought to change the community's perceptions of the place of sexual speech within the nation's political culture. The language used by ordinary New Yorkers to decry government officials' actions against burlesque and Broadway reflects most strongly the procedural arguments put forth by the activists of the National Council on Freedom from Censorship: that average people should make decisions about which sexual portrayals were permissible, that any form of regulation of obscenity aside from trial by jury was illegitimate, that those involved in commercial culture were entitled to democratic protection of their freedom of speech. If anticensorship activists could not or did not wish to do away entirely with the concept of obscenity at this time, they succeeded in expanding the safeguards against the suppression of speech in New York's entertainment industry. And if their success in convincing substantial numbers of New Yorkers to adopt this stance in 1945 was in part an effect of wartime discourse, still it pointed to a future in which such arguments constituted the dominant framework for contro-versies about obscenity and pornography.

GENDER, DEMOCRATIC CITIZENSHIP, AND THE STATE

Anticensorship activists' articulation of democratic moral authority reflected their deeply felt commitment to a culture that honored the freedom of choice of both the producers and consumers of entertainment, one that denied that the few had the right to prohibit portrayals of sex countenanced by the many. But their arguments had consequences beyond offering new ways to talk about the regulation of sex in commercial culture. When anticensorship activists in-vented the legal fiction of the average person, they forged a new link between "democracy" and "authority" in the fictive body of this person. That link had implications for how democracy was constructed, how citizenship enacted, and how authority over sex was understood in modern America.[64]

From the volunteer censor committees of the National Board of Censorship, to the citizens' play jury, to the state-centered obscenity regime envisioned by the National Council on Freedom from Censorship, each of these schemes prof-itably can be understood as a variation on the theme of the jury. For anticen-sorship activists, the jury, whether an aspect of state power or a corrective to it, was organized around the figure of the average person as both the standard for defining obscenity and the mechanism for regulating it. A model of direct democracy, it brought together ordinary citizens to deliberate and collectively make decisions that authorized or prohibited the exercise of social, cultural, and state power. Situating the jury at the center of democratic moral authority, anticensorship activists cast citizens less as individual bearers of rights, who looked to the state to protect those rights, than as members of a collectivity with the power to make the rules by which they would govern themselves. In this sense, the jury *was* democratic moral authority.[65]

Since the average person who deliberated on these juries, voluntary and of-ficial, was a legal fiction, however, the articulation of democratic moral author-ity could obscure some profoundly antidemocratic effects. Not all citizens in a democracy are equal, nor are all individuals within a democracy necessarily rec-ognized as citizens. For example, voluntary regulatory schemes such as those enacted by the National Board of Censorship or the advocates of the citizens' play jury tended to employ women and men of a social and cultural elite as their "average citizens," thus eliding class and race privilege while pretending to resist it. Such schemes could be advanced as models of democratic practice when, *in practice*, they constituted some individuals as more capable of exercising the prerogatives of citizenship than others.

Further, as democratic moral authority evolved, it increasingly operated to exclude women as a group from the regime for regulating obscenity. The average person standard, invented against both the child and those who spoke from the subject position of protecting the child, embedded into the legal regime a gendered ideal for judging obscenity. It was intended to displace maternalists, vice reformers, and clerics from their privileged position as moral and cultural arbiters. Understood against these more or less feminized figures (where "feminized" can mean maternal and/or prudish), the average person is more clearly seen as a masculinized one, whose relationship to the obscene comes to constitute the rational measure of what is truly beyond the pale. This sense of the gender of the average person — and hence of democratic moral authority and its citizen — is confirmed by the district court's decision in the *Ulysses* case, in which NCFC lawyers first established that whether a work was obscene depended upon its effect "on a person with average sex instincts." The presiding judge's standard derived from his translation of the French *l'homme moyen sensuel,* which refers particularly to the *man* of average sex instincts. Explicitly comparing the average person to the "reasonable man" in tort law, Judge Woolsey evaluated *Ulysses'* prurience by asking two of his male friends to read the book.[66] The average person standard maintained the illusion of gender neutrality, but it operated to undermine presumptions that those whose expertise derived from their child-protection activities ought to guide public policy concerning obscenity; no longer could they claim to be the voice of reason. Maternalist women were prominent within this now discredited group.

The shift to a state-centered obscenity regime escalated this trend, for resituating the average person in the trial jury box excluded female bodies. Most of the National Board's volunteer censors were women, and women constituted from one-fourth to three-fourths of the membership of each citizens' play jury convened. At the time that advocates of democratic moral authority first sought to restrict the regulation of obscenity to jury trials, however, women in New York state were prohibited from sitting on juries. Anticensorship activists could not have known they would be accorded that right in 1937.[67] Their acclaim for democratic trial juries, coupled with their silence about women's exclusion from those juries, raises questions about the breadth of their vision of democracy. Besides, the district attorneys, police officers, and judges whom anticensorship activists identified as the appropriate authorities to execute and supervise the prosecution of obscenity violations were overwhelmingly men, as were the licensing officials who exercised a regulatory power despite the criticisms of the anticensorship coalition. In contrast, when sites both in and outside of the state were part of an obscenity regime, even women who did not participate in government regulation could share in enacting public policy. Ironically, then, as it evolved, democratic moral authority became less democratic. While formally a democratic moral authority encompassed female citizens, in reality its defining characteristics — the rejection of voluntary regulation, the empowerment of a sector of the state from which women were by and large excluded, and the emphasis upon the average person standard — moved women even farther from the center of New York's system of sexual regulation.

As a consequence, female anti-obscenity activists fared less well than some other maternalists in making claims upon the state. Feminist historians recently have traced the roots of the U.S. welfare state to middle-class women's advocacy of a range of social welfare measures during the Progressive era and even earlier, exposing the institutional connections that linked Progressive reform with Depression-era public policy. Much of this work has demonstrated, in historian Robyn Muncy's words, the creation of a "female dominion" encompassing federal bureaucracies that administered social policy concerning women and children, most notably the Women's Bureau and the Children's Bureau. Through the creation of this dominion women found within government a refuge, however circumscribed, from which they could advance or at least sustain the maternalist concerns that had motivated their political activism since the nineteenth century. Of course, that refuge was a temporary one. Male bureaucrats expanded their jurisdiction over welfare policies as these policies became more important to the workings of the state, and consequently women lost their leadership roles.[68]

However, even after women activists lost power within the federal government, the emerging welfare state was indelibly marked by their earlier activism. If failure to reenact landmark child and maternal health legislation in 1928 signaled the waning of women's power within the federal government, still the Women's Bureau and the Children's Bureau remained as small pockets of female influence; still female activists' understandings of the purpose of government assistance to mothers and children shaped New Deal welfare policies; still women with roots in the dominion held important positions within state and federal agencies.[69] This was less true in the case of obscenity regulation, where women could not be said to have established even a short-lived dominion. While female anti-obscenity activists in New York state did accomplish their goal of government censorship of the movies, this policy-making apparatus was largely male dominated. Similarly, government regulation of other forms of commercial culture was administered almost entirely by men. Nor were female censorship advocates able to obtain federal control over the motion picture industry.

The particular constructions of democratic moral authority lessened the likelihood that women might use maternalism to carve out a place for themselves in a system of obscenity regulation, even as it remained a vital justification for their welfare activism. As we have seen, women's advocacy of censorship had unintended consequences, for when female anti-obscenity activists appealed to the state to protect their children from representations of illicit sexuality in commercial culture, they reinforced the perception that their moral authority was limited to their guardianship of children. Once the further elaboration of democratic moral authority helped to remove the protection of children as the legal standard for government regulation of obscenity, maternalism was of limited usefulness in justifying a special role for women in controlling sexual portrayals in commercial culture.

Yet it would be too simple to conclude that the rise of democratic moral authority and the increasing permissiveness subsequently accorded commercial culture were detrimental to "women's" interests. Women in New York City identified for themselves diverse interests. Many endorsed the emerging restrictions on regulatory capacity. Women filled the National Board of Censorship's review committees, helped found the National Committee for Better Films, and belonged to theatrical unions that opposed government regulation. They constituted about 20 percent of the membership of the National Council on Freedom from Censorship and were among the citizens who complained about overzealous municipal officials. Women may have had limited ability to influence policy in these male-dominated organizations, but their embrace of democratic moral authority cautions against overstating women's loss of regulatory power during the twentieth century. It must be remembered that women's role in earlier regulatory systems was never equal to men's.

Further, many New York City women benefited from the greater freedom intended commercial culture by the proponents of democratic moral authority. Women who worked in the entertainment industry — as performers, producers, authors, ticket takers, or designers, among other positions — had a material interest in preventing government censorship from interfering with their livelihoods. Unlike most female censorship proponents, many of these women, especially those employed in burlesque, were of working-class origins; working on the stage might be one of their better options. While it is possible that, as censorship advocates charged, lax supervision of sexual portrayals permitted exploitation of female employees, in fact these employees almost never called for strict government regulation of content, nor did they agree, at least publicly, that they were being exploited or degraded by their work. Indeed, they frequently protested against government suppression.[70]

Some of the women employed in the entertainment industry had additional reasons for opposing regulation. For example, NCFC member Helen Arthur was a feminist who encountered government interference because she tried to produce on the stage what was in her view a realistic portrayal of prostitution. Others, like actress/director Margaret Webster, were lesbians: they endorsed the increased permissiveness promised by democratic moral authority because it would permit the portrayal of diverse sexualities. Webster, for example, resigned from the board of directors of a city-owned performing arts center to protest the closing of *Trio*. For these women, as undoubtedly for others less prominent, greater laxity in commercial culture seemed to promise heightened freedom for themselves.[71]

Unfortunately, this promise remained largely unrealized. The proponents of democratic moral authority maintained that enhanced permissiveness for the entertainment industry would mean greater freedom for those artists who desired to challenge the sexual and gender status quo, and the presence of several feminists among the founders of the NCFC suggests that they believed the feminist demand for "sex rights" could be pursued through this activism. But in fact the expanded scope for sexual portrayals mainly confirmed sexual difference and female inequality, as latitude for the entertainment industry translated into an enhanced ability to profit from the commodification not just of sexuality but more particularly of female sexuality. Burlesque comedy may have acknowledged and made fun of both male and female sexuality, but the dominant effect of the striptease was to set women's sexuality apart as other. The same was true of theatrical depictions of lesbianism, which helped to popularize an emerging heterosexual norm and to denigrate female same-sex intimacy. And the National Board of Censorship had to contend with controversy over the portrayal of the female nude but not the male nude — not because male nudity was not controversial but because it rarely, if ever, occurred in films. Any advance in women's sexual freedom fostered by New York's commercial culture was countered by the restrictive norms and expectations broadcast by plays, movies, and magazines.

The discourse of democratic moral authority also yielded mixed blessings for women by changing the conventions for judging and regulating obscenity.

In elevating democratic procedure as the overriding matter for policy makers, it sought to remove from consideration concerns about the *effects* of speech that had previously guided debates about obscenity. Some latter-day feminists would decry this result, claiming that obscenity (or pornography) has real effects in structuring women's experience of sexuality and sexual violence. Whether or not this contention is true, the emphasis upon process rather than effects altered the balance of power between the (mostly male) producers of commercial culture and its critics (women among them), even if it also laid the foundation for the defense of unpopular, including feminist, portrayals of sex. Further, the creation of the superficially gender-neutral average person standard abetted the suppression of some women's specific concerns about sexual representation in a sexist society. Although democratic moral authority gave voice to one group of women by offering a theoretical foundation for those who demanded a wider space for discussions of sexuality, it simultaneously helped to silence another group — those who based their right to speak about regulation on their special characteristics or unique experiences as women.

While some New York women collaborated with men to create democratic moral authority, then, they participated in developing an obscenity regime that affected them in discrete ways. It was a regime that depended to a degree on their invisibility as women and that institutionalized their physical exclusion. When women anticensorship activists assumed the mantle of the average person, they had to forsake their gender identity in a way that men did not. In this sense democratic moral authority, for all its value in securing more freedom to the purveyors of commercial culture, constituted a gendered ideology in the same way that, historian Joan Landes tells us, democracy itself has been gendered historically. She shows that

> from the outset, democracy in the modern world produced not only a discourse but a practice of gender difference. . . . The representation of power in the democratic public sphere was premised on the fiction of a neutral, but embodied (because natural) subject; one capable of subjecting (his) individual passions and interests to the rule of reason.[72]

Such was the fate of women under democratic moral authority, as men's (presumed) standards came to signify the "average" and the reasonable and as men's participation in regulation became the manifestation of "democratic" practices of deliberation, the means by which citizens could make themselves heard. In formulating a discourse of democracy without critically examining who was the democratic citizen, anticensorship activists laid the foundations for the emergence in the late twentieth century of a feminist antipornography movement that could mobilize large numbers of women in the purported quest to reclaim their own right to participate, as citizens, in the democratic regulation of sex.

CONCLUSION

N ew Yorkers were not the only Americans who struggled over describing and delimiting obscenity in the first half of the twentieth century. In Chicago Catholics warned of a boycott of the stage if plays about divorce and infidelity were not abolished; in Massachusetts clubwomen successfully pressed the state legislature to enact motion picture censorship in 1920, only to see it vetoed by the governor. In 1921, the same year that Philadelphia clergy asked their mayor for local theater and movie censorship, residents of Los Angeles disagreed among themselves about the wisdom of film censorship in their own city. Plays such as *The Captive* and *Desire Under the Elms* were closed by police after complaints in San Francisco, Los Angeles, and Detroit; in Pittsburgh a civic committee succeeded in eliminating thirty "salacious" magazines from the city's newsstands.[1] These local debates also had their national counterparts. During the 1910s, for example, there were congressional hearings on the possibility of establishing a federal motion picture censorship board; the Depression decade gave rise not just to the Legion of Decency and the National Organization for Decent Literature but also to debate about their legitimacy.[2]

During the 1950s disagreement over what to do about the obscene erupted onto the national scene in new and more insistent ways. In a series of congressional hearings that spanned the decade and continued into the next, in best-selling books and in magazines like *Reader's Digest*, and in the nation's highest court, something called *pornography* entered the national imagination. Over the remainder of the century, as Americans continued the contests over sexually explicit materials, the problems inherent in the concept of democratic moral authority became clear.

The postwar nationalization of the debate about obscenity and pornography had several causes. In part it reflected a rise in the easy availability of sexually explicit matter attributable to the growth of certain forms of mass media. The magazine industry was expanding rapidly, with much of the increase occurring in two sectors that were certain to draw attention: comic books, aimed ostensibly at children, and the men's sophisticates, an older genre that had been revitalized with the appearance of *Esquire* in 1933. Soon *Esquire*'s drawings of voluptuous but mostly clothed "Vargas girls" were joined by *Pic*'s "photos of young women not far removed from nudity" and, in 1953, *Playboy*'s centerfold photographs of nude, if heavily airbrushed, women.[3] These "girlie books" were mainly purchased by men, but there were also true crime and scandal magazines, read by both sexes, featuring tales of murder and rape that far exceeded earlier magazines in their grisliness. At the same time, the pulp novel trade had taken off, and many of these inexpensive paperbacks also plied sexual wares. By the early 1950s millions of Americans were, for the price of a quarter or so, buying books like *Women's Barracks*, a purported exposé of life in the French army featuring several lesbian scenes.[4] As the mass media proliferated, reformers and government officials called for remedies that would suppress their portrayals of sex and violence at the source.

The increasing importance of the mass media themselves to national politics also helped make the debates about obscenity more visible. In 1950 Senator Estes Kefauver broadcast to a nationwide television audience the hearings of his Special Committee to Investigate Organized Crime. Among the first of a series of televised congressional investigations during the 1950s, these portended the increasingly important role television would play in the making and breaking of political careers. Kefauver, harboring ambitions for the presidency, understood the value of the national publicity afforded by such a medium: estimates of spectators for his organized crime hearings ranged up to 86 percent of the television audience. It is perhaps not coincidental that testimony about the dangers of mass media — in particular, the so-called crime comics — surfaced in these early broadcasts.[5] They would become even more prominent in mid decade, when the Senate Subcommittee to Investigate Juvenile Delinquency televised hearings focusing on comic books and pornographic materials.

More generally, concern over the dangers of obscenity and pornography echoed the fears that shaped postwar national and international politics. As early as 1942 New York's Archbishop Spellman had labeled obscenity a "filth column" that represented the most dangerous sort of subversion from within. Such thinking flourished in cold war America as the endeavor to contain Communism abroad and to prevent its infiltration into national life was matched by an equally serious effort at what scholar Elaine Tyler May has called domestic containment.[6] Maintenance of an idealized family came to be seen as essential to the preservation of the "American way of life" — an ideological configuration that collapsed capitalism, consumerism, democratic institutions, and a nuclear family composed of breadwinning father, stay-at-home mother, and obedient children. Within such a context it is no surprise that pornography became such an issue of concern, for porn took sex — which ought to be contained safely within the family — and inappropriately cast it into the public sphere, where it degraded both capitalism and consumerism.

Indeed, traditions of identifying obscenity as a source of contamination and corruption made an almost natural fit between talk about pornography and fear of Communist infiltration and domestic subversion. At the same time that some self-proclaimed patriots pointed to the presence of homosexuals in government office as an alleged weakness in the nation's defenses, contending that Communists could exploit their supposed lack of moral fibre to gain access to state secrets, they also warned that "part of the Communist conspiracy was to print and deposit for mailing and delivery obscene, lewd, lascivious, and filthy books." For example, the Minnesota Juvenile Court Judges Association counseled parents that through such means Communists planned to "despoil your children, to rob them of their respect for law and the teachings of morality, to enslave them with sex and narcotics. When that happens, the seeds of communism will fall on fertile ground."[7] Obscenity, like homosexuality and drug addiction (both also matters of national concern during the 1950s), possessed an inexorable logic of contamination: just as "one homosexual can pollute a Government office," obscene literature would lead to "the pollution of our thought supply";[8] just as youthful experimentation with marijuana inevitably produced a dope addict, youthful perusal of comics and girlie magazines followed the "same pattern of progression," resulting in addiction to pornography.[9] Even worse, critics alleged that pornographic materials, like the paperback *Lady of the Evening*, taught readers how to use drugs as well as instructing them about a range of perversions, from homosexuality and lesbianism to sadomasochism and fetishism.[10] Thus an ever spreading web of corruption and contamination threatened the integrity of American life.

The defense of the "traditional" family that gave rise to these warnings also contributed to the return of women's organizations to a prominent position within anti-obscenity organizing. Groups such as the General Federation of Women's Clubs remained interested in the issue of mass media's effect on children in the years after World War I, but much of their participation had remained within the sphere of better films work. From the late 1920s through the 1940s they enjoyed a more friendly relationship with the film industry than did more outspoken critics like the Catholic Church. By the mid-1950s, however, the GFWC launched an all-out attack upon crime comics, followed by campaigns to eliminate lurid magazines and "abolish pornography." Dozens of local groups reported back to national headquarters on their success in persuading newsdealers to stop carrying objectionable magazines, their fruitful lobbying for new laws to ban horror comics and other publications "considered likely to corrupt the morals of minors," and their efforts to strengthen enforcement of the Comstock Act. Colorado clubwomen even claimed credit for convincing officials of the Safeway grocery chain to stop selling comic books and paperback novels in all of its 137 stores in the Rocky Mountain region.[11]

Maternalist activism of the sort embraced by members of the GFWC is not surprising in an era characterized by familialist politics. Yet the constellation of social and political concerns that predominated in the late 1940s and early 1950s was especially conducive to women's focus on mass media. Nationwide concern over juvenile delinquency that emerged during the 1940s was in large part an articulation of anxiety over wartime disruption of families, particularly the perceived vices of working mothers and absent fathers; the campaign against juvenile crime that continued through the 1950s was "one element in the postwar disciplining of the family."[12] In this light women's anti-obscenity activism expressed their eagerness to lay the blame for juvenile delinquency where they believed it properly belonged: outside the family, in the broader culture. If negligent mothers are being blamed for the crimes of their children, then a mothers' campaign against mass media functions as more than a demonstration of its participants' status as good mothers. It also declares that juvenile crime is a problem beyond the control of individual mothers, both those who work outside the home and those who do not. Women's anti-obscenity activism represented a defense of mothers against their cold war critics.[13]

The expanded role of women's and parents' groups in the anti-obscenity activism of this period demonstrates the continuing importance of concern over children to the debates over regulating media. But in certain ways this focus on the child was a defensive strategy. In the years after World War II, democratic moral authority, with its emphasis on the average person, became increasingly influential not just in New York City but in jurisdictions across the country. As a consequence, the national paradigm that had governed obscenity regulation for the previous one hundred years grew ever more tenuous. In large part it was because of the encroachment of democratic moral authority that the debates about obscenity burst upon the national scene.

~

The tone for the congressional hearings of the 1950s was set in 1948, when New York City psychiatrist Fredric Wertham first published his "findings" on the relationship between juvenile delinquency and comic books. He elaborated on these ideas in 1954 in his bestselling book, *Seduction of the Innocent.* Both his earlier article (afforded a wide audience when it was reprinted in *Reader's Digest*) and the book were greeted with enormous skepticism by his colleagues in psychiatry and child welfare, but parents throughout the nation rallied to his cause, and politicians were soon to follow. In the wake of Wertham's writings, a number of cities and states launched investigations into the effects of comic books and in several instances passed legislation banning the sale of crime, horror, and/or sex comic books to children.[14]

Wertham's crusade is notable for its impact, but more significant is the way in which his rhetoric rehearsed much of the forthcoming debate about pornography. Most obviously, Wertham sought to recenter around children the debate about media's effects. He argued explicitly that adults were adequately protected from obscenity: "There is a whole machinery to protect adults from seeing anything that is obscene or too rough in the theater, in the movies, in books and even in night clubs." But "children are left entirely unprotected." This created a ludicrous disparity in the law, according to Wertham, who contended that

> the contrast between censorship for adults and the lack of it for children leads to such fantastic incongruities as the arrest of a girl in a nightclub for obscenity because she wrestles with a stuffed gorilla, when any six-year-old, for ten cents, can pore for hours or days over jungle books where real gorillas do much more exciting things with half-undressed girls than just wrestling.[15]

Indeed, Wertham's genius as a rhetorician seems to have been his ability to cast himself not as a critic of but as an advocate for the child. He argued that America's children, even the troubled and the delinquent, were true innocents who had been "tempted and seduced" to bad behavior by the violence and sex they encountered in comic books. Proclaiming himself "defense counsel for the children who were condemned and punished by the very adults who permitted" their seduction, Wertham focused national attention on what he labeled "the new pornography, the glorification of violence and sadism" that, he believed, lured children down the paths of crime and sexual abnormality.[16]

The bulk of Wertham's criticism was directed at the brutality, gore, and crime that he found in comic books, but the very language of seduction that he used to describe the problem suggests that sex lay not far beneath the surface of his concerns. Crime comics' most pervasive effect, Wertham wrote, encompassed both violence and sex, for the books induced a "moral disarmament

. . . a blunting of the finer feelings of conscience, of mercy, of sympathy for other people's suffering and of respect for women as women and not merely as sex objects to be bandied around or as luxury prizes to be fought over."[17] Wertham contended that this "admixture of sensuality with cruelty" was "the keynote of the comic books' sexual message, drummed into children from a tender age on. . . . It is a special perversion that they cultivate most of all, sadism." He listed, nonetheless, a wide range of perversions and sexual problems that the typical crime comic cultivated: sadomasochistic fantasies prompted by flagellation and rape scenes, "fetichistic tendencies," encouraged by drawings that emphasized breasts, buttocks, genitalia, and high heels, masturbation problems, and "sex fears of all kinds," leading sometimes to frigidity in girls.[18] Wertham provided an extended analysis of the ways in which comic books, especially those featuring the "muscular male supertype" or the "sadistic" female heroine, seduced children into homoerotic fantasies and relationships. He argued, for example, that the Batman stories were "like a wish dream of two homosexuals living together":

> They are Bruce Wayne and "Dick" Grayson. They live in sumptuous quarters, with beautiful flowers in large vases and have a butler, Alfred. Batman is sometimes shown in a dressing gown. . . . Robin is . . . devoted to nothing on earth or in interplanetary space as much as to Bruce Wayne. He often stands with his legs spread, the genital region discreetly evident. . . . In these stories there are practically no decent, attractive successful women. . . . If [a girl] is after Bruce Wayne, she will have no chance against Dick.

Batman's lesbian counterpart, Wonder Woman, provided another "morbid ideal" for her girl readers. Wertham added that the homosexuals treated in his clinic confessed that the Batman stories were their favorite reading.[19]

Although Wertham's most vociferous criticisms were reserved for the entwining of violence and sex that he found in comic books, his writings paved the way for a decade of congressional investigation that focused not so much on his "new pornography" of violence and sadism but on the old obscenity of sexual explicitness. The House Select Committee on Current Pornographic Materials, the House and Senate Committees on the Judiciary, and the House Committee on Post Office and Civil Service all held hearings, issued reports, and recommended legislation. Warning of a traffic in sexually explicit materials of "staggering proportions," congressional representatives and the citizens who testified before their committees brought the term *pornography* into popular use and made the problem of the "smut peddler" one of national concern. Like Wertham, most participants in these hearings located the dangers of sexual portrayals in the very child that proponents of democratic moral authority had done their best to displace from these debates. Although congressional scrutiny shifted from comic books to paperback novels, girlie magazines, and "outright pornography," all of which were directed toward an adult audience, it was children who were deemed at risk. Thus, the assertion by members of the Senate Subcommittee on Juvenile Delinquency that pornography was "big business depending for much of its profits on the lunch money and the allowances of schoolchildren" reflected a more pervasive sense that pornography was especially alluring to children and that its purveyors targeted children as consumers. By the end of the decade the assertion that 75 percent of pornography in the United States was "sold directly to juveniles" was accepted as fact by those conducting the hearings.[20] A relatively broad definition of pornography facilitated this belief, as did newer methods of distribution. The affordability of paperback books meant that a wide range of literature could conceivably fall into the hands of adolescents who would not have had access to higher-priced under-the-counter pornography. The continuing growth of a mail-order trade in sexually explicit books raised the possibility that children might "receive pornographic filth in the family mailbox"; critics suggested that obscene materials need not even be purchased, as suggestive advertising flyers were sent indiscriminately to children and thereupon invaded the heretofore sacrosanct home.[21]

Despite their agreement on the seriousness of the problem of pornography and its threat to children, many participants in these hearings admitted a fundamental confusion about what exactly obscenity was and what could be done about it. This was an especially common refrain among those responsible for enforcing the laws. Local police officials complained that different judges applied different standards; a representative of newsdealers, who were under fire for selling salacious magazines, objected that "there are no standards and there are no guides and I, as an attorney, cannot define to you what is lewd, obscene and indecent. Our courts have differed." A postal employee charged with enforcing the Comstock Act also called for clearer guidelines as to what "Congress wants kept out of the mails. . . . They say 'obscene.' I can't add any more words. It is lewd, lascivious, filthy, indecent, but they all mean the same thing, and it is applying that, and that is our trouble."[22] Such confusion reflected the erosion of the older paradigm for regulating obscenity.

That erosion had gained momentum with the 1933 *Ulysses* case, in which Judge John Woolsey rejected the traditional standard that judged obscenity by the effect of isolated passages upon the most vulnerable readers. Woolsey's ruling had influence far beyond New York. Increasingly, judges in far-flung jurisdictions determined whether or not a particular representation was obscene on the basis of its effect upon "normal" adults rather than juveniles or abnormal individuals; they required that the work be judged as a whole and they admitted expert testimony as to its artistic or scientific value. By the late 1940s one Pennsylvania judge, in an influential opinion, called the *Ulysses* decision the "keystone" of a "modern American rule" of obscenity. Only a few years later two proponents of the extension of constitutional protections to sex literature proclaimed that "relatively sane standards" had come to characterize most courts' approach to obscenity litigation.[23] Nonetheless, some judges in some jurisdictions remained wedded to aspects of the Hicklin Rule, as did many citizens. As a result, confusion and frustration were the order of the day, as the testimony in congressional hearings attested. It was because the nation's obscenity regime was already changing that the U.S. Supreme Court found it necessary to issue a series of opinions on the question in the 1950s.

Three cases in particular demonstrated that, in significant ways, the system of obscenity regulation that had governed the nation in the early part of the century was to be no more. First, in a 1952 case concerning the New York State Board of Censors' refusal to permit exhibition of the Italian film *The Miracle*, the Supreme Court explicitly rejected the finding of the 1915 *Mutual* decision that there was no constitutional question involved in government censorship of motion pictures, concluding that the movies were indeed "a significant medium for the communication of ideas." While the justices did not rule on whether censorship of films was unconstitutional on its face, they began to strike down certain acts of censorship on the grounds that they impinged the rights to free expression guaranteed through the First and Fourteenth Amendments.[24] Five years later, in *Butler v Michigan*, the Court assayed its first direct blow against the Hicklin Rule. In this case the justices voided a Michigan obscenity conviction under a statute that outlawed the distribution of matter "tending to incite minors to violent or depraved or immoral acts, manifestly tending to the corruption of the morals of youth." Ruling that such a statute "reduces the adult population of Michigan to reading only what is fit for children," the Court undermined an important foundation of the earlier obscenity regime, that materials should be judged by their effect upon those whose minds were open to immoral influences.[25] But not until their decision in *Roth v United States*, several months later, did the justices articulate a new standard to take the place of the threadbare Hicklin Rule.

What became known as the *Roth* decision arose out of two prosecutions — one in California under state law, another in New York under the Comstock Act — of mail-order pornographers, a sector of the trade in sexually explicit materials that had been of great interest to congressional investigators. The Court sustained both convictions, the majority agreeing with Justice William Brennan that obscenity was by definition material "utterly without redeeming social importance" and therefore was not constitutionally protected speech. In so ruling, the justices generally affirmed the traditional approach of Anglo-American law to the obscene, dealing a blow to those civil libertarians who had begun urging that speech about sex should be afforded the same constitutional protection as other forms of speech.[26] *Roth* did, however, confirm the changes in determining the standards for obscenity that had been occurring in courts throughout the nation. The majority opinion explicitly rejected the Hicklin Rule and set forth a new test: material could be considered obscene only if "to the average person, applying contemporary community standards, the dominant theme of the material taken as a whole appeals to prurient interest." Because the trial judges in each of these cases had in fact employed this standard — the jury weighing Samuel Roth's fate had been instructed that it should articulate the "common conscience of the community" — most of the Supreme Court justices agreed that the defendants had illegally purveyed obscene material. Thus, the two concepts at the core of democratic moral authority — the average person rule and the jury as representative of community standards — received the imprimatur of the nation's highest tribunal, as did the basic presumption of moral relativism — that the relevant standards were contemporary and local, not eternal and universal.[27]

Yet, in a less noted case decided on the same day, the Court rejected another of democratic moral authority's principles: that obscenity regulation should be restricted to criminal proceedings, with the trial jury as the *sole* arbiter of the obscene. *Kingsley Books Inc. v Brown* concerned the attempt to prohibit sale in Times Square bookshops of a series of paperback books entitled *Nights of Horror*. If the description of the booklets offered by a state judge is in any degree accurate, the stories represented the worst of the pornography of the day, for they included "such horrors as cauterizing a woman's breast with a hot iron, placing hot coals against a woman's breasts, tearing breasts off, placing hot irons against a woman's armpits," and other acts equally abhorrent.[28] Such was their offensiveness that New York officials elected to proceed against the booklets not by arresting the bookseller but by obtaining an injunction against their distribution. This was possible under a section of the New York Code of Criminal Procedure that permitted local officials to procure a temporary injunction prohibiting the sale of material believed to be "obscene, lewd, lascivious, filthy, indecent, or disgusting." The law provided for an expedited hearing to determine whether the material was in fact obscene. If it was so found by a judge (or a jury, at the judge's discretion) it was to be destroyed. The procedure differed from criminal prosecution in its capacity to prevent dissemination of allegedly obscene materials before they were actually adjudged to be obscene.[29]

When the publishers of *Nights of Horror* challenged the constitutionality of this law, alleging that it constituted an illegal form of prior restraint on speech, the U.S. Supreme Court upheld the statute in a 5–4 decision. Writing for the majority, Justice Felix Frankfurter maintained that the Court could not restrict a state "to the criminal process in seeking to protect its people against the dissemination of pornography." Three dissenting opinions raised a variety of objections, among them that the statute's lack of guarantee of a jury trial was a fatal flaw. Despite the split decision, however, *Kingsley* established that states were entitled to preserve a broad range of remedies in the fight against obscenity and that a jury trial was not mandated to ensure due process.[30]

Supreme Court attention to the problem of obscenity regulation shifted the national debate in subtle ways. Much, of course, remained the same. In the congressional hearings that went on into the late 1950s and 1960s, irate citizens continued to warn of the dangers to children posed by pornography, now estimated as a one- to three-billion-dollar-a-year industry.[31] In the wake of the Court's rulings that general obscenity laws could not be drawn to protect the most vulnerable individuals, in fact, attention to guarding children redoubled: admonitions that "purveyors of filth are aiming their products more and more at the youth of our land" were accompanied by legislative proposals such as one that would make illegal the mailing of "arousing" materials to individuals under the age of nineteen.[32] Many individuals testifying before Congress stressed that, after the *Butler* and *Roth* rulings, new strategies for protecting the most vulnerable must be found. In response, representatives of the ACLU and the mass media insisted that the principles of the average person standard and the jury trial provided the appropriate foundation for an obscenity regime in a democratic nation.

Yet, when the Supreme Court endorsed a version of democratic moral authority, the justices left open a door that had been unanticipated by its advocates. Anti-obscenity activists seized upon the Court's pronouncement in *Roth* that contemporary community standards had a role to play in the determination of the obscene to justify their own efforts. This was the principle on which

Cincinnati's Citizens for Decent Literature was founded in 1957. Directed by Charles S. Keating Jr., this very successful group aimed to show local law enforcement officials that attempts to suppress obscenity would be supported by the community. Soon the Cincinnati group had gone national, and its efforts were praised by civic leaders. For example, a 1959 report by the House Subcommittee on Postal Operations (chaired by Pennsylvania Representative Kathryn Granahan, who made a career of the crusade against obscenity in the mails) contained a long section on "community action." The Northern Virginia Citizens for Decent Literature was cited approvingly as a model for the ways that "each community [may reserve] to itself the right of setting standards which reflect its own moral climate." This group established a "Committee on Standards . . . to develop criteria representing the 'average citizen applying contemporary community standards' " and then visited newsstands with the demand that their proprietors stop selling fifty objectionable magazines. If the *Roth* decision emphasized the contemporary standards of the community, it was reasoned, a mechanism for clarifying those standards was required. Community action would "have a bearing on the verdicts reached by the triers of the facts, the juries and judges, by making them aware of what their community's standards are." After *Roth* an increasing number of opponents of obscenity justified their activism as necessary to the proper (democratic) operation of the legal process laid out by the Supreme Court.[33]

Efforts to tighten obscenity laws were also championed as a necessary response to the Court's emphasis on community standards. At the end of the decade, for example, the Comstock Act was amended to allow the government to prosecute mailers of obscene matter in the jurisdiction where the mail was received. Previously, prosecution could occur only in the jurisdiction where the matter was deposited in the mail, a sore point for anti-obscenity activists and postal officials, who contended that the great bulk of such matter was mailed from Los Angeles and New York, two jurisdictions notoriously loathe to convict on obscenity charges. Lobbying for this change, an official of the National Association of Evangelicals argued that the proposed bill "simply allows the application of community standards in those areas where the materials are apt to do the damage."[34] In sum, while some anti-obscenity activists bemoaned the Supreme Court's accent on contemporary community standards (a representative of New York's now-Cardinal Spellman criticized this aspect of the *Roth* decision for ignoring "lasting moral values and . . . absolutes"),[35] the vast majority interpreted this part of the ruling as a summons to action. By the early 1960s Citizens for Decent Literature's Charles Keating testified before Congress that *he* was the average person, a representative of the "community of the United States."[36]

⌒

A decade after *Roth* the agitation about pornography moved into a new arena. Responding to insistent appeals by Charles Keating, Cardinal Spellman, and others, in 1967 Congress created the Presidential Commission on Obscenity and Pornography. Its eighteen members were instructed to gather information about the organization of the smut industry, to devise definitions of obscenity and pornography, to ascertain whether these materials caused adults or youth to engage in criminal or other "antisocial" behavior, and to recommend action to regulate the traffic in sexually explicit matter. Although Congress created the commission in response to the concerns of antipornography activists and intended it to reflect their concerns, President Lyndon B. Johnson's appointment of William B. Lockhart as chairman (and exclusion of Keating from membership) suggested that other groups would wield greater influence. Lockhart was a prominent legal scholar who had been among the first to argue that alleged obscenity should be governed, as other speech, by a clear and present danger test. In mid-1969 a vacancy allowed Richard Nixon to appoint Charles Keating as his sole representative on the commission. Keating's combative presence ensured that the opposing arguments about how (indeed, whether) to define and regulate obscenity would be brought into sharp relief.[37]

To no one's surprise, as time neared for the commission to issue its report, all-out war erupted. Keating went so far as to go to court to try to suppress the publication of the majority report, which among other things recommended the repeal of all local, state, and national laws "prohibiting the sale, exhibition, or distribution of sexual materials to consenting adults." Two other dissenting commissioners organized their own public hearings in eight cities, at which citizens denounced obscenity and pornography. Even before the majority report was officially published, the Senate rejected it by a 60–5 vote, and Vice President Spiro Agnew concurred, declaring that "as long as Richard Nixon is President, Main Street is not going to turn into smut alley." Contemporary observers pointed out that the Nixon administration's posturing was part of the Republican law-and-order strategy in midterm elections. But the conflict within and about the commission is more interesting for what it reveals about both the effects of the sexual revolution upon the debate about obscenity regulation and the continuing struggles over the meanings of democratic moral authority.[38]

The entire thrust of the commission's majority report was to portray the use of sexually explicit materials as an aspect of normal everyday life. Observing that "much of the 'problem' regarding materials which depict explicit sexual activity stems from the inability or reluctance of people in our society to be open and direct in dealing with sexual matters,"[39] the commissioners argued that the solution lay in greater openness. In addition to repealing legislation regulating the dissemination of "erotica" to consenting adults, they recommended a "massive sex education effort" that would aim for pluralism rather than orthodoxy and allow the proliferation of information about sex.[40] Greater openness also would mandate recognition of what the commissioners surmised from their studies: that most Americans enjoyed sexually explicit materials. The majority report emphasized that 85 percent of American men and 70 percent of women had seen pornography at some point in their lives, that this exposure was voluntary and often occurred in social settings, shared by friends and acquaintances, that it appeared that women as well as men were aroused by erotica, and that there was insufficient evidence to conclude that such exposure caused criminal behavior. Exposure to erotica was, however, productive of other attitudinal changes:

> Persons with more recent erotica experience tend to hold liberal sexual attitudes, are more *tolerant* of the sexual activities and preferences of others, and are less likely to respond punitively with either social ostracism or the demand for activation of legal sanctions. . . . Highly experienced persons, as compared with others, are more supportive of First Amendment rights, less restrictive regarding the availability of erotica, and more active in local and national politics. They are also more highly educated and more frequently read books and magazines and view motion pictures.

In light of the commissioners' position that "we live in a free, pluralistic society which places its trust in the competition of ideas in a free market place. . . . Coercion, repression and censorship in order to promote a given set of views are not tolerable," this relationship between use of pornography and greater tolerance was offered as a positive outcome.[41]

The commissioners also funded a series of social scientific studies intended to gauge "erotica's" social effects, from which they concluded there was "no evidence to date that exposure to explicit sexual materials plays a significant role in the causation of delinquent or criminal behavior among youth or adults."[42] The appeal to social science evidence about the harms of sexual explicitness can be traced back at least to the 1930s, when under Payne Fund auspices sociologists, psychologists, and educators studied motion pictures' effect on children.[43] It had also played an important role in the writings of Fredric Wertham, who claimed that his conclusions about the dangers of comic books were substantiated by (his own) rigorous psychological research. In previous cases the emphasis on scientific proof of mass media's destructive effects provided a way to justify the demand for censorship even as the cultural climate fostered skepticism toward such demands. Specification of harms, and proof of them, was a necessary response to the growth of an anticensorship coalition and its advocacy of democratic moral authority. Yet this strategy had its dangers, which became obvious in the President's Commission's majority report: if social science could offer no proof of a causal relationship between sexually explicit materials and bad behavior, then the argument for regulation was undermined. Commissioners who advocated stricter regulation of obscenity realized this and sought to change the parameters of the debate, insisting that "the government interest in regulating pornography has always related primarily to the prevention of moral corruption and *not* to prevention of overt criminal acts and conduct." But theirs was a minority voice, and recourse to social science became a permanent feature of debates over obscenity in the wake of the commission's report.[44]

Conspicuous by their relative absence from the debate generated by the commission were American youth. The commissioners who concurred in the majority report did bow to what they saw as a consensus among the nation's citizens, drafting a model ordinance that would prohibit the commercial dissemination of certain sexually explicit materials to young people.[45] Nonetheless, their brief discussions of the (generally benign) role of pornography in adolescent sex education and of the lack of evidence that sexually explicit materials caused juvenile delinquency only highlighted the focus on adults. Children also played almost no role in the minority reports submitted by Charles Keating, Methodist minister Winfrey Link, and Morton A. Hill, a Catholic priest and president of the New York-based Morality in Media. Perhaps because the majority report nodded to the legitimacy of protecting children, the bulk of their criticism was directed at the commission's "undemocratic" leadership and at the assumption that the only grounds for regulating adults' access to pornography was the proven presence of a "cause-effect relationship between pornography and criminal behavior."[46] They also directed a good deal of attention toward demonstrating that concerns for the average person mandated laws against obscenity. For example, Link explained,

Not only does every individual reflect a certain moral character, but so does every group of individuals, a club, a city, a state, or even a nation — *the essence of which is determined by a general consensus of individual standards.* It is, stated another way, the distillation of all the individual moralities or the *level* of morality generally. It is this level, this distillation, this average, this essence, which the state has an interest in protecting.[47]

It was crucial to protect this average morality because it was the average person who ought to make decisions about what was obscene. In their specific recommendations, Hill, Link, and Keating embraced this aspect of democratic moral authority and sought to use to it their own ends. Hill and Link, for example, offered a model state obscenity statute that required a jury trial unless it was waived by both parties and that limited judges' discretion to dismiss charges in obscenity prosecutions, noting that "the jury . . . has a special aptitude for expressing the view of the average person. As the trier of fact, it is the exclusive judge of the common conscience of the community and the embodiment of community standards." Charles Keating provided only one specific legislative recommendation: a federal law mandating these same requirements and prohibiting federal courts from reviewing state court proceedings in obscenity actions.[48] All these recommendations were intended to construct a central role in obscenity regulation for the "community," but a particular conception of the community. Keating articulated this conception in his rebuttal to the majority's conclusions:

> Far from needing repeal of legislation controlling pornography, what is called for is a return to law enforcement which permits the American to determine for himself the standards of acceptable morality and decency in his community. Our law enforcement in the area of obscenity has been emasculated by courts, seemingly divorced from the realities of our communities, determining from afar the standards of those communities. The law is capable of coping with the problem of pornography and obscenity, but it must be law, coupled with the logic that an American is innately capable of determining for himself his standards of public decency and, beyond that, he has a right to make that determination.[49]

As anti-obscenity activists had learned, an obscenity regime that put "the people" and "the community" at its center could be very useful.

That, of course, is exactly what the Supreme Court did in 1973, when it decided *Miller v California*. On the whole, this decision endorsed *Roth*'s standards for judging obscenity, while adding two requirements: that, to be obscene, work must be "patently offensive" and lack "serious literary, artistic, political, or scientific value" (this overturned an earlier ruling that obscene material must be "utterly without redeeming social value"). As important, *Miller* established that contemporary community standards ought to be judged according to the *local* community. Writing for the majority, Chief Justice Warren Burger opined that "it is neither realistic nor constitutionally sound to read the First Amendment as requiring that the people of Maine or Mississippi accept public depiction of conduct found tolerable in Las Vegas or New York City. . . . People in different states vary in their tastes and attitudes, and this diversity is not to be strangled by the absolutism of imposed uniformity." His pronouncement used the position of anti-obscenity activists to settle an ongoing debate within the court about whether community standards ought to be national or local.[50]

The *Miller* decision can be read, in part, as a rejection of the majority report of the President's Commission on Obscenity and Pornography. Not only did the decision echo the demands of the dissenting commissioners for a return to local control, it also refuted the majority's contention that the Supreme Court was moving toward the view that consenting adults' use of pornography constitutionally could not be regulated.[51] While scholars have debated whether the *Miller* rule substantially altered the effectiveness of obscenity prosecution, its significance lies as much in the legitimation it offered for a particular interpretation of democratic moral authority — and the impetus thereby given to community organizing around pornography — as in its consequences for law enforcement efforts. In this sense, it paved the way for the Attorney General's Commission on Pornography, convened in 1985 by President Ronald Reagan. The Meese Commission, as it was popularly known, issued a *Final Report* that completely repudiated the findings of the President's Commission that preceded it by less than twenty years. Its conclusions have been ridiculed by civil libertarians and rejected by social scientists; scholars have labeled it a reincarnation of Victorian prudishness, an attempt to "return the United States to the days of Comstockery."[52] Yet to see the report of the Meese Commission merely as part of an effort to turn back the clock to a mythical past is to miss what makes late-twentieth-century debates about obscenity distinctly modern. Within this document the instability of democratic moral authority — its final inability to displace the "vulnerable viewer" as well as the ease with which the "average person" becomes transformed into a specific community, and a specific citizen — becomes exceedingly clear.

In nineteen-hundred-plus pages the Meese Commission *Final Report* essentially makes two assertions: pornography is harmful to individuals and society and needs to be controlled through law enforcement and citizen action. Commission members delineated the harms by distinguishing between three categories of pornography: "sexually violent material," which they concluded "bears a causal relationship to antisocial acts of sexual violence and, for some subgroups, possibly to unlawful acts of sexual violence," nonviolent but degrading materials, which they alleged caused discrimination against women and induced viewers to "view rape or other forms of sexual violence as less serious than they otherwise would have," and "non-violent and non-degrading materials." The commissioners reported that this final category was the smallest of the three, and while they concluded that it probably does not cause sexual violence it was threatening in another way: "We have little doubt that much of this material does find its way into the hands of children, and to the extent that it does we all agree that it is harmful."[53] While individual members of the commission saw other harms in pornography — in particular, several were concerned about the ways in which porn undermines "the strongest unit of society — the family"[54] — the main body of the report, as this elucidation of harms suggests, is concerned with its dangers to women and children.

These two groups figured very differently in the two commissions' reports. In 1970 children were barely mentioned at all.[55] In 1986 they constituted one of the primary groups victimized by pornography, but their victimization occurred not in their role as consumers (as the Hicklin Rule would have had it) but in their role as exploited performers. Child pornography was a central concern of the Meese Commission, and its members were unanimous that enforcement of laws against child porn should be accorded the highest priority by law enforcement officials. As for women, in the 1970 *Report* the little attention paid to them was intended to incorporate the female consumer into a preexisting notion of the average citizen. Women, it was asserted, could be turned on by pornography just like men; they might welcome it as an aid to marital satisfaction.[56] The notion that pornography promoted "sex-calloused attitudes toward women" was discounted.[57] In 1986, despite the concern for child pornography, most of the analysis of the harms of pornography focused upon the harms to women. In effect, in 1970 women were considered, with men, as adults; in 1986, "women and children" were collapsed into one category of victims.

The Meese Commission's *Final Report* echoed to a striking degree the criticisms of pornography that a segment of the feminist movement had been developing since the mid-1970s. Originating in grassroots activism in large cities like Los Angeles and New York, the feminist antipornography movement quickly spread across the nation, aided by its eloquent defense in books such as *Take Back the Night: Women on Pornography* and the writings and speeches of Andrea Dworkin and Catherine MacKinnon. These women advanced the hypothesis that pornography provides a blueprint for the discrimination and violence that millions of women experience in their daily lives. Although much of their early activism was directed toward images emphasizing sexualized violence, antiporn feminists did not hesitate to censure an immense spectrum of sexual materials. An article authored by members of one of the earliest groups, Women Against Violence in Pornography and Media, demonstrates the breadth of their critique:

> Not all pornography is violent, but even the most banal pornography objectifies women's bodies. An essential ingredient of much rape and other forms of violence to women is the "objectification" of the woman. This is not just rhetoric. It means that women are not seen as human beings but as things. Men are reared to view females in this way, pornography thrives off this and feeds it, and rape is one of the consequences.[58]

Antiporn feminists claimed to distinguish between obscenity, which they characterized as an issue of morality and basically harmless, and pornography, which they called a "political practice" of male supremacy.[59] To solve the problem of pornography, they advocated, by the early 1980s, passage of a civil rights ordinance that permitted women who claimed to be injured by specific pornographic materials to sue for their suppression and for monetary damages.[60] But the antiporn feminists' definition of pornography seemed to many, including other feminists, to encompass that which had traditionally been labeled obscene, and their willingness to entrust pornography interdiction to government brought accusations that they were both "anti-sex" and "pro-censorship."[61]

The majority of members of the Meese Commission found much of this feminist discourse on pornography very useful. Carole S. Vance argues convincingly that the commission's discourse on harm, which drew upon both feminist and social scientific arguments, reflected the belief that "the attack on sexually explicit material had to be modernized." Commenting on the collaboration between the social conservatives who directed the commission and the feminists who testified before it, she points out that "the notion that pornography degrades women proved to be a particularly helpful unifying term, floating in and out of fundamentalist as well as antipornography feminist testimony."[62]

Certainly, one of the most bizarre features of the 1986 *Final Report* — a cultural production of the Reagan administration, after all — is its trumpeting of the antipornography feminist critique. In their individual statements some commissioners witnessed to the emotional power and persuasiveness of feminist testimony. Psychiatrist Park Dietz, for example, recounted the effect that Andrea Dworkin's statement to the commission had upon him:

> When Andrea Dworkin challenged us to find the courage "to go and cut that woman down and untie her hands and take the gag out of her mouth, and to do something, to risk something, for her freedom," I cried. . . . I ask you, America, to strike the chains from America's women and children, to free them from the bonds of pornography, to free them from the bonds of sexual slavery, to free them from the bonds of sexual abuse, to free them from the bonds of inner torment that entrap the second-class citizen in an otherwise free nation.[63]

And no less than James Dobson, president of the conservative group Focus on the Family, intoned that "pornography is the theory; rape is the practice" in his contribution to the *Final Report*.[64] In the report itself the analysis of pornography that had been articulated by the feminist antipornography movement took center stage. The commission concluded that

> the pornography industry systematically violates human rights with apparent impunity. The most powerless citizens in society are singled out on the basis of their gender — often aggravated by their age, race, disability, or other vulnerability — for deprivations of liberty, property, labor, bodily and psychic security and integrity, privacy, reputation, and even life. . . . We therefore conclude that pornography, when it leads to coerced viewing, contributes to an assault, is defamatory, or is actively trafficked, constitutes a practice of discrimination on the basis of sex.[65]

As Vance suggests, one way to explain the prominence of a radical feminist[66] analysis within a document meant to serve a social conservative agenda is that each group was "strategizing how best to use the other."[67] But we also need to ask, What makes it possible for each to use the other in this specific context? How do the presumptions underlying the current obscenity regime enable this mutually exploitative relationship?

A good part of the answer is to be found in the rise of democratic moral authority. For when anticensorship activists focused their efforts on this concept they brought the question of obscenity regulation into the realm of citizenship in an entirely new way. When the "average person" was inscribed at the center of the system of obscenity regulation, an exceedingly unstable legal regime was invented, one that depended upon a legal fiction whose meanings were up for grabs. By the 1980s, those who were at first excluded from this conception of the average person were asserting the fact of their inclusion, by claiming their rights as citizens.

The testimony of Andrea Dworkin before the Meese Commission is a case in point. Dworkin began her testimony with the words, "My name is Andrea Dworkin. I am a citizen of the United States, and in this country where I live, every year millions of pictures are being made of women with our legs spread." Throughout her testimony Dworkin returned again and again to the fact of her citizenship:

> In this country where I live as a citizen real rapes are on film and are being sold in the marketplace. . . . In this country where I live as a citizen, women are penetrated by animals . . . urinated on and defecated on. . . . In the country where I live as a citizen, there is a pornography of the humiliation of women where every single way of humiliating a human being is taken to be a form of sexual pleasure for the viewer and the victim. . . . I live in a country where if you film any act of humiliation or torture, and if the victim is a woman, the film is both entertainment and it is protected speech. Now that tells me something about what it means to be a woman citizen in this country, and the meaning of being second class.[68]

Dworkin's testimony was quoted at length within the commission's report as representative of those many "victims whose voices were not heard,"[69] limiting the import of her words to a plea on behalf of those allegedly harmed by pornography. Of course they were that, but they were also the words of a citizen demanding the right to be represented within the community that determines standards, to make the decisions about how pornography will be regulated. Dworkin's authority lies in her claim to speak both for those whom she understands to be the powerless victims of pornography and for herself — and, by extension, for all women — as citizen.[70] Ironically, what makes this rhetoric powerful is exactly what makes it dangerous. For in trying to reclaim democratic citizenship in the arena of sexually explicit materials, activists such as Dworkin reconstituted themselves vulnerable viewers,[71] at the same moment that the religious right was seeking to refocus attention on mass media's effect on that more venerable vulnerable viewer, the child.[72] In the process they cemented the link between women and children, positioning women as objects rather than subjects of the law. The rhetoric of feminist antipornography activists in fact undermines their claim to citizen status.[73]

Nonetheless, Dworkin's rhetoric has much in common with that of Charles Keating, founder of Citizens for Decent Literature, who stood before congressional committees twenty-five years earlier and claimed "to speak for most of our American citizens." The very name of Keating's group — the first secular national organization dedicated specifically to combating obscenity — suggests the increasing importance of the concept of citizenship in legitimating anti-obscenity activism, and it has remained central for both social conservatives and antiporn feminists into the 1990s. Indeed, one of the grounds on which the 1986 *Final Report* was criticized was that it offered a blueprint for antipornography organizing by community groups. In a chapter entitled "Citizen and Community Action and Corporate Responsibility" the commissioners gave step-by-step instructions on how to implement a "citizen action" program on pornography, including questionnaires for surveying local law enforcement officers on their efforts and identifying the extent of the pornography problem in a community. Unlike the 1970 *Report*, which endorsed community action only as a process for establishing a "pluralistic" dialogue among community members, the 1986 version suggested that letter-writing campaigns, picketing, and boycotts could help consolidate a "solid collective community standard" that would aid in law enforcement efforts.[74] The emphasis on ascertaining public opinion that had been so important to early anticensorship activists was now taken up by a government commission in support of the battle against pornography.

From "pluralism" to a "solid collective community standard" — the relationship between citizenship and obscenity regulation constructed within democratic moral authority made for an enormous amount of instability and contestation. Democracy is itself an unstable system, and the citizen, like the average person, is a legal fiction. The formulators of democratic moral authority envisioned this fictional person as one who would advance the battle against the sexual prudery and censorship advocated by those women activists and ministers who claimed to speak in defense of children, family, and church. They could not foresee the emergence of a feminist movement whose own democratic quest would lead some of its constituents to identify their exclusion from average personhood as both a cause and effect of women's subordination. Nor, it seems, did they imagine that the very ministers and lay activists whom they sought to subdue could convincingly reclaim for themselves the power to speak for a community. Far from settling the question of who was to be protected from obscenity, who was to do the protecting, and what was at stake, the invention of democratic moral authority as the paradigm for obscenity regulation ensured that these contests will continue for a very long time.

NOTES

Introduction

1. Davis, *The Exploitation of Pleasure*, pp. 44–45.

2. In addition to Davis, see Addams, *The Spirit of Youth and City Streets*. For an overview of these concerns, see Boyer, *Urban Masses and Moral Order in America*.

3. Throughout this study I will use the terms *obscene* and *obscenity* to describe all those materials which individuals tried to suppress or regulate on their belief that the materials were lewd or not fit for public display. My use of these terms, without quotation marks, is not intended to endorse the position that the materials were in fact obscene.

4. On Comstock and the vice society movement, see Boyer, *Purity in Print*; Gilfoyle, "The Moral Origins of Political Surveillance"; Beisel, *Imperiled Innocents*; Johnson, "Anthony Comstock." On the history of obscenity generally, see also Kendrick, *The Secret Museum*; Hunt, *The Invention of Pornography*; Gurstein, *The Repeal of Reticence*; De Grazia, *Girls Lean Back Everywhere*; Marcus, *The Other Victorians*; Haney, *Comstockery in America*. For a study that places twentieth-century regulation of obscenity in New York in a broader context of sexual regulation, see Nelson, "Criminality and Sexual Morality."

5. The most complete work on the social purity movement remains Pivar, *Purity Crusade*. See also Odem, *Delinquent Daughters*, especially chapter 1; DuBois and Gordon, "Seeking Ecstasy on the Battlefield"; Ginzberg, *Women and the Work of Benevolence*, especially chapter 6; D'Emilio and Freedman, *Intimate Matters*, especially pp. 150–167; Valverde, *The Age of Light, Soap, and Water*. On the WCTU's involvement see Parker, *Purifying America*.

6. Pascoe's articulation of the notion of female moral authority has been important to my own conceptualization of this project. See Pascoe, *Relations of Rescue*.

7. Stansell, *City of Women*; Peiss, *Cheap Amusements*; Meyerowitz, *Women Adrift*.

8. Singal, "Toward a Definition of American Modernism"; Pascoe, *Relations of Rescue*, pp. 192–201; Douglas, *Terrible Honesty*; Purcell, *The Crisis of Democratic Theory*.

9. Here I am using the term *censorship* in the broad sense in which it was used by participants in these debates — as signifying any effort to prohibit or punish speech.

10. Douglas, *Terrible Honesty*, pp. 6–8 and passim. Douglas, however, overestimates the real cultural power of this so-called matriarch, and her identification of the process of "masculinization" with an uncritically defined democratization suggests that the masculinization of American culture is essentially beneficial. In contrast, I argue that the construction of a particular understanding of democracy within debates about culture and sex during these years is itself a gendered process with contradictory consequences, a process that is neither essentially "good" nor "bad."

11. It is important to note that "female moral authority" took many forms, and could be marshaled to support a variety of political positions, ranging from opposition to prostitution to support for labor reform and the labor movement to criticism of lynching and Prohibition. Among opponents of censorship, however, it was believed to represent a specific repressive stance toward cultural regulation, and they formulated their own strategies within the context of that belief.

12. For examples, see May, *Screening Out the Past*; Rosenzweig, *Eight Hours for What We Will*; Couvares, *The Remaking of Pittsburgh*; Allen, *Horrible Prettiness*; Peiss, *Cheap Amusements*; Levine, *Highbrow/Lowbrow*; Richard Butsch, ed., *For Fun and Profit: The Transformation of Leisure into Consumption* (Philadelphia: Temple University Press, 1990); Richard W. Fox and T. J. Jackson Lears, eds., *The Culture of Consumption: Critical Essays in American History, 1880–1930* (New York: Pantheon, 1983).

13. See, for example, William R. Taylor, "The Launching of a Commercial Culture: New York City, 1860–1930," in Mollenkopf, *Power, Culture, and Place*, pp. 107–133. But, for an analysis emphasizing the creative tension between "the economic imperatives of the industry" and consumers' desires, see Francis G. Couvares, "Introduction," in Couvares, *Movie Censorship and American Culture*, pp. 1–15.

14. D'Emilio and Freedman, *Intimate Matters*, pp. 233, 239–260.

15. This characterization of Broadway revues is found in *New York American*, December 2, 1923.

16. On Bara, see May, *Screening Out the Past*, pp. 105–109; Staiger, *Bad Women*, pp. 147–162.

17. See *The Rubicon* clipping file and *The Virgin Man* clipping file, both in the Billy Rose Theatre Collection, Lincoln Center Library for the Performing Arts.

18. A general overview can be found in Curtin, *"We Can Always Call Them Bulgarians"*; see also Chauncey, *Gay New York*, especially chapter 11. The appearance of homosexuals on stage should not be confused with a longstanding tradition of female impersonation. See Geraldine Maschio, "Female Impersonation on the American Stage, 1860 to 1927," *Performing Arts Resources* 12 (1987): 156–170.

19. This interpretation draws on the analysis offered by Freedman in "'Uncontrolled Desires'"; and Freedman and John D'Emilio in *Intimate Matters*, especially chapter 12. It should be noted that under the Production Code motion pictures presented something of an exception to this pattern; even marital sexuality was limited in its portrayal by Hollywood.

20. For an excellent discussion of primitivism, see duCille, "Blues Notes on Black Sexuality"; on Harlem nightclubs see Erenberg, *Steppin' Out*, pp. 253–258.

21. Davis, *The Exploitation of Pleasure*, especially pp. 30 and 33. On commercial culture in New York City, see Allen, *Horrible Prettiness*; Snyder, *The Voice of the City*; Erenberg, *Steppin' Out*; Peiss, *Cheap Amusements*. An important source on the early motion picture industry is Ramsaye, *A Million and One Nights*.

22. Hugh McLeod, "Secular Cities? Berlin, London, and New York in the Nineteenth and Early Twentieth Centuries," in Bruce, *Religion and Modernization*, pp. 59–89.

23. At the same time, this diversity, especially the substantial Jewish population,

placed some limits on Catholic influence, so that New York was distinct from a city like Boston, where book and stage censorship was firmly established.

24. For examples, see *New York Times*, October 4, 1923, p. 22, February 13, 1925, p. 19, May 21, 1925, p. 27, February 20, 1926, p. 19, January 31, 1917. Typescript regarding nudity in films, Box 140, National Board of Review of Motion Pictures Collection, Rare Books and Manuscripts Division, New York Public Library, Astor, Lenox and Tilden Foundations.

25. Schauer, *The Law of Obscenity*, p. 9.

26. Lynn Hunt, "Obscenity and the Origins of Modernity, 1500–1800," in Hunt, *The Invention of Pornography*, p. 35.

27. Quoted in Bryan, *American Theatrical Regulation*, p. 7.

28. Bryan, *American Theatrical Regulation*, p. 32. See also Agnew, *Worlds Apart*; Wertheimer, "Mutual Film Reviewed"; Czitrom, "The Politics of Performance."

29. Two early prosecutions under the common law were *Commonwealth v Sharpless* (1815), a Pennsylvania case concerning the display of an obscene painting, and *Commonwealth v Holmes* (1821), in which the Massachusetts Supreme Court upheld the conviction of a publisher of *Fanny Hill*. State obscenity statutes included Vermont (1821); Connecticut (1834), Massachusetts (1835), and Pennsylvania (1860). For an overview see Schauer, *The Law of Obscenity*, pp. 8–10; and Blanchard, "The American Urge to Censor," especially p. 746.

30. Boyer, *Purity in Print*, p. 3; Boyer, *Urban Masses and Moral Order*.

31. Quoted in Broun and Leech, *Anthony Comstock*, p. 78.

32. Ibid., p. 81.

33. The 1873 law added a prohibition on contraceptive devices, stiffened the penalties for violating the statute (with a provision that offenders could be imprisoned at hard labor for up to ten years), and appointed Comstock as a postal inspector, thus enhancing enforcement. On the history of federal enactments against obscenity and the subsequent passing of "Little Comstock" laws in the states, see Blanchard, "The American Urge to Censor," pp. 746–748.

34. On the vice society movement, see Boyer, *Purity in Print*; the Massachusetts law is quoted on p. 11. Nicola Beisel has argued recently that the entire antivice movement is best understood as an effort to ensure the maintenance of class status through the "reproduction of the next generation. . . . Crusades to protect children from vice address parents' fear that vice will render children unfit for desirable jobs and social positions." See Beisel, *Imperiled Innocents*, pp. 4–5 and passim.

35. Parker, *Purifying America*, p. 128 and passim; see also Pivar, *Purity Crusade*; and Beisel, *Imperiled Innocents*, especially chapter 3.

36. *Regina v Hicklin*, L.R. 3 Q.B. 36; Schauer, *The Law of Obscenity*; Rabban, "The Free Speech League"; Wertheimer, "Free-Speech Fights," especially chapter 2; Blanchard, "The American Urge to Censor."

37. Anthony Comstock, *Frauds Exposed* (1880), quoted in Broun and Leech, *Anthony Comstock*, pp. 80–81. On Comstock's views about the relation between masturbation and erotic books (alluded to here), see Beisel, *Imperiled Innocents*, pp. 54–56.

38. Quoted in Beisel, *Imperiled Innocents*, p. 39.

39. Johnson, "Anthony Comstock," pp. 75–76; Gurstein, *Repeal of Reticence*, p. 181 and passim.

40. Gilfoyle, *City of Eros*.

41. D'Emilio and Freedman, *Intimate Matters*, pp. 130–133.

42. Brodie, *Contraception and Abortion in Nineteenth-Century America*, especially chapter 3; James C. Mohr, *Abortion in America: The Origins and Evolution of National Policy, 1800–1900* (New York: Oxford University Press, 1978), especially chapter 4.

43. On the increasing importance of heterosociality and heterosexuality in commercial culture, see Peiss, *Cheap Amusements*; Erenberg, *Steppin' Out*; Kasson, *Amusing the Million*; Rabinovitz, "Temptations of Pleasure."

44. Quoted in Rabban, "The Free Speech League," p. 62.

45. D'Emilio and Freedman, *Intimate Matters*, pp. 161–166; Jesse F. Battan, "'The Word Made Flesh': Language, Authority, and Sexual Desire in Late Nineteenth-Century America," *Journal of the History of Sexuality* 3, 2 (October 1992): 223–244; see also Hal D. Sears, *The Sex Radicals: Free Love in High Victorian America* (Lawrence: Regents Press of Kansas, 1977).

46. Quoted in Rabban, "The Free Speech League," p. 80.

47. Schroeder, *"Obscene" Literature*, p. 256.

48. Members of the Free Speech League provided financial, legal, and emotional support to birth control activists Goldman and Sanger, sex reformers Moses Harman and Ida Craddock, *Masses* publisher Max Eastman, and various anarchists and labor activists, particularly members of the IWW. Hecklers at a 1902 speech delivered by Anthony Comstock in Brooklyn were likely FSL members, although they were not identified as such in newspaper reports. See Rabban, "The Free Speech League," pp. 88–98; *New York Times*, December 8, 1902, p. 2.

49. *New York Times*, October 31, 1906, p. 7, August 4, 1906, p. 6. See also Broun and Leech, *Anthony Comstock*, pp. 216–219. Other controversial actions by Comstock included his participation in the campaign to suppress George Bernard Shaw's play, *Mrs. Warren's Profession*, in 1905, and his arrest of physical culture entrepreneur Bernarr MacFadden in the same year. On Comstock's earlier forays against art, see Beisel, *Imperiled Innocents*, chapter 7.

50. *New York Times*, August 7, 1906, p. 6, January 1, 1907, p. 8.

51. See Budke, "Assessing the 'Offense of Public Decency,'" chapter 4; Laufe, *The Wicked Stage*, chapter 3.

52. *New York Times*, April 6, 1900, p. 7.

53. Ibid., July 7, 1906, p. 7.

1. "To Protect the Morals of Young People"

1. *New York Times*, December 27, 1908, p. 1.

2. The history of the National Board of Censorship of Motion Pictures has been recounted by numerous scholars. See May, *Screening Out the Past*; Sklar, *Movie-Made*

America; Jowett, *Film*; Rosenbloom, "Between Reform and Regulation"; Rosenbloom, "In Defense of the Moving Pictures"; Rosenbloom, "Progressive Reform"; Feldman, *The National Board*; Fisher, "Film Censorship and Progressive Reform"; Czitrom, "The Redemption of Leisure."

3. General statistics about moviegoing in New York may be found in May, *Screening Out the Past*, p. 35; Sklar, *Movie-Made America*, p. 16; Robert C. Allen, "Motion Picture Exhibition in Manhattan, 1906–1912: Beyond the Nickelodeon," in Gorham Kindem, ed., *The American Movie Industry* (Carbondale, Ill.: Southern Illinois University Press, 1982), pp. 12–24; Russell Merritt, "Nickelodeon Theaters, 1905–1914: Building an Audience for the Movies," in Tino Balio, ed., *The American Film Industry* (Madison: University of Wisconsin Press, 1976), pp. 59–79; Davis, *The Exploitation of Pleasure*. On concern about children and the movies, see also Sklar, *Movie-Made America*, especially chapter 8; Jowett, *Film*, chapter 4; deCordova, "Ethnography and Exhibition." For an excellent summary of the debate over the class of the cinema audience, see Hansen, *Babel and Babylon*, chapter 2.

4. Platt, *The Child Savers*; Joseph Kett, *Rites of Passage: Adolescence in America, 1790 to the Present* (New York: Basic, 1977); Mennel, *Thorns and Thistles*; Linda Gordon, *Heroes of Their Own Lives: The Politics and History of Family Violence, Boston, 1880–1960* (New York: Viking, 1988); Dominick Cavallo, *Muscles and Morals*; David Nasaw, *Children of the City*.

5. Peiss, *Cheap Amusements*; Addams, *The Spirit of Youth and City Streets*; Davis, *Exploitation of Pleasure*.

6. On the invention of childhood innocence, see Phillipe Aries, *Centuries of Childhood: A Social History of Family Life*, trans. Robert Baldick (New York: Vintage, 1962).

7. For articulation of concerns about motion pictures' effects on patrons' physical health, see Addams, *The Spirit of Youth and City Streets*; and Collier, "Cheap Amusements." The quote is from *New York World*, December 24, 1908, p. 10.

8. Another typical film, *Too Much Champagne*, made intemperance the subject of humor, portraying the difficulties of a drunken man trying to make his way home. See reviews in *Variety*, February 1, 1908, March 14, 1908, August 29, 1908, September 5, 1908.

9. *New York World*, December 21, 1908, p. 16, and December 24, 1908, p. 10; *New York Tribune*, December 24, 1908, p. 4; *New York Times*, December 24, 1908, p. 2.

10. *New York World*, December 24, 1908, p. 10; see also *New York Tribune*, December 24, 1908, p. 4, December 27, 1908, p. 2, November 16, 1911, p. 8; *New York World*, December 25, 1908, p. 1; *New York Times*, December 24, 1908, p. 4; Board of Aldermen Proceedings, November 29, 1910, p. 742, Municipal Research Library, City of New York (hereafter cited as Proceedings); *New York Times*, March 16, 1911, p. 8, July 2, 1911, 5:15, November 16, 1911, p. 8; May, *Screening Out the Past*, chapter 3. For a different analysis of the "temptations" of moviegoing for young women, see Rabinovitz, "Temptations of Pleasure."

11. The campaign against Sunday entertainment can be traced in the *New York Times*; see especially March 1, 1906, p. 1, November 5, 1906, p. 6, December 1, 1906, p. 5, January 29, 1907, p. 3, May 2, 1907, p. 8, October 14, 1907, p. 2, December 5, 1907, p. 16, December 20, 1907, p. 7, July 1, 1908, p. 3, December 3, 1908, p. 9. On the complex relationship be-

tween blue law campaigns and the agitation against the movies see Armour, "Effects of Censorship Pressure"; and Czitrom, "The Politics of Performance."

12. June 25, 1908, Theo. Bingham to Mayor George McClellan, Box MGB52, McClellan Collection, Mayors' Papers, Municipal Archives, Department of Records and Information Services, City of New York (hereafter cited as Mayors' Papers); "Cheap Amusement Shows in Manhattan, Preliminary Report," Box 170, National Board of Review of Motion Pictures Collection, Rare Books and Manuscripts Division, New York Public Library, Astor, Lenox and Tilden Foundations (hereafter cited as NBRMPC); Collier, "Cheap Amusements;" Peiss, *Cheap Amusements*, p. 159.

13. January 17, 1908, Theo. Bingham to Mayor McClellan, Box MGB52, McClellan Collection, Mayors' Papers; *New York World*, December 21, 1908, p. 16, December 24, 1908, p. 10; *New York Times*, December 21, 1908, p. 2, December 24, 1908, p. 4; *New York Daily Tribune*, December 24, 1908, p. 4; Hearing Transcript, Box MGB51, McClellan Collection, Mayors' Papers.

14. Hearing Transcript, Box MGB51, McClellan Collection, Mayors' Papers.

15. Ibid.

16. *New York Tribune*, December 24, 1908, p. 4, December 25, 1908, p. 1, December 27, 1908, p. 2; *New York World*, December 21, 1908, p. 16, December 24, 1908, p. 10, December 25, 1908, p. 1, December 26, 1908, p. 2, p. 8; *New York Times*, December 21, 1908, p. 2, December 24, 1908, p. 4, December 26, 1908, p. 8; Ramsaye, *A Million and One Nights*, 2:477; May, *Screening Out the Past*, p. 2.

17. Armour, "Effects of Censorship Pressure," pp. 113–121; Czitrom, "The Politics of Performance," pp. 32–33; Staiger, *Bad Women*, pp. 93–103.

18. These included the passage of legislation that would prohibit the admission of "unescorted" children under the age of sixteen from attending the movies, a prohibition that already existed for vaudeville theaters. See Resolution 128, City Clerk Approved Papers, December 1908-February 1909, Municipal Archives, Department of Records and Information Services, City of New York; Proceedings, January 26, 1909, p. 472. Such legislation reserved to the state what had previously been a parental right to regulate children's access to motion pictures and attempted to subject the children of working-class families to native-born middle-class standards of child rearing. However, because so many parents ignored it, the unescorted children law was rarely enforced. See Nasaw, *Children of the City*, chapter 8, regarding newsboys' frequent unauthorized attendance at movies.

19. Czitrom, "The Politics of Performance," p. 34.

20. In 1916 the National Board of Censorship of Motion Pictures changed its name to the National Board of Review of Motion Pictures, a name that it retains to this day. Throughout the book, however, I will refer to the agency by its original name.

21. Feldman, *The National Board*, pp. 22–24; March 1, 1909, John Collier to Gustavas A. Rogers, Box 170, NBRMPC.

22. Feldman, *The National Board*, pp. 28–31; "Report of Committee on Plan of Action," Box 120, NBRMPC. At first the exhibitors and Motion Picture Patents Company

paid only part of the board's expenses. The People's Institute also subsidized the board, through the provision of office space and staff time. Later the board was supported through a fee, paid by producers, for every reel of film reviewed.

23. February 3, 1910, Certificate of Conducting Business, Box 170, NBRMPC.

24. Czitrom, "The Redemption of Leisure," analyses the community of interests between motion picture exhibitors and Progressive activists.

25. Data on the board's volunteer censors can be found in "Schedule of Classification, 1921," Box 164, NBRMPC.

26. June 18, 1909, "Report of Committee on Plan of Action," Box 120; January 5, 1914, John Collier to Orrin Cocks, Box 170; both NBRMPC.

27. This contradiction could cause disagreement among National Board members themselves as to whether or not they engaged in "censorship." See February 5, 1915, "Report of Meeting at Mechanics Institute," Box 170, NBRMPC.

28. On democratic ideology in the Progressive era, see Rodgers, *Contested Truths*, especially pp. 179–183; and "In Search of Progressivism." See also Ellis, *American Political Cultures*, pp. 22–23. On settlement workers' advocacy of cultural pluralism, see Carson, *Settlement Folk*. National Board members' embrace of democracy and cultural pluralism is noted in Fisher, "Film Censorship and Progressive Reform"; and Rosenbloom, "In Defense of the Moving Pictures."

29. N.d. n.a. memo, Box 170; March 30, 1916, William McGuire to Mrs. R. L. McCann; "The Policy and Standards of the National Board of Censorship of Motion Pictures," revised May 1914, Box 171; both NBRMPC. References to "public opinion" and the board's democratic nature are abundant in board records. For examples, see January 15, 1914, John Collier to Orrin Cocks, May 1915 speech by Orrin Cocks, March 29, 1916, press release, "The National Board's Opposition to 'Legal Censorship,'" Box 170; October 1, 1914, Bulletin, Box 171; 1912 Annual Report, Box 143; June 5, 1916, Spring Conference Transcript, Box 86; all NBRMPC. For later examples, see January 1921 "Activities of the National Board of Review of Motion Pictures," Box 143; March 1921 typescript beginning "Fair-minded people," Box 151; both NBRMPC.

30. "A City Ordinance for a Motion Picture Commission," Box 143; "Relation of the National Board of Censorship to Motion Picture Regulation," Box 172; March 22, 1916, memo by Mrs. Redding; and "Public Amusements Safe-Guarded for Moral Health," Box 170; "The Policy and Standards of the National Board of Censorship of Motion Pictures revised May 1914," Box 171; April 15, 1916, circular letter (re: Christman-Wheeler Bill), Box 64; [1919] typescript beginning "In answer to," and March 1921 typescript beginning "Fair-Minded People," Box 151; all NBRMPC.

31. May, *Screening Out the Past*; Sklar, *Movie-Made America*; Peiss, *Cheap Amusements*, especially pp. 154–158.

32. [1919] typescript beginning "In answer to . . . ," Box 151; 1 January 1921 "Activities of the National Board of Review of Motion Pictures," Box 143; both NBRMPC.

33. N.d. n.a. memo, Box 170; September 20, 1910, John Collier to Editor; and April 15, 1916, circular letter [re: Christman-Wheeler Bill], Box 64; March 1921 typescript begin-

ning "Fair-minded people," Box 151; all NBRMPC. Rarely, National Board members recognized that their own standards might differ from those of the people they sought to represent. See Orrin Cocks, "Motion Pictures and Their Regulation," *General Federation Magazine*, September 1918.

34. "The Standards of the National Board of Censorship of Motion Pictures" [n.d.], in file MFL n.c. 349, Billy Rose Performing Arts Collection, New York Public Library at Lincoln Center (hereafter cited as Lincoln Center).

35. Collier, "Cheap Amusements."

36. It should be noted that the "rationalization" of licensing laws would also increase the economic barriers to becoming a motion picture exhibitor, thus protecting the financial interests of exhibitors whose previously established theaters would likely be exempted from new regulations.

37. Proceedings, October 4, 1910, p. 66, October 18, 1910, p. 115, October 18, 1910, p. 532; *New York Times*, October 11, 1910, p. 7, October 27, 1910, p. 8, November 17, 1910, p. 16.

38. *New York Times*, July 7, 1912, p. 10.

39. May 23, 1913, William Gaynor to Thomas J. Bannon, Box GWJ80, Gaynor Collection, Mayors' Papers; Collier, "Film Shows and Lawmakers"; Staiger, *Bad Women*, pp. 110–112.

40. Fosdick, *A Report on the Condition of Moving Picture Shows*; December 24, 1912, William Gaynor to Frederick C. Howe, Box GWJ80, Gaynor Collection, Mayors' Papers.

41. Women's Municipal League *Bulletin*, June 1909, p. 4, September 1910, p. 7, November 1910, p. 17, and November 1911, pp. 21–27; April 2, 1911, General Committee Special Meeting Minutes, Box 120, and October 21, 1911, General Committee Minutes, Box 121, both NBRMPC; *New York Times*, November 7, 1911, p. 12, November 8, 1911, p. 8.

42. Paula Baker suggests that female Progressive reformers were more willing than their male compatriots to trust in state regulation. See "The Domestication of Politics"

43. *New York Times*, November 9, 1911, p. 8; November 8, 1911 [Dr. Slicer] to Editor, Box 47, NBRMPC; *New York Times*, November 16, 1911, p. 8.

44. *New York Times*, November 29, 1911, p. 5; Proceedings, December 5, 1911, p. 458, January 9, 1912, p. 83, April 2, 1912, p. 90, June 11, 1912, p. 744, December 17, 1912, p. 732, March 11, 1913, p. 1040, June 3, 1913, p. 593, June 17, 1913, p. 1031.

45. The proposed ordinance requiring censorship by the police commissioner can be found in Proceedings, December 5, 1911, p. 458; that creating a censorship in the Department of Licenses is in Proceedings, April 2, 1912, p. 90; and the ordinance that would require inspection by Department of Education employees can be found in Proceedings, June 11, 1912, p. 748.

46. Proceedings, January 9, 1912, p. 83; December 29, 1911, John Collier to *New York Times*, Box 47, NBRMPC.

47. Proceedings, January 6, 1913, p. 3. Gaynor discusses his veto in correspondence contained in Box GWJ80, Gaynor Collection, Mayors' Papers; see, for example, December 27, 1912, William Gaynor to H. N. Niles, December 24, 1912, William Gaynor to Alvin Summers, and March 20, 1913, William Gaynor to Horace H. Baker. Several years later the

U.S. Supreme Court rejected Gaynor's argument that motion pictures were entitled to free speech protection.

48. Proceedings, May 7, 1912, p. 426; *New York Times*, May 13, 1912, p. 9, June 15, 1912, p. 10, December 15, 1912, p. 10, December 17, 1912, p. 14.

49. *New York Times*, May 10, 1912, p. 11; Women's Municipal League *Bulletin*, November 1912, p. 18; Society for the Prevention of Crime Bulletin no. 23, Box 151, NBRMPC.

50. On the campaign to override the veto and to repass the legislation, see "Reasons for Passing," Box 151, NBRMPC; Proceedings, January 21, 1913, p. 236, June 13, 1913, p. 593, July 1, 1913, p. 97; see also Staiger, *Bad Women*, pp. 113–114.

51. See Collier, "Film Shows and Lawmakers." In fact, the panic was caused by a false cry of fire and exacerbated by inadequate emergency exits.

52. "Collier's Statement of Standards" and "The Policy and Standards of the National Board of Censorship of Motion Pictures," Box 171; n.a. 1913 speech, Box 170; both NBRMPC; *New York Times*, October 23, 1915, p. 10. In contrast to critics of the motion pictures, who usually asserted that children constituted the majority of the motion picture audience, board representatives estimated at various times that children under sixteen made up as little as 11 percent and not more than 25 percent of the film audience. Available statistics indicate that such lower estimates more nearly reflected reality, but the view that children dominated the film audience was widespread.

53. N.d. typescript (in "questionnaires, juvenile standards, AL-KY, 1915" file), Box 146, NBRMPC.

54. This strategy, which was institutionalized in the better films movement created by the board in 1916, became crucial to the battle against state censorship. It is discussed in detail in chapter 5, this volume.

55. N.a. 1913 speech, Box 170; National Board of Censorship of Motion Pictures *Annual Report*, 1912, Box 143; "Collier's Statement of Standards," n.d. Box 171; all NBRMPC.

56. Cassady, "Monopoly in Motion Picture Production"; Hampton, *History of the American Film Industry*.

57. "The Policy and Standards of the National Board of Censorship of Motion Pictures," Box 171, NBRMPC. Also related to sexual morality were sections on "women smoking and drinking" and "vulgarity."

58. "The Policy and Standards of the National Board of Censorship of Motion Pictures," Box 171, NBRMPC.

59. Ibid.

60. "Special Bulletin on Motion Picture Comedies," Box 170; February 4, 1915, Oscar O. Ballin to Wilton Barrett, and February 6, 1915, Barrett to Ballin, Box 105; August 15, 1918, Report on *Agonies of Agnes*, Box 155; all NBRMPC.

61. "The Policy and Standards of the National Board of Censorship of Motion Pictures," Box 171, NBRMPC. I saw no evidence of concern with lesbianism — the behavior encompassed within the terms "degeneracy" or "perversion" seemed to refer only to men.

62. June 17, 1914, Minutes, Box 121; February 10, 1917, Report, *Jerry's Winning Way*, and March 2, 1918, Report, *The Rogue*, Box 157; both NBRMPC.

63. "Special Bulletin to Motion Picture Producers" [re: "sexual perverts"], Box 171, NBRMPC.

64. For examples, see July 5, 1916, Report, *A Gambler's Gambol*, Box 156; November 13, 1916, Report, *Behind the Screen*, Box 155; July 7, 1919, Report, *Yankee Doodle in Berlin*, Box 158; all NBRMPC.

65. February 23, 1917, Secretary's Report on *Caught with the Goods*, and March 2, 1917, General Committee Minutes, Box 121, NBRMPC.

66. Chauncey, "From Sexual Inversion to Homosexuality."

67. *Caught with the Goods* (Triangle Film Corporation, 1917), Motion Picture Division, Library of Congress; February 23, 1917, Secretary's Report on *Caught with the Goods*, and March 2, 1917, General Committee Minutes, Box 121; February 28, 1917, W. D. McGuire Jr. to Members of the General Committee, Box 120; March 21, 1918, Correspondent's Report, Box 155; all NBRMPC.

68. "The Policy and Standards of the National Board of Censorship of Motion Pictures," Box 171, NBRMPC, p. 17; "Standards of the National Board of Censorship of Motion Pictures," n.d., Lincoln Center.

69. February 23, 1916, Report of the Committee on Standards, Box 120; "Special Bulletin to Motion Picture Producing Directors" [re: nudity], Box 171; both NBRMPC. I could find no extant print of *Purity*. The term *nudity,* as used by National Board of Censorship members as well as critics of motion pictures, could have a number of meanings. However, on the basis of their statements and reviews of the film, I believe that there was substantial, if not total, nudity in this film. See, for example, the July 7, 1916, review in *Variety*, which notes that the motion picture "gives an audience about eighteen good peeks at the girl [Audrey Munson], in just the same state of undress as she would be on entering her morning tub." See also a photo still in Brownlow, *Behind the Mask of Innocence*, p. 7.

70. The board's decision on the film came only after extensive negotiations with the filmmakers regarding the extent of nudity that would be permitted; close-ups of the unclothed Audrey Munson and "suggestive" leers on men's faces were prohibited by board censors. "Report on Review of *Purity*," July 13, 1916, Box 121; August 1916 William D. McGuire to Sir/Madam, July 18, 1916, Executive Secretary to Mutual Film Corp., August 2, 1916, Special Bulletin — *Purity*, Box 106; both NBRMPC.

71. *New York Times*, January 11, 1917, p. 13; January 31, 1917, n.a. typescript and April 21, 1917, press release, Box 140; "Standards and Policy of the National Board of Review of Motion Pictures, 1 October 1916" and "Special Bulletin to Motion Picture Producing Directors," Box 171; both NBRMPC.

72. November 29, 1918, General Committee minutes, Box 120, NBRMPC.

73. *The Girl Alaska* (World Pictures, 1919), Motion Picture Division, Library of Congress. National Board censors had ordered that the nude scenes of Mollie be shortened to a "flash," but, at least in this version, they are quite lengthy. See August 19, 1919, Report on *The Girl Alaska*, Box 156, NBRMPC.

74. I will use the term *white slavery* without enclosing it in quotations. It is important to recognize, however, that the term carried with it racial and sexual stereotypes, em-

phasizing the purity and innocence of the young native-born girls who were allegedly sold into prostitution by Jewish, Chinese, and other foreign-born procurers.

75. Roy Lubove, "The Progressives and the Prostitute," *Historian* 24 (1962): 303–330; Rosen, *The Lost Sisterhood*, p. 124. For general information about "white slavery," see also Connelly, *The Response to Prostitution in the Progressive Era*. For information on prostitution in New York City, see Gilfoyle, *City of Eros*. On the proliferation of public speech about venereal disease and prostitution, especially in plays, see Burnham, "The Progressive Era Revolution."

76. Sloan, *The Loud Silents*, pp. 80, 84; Brownlow, *Behind the Mask of Innocence*, pp. 70–85; Staiger, *Bad Women*, chapter 5.

77. *New York Times*, December 9, 1913, p. 8, December 20, 1913, p. 1, December 21, 1913, 2:5, December 22, 1913, p. 16, December 25, 1913, p. 16. For a description of the film, see Brownlow, *Behind the Mask of Innocence*, pp. 80–84.

78. The campaign against *The Inside of the White Slave Traffic* can be traced in *New York Times*, December 27, 1913, p. 18, December 28, 1913, 2:2, December 29, 1913, p. 7, January 17, 1914, p. 2, March 5, 1914, p. 2, March 6, 1914, p. 6. New York police and judges also objected to the movie because it contained a scene "which showed a policeman and a cadet [pimp] in a police court using their influence with the Magistrate to have the cadet discharged." See *New York Times*, December 22, 1913, p. 16. See *New York Times*, January 16, 1914, p. 9, on *A Victim of Sin*.

79. Transcript of October 27, 1913, review meeting for *A Traffic in Souls*, Box 121, NBRMPC. For a synopsis of the film, see Steven Higgins, "A Traffic in Souls," *Classic Images* 64 (July 1979): 24–27. For a comparison of the board's treatment of these two films, see Couvares, "The Good Censor."

80. December 18, 1913, Assistant Secretary to Samuel London, Box 105; "Remarks Made at General Committee Meeting," Box 121; both NBRMPC.

81. December 22, 1913, Assistant Secretary to Samuel London and February 17, 1914, Executive Secretary to Dr. Robinson, Box 105; December 22, 1913, Minutes, Box 121; both NBRMPC. Extant copies of this film demonstrate the results of censorship by the National Board: the motion picture has no continuity, its plot is almost impossible to follow, and the final shot of "Potters' Field" seems to have absolutely no connection with the rest of the story. The film can be viewed at the Motion Picture Division, Library of Congress, and at the Wisconsin Center for Film and Theater Research.

82. *New York Times*, December 17, 1913, p. 4 and February 4, 1914, p. 8. Simultaneously, New York City feminists were battling city officials' efforts to censor two Broadway productions about white slavery, *The Lure* and *The Fight*. See chapter 5, this volume.

83. February 7, 1914, Special Bulletin, Box 170, NBRMPC.

84. Carrow, *The Licensing Power in New York City*. On the expansion of administrative regulation at the federal level, see Skowronek, *Building a New American State*; for a contemporary analysis of this development at all levels of government, see Freund, *The Growth of American Administrative Law*.

85. September 9, 1917, W. D. McGuire to Stephen Bush, Box 32; March 8, 1910 [John Collier] to Dr. J. P. Warbasse, Box 64; both NBRMPC.

86. The operation of this system can be seen in June 22, 1914, July 9, 1914, July 21, 1914, August 12, 1914, and August 19, 1914, Executive Secretary to George Bell, August 24, 1914, George Bell to Orrin Cocks, Box 32, NBRMPC.

87. An exception to this "smooth functioning" was the exhibition of *The Birth of a Nation* in 1915, which prompted members of New York's African American community to protest to Bell and the National Board. Although the furor over this film was framed as a conflict over racial stereotypes, those scenes most objected to, including two scenes portraying attempted rapes of white women by black men, concerned sexual stereotypes about black men. It is likely, however, that the view of sexuality presented within the film, because it fit so well with racist sexual ideologies, did not arouse the ire of municipal officials or white moral reformers. For a discussion of the controversy over this film and the role of the National Board of Censorship, see Thomas R. Cripps, "The Reaction of the Negro to the Motion Picture *Birth of a Nation*," *Historian* 25 (May 1963): 334–362; Couvares, "The Good Censor."

88. "18 February 1916 Memo on discussion in the Office of Mr. Bell," Box 170, NBRMPC; see also Couvares and Peiss, "Sex, Censorship and the Movies," p. 15.

89. Bell's closer supervision of and cooperation with the National Board can be traced in March 22, 1916, William McGuire to Frederick H. Whitin, Box 21; "Report to the General Committee, June-October 1916," May 25, 1916, Notice and June 22, 1916, General Committee Minutes, Box 120; March 28, 1916, W. D. McGuire to Motion Picture Theatre Managers, and March 21, 1916, William McGuire to Mrs. Margaret Browning, Box 163; May 15, 1916, Deputy Commissioner [Kaufmann] to Universal Film Manufacturing Co., and May 18, 1916, Deputy Commissioner to Universal Film Manufacturing Co., Box 32; all NBRMPC. Some of this "help" was probably welcomed by the National Board because its own statistics suggested that 15–20 percent of films shown in New York City were not censored according to its instructions; members of the board claimed that this was due to the fact that films shown in New York were usually sample copies released in that city before being exhibited in the rest of the nation.

90. January 17, 1916, George Bell to "Licensees of places of public amusement in which motion pictures are exhibited," Box 32, NBRMPC.

91. New York City Department of Licenses *Annual Report*, 1916, p. 23; *New York Times*, September 1, 1916, p. 20. On birth control activism in New York during 1916, see D'Emilio and Freedman, *Intimate Matters*, pp. 232–233.

92. August 1916 Executive Secretary's Report, Box 2, Folder 7, John Saxton Sumner Papers, State Historical Society of Wisconsin Archives (hereafter cited as Sumner Papers); September 5, 1916, Membership Secretary to Ephraim Kaufmann, and September 6, 1916, George Bell to W. M. Covill, Box 32; September 20, 1916, William McGuire to James Bronson Reynolds, Box 105; both NBRMPC. The allegation was made by Yushe Botwin, whose participation in organized prostitution was in fact detailed in the film; National Board censors had approved the picture on the condition that those scenes showing him were excised. See *New York Times*, August 13, 1916, 7:1. Just two months earlier the Kings County (Brooklyn) district attorney declared his intention to "do away with pictures

that deal with sex problems," in response to the exhibition of *Where Are My Children?* See *New York Times*, June 18, 1916, 8:3.

93. September 20, 1916, Executive Secretary to James Bronson Reynolds, Box 105, NBRMPC; New York City Department of Licenses *Annual Report*, 1916, pp. 16–18; *New York Times*, September 12, 1916, p. 9, September 23, 1916, p. 4.

94. October 3, 1916, John Sumner to D.M. [sic] McGuire, Box 105, NBRMPC. Through 1916 Sumner collaborated with the license commissioner in this campaign, viewing films at the commissioner's request and proclaiming many of them "not proper for public exhibition." Sumner and his colleagues at the New York Society for the Suppression of Vice also helped to widen Bell's campaign; for example, they sent notice of Bell's prohibition of the film *Corruption* to other vice groups around the country "in order that they may be prepared to deal with this picture in their locality . . . and warning them that in spite of its objectionable character the film was favorably passed by the so-called National Board of Review." This cooperation continued with Bell's successor, John Gilchrist. See NYSSV Executive Secretary's Reports for July-November 1916, April 1917, September 1917, June 1918, and June 1919, Box 2, Sumner Papers. On *Where Are My Children?* see Sloan, *The Loud Silents*, chapter 4; Kuhn, *Cinema, Censorship and Sexuality*, chapter 3.

95. January 17, 1916, Bell to "the licensees of places of public amusement in which motion pictures are exhibited," Box 32; "The Hand That Rocks the Cradle" file, Box 104; both NBRMPC; New York City Department of Licenses *Annual Report*, 1916, pp. 18–19; *New York Times*, May 7, 1917, p. 18, May 10, 1917, p. 11, June 7, 1917, p. 10, and July 14, 1917, p. 7; *New York Dramatic News*, May 12, 1917, clipping in Box 32, NBRMPC. On the *Sex Lure* campaign see also November 20, 1916, W. M. Covill to W. D. McGuire and December 11, 1916, George Bell to Lester Scott, Box 32, NBRMPC.

96. October 3, 1917, Executive Secretary to George Bell and September 19, 1917, W. D. McGuire to Stephen Bush, Box 32, NBRMPC. On *The Finger of Justice*, see "The Finger of Justice" file, Box 104, NBRMPC, especially July 2, 1918, W. D. McGuire to James Orloff Spearing; see also *New York Times*, July 3, 1918, p. 11 and July 4, 1918, p. 13. The advertisement for *The Finger of Justice* can be found in the *New York Catholic News*, June 29, 1918, p. 17. The advertisement went on to put forth the question that, it was claimed, prostitutes put to Reverend Smith during the clean-up campaign: "If you take away our only means of subsistence, what are you going to do with us?" The presence of this ad in the *Catholic News* is startling, given that many Catholic activists protested against the film. Perhaps they learned of it from this ad.

97. October 3, 1916, John Sumner to D. M. [sic] McGuire, Box 105, NBRMPC.

98. Information on Ellen O'Grady is from her obituary in *New York Times*, December 29, 1949, p. 25.

99. June 29, 1918, Ellen O'Grady to John Gilchrist, Box 20, John Hylan Collection, Mayors' Papers.

100. See *New York Times*, June 29, 1919, 4:2; and *New York Catholic News*, July 19, 1919, p. 14, on *Fit to Win*; Report to General Committee, April 1919, Box 120, NBRMPC, on *The*

End of the Road; April 11, 1919, General Committee Minutes, May 5, 1919, F. Ernest Johnson to W. D. McGuire, May 7, 1919, Orrin Cocks to F. Ernest Johnson, and May 8, 1919, F. Ernest Johnson to Orrin Cocks, Box 25, NBRMPC, on *The Solitary Sin*. The campaign against venereal disease films can also be traced in *New York Times*, June 5, 1920, p. 26, and New York City Department of Licenses *Annual Report*, 1918–1920, pp. 6–12. See Brownlow, *Behind the Mask of Innocence*, pp. 61–63 and 66–70, and Brandt, *No Magic Bullet*, for discussion of *The End of the Road* and *Fit to Win*.

101. For the argument that concern about children masked class antagonism, see Sklar, *Movie-Made America*; for the revisionist position that talk about children should be considered on its own terms, see deCordova, "Ethnography and Exhibition"; and, on debates about obscenity generally, Nicola Beisel, *Imperiled Innocents*.

102. Their approval could be qualified, however, if they believed such propaganda films lacked "truthfulness."

103. Report of Investigations by Mrs. Benzecry, Box 20; January 18, 1917, Women's City Club Meeting transcript, Box 47; both NBRMPC.

104. January 18, 1917, Women's City Club Meeting transcript, Box 47, NBRMPC.

105. Proceedings, April 22, 1919, pp. 256–257; *New York Catholic News*, April 19, 1919, p. 4; *New York Times*, May 29, 1919, p. 9. Those testifying in favor of the legislation also included John Sumner, Canon William S. Chase, and a representative of the Catholic Federation. See May 1919 NYSSV Executive Secretary's Report, Box 2, Folder 7, Sumner Papers.

106. "The National Board's Opposition to 'Legal Censorship,'" Box 170; n.d., n.a. typescript ["in answer to . . ."], Box 151; both NBRMPC; Proceedings, June 10, 1919 pp. 489–491; *New York Times*, June 11, 1919, p. 16.

107. *New York Times*, May 12, 1916, p. 17, and May 21, 1916, p. 12. On lobbying by the National Board see "Manhattan, 1910–1919" file, Box 64, NBRMPC.

108. *New York Times*, January 19, 1918, 4:6, and April 16, 1919, p. 4; "Motion Pictures" pamphlet (report of committee to the New York State Conference of Mayors), Box 150, NBRMPC; article in *Moving Picture World* quoted in Feldman, *National Board of Censorship*, p. 168.

109. *New York Times*, February 17, 1921, p. 3; see Feldman, *National Board of Censorship*, pp. 168–191, for an extended discussion of Stevenson's attack on the board and the successful campaign for state censorship. On the Supreme Court ruling, see Jowett, "'A Capacity for Evil.'"

110. *New York Times*, February 8, 1921, p. 11, April 6, 1921, p. 19, May 1, 1921, 8:2, May 6, 1921, p. 18; Feldman, *National Board of Censorship*, p. 184; March and April 1921 NYSSV Executive Secretary's Reports, Box 2, Folder 7, Sumner Papers. Clayton is quoted in Feldman, *National Board of Censorship*, p. 19. Others who proclaimed that censorship would protect not only children were Stevenson and Mayor John Hylan, who were concerned with "impressionable foreigners," as was Mrs. O'Grady (all quoted in Feldman, *National Board of Censorship*, pp. 170, 171); and Mrs. Clarence Waterman, who protested films' disrespect to women. *New York Times*, April 6, 1921, p. 19.

111. *New York Times*, February 21, 1921, p. 17 and April 1, 1921, p. 17.

112. *Film Progress,* 5, 2 (February 1921) and 5, 5 (May 1921), Box 96; March 31, 1921, Executive Secretary to Samuel Calvert, Box 25; both NBRMPC.

113. *New York Times,* May 15, 1921, p. 1.

114. On New York state politics during this period, see Paula Baker, *The Moral Frameworks of Public Life: Gender, Politics, and the State in Rural New York, 1870–1930* (New York: Oxford University Press, 1991).

115. *New York Times,* April 28, 1921, p. 12.

116. See Feldman, *National Board of Censorship;* Jowett, *Film,* p. 135; Randall, *Censorship of the Movies,* p. 16.

2. "The Habitats of Sex-Crazed Perverts"

1. *In the Matter of Bonserk Theatre Corporation* (1942). This is an unpublished decision, but copies of Levy's opinion can be found in Box 3629, LaGuardia Collection, Mayors' Papers Collection, Municipal Archives, Department of Records and Information Services, City of New York (hereafter cited as Mayors' Papers), and in vol. 2350, American Civil Liberties Union Papers, Seeley G. Mudd Library, Princeton University (hereafter cited as ACLU).

2. Brief reports on burlesque inspections are to be found in the NYSSV Executive Secretary Reports, including the following months: September 1916, December 1920, June-July 1924, January, March 1926, March 1928, September 1928, June, October 1929, January-May, November, December 1930, January-July, December 1931, January-December 1932, January-March, September-November 1933, July 1934, January-November 1936, March-April, August-November 1937, August 1938, March, August, and December 1939, July 1940, February, June, and November 1941, January, April 1942. These are located in Boxes 2 and 3, John Saxton Sumner Papers, State Historical Society of Wisconsin Archives (hereafter cited as Sumner Papers). See also June 28 entry, Diary 1915, Box 1, Folder 3, Sumner Papers.

3. Because traditional burlesque no longer exists, it is difficult for the historian to reconstruct what burlesque looked like and how performers and audience experienced it in the 1930s. Still, some sources exist that permit an approximation of the performances that took place on burlesque stages in New York City. These sources include descriptions of burlesque to be found in theater reviews, in the testimony of burlesque foes and friends at license renewal hearings, and in affidavits filed in legal actions, as well as in the reminiscences of performers. Burlesque scripts, located in the Chuck Callahan Collection of the Walter Hampden-Edwin Booth Theatre Collection at the Players' Club in New York City (hereafter cited as Chuck Callahan Collection), have also proved useful in reconstructing comic bits.

4. On the "vulnerable viewer," see Francis G. Couvares, "Introduction" in Couvares, *Movie Censorship and American Culture,* pp. 1–15.

5. Simmons, "Modern Sexuality and the Myth of Victorian Repression"; Clyde Griffen, "Reconstructing Masculinity from the Evangelical Revival to the Waning of Progressivism: A Speculative Synthesis," in Carnes and Griffen, *Meanings for Manhood,* pp.

183–204; Gail Bederman, *Manliness and Civilization: A Cultural History of Gender and Race in the United States, 1880–1917* (Chicago: University of Chicago Press, 1995).

6. My analysis differs from that of other historians by exploring the Great Depression not as cause of this antiburlesque campaign but as context for it. For the argument that this campaign was essentially a turf war between burlesque entrepreneurs and Times Square commercial interests, see Allen, *Horrible Prettiness*; Laurence Senelick, "Private Parts in Public Places," in Taylor, *Inventing Times Square*, pp. 329–353.

7. Hanley, "Popular Culture and Crisis."

8. On burlesque's early years, see Allen, *Horrible Prettiness*; Buckley, "The Culture of 'Leg-Work.'" On twentieth-century burlesque see Zeidman, *The American Burlesque Show*; Corio, *This Was Burlesque*; Minsky and Machlin, *Minsky's Burlesque*; Sobel, *A Pictorial History of Burlesque*.

9. Allen, *Horrible Prettiness*, especially p. 21; see also Buckley, "The Culture of 'Leg-Work.'"

10. Zeidman, *The American Burlesque Show*, chapter 4.

11. Allen, *Horrible Prettiness*, pp. 244–249. Of course, the prices at the Broadway revues were quite a bit higher than those for burlesque shows. This suggests that the burlesque audience at this time included middle-class patrons.

12. Minsky and Machlin, *Minsky's Burlesque*, p. 33; Allen, *Horrible Prettiness*, pp. 244–245.

13. Minsky and Machlin, *Minsky's Burlesque*, p. 60.

14. Ibid., pp. 33–34; Corio, *This Was Burlesque*, p. 72.

15. The extent to which strippers removed their clothing varied by theaters, performers, and performances. Some theaters such as the New Gotham Theatre on 125th Street had a reputation for offering very "raw" shows, while the Republic Theatre on 42nd Street was reported to have a relatively "clean" show with little nudity. Furthermore, each theater had both a "whore show" (its regular show) and a "Boston" or "parlor" show, offered when police or other city officials were suspected of being in attendance. On the New Gotham, see Minsky and Machlin, *Minsky's Burlesque*, p. 184; on the Republic's show, see *Zit's Entertainment Weekly*, December 12, 1931.

16. My discussion of the forms and content of the striptease is derived from a variety of sources, including testimony to be found in the Burlesque Hearing Transcript (especially testimony of John S. Sumner, James Danahy, Nathaniel K. Miller, Sidney Irving Rankin, Charles M. Feldheim, and Max Rudnick), Box 242, James J. Walker Collection, Mayors' Papers (hereafter cited as Burlesque Hearing Transcript). See also reviews of burlesque in *Zit's Entertainment Weekly*, for example, April 5, 1930, November 14, 1931, November 21, 1931, and December 12, 1931. For a description of strippers' costumes as well as the claim of stripping only to panties or leotard, see Corio, *This Was Burlesque*, p. 78. For general discussions of the striptease, see also Corio, *This Was Burlesque*; Zeidman, *The American Burlesque Show*; Minsky and Machlin, *Minsky's Burlesque*, and Sobel, *A Pictorial History of Burlesque*.

17. Burlesque Hearing Transcript, Testimony of Max Rudnick, p. 1061.

18. Corio, *This Was Burlesque*, p. 78.

19. Minsky and Machlin, *Minsky's Burlesque*, p. 184.

20. Corio, *This Was Burlesque*, p. 90.

21. Burlesque Hearing Transcript, testimony of John S. Landes, p. 692. Indeed, as Karen Booth suggests, the uncertainty of not knowing whether to trust the evidence of one's own eyes may have contributed to the titillation of watching a striptease. Personal communication to author.

22. Minsky and Machlin, *Minsky's Burlesque*, p. 184.

23. Burlesque Hearing Transcript, testimony of George Moeller, pp. 191–192.

24. "The Beautiful Fairy Scene," Chuck Callahan Collection.

25. On the use of the term *fairy* in New York City, see Chauncey, *Gay New York*.

26. Dressler, "Burlesque as a Cultural Phenomenon," p. 77.

27. "The Bull Fight," Chuck Callahan Collection.

28. On West, see Hamilton, *When I'm Bad I'm Better*. She suggests, in fact, that "Mae West brought burlesque humor to Broadway," p. 53. On nightclubs, see Erenberg, *Steppin' Out*.

29. In a sense, burlesque constituted an "alternative" culture. On this concept, see Rosenzweig, *Eight Hours for What We Will*, p. 64 and passim. However, the extent to which burlesque also shared much with the dominant culture, including pervasive misogyny and racial and ethnic prejudice, should not be minimized. A more detailed discussion of the misogyny of burlesque humor can be found in Dolan, "'What, No Beans?'"

30. Freedman, "'Uncontrolled Desires,'" p. 201.

31. In *Horrible Prettiness* Allen discusses burlesque's lack of "monovocality" at p. 28 and passim.

32. Robert Allen has observed that economic crises had similar effects on the burlesque industry in the nineteenth century as well. See Allen, *Horrible Prettiness*, p. 249.

33. Poggi, *Theater in America*; Glenn Loney, *Twentieth-Century Theatre*, vol. 1 (New York: Facts on File, 1983), pp. 180, 185; Samuel L. Leiter, *The Encyclopedia of the New York Stage, 1930–1940* (Westport, Conn.: Greenwood, 1989), p. xxvi. See also the essays in Taylor, *Inventing Times Square*, especially Eric Lampard, "Introductory Essay," pp. 16–35; David C. Hammack, "Developing for Commercial Culture," pp. 36–50; and Brooks McNamara, "The Entertainment District at the End of the 1930s," pp. 178–190.

34. Zeidman, *The American Burlesque Show*, p. 171.

35. Ibid., p. 217.

36. Minsky and Machlin, *Minsky's Burlesque*, p. 127; Zeidman, *The American Burlesque Show*, p. 217.

37. Zeidman, *The American Burlesque Show*, p. 191.

38. Ibid., pp. 169, 171.

39. See Allen, *Horrible Prettiness*, especially pp. 127–132, and Buckley, "The Culture of 'Leg-Work,'" p. 122.

40. Information about raids on burlesque theaters can be found in *New York Times*, March 4, 1915, p. 9, November 3, 1915, p. 15, December 7, 1924, p. 23, March 12, 1926, p. 21, May 27, 1926, p. 2, September 21, 1926, p. 15, February 25, 1927, p. 24, March 30, 1927, p. 13,

June 30, 1927, p. 32, January 15, 1928, p. 3. For the disposition of some of these cases, see *New York Times,* May 11, 1926, p. 12, March 5, 1927, p. 12, May 5, 1927, p. 10, May 28, 1927, p. 15.

41. For a contemporary description of Times Square, see Burlesque Hearing Transcript, p. 501. The Depression-era decline in Times Square property values must have seemed all the more frightening because the rate of appreciation of district property values had previously been among the highest in the city. See Betsy Blackmar, "Uptown Real Estate and the Creation of Times Square" in Taylor, *Inventing Times Square,* pp. 51–65.

42. February and April 1932 NYSSV Executive Secretary Reports, Box 3, Folder 1, Sumner Papers; *New York Times,* March 25, 1932, p. 22, and April 7, 1932, p. 29. The POA did manage to have a burlesque theater barker convicted for maintaining a public nuisance; see *New York Times,* April 21, 1932, p. 23, and April 22, 1932, p. 17. The previous year a raid on the Republic Theatre, instigated by the NYSSV, had also resulted in dismissed charges against six performers, including Gypsy Rose Lee, and two other theater employees. See April and May 1931 NYSSV Executive Secretary Reports, Box 3, Folder 1, Sumner Papers.

43. *A. H. Woods Theatre Co. v Gilchrist,* 193 N.Y.S. 259, aff'd. 135 N.E. 941. This decision applied only to theatrical licenses. License commissioners had the power to revoke motion picture theater licenses, which were governed by a different section of the city Code of Ordinances.

44. These developments will be discussed at greater length in chapter 3, this volume.

45. *New York Telegram,* May 18, 1932, clipping in vol. 604, ACLU; see also Burlesque Hearing Transcript, p. 412.

46. Allen, *Horrible Prettiness.*

47. Ibid., p. 192.

48. On the composition of the burlesque audience, see Dressler, "Burlesque as a Cultural Phenomenon," especially chapter 5; Allen, *Horrible Prettiness,* p. 192; Minsky and Machlin, *Minsky's Burlesque,* pp. 98–99. This strategy for attracting a new audience paralleled that pursued by nightclub owners during the same period, as described by Erenberg, "From New York to Middletown." Nightclub owners, unlike burlesque entrepreneurs, successfully integrated their businesses "into the reputable public culture of urban life" (p. 766).

49. Reports of women in the audience, often coexisting with characterizations of burlesque as a "man's world," can be found in Dressler, "Burlesque as a Cultural Phenomenon," especially chapter 5. Ann Corio also provides contradictory accounts of women in the audience; see *This Was Burlesque,* pp. 158–159.

50. "The Business of Burlesque," *Fortune* (February 1935), quoted in Dressler, "Burlesque as a Cultural Phenomenon," p. 160. Dressler observes that while its humor, which "glorif[ied] the laborer," made the burlesque house "a world for the proletariat," by the mid-1930s "the patron [was] no longer exclusively of that group" (p. 80).

51. Ibid., chapter 5. Dressler's estimates are calculated from a nonrandom sample, and thus must be used advisedly. In addition, his study, completed in 1939, may reflect changes in the burlesque industry that occurred as a result of the regulatory campaigns

described here. Nonetheless, his dissertation remains the best source on the burlesque audience of the 1930s.

52. Freedman, "Uncontrolled Desires," p. 203.

53. On the "marginal man," see Susman, *Culture as History*, pp. 170–171.

54. Burlesque Hearing Transcript, testimony of Edmund Waterman, pp. 176, 179; Donald G. Price, p. 547; Thomas O. Young, p. 553; Edward R. Forrest, p. 1248; Louis A. Kissling, pp. 1446–1448; Alfred Taub, p. 248.

55. Burlesque Hearing Transcript, testimony of Henry Moskowitz, p. 53; Edmund Waterman, p. 180; Statement of Commissioner Geraghty, p. 412; testimony of Louis Fehr, pp. 270–272.

56. Burlesque Hearing Transcript, Testimony of Father Burke, p. 25; Patrolman Francis J. Houghton, pp. 394–403; Frank J. Donovan, p. 448; Edward R. Forrest, pp. 1226–1229, 1248–1260, 1327; Donald G. Price, p. 547.

57. Burlesque Hearing Transcript, testimony of William M. McCarthy, p. 234.

58. Burlesque Hearing Transcript, testimony of Louis A. Kissling, p. 1428.

59. Burlesque Hearing Transcript, testimony of Frederick J. Stewart, p. 71; Oscar D. Dike, p. 91; Alfred Taub, pp. 247–248.

60. Burlesque Hearing Transcript, testimony of Edmund Waterman, pp. 176–184; William McCarthy, pp. 228–231; Alfred Taub, p. 248; James Danahy, p. 153; J. W. MacDowell, p. 241; Donald G. Price, p. 547.

61. Burlesque Hearing Transcript, Ferdinand Pecora's opening statement, p. 12; testimony of Borden R. Putnam, pp. 147–148; Oscar D. Dike, p. 88; Alfred Taub, p. 248. Sometimes burlesque opponents resorted to less than honest means to demonstrate women's distaste for burlesque. For example, License Commissioner Geraghty received a telegram, allegedly from prominent actress Jane Cowl, which stated that she had refused to walk into the Eltinge Theatre "due to deplorable and shocking conditions" in the front of the theater. Cowl denounced the telegram as a hoax, and several days later it was learned that the message had been sent by someone in the Selwyn theater office — one of the legitimate theater interests that the burlesque entrepreneurs claimed were conspiring to eliminate them as competition. Clearly, the telegram's author believed that it would suggest that respectable women were offended by the posters before the theaters and, perhaps, even afraid of the men who stopped to look at them. See *New York Times*, May 6, 1932, p. 19, May 7, 1932, p. 11, May 10, 1932, p. 25; Burlesque Hearing Transcript, pp. 1022–1024, 1089–1090, 1191.

62. The National Council on Freedom from Censorship was founded in 1931 by the American Civil Liberties Union. It will be discussed at greater length in chapter 5, this volume.

63. Burlesque Hearing Transcript, testimony of Annie Elms, pp. 281–288. See also testimony of Beatrice Shiller, pp. 656–659, and Winifred Alsten, pp. 901–909. Such testimony was intended to offset burlesque critics' suggestion that, because "the shows given are not of a character to appeal especially to women" they must be immoral. See, for example, testimony of Elias Sugarman, pp. 934–935.

64. See Burlesque Hearing Transcript, testimony of Louis W. Fehr, pp. 278–281;

Nathaniel K. Miller, pp. 575–576; Herbert B. Benjamin, p. 655; Victoria Krikorian, pp. 661–662; Louise Labrutto, p. 665; John S. Landes, p. 689; Sophie Kelly, pp. 721–723; Edwin Rowland, p. 791; Harold Lawrence Young, p. 822; Benjamin Kaufman, p. 900; Elias Sugarman, pp. 933–934; Carl Schlanger, pp. 937–938; Albert Strauss, pp. 941–942; David Berk, p. 953; Milton Jones, p. 1014; Max Rudnick, p. 1049; Joseph G. Abramson, p. 1094; Samuel Lipman, p. 1101; Charles Hertzig, pp. 1123–1127. Opponents of burlesque also admitted, under cross-examination, that women attended the shows. See testimony of Henry Moskowitz, p. 51; Frank J. Donovan, p. 469; and Thomas Kavanaugh, pp. 485–489.

65. Burlesque Hearing Transcript, testimony of Ira Wilens, p. 597 and Cleon Throckmorton, p. 625. Evidence about the "regularity" of the audience can also be found in the testimony of Frank J. Donovan, p. 469; Nathaniel K. Miller, pp. 567–568; Irving S. Whiting, p. 614; Leonard Stewart Smith, p. 620; Herbert B. Benjamin, pp. 655–656; James McKernan, pp. 684–685; Harold Lawrence Young, p. 819; Charles Feldheim, p. 861; Albert Woods, p. 886; Heyworth Campbell, p. 913; Elias Sugarman, pp. 928–929; Albert Strauss, p. 942; David Berk, p. 952; Joseph G. Abramson, p. 1095.

66. Simultaneously attorneys for the burlesque theaters sought to use assumptions that burlesque was "a poor man's theater" to their advantage. They argued that burlesque was no different than the Broadway revues, and they intimated that the attack on it was a reflection of reformers' distaste for working-class recreation rather than any real difference in the performances. See Burlesque Hearing Transcript, testimony of Louis W. Fehr, pp. 266–271; Cleon Throckmorton, p. 635; Leonard Stewart Smith, pp. 619–622; Heyworth Campbell, p. 912.

67. Burlesque Hearing Transcript, testimony of Frank J. Donovan, p. 469; George M. Stoll, pp. 512–523; Nathaniel K. Miller, pp. 564–567; Beatrice Shiller, p. 658; Victoria Krikorian, p. 662; Louise Labrutto, p. 665; Sophie Kelly, pp. 719–721; Joseph G. Abramson, p. 1093.

68. Burlesque Hearing Transcript, testimony of David Berk, pp. 961–964; Cleon Throckmorton, pp. 627–642; Nathaniel K. Miller, pp. 576–577, 580–581; Harold Lawrence Young, pp. 828, 838; Charles M. Feldheim, p. 875; Heyworth Campbell, pp. 920–921.

69. Burlesque Hearing Transcript, testimony of Cleon Throckmorton, p. 642; William M. McCarthy, p. 235; Patrolman Hugo Harris, p. 315; Ira Wilens, pp. 602–603; James Danahy, pp. 168–174.

70. For a summary of the debates about mass culture, see Denning, "The End of Mass Culture," and the responses by Janice Radway, Luisa Passerini, and William R. Taylor, pp. 19–31. On *Our Movie-Made Children* and the Payne Fund Studies that it popularized see Sklar, *Movie-Made America*, pp. 134–140.

71. On the theme of the average man and the average American during the Depression, see Susman, *Culture as History*, especially "Culture and Containment," pp. 184–210, and "The People's Fair: Cultural Contradictions of a Consumer Society," pp. 211–229.

72. *New York Catholic News*, September 3, 1932, p. 4; *New York Herald-Tribune*, September 20, 1932, clipping in vol. 604, ACLU; *New York Times*, September 18, 1932, p. 1, and September 20, 1932, p. 1. On the investigation of the Walker administration, see Kessner, *Fiorello H. LaGuardia*. McKee, who was the president of the Board of Aldermen, had

long favored state action against the theater. In 1926, as acting mayor, he ordered raids on three Broadway plays: *The Captive, The Virgin Man*, and *Sex*.

73. During the investigations of the Walker administration, the License Department was criticized as one of the most corrupt municipal divisions. It may be that the renewal of burlesque licenses resulted from burlesque producers' "good connection with the police and politicians." See Minsky and Machlin, *Minsky's Burlesque*, p. 92.

74. *New York Times*, May 16, 1933, p. 19; *New York Herald-Tribune*, May 16, 1933, clipping in scrapbook MWEZ-x-n.c.7393, Billy Rose Theatre Collection, Lincoln Center Library for the Performing Arts; *New York World-Telegram*, May 17, 1933, clipping in vol. 514, ACLU; *New York Catholic News*, May 20, 1933 p. 4; *Zit's Entertainment Weekly*, May 27, 1933, p. 11.

75. October 21, 1933, Sidney S. Levine to American Civil Liberties Union, vol. 603b, ACLU; *New York Times*, October 12, 1933, p. 30, October 15, 1933, p. 25, October 17, 1933, p. 23, November 29, 1933, p. 22; *New York Catholic News*, October 21, 1933, p. 3; *Billboard*, November 4, 1933, clipping in vol. 591, ACLU; *Zit's Entertainment Weekly*, May 19, 1934, p. 7.

76. *New York Times*, January 21, 1934, p. 1, March 28, 1934, p. 26; *Zit's Entertainment Weekly*, May 19, 1934, p. 7; Zeidman, *The American Burlesque Show*, pp. 143, 164–166.

77. These regulations were formulated through negotiations with clergy and burlesque producers. The negotiations can be traced in September 12, 1934, John Q. Tilson to LaGuardia, September 13, 1934, J. A. McCaffrey to Paul Moss, September 17, 1934, Moss to McCaffrey, September 22, 1934, Moss to LaGuardia, November 10, 1934, LBD to Mayor, November 15, 1934, John Q. Tilson to LaGuardia, and November 20, 1934, Moss to LaGuardia, Box 3126, LaGuardia Collection, Mayors' Papers. The Department of Licenses Regulation Concerning Theatres and Concerts can be found in vol. 1077, ACLU, and is also partially reprinted in Minsky and Machlin, *Minsky's Burlesque*, p. 139. On LaGuardia, see Kessner, *Fiorello H. LaGuardia*.

78. *In re Rudhlan Amusement Corporation*, 262 N.Y.S. 269, 281.

79. In 1931 the New York City Code of Ordinances had been amended to provide the license commissioner with the power to *revoke*, after an administrative hearing, the license of any "place of public amusement or sport, outdoor or indoor, not heretofore specified." On the basis of this amendment the city's license commissioners rejected the distinction between renewal and revocation and claimed the right to revoke theater licenses for violation of administrative rules after a hearing.

80. *Holly Holding Corporation v. Moss*, 284 N.Y.S. 216, aff'd. 1 N.E.2· 359. The New York Court of Appeals ruled that the 1931 amendment did not apply to theater licenses.

81. Successful prosecution was not, however, impossible. For example, early in 1931, on complaint of the New York Society for the Suppression of Vice, eight performers at the Gotham Theatre were convicted on obscenity charges in the Court of Special Sessions. See Executive Secretary Reports, January-February 1931, Box 3, Folder 1, Sumner Papers.

82. *New York Times*, April 7, 1935, p. 17; *New York Catholic News*, April 13, 1935, p. 4.

83. It may have been as well that cognizance of legal limitations on municipal authority produced uncertainty within government circles, resulting in a situation in

which licensing officials both sought to establish their power to revoke theater licenses and hesitated to exercise their power to refuse to renew them. In American law the powers of a city were limited to those that had been granted "in specific and unambiguous statutory language" by the state legislature. This understanding of the limited nature of municipal authority was known as Dillon's Rule. Both licensing authority and criminal prosecution were founded upon the police power, and, while municipalities generally were granted extensive police powers to protect public welfare, legal scholars held that the protection of morals provided "less urgent" grounds for the exercise of the police power than did the protection of public safety and order. Although in 1932 a New York Supreme Court justice had affirmed licensing authorities' power to refuse to renew theater licenses, the fact that the state legislature had never *explicitly* granted that right may have made city officials reluctant to assert it, especially when their grounds for doing so were based upon the protection of public morals rather than public safety. At the same time, administrative officials such as the commissioner of licenses were granted wide discretionary powers, and courts were loathe to interfere with their decisions unless they were "grossly arbitrary." All of this made for a very unsettled regulatory context. See Hendrik Hartog, *Public Property and Private Power: The Corporation of the City of New York in American Law, 1730–1870* (Chapel Hill: University of North Carolina Press, 1983), p. 223; Frug, "The City as a Legal Concept"; Freund, *The Police Power*; Cuthbert W. Pound, "Constitutional Aspects of Administrative Law" in Freund, *The Growth of American Administrative Law*, pp. 100–135.

84. *New York Times*, June 21, 1943, p. 1; August 19, 1940, "Address by Mayor LaGuardia to Meeting of Publishers and News Distributors," February 27, 1941, Lois Holz to Mayor LaGuardia, and [1940] *Catholic Mirror* clipping, all in Box 3569, LaGuardia Collection, Mayors' Papers.

85. Senelick, "Private Parts in Public Places," p. 337; 1 March 1945 Transcript, League of New York Theatres meeting, vol. 2638, ACLU.

86. September 22, 1934, Paul Moss to LaGuardia, Box 3126, LaGuardia Collection, Mayors' Papers. On Moss's career, see John Simons, ed., *Who's Who in American Jewry*, vol. 3 (New York: National News Association, 1938), p. 762, and his obituary in the *New York Times*, February 26, 1950, p. 76. On ethnic politics during LaGuardia's tenure as mayor, see Bayor, *Neighbors in Conflict*; McNickle, *To Be Mayor of New York*. The estimate of Catholic population is from Rosenwaike, *Population History of New York City*.

87. May 15, 1936, Paul Moss to LaGuardia, Box 3167, LaGuardia Collection, Mayors' Papers.

88. December 9, 1936, Paul Moss to Mayor, Box 3167; April 21, 1937, Thomas Scanlon to Mayor LaGuardia, and follow-up letter of the same day, Box 3399; both LaGuardia Collection, Mayors' Papers; *New York Times*, April 9, 1937, p. 23, and April 16, 1937, p. 27. Morton Minsky recalls that the act incurring the wrath of the New York Society for the Suppression of Vice, which filed the complaint against the theater, "consisted of a stripper on a trapeze taking her clothes off gradually and dropping each item to the stage." Minsky and Machlin, *Minsky's Burlesque*, p. 256.

89. *New York Times*, April 16, 1937, p. 27, April 29, 1937, p. 1, April 30, 1937, p. 1; *New York*

Catholic News, April 24, 1937, p. 4; *New York Journal*, April 29, 1937, clipping in vol. 962, ACLU. Contrary to Laurence Senelick's assertion in "Private Parts in Public Places," I have found no evidence to indicate that the 42nd Street Property Owners' Association was active in the 1937 drive. Indeed, in 1936 an article in the POA's official publication exhibited a markedly cordial attitude toward the Times Square burlesque theaters. Other commercial organizations submitted letters opposing the renewal of the licenses, but it appears that their support of the antiburlesque campaign was merely nominal. See Forty Second Street Property Owners and Merchants Association "Activities," Spring 1936, New York Public Library Annex; "List of Letters sent to Corp. Counsel to be Used in Action Against Burlesque Theatres," Box 3570, LaGuardia Collection, Mayors' Papers.

90. Freedman, "Uncontrolled Desires." In referring to a "panic" I intend neither to call into question the existence of sex crimes nor to denigrate concern about them. What I am interested in is the way in which increased attention to sex crimes, even in the absence of substantial evidence about an increase in such crimes, was exploited to facilitate state control over sex performance in the theater.

91. On the murder of Nancy Titterton, see *New York Times*, including April 11, 1936, p. 1, and April 22, 1936, p. 1. Jean Morvan, four years old, was diagnosed as having died from peritonitis that resulted from a criminal assault. A relative confessed to the rape and was subsequently committed to the Mattewan State Hospital for the Criminally Insane. See *New York Times*, March 3, 1937, p. 48, March 4, 1937, p. 48, April 30, 1937, p. 45, June 25, 1937, p. 46. Nine-year-old Einer Sporrer was beaten with a hammer and allegedly raped after her death. Salvatore Ossido, who was free on bail on charges of sexually assaulting a twelve-year-old girl, was convicted of the murder. See *New York Times*, March 21, 1937, p. 24, and April 24, 1937, p. 36.

92. It seems likely, but I have found no direct evidence, that the New Gotham conviction was itself made possible by the sex crime panic.

93. Freedman, "Uncontrolled Desires," p. 203.

94. 1936 New York Society for the Suppression of Vice *Annual Report*, p. 5.

95. Frank J. Williams to Editor, *New York Times*, April 25, 1936; quoted in *New York Catholic News*, May 16, 1936, p. 47.

96. *New York Times*, April 16, 1937, p. 27; *New York Catholic News*, April 24, 1937, p. 4; *New York American*, April 26, 1937, clipping in vol. 962, ACLU.

97. *New York Times*, April 29, 1937, p. 1.

98. *New York Times*, April 30, 1937, p. 1, and May 1, 1937, p. 1.

99. May 4, 1937, John Warren Hill to Fiorello H. LaGuardia, Box 3185, LaGuardia Collection, Mayors' Papers.

100. *New York Journal*, April 29, 1937, clipping in vol. 962, ACLU.

101. May 3, 1937, Horace C. Smith to "Hon. F. H. LaGuarder," Box 3190; see also May 3, 1937, Albina L. D'Attoro [D'Attore?] to Mayor LaGuardia, Box 3399; both LaGuardia Collection, Mayors' Papers. Note the similarity between Mr. Smith's description of the effect of burlesque on his sons and nineteenth-century descriptions of the results of masturbation.

102. *New York Times*, May 1, 1937, p. 1.

103. *New York Journal*, April 29, 1937, clipping in vol. 962, ACLU; *New York Times*, April 30, 1937, p. 1.

104. The quote is from April 30, 1937, Bobbie Duke to LaGuardia, Box 3190, LaGuardia Collection, Mayors' Papers. Correspondence in favor of license renewal can be found here.

105. Linking burlesque and sex crimes gave municipal authorities a stronger rationale for their administrative actions. Legal scholar Ernst Freund has noted that "the interference of the state [in regulating morality] is made more plausible and acceptable by taking the view that acts and conditions which primarily violate only morality, are apt, in their more remote and indirect consequences, to produce physical disorder and crime, and thus to endanger the public safety" (Freund, *Police Power*, sec. 187). Here the consequences were alleged to be very direct.

106. *New York Times*, May 6, 1937, p. 26, May 8, 1937, p. 21, May 11, 1937, p. 30, May 12, 1937, p. 48, May 15, 1937, p. 23, May 17, 1937, p. 22, May 20, 1937, p. 1.

107. *New York Journal*, April 30, 1937, clipping in vol. 962, ACLU; *New York Catholic News*, May 1, 1937; *New York Times*, May 4, 1937, p. 28.

108. June 8, 1937, Archibald Palmer to Fiorello LaGuardia, June 12, 1937, Howard S. Cullman to LaGuardia, June 14, 1937, telegrams from Daniel Frohman and Frank Gilmore to LaGuardia, June 30, 1937, Charles H. Tuttle to Lester Stone, Box 3399, LaGuardia Collection, Mayors' Papers; *New York Times*, June 29, 1937, p. 18.

109. Press Release, Box 3399, LaGuardia Collection, Mayors' Papers; *New York Times*, July 11, 1937, p. 1.

110. July 11, 1937, Press Release, Box 3399, LaGuardia Collection, Mayors' Papers.

111. Constitution and By-Laws of the Variety Revue Theatre Association of New York, and July 11, 1937, Press Release, Box 3399, LaGuardia Collection, Mayors' Papers. The first Board of Governors included two Catholic, two Protestant, and two Jewish men. Besides the Knights of Columbus officer, one of these men was the brother of Reverend Joseph McCaffrey, the most vocal opponent of burlesque theaters; others were affiliated with Brooklyn Big Brothers, the Federation of Jewish Charities, and the YMCA.

112. *New York Times*, July 13, 1937, p. 22.

113. These agreements can be found in Box 3189, LaGuardia Collection, Mayors' Papers.

114. September 7, 1935, Paul Moss to LaGuardia, LaGuardia Collection, Mayors' Papers.

115. May 27, 1937, and June 19, 1937, Thomas J. Phillips to Clendenin J. Ryan, Jr., June 16, 1937, Ralph Whitehead to Tom Phillips, July 2, 1937, Ralph Whitehead to Lester Stone, July 3, 1937, Ralph Whitehead to LaGuardia, July 13, 1937, Ralph Whitehead to LaGuardia, Box 3399, LaGuardia Collection, Mayors' Papers.

116. Agreement between Employer and the American Federation of Actors, Box 3399, LaGuardia Collection, Mayors' Papers; *New York Times*, December 1, 1937, p. 26, December 28, 1937, p. 7, June 23, 1938, p. 27, December 14, 1938, p. 33. Later the name of the union was changed to Brotherhood of Artists and Actors. A brief account of the controversy

can be found in January 1954 "B.A.A. Bits of News," located in Box MA-2, Actors Equity Association Collection, Robert F. Wagner Labor Archives, New York University.

117. *New York Times*, July 12, 1937, p. 19, July 13, 1937, p. 22, August 26, 1937, p. 23.

118. See, for example, Allen, *Horrible Prettiness*; Corio, *This Was Burlesque*; Minsky and Machlin, *Minsky's Burlesque*. Alone among chroniclers of burlesque, Zeidman, *The American Burlesque Show*, notes the continuation of burlesque in some form until 1942.

119. *New York Times*, July 21, 1937, p. 19, November 26, 1937, p. 26; Zeidman, *The American Burlesque Show*, pp. 234–235; Minsky and Machlin, *Minsky's Burlesque*, p. 281. The financial difficulties of the theaters are discussed in *New York Times*, June 27, 1940, p. 25. On the content of variety revue shows, see Executive Secretary Reports, August 1938, March 1939, August 1939, December 1939, February 1941, April 1942, Box 3, Folders 2 and 3, Sumner Papers.

120. *New York Times*, December 11, 1937, p. 22, February 4, 1939, p. 13; *New York World-Telegram*, February 3, 1939, clipping in vol. 2062, ACLU; December 26, 1940, Harry L. Bowlby to Paul Moss, December 27, 1940, and March 26, 1941, Bowlby to Thomas Dewey, April 10, 1941, Bowlby to Paul E. Lockwood, all in Box 307, District Attorneys Collection, Municipal Archives, Department of Records and Information Services, City of New York.

121. *New York Times*, December 2, 1941, p. 17, February 1, 1942, p. 45, February 2, 1942, p. 10, February 22, 1942, p. 29, February 25, 1942, p. 21.

122. There were some reports that the striptease, ostensibly banned in 1937, was again being performed, although strippers were taking less off. Yet most commentators agreed that there had been little change in the performances since the institution of the variety revue policy. On the content of burlesque shows in 1942, see untitled typescript of police reports on burlesque, and March 4, 1942, F. Leopold Schmidt to LaGuardia, Box 3629, La-Guardia Collection, Mayors' Papers.

123. On LaGuardia's sagging popularity, see Kessner, *Fiorello H. LaGuardia*, chapter 13 and passim.

124. January 30, 1942, draft of press release, Box 3297, LaGuardia Collection, Mayors' Papers.

125. Ben Barker-Benfield, "The Spermatic Economy: A Nineteenth-Century View of Sexuality," *Feminist Studies* 1, 1 (1972): 45–66; Mumford, "'Lost Manhood' Found."

126. March 25, 1942, John A. O'Brien to LaGuardia, n.d. Mr. Benson to LaGuardia, F. Leopold Schmidt to LaGuardia, Box 3629, LaGuardia Collection, Mayors' Papers. Letters mentioning youth in general include April 18, 1942, Archbishop Spellman to LaGuardia, May 18, 1942, Sister Mary Rinaldo to LaGuardia, n.d. Mrs. M. L. to LaGuardia, Box 3629, LaGuardia Collection, Mayors' Papers.

127. March 21, 1942, "A Praying Soldier" to LaGuardia, Box 3629, LaGuardia Collection, Mayors' Papers.

128. On attitudes toward venereal disease during wartime, see Brandt, *No Magic Bullet*.

129. Representatives of the legitimate theater, burlesque consumers and employees and, after some hesitation, civil libertarians all condemned this final assault against bur-

lesque. Theatrical groups that lobbied the city administration to restore the burlesque licenses included Equity, the Authors' League of America, and the League of New York Theatres, representing theater owners and producers. See March 3, 1942, Howard Lindsay to LaGuardia, March 16, 1942, Frank Gillmore to Paul Moss, Box 3629, LaGuardia Collection, Mayors' Papers; *New York Times*, February 25, 1942, p. 21, March 4, 1942, p. 4, March 18, 1942, p. 28.

130. See, for example, March 22, 1942, "Commuter" to LaGuardia, June 26, 1942, "One Who Likes Shows" to LaGuardia, n.d. Joseph Cella to LaGuardia, n.d. "A Jerk That Voted for You" to LaGuardia, Box 3629, LaGuardia Collection, Mayors' Papers.

131. February 26, 1942, press release, vol. 2350, ACLU; March 16, 1942, Frank Gillmore to Paul Moss, Box 3629, LaGuardia Collection, Mayors' Papers.

132. March 13, 1942, Miss Juliet M. Bartlett to LaGuardia, and William I. Graham to LaGuardia, Box 3629, LaGuardia Collection, Mayors' Papers; *New York World-Telegram*, February 24, 1942, clipping in vol. 2348, ACLU; *New York Times*, February 25, 1942, p. 21, March 18, 1942, p. 28.

133. [Frederick Woltman], n.d *New York World-Telegram* clipping, vol. 2348, ACLU.

134. March 3, 1942, Howard Lindsay et al. to LaGuardia, and March 23, 1942, Morris Ehrlich to LaGuardia, Box 3629, LaGuardia Collection, Mayors' Papers; see also letter from "four soldiers," *New York Daily News*, August 29, 1942, clipping in Box 3629, LaGuardia Collection, Mayors' Papers; *New York Times*, March 4, 1942, p. 4, March 30, 1942, p. 21.

135. LaGuardia quoted in "Petition of Bonserk Theatre Corporation," Box 3629, LaGuardia Collection, Mayors' Papers.

136. *Bonserk Theatre Corporation v Moss*, 34 N.Y.S.2· 541.

3. "In the Clutches of Lesbians"

1. February 20, 1945, John Sutherland Bonnell to Fiorello LaGuardia, Box 3352; n.d. press release, Box 3351; both LaGuardia Collection, Mayors' Papers Collection, Municipal Archives, Department of Records and Information Services, City of New York (hereafter cited as Mayors' Papers).

2. Studies of the regulation of the legitimate theater during the twentieth century include Laufe, *The Wicked Stage*; Curtin, *"We Can Always Call Them Bulgarians"*; Wainscott, "Attracting Censorship to the Popular Theatre"; Rod, "Trial by Jury"; Hamilton, *When I'm Bad I'm Better*, especially chapter 4.

3. Levine, *Highbrow/Lowbrow*; Allen, *Horrible Prettiness*; Snyder, *The Voice of the City*; Peiss, "Commercial Leisure and the 'Woman Question' "; Gunther Barth, *City People: The Rise of Modern City Culture in Nineteenth-Century America* (New York: Oxford University Press, 1980). A similar process is described for cabarets in Erenberg, *Steppin' Out*. The extent to which Broadway may also have become integrated into a developing "middlebrow" culture is beyond the scope of this study. One might speculate, however, that middlebrow cultural forms would be positioned similarly to "high art" with regard to state regulation. See Joan Shelley Rubin, *The Making of Middlebrow Culture* (Chapel Hill: Uni-

versity of North Carolina Press, 1992). For early twentieth-century statistics on theater attendance in New York City, see Davis, *The Exploitation of Pleasure*, pp. 36–37.

4. "Statement of Acting Mayor Murray Hulbert on Theatre Regulation," Box 195, John Hylan Collection, Mayors' Papers. Here, Hulbert referred to this oft-voiced opinion but rejected it.

5. *New York Catholic News*, September 20, 1930, p. 3.

6. Allen, *Only Yesterday*, especially p. 93; Laufe, *The Wicked Stage*; Churchill, *The Theatrical Twenties*; Hamilton, *When I'm Bad I'm Better*, chapter 4.

7. Laufe, *The Wicked Stage*, p. 50.

8. Demastes, *Beyond Naturalism*, p. 16. See also Murphy, *American Realism and American Drama*; Tom F. Driver, *Romantic Quest and Modern Vision: A History of the Modern Theatre* (New York: Delacorte, 1970); Gary A. Richardson, *American Drama From the Colonial Period Through World War I: A Critical History* (New York: Twayne, 1993).

9. On O'Neill, see Murphy, *American Realism and American Drama*, pp. 112–131; Demastes, *Beyond Naturalism*, p. 21.

10. On early attitudes toward theater, see Agnew, *Worlds Apart*; Richardson, *American Drama*, pp. 2–4. On the transformation of a Protestant critique of the theater, see Richard Wightman Fox, "The Discipline of Amusement" in Taylor, *Inventing Times Square*, pp. 83–98.

11. "Statement of Acting Mayor Murray Hulbert on Theatre Regulation," Box 195, John Hylan Collection, Mayors' Papers. See also *New York Catholic News*, November 2, 1929, p. 5, September 20, 1930, p. 3; *New York Times*, December 17, 1923, p. 11, May 26, 1927, p. 16; *New York Herald-Tribune*, January 25, 1931, clipping in vol. 604, American Civil Liberties Union Papers, Seeley G. Mudd Library, Princeton University (hereafter cited as ACLU); March 5, 1945, Thomas A. Madden to Paul Moss, Box 3352, LaGuardia Collection, Mayors' Papers.

12. Examples of the linking of obscenity and commerciality can be found in the *New York Times*, May 7, 1922, p. 16, February 23, 1925, p. 5, May 26, 1927, p. 16, January 29, 1931, p. 21; *New York American*, December 2, 1923, clipping in MWEZ+n.c. 6521, Billy Rose Theatre Collection, Lincoln Center Library for the Performing Arts (hereafter cited as Lincoln Center); New York City Department of Licenses *Annual Report* (1924), p. 7; *New York World*, November 17, 1930, clipping in vol. 385, ACLU; *New York Catholic News*, January 27, 1934, p. 4; "Moss Did RIGHT," n.d., *New York Journal-American* clipping, Box 3352, LaGuardia Collection, Mayors' Papers.

13. I use *modernist* here to suggest anti-obscenity activists' unhappiness with a broadly defined modern worldview rather than a specific literary style or theological perspective.

14. *New York World*, December 20, 1930, clipping in vol. 385, ACLU; *New York Times*, February 4, 1927, p. 17; *New York Catholic News*, November 21, 1942. For similar examples, see also New York Society for the Suppression of Vice *Annual Report, 1929*; *New York Catholic News*, November 17, 1934, p. 4; *New York American*, December 7, 1923, clipping in MWEZ+n.c.6521, Lincoln Center; *New York Times*, March 16, 1925, p. 21, and January 17, 1931, p. 22.

15. *New York Catholic News*, October 31, 1925, p. 1, May 15, 1926, p. 1; *New York Times*, February 28, 1925, p. 15. Other criticisms of realism can be found in New York Society for the Suppression of Vice *Annual Report 1926*; *New York World*, November 17, 1930, and December 20, 1930, clippings in vol. 385, ACLU; *New York Times*, March 5, 1925, p. 21 (in which District Attorney Joab Banton condemned those persons "Bolshevist in temperament" who would "allow realism to run riot"), May 11, 1927, p. 28.

16. *New York Catholic News*, April 1, 1933, p. 24; see also *New York World*, November 17, 1930, clipping in vol. 385, ACLU; *New York Catholic News*, December 8, 1923, p. 1, August 23, 1929, p. 3, and September 2, 1933, p. 4; *New York Tribune*, May 24, 1923, in "God of Vengeance" clipping file, Lincoln Center; New York Society for the Suppression of Vice *Annual Report 1926*.

17. *New York-Herald Tribune*, December 20, 1930, clipping in vol. 385, ACLU.

18. *New York Times*, December 13, 1912, p. 10, and December 19, 1912, p. 9.

19. *New York Catholic News*, October 21, 1916, p. 6, November 25, 1916, p. 1, December 30, 1916, p. 5.

20. *New York Catholic News*, July 7, 1917, p. 10.

21. Laufe, *The Wicked Stage*, pp. 24–27; *New York Times*, April 6, 1900, p. 7, November 1, 1905, p. 1, July 7, 1906, p. 7. Despite their lack of success in prosecuting *Mrs. Warren's Profession*, after the arrests the producer withdrew the play, and it was not revived in New York until 1907. On the campaigns against each of these plays, see Budke, "Assessing the 'Offense of Public Decency.'"

22. See chapter 5, this volume.

23. For descriptions of the play see "The Theme of Aphrodite" and clippings contained in "Aphrodite" clipping file and in scrapbook MWEX+++n.c. 24,274, both at Lincoln Center.

24. *New York American*, December 4, 1919, and December 2, 1919, in "Aphrodite" clipping file, Lincoln Center.

25. Notable among these changes, the producers agreed to dim the lights on an actress who was supposed to represent a nude statue. While this statue also occasioned much comment in the press, most drama critics agreed that it was not lewd. On the results of this campaign, see December 2, 1919, Mayor Hylan to John Gilchrist, Box 208, Hylan Collection, Mayors' Papers; *New York Tribune*, December 3, 1919, *New York American*, December 4, 1919, and unidentified clipping, December 4, 1919, all in scrapbook MWEX+++n.c. 24,274, Lincoln Center; December 1919 Executive Secretary's Report, Box 2, Folder 7, John Saxton Sumner Papers, State Historical Society of Wisconsin Archives (hereafter cited as Sumner Papers).

26. January 20, 1920, John Sumner to John F. Hylan, and January 29, 1920, John Gilchrist to John F. Hylan, both Box 61, Hylan Collection, Mayors' Papers; September 1919, October 1919, February 1920, March 1920, May 1920, March 1921, May 1921 Executive Secretary's Reports, Box 2, Folder 7, Sumner Papers.

27. On *The Demi-Virgin*, see Wainscott, "Attracting Censorship to the Popular Theatre"; and Rod, "Trial by Jury." For contemporary descriptions of the play, see the *New*

York Sun, October 19, 1921, *New York Clipper*, October 26, 1921, and scraps of clippings, all in "The Demi-Virgin" clipping file, Lincoln Center.

28. The role of the better public shows movement is reflected in NYSSV Executive Secretary Reports, October 1921-January 1922. The case's progress through the courts can be traced in the *New York Times*, November 3, 1921, p. 22, November 8, 1921, p. 19, November 15, 1921, p. 9, November 23, 1921, p. 10, November 25, 1921, p. 18, November 26, 1921, p. 18, December 13, 1921, p. 24, December 24, 1921, p. 5, March 19, 1922, p. 8, May 3, 1922, p. 3. The court ruling is *A. H. Woods Theatre Co. v Gilchrist*, 192 N.Y.S. 417, aff'd. 135 N.E. 941. Commissioner Gilchrist's power was upheld by the New York Supreme Court, but that decision was reversed by the Appellate Division; the Court of Appeals affirmed without comment. For attendance figures see Wainscott, "Attracting Censorship to the Popular Theatre," p. 136.

29. See, for example, Alexander Woolcott's column, *New York Times*, January 1, 1922, 6:1; *New York Times*, December 24, 1921, p. 7.

30. Groups involved in formulating the play jury plan included Equity, the Dramatists' Guild, and the Producing Managers' Association, and Sumner's Better Public Shows Movement, which consisted of representatives of a number of civic organizations, among them the Girl Scouts, YMCA, YWCA, and clerics' associations. See New York Society for the Suppression of Vice *Annual Report 1921*; New York City Department of Licenses *Annual Report* (1922); *New York Times*, January 25, 1922, p. 16, March 3, 1922, p. 15, March 11, 1922, p. 1, March 18, 1922, p. 12, April 18, 1922, p. 15, May 21, 1922, 7:1, May 24, 1922, p. 22, September 13, 1922, p. 18, October 8, 1922, 2:5. On theater organizations' motivations for supporting the plan, see Rod, "Trial by Jury," p. 50; *New York Times*, May 21, 1922, 7:5 and October 8, 1922, 2:5.

31. Program of the Joint Committee Opposed to Political Censorship, Box 3, Folder 10, Sumner Papers.

32. Rod, "Trial by Jury," pp. 51–52.

33. *New York Times*, February 3, 1927, p. 1.

34. It was rumored that some of these complaints were actually instigated by producers seeking publicity. On the suspicion that William Brady, producer of *A Good Bad Woman*, had intentionally produced a "dirty" play, either to make more money or to create a "clean-up" movement, see the *New York Times*, February 14, 1925, p. 1, February 17, 1925, p. 1, February 20, 1925, p. 19, February 27, 1925, p. 7.

35. *New York Times*, March 14, 1925, p. 15, and March 15, 1925, p. 17; *New York World*, March 14, 1925, and *New York Telegraph*, March 15, 1925, clippings in MWEZ-x-n.c.22,510, Lincoln Center.

36. Edwin Justus Mayer, *The Fire Brand*, script located at Lincoln Center. Schildkraut quoted in *New York Telegraph*, November 10, 1924, clipping in scrapbook MWEZ +n.c. 22,510, Lincoln Center.

37. *New York Telegram*, November 25, 1924, clipping in scrapbook MWEZ +n.c. 28,130, Lincoln Center.

38. Sidney Howard, *They Knew What They Wanted*, script located at Lincoln Center.

39. "Program Notes on *They Knew What They Wanted*," mimeograph for 1949 revival, located in scrapbook MWEZ +n.c. 28,130, Lincoln Center.

40. *New York Times*, February 21, 1925, p. 1, and February 22, 1925, p. 1; *New York Review*, February 21, 1925, clipping in "A Good Bad Woman" scrapbook, Lincoln Center.

41. *New York Times*, March 22, 1925, 9:6. Those involved in the arts included the editor of *Scribner's Magazine*, a musician, a photographer, a writer, and one woman who was identified as the wife of a novelist.

42. *New York Times*, February 18, 1925, p. 18, March 16, 1925, p. 18, May 4, 1925, p. 22.

43. *New York Times*, March 16, 1925. Indeed, the class composition of the play jury was cited by the producers of *The Bunk of 1926* as reason for rejecting its condemnation of their play: "Eight of the eleven jurors that passed on my case are named in the Social Register," stated Ramsey Wallace, "and they take it upon themselves to decide arbitrarily what the masses shall see and approve." See the *New York Times*, June 9, 1926, p. 1. Similar assumptions that "uneducated" persons are unable to make judgments about art, or are more likely to condone censorship, were articulated during the trial of Dennis Barrie, director of the Cincinnati Contemporary Arts Center, for displaying sexually explicit photographs by Robert Mapplethorpe. See for example, *Christian Science Monitor*, October 24, 1990, p. 20; *New York Times*, October 6, 1990, p. 6.

44. The two productions in which changes were ordered were *The Great Temptations* and *Bunk of 1926*. At first the latter play closed because the actors abided by a clause in their contract that required them to walk out on any production condemned by a play jury. This clause had been inserted as one means of ensuring that the jury system would work. However, the producers obtained a court order enjoining not only city officials but also Actors' Equity from interfering with the play, and the performers returned. The scene that had offended play jurors was removed, however; furthermore, the play failed soon thereafter (perhaps because it had been cleaned up). See *New York Times*, June 8, 1926, p. 1, June 9, 1926, p. 1, June 22, 1926, p. 21; "Theatre Regulation in New York City," Box 3568, LaGuardia Collection, Mayors' Papers.

45. *New York Times*, June 9, 1926, p. 1. The script for *Sex* is published in Schlissel, *Three Plays by Mae West*. On the play and the campaign against it see Hamilton, *When I'm Bad I'm Better*, chapters 3 and 4. *The Shanghai Gesture*, authored by John Colton, exploited racist ideas of degenerate Asian sexuality and pure white womanhood to become one of the hits of the season. Its central character was Mrs. Goddam, a Chinese madame who was "ruined" in her youth by a British businessman. She exacted her revenge by selling his daughter into prostitution, but saw her own daughter become a sexual degenerate and drug addict in turn. One scene portrayed a "white slave" auction, where Mrs. Goddam invited Chinese pimps to bid on the businessman's daughter: "This is a white girl, not a yellow one. What am I bid? Think of your hairy chest against her lovely young breasts. Think of your mouth against her soft red lips." Quoted in Churchill, *The Theatrical Twenties*, p. 202. These two plays were considered by play juries in June 1926. *The Captive*, which was reviewed in November, will be discussed in greater detail below.

46. On perceptions of and attitudes toward lesbianism in the early twentieth century, see Christina Simmons, "Companionate Marriage and the Lesbian Threat"; Faderman,

"The Morbidification of Love"; Chauncey, "From Sexual Inversion to Homosexuality";
Faderman, *Odd Girls and Twilight Lovers*, especially pp. 88–92; Carroll Smith-Rosenberg,
"The New Woman as Androgyne: Social Disorder and Gender Crisis, 1870–1936," in
Smith-Rosenberg, *Disorderly Conduct*, pp. 245–296; Esther Newton, "The Mythic Man-
nish Lesbian: Radclyffe Hall and the New Woman" in Duberman, Vicinus, and Chauncey,
Hidden From History, pp. 281–293. For an extremely helpful overview of plays featuring
gay and lesbian characters, see Curtin, *"We Can Always Call Them Bulgarians."*

47. Asch (Sholom Ash), *The God of Vengeance*.

48. Ibid., pp. 35–36, 58–65.

49. Ibid., p. 99. The endings of the published play and the 1923 production varied
slightly. In the former, Yekel drags Rifkele down into his brothel; in the latter, he merely
banishes her and her ex-prostitute mother from his home, leaving the audience to imagine her fate. Further, there is some evidence that the love scenes between Rifkele and
Manke may have been truncated when the play was produced on Broadway. On the differences between the published play and the staging for the 1923 English-language production, see Curtin, *"We Can Always Call Them Bulgarians,"* especially pp. 30, 32–33, 39;
and Erdman, "Jewish Anxiety in 'Days of Judgment.' "

50. Quoted in Curtin, *"We Can Always Call Them Bulgarians,"* p. 29. See pp. 32–33 for
discussion of others involved with the production who denied that the relationship between Manke and Rifkele was sexual.

51. Arthur Hornblow, "Mr. Hornblow Goes to the Play," *Theatre Magazine* (April
1923), pp. 20, 68. See also reviews in *New York Telegraph*, December 31, 1922; *New York Tribune,* December 20, 1922; *New York Sun*, December 20, 1922; *New York Globe*, December
20, 1922; *New York Telegram*, December 20, 1922; *New York Call*, December 20, 1922 (all
contained in *The God of Vengeance* clipping file, Lincoln Center); unnamed reviewer for
the *Baltimore Sun*, quoted in Curtin, *"We Can Always Call Them Bulgarians,"* p. 33; reviews in the *New York World* and the *New York Evening Post*, quoted in Curtin, *"We Can
Always Call Them Bulgarians,"* p. 30.

52. Hornblow, "Mr. Hornblow Goes to the Play"; *New York Tribune*, May 24, 1923, in
The God of Vengeance clipping file, Lincoln Center.

53. Asch, *God of Vengeance*, p. 95. Indeed, the play, at least in published form, is ambiguous enough to make possible the interpretation that Rifkele had been corrupted by
a man during the night she spent away from home. For example, Manke tells Rifkele that
they will go to a house where there will be "young folks aplenty, — army officers."
Nonetheless, when Yekel asks Rifkele whether she is "still a chaste Jewish daughter," she
can only reply "I don't know." Asch, *God of Vengeance*, pp. 64, 94.

54. As a Yiddish-language production, it might have escaped the notice of vice reformers; however, these reformers had complained about raciness in the foreign-lan-
guage theater several times in the past.

55. On the problem of presenting Yiddish theatrical productions before English-language audiences, see Ellen Schiff, "Shylock's *Mishpocheh*: Anti-Semitism on the American Stage" in Gerber, *Anti-Semitism in American History*, pp. 79–99. Sexuality in the Yiddish theater is briefly discussed in Howe, *World of our Fathers*. There may well have been

similar differences of interpretation within Yiddish-language audiences as well. It seems likely that many in the Berlin audience before which *The God of Vengeance* had its premiere in 1910 might have interpreted the women's relationship as lesbian, given the large and visible lesbian community in that city at the time.

56. Faderman, "The Morbidification of Love Between Women."

57. *New York Times*, May 24, 1923, p. 1. In 1897 the actors in a burlesque show were convicted of maintaining a public nuisance, but there had been no previous convictions under the city's obscenity ordinance (sec. 1140a).

58. *New York Times*, March 7, 1923, p. 6, March 8, 1923, p. 8, May 24, 1923, p. 1, May 29, 1923, p. 2; January-March 1923 Executive Secretary Reports, Box 2, Folder 8, Sumner Papers; Zosa Szajkowski, *Jews, Wars, and Communism*, vol. 2 (New York: Ktav, 1974), pp. 143–147; February 16, 1931, Harry Weinberger to Forrest Bailey, vol. 516, ACLU.

59. The rabbi was Joseph Silverman of Temple Emanuel. See Curtin, *"We Can Always Call Them Bulgarians,"* p. 36.

60. My argument here is based upon my reading of the New York Supreme Court's opinion overturning the conviction in the *God of Vengeance* case, *People v Weinberger*, 239 NY 307. For the relevant scenes in the play, see *God of Vengeance*, pp. 35–36 and 61–62. See also Joseph Schildkraut, *My Father and I* (New York: Viking, 1959), p. 181, quoted in Curtin, *"We Can Always Call Them Bulgarians,"* p. 33. A slightly different interpretation is offered in Erdman, "Jewish Anxiety in 'Days of Judgment.'" The conviction was overturned on procedural grounds.

61. Notably, the word *lesbian* never appears in this play or in any of the others considered here.

62. Bourdet, *The Captive*, p. 171.

63. Ibid., pp. 169, 171. A number of reviewers commented on Mencken's "ghastly" white face makeup, which she chose to suggest the extent of Irene's torment.

64. Ibid., pp. 149–150.

65. See, for example, *New York Times*, January 21, 1927, p. 14 (letter to Editor from Elsie McCormick), March 7, 1927, p. 11, May 11, 1927, p. 28; *New York Evening Post*, March 8, 1927, in scrapbook MWEZ+n.c. 17,072, Lincoln Center.

66. Nathan, "The Theatre," p. 374. It should be noted that the published play suggests that Irene had not yet consummated a physical relationship with Madame d'Aiguines.

67. Ibid., pp. 373–374.

68. November 1926 Executive Secretary Report, Box 2, Folder 9, Sumner Papers; *New York Law Journal*, March 9, 1927, decision of Justice Mahoney in *Liveright v Banton*, Box 3352, LaGuardia Collection, Mayors' Papers (also noting that young men "in pairs" attended the performances). Concerns about the attendance of women are also articulated in Minnie L. Coffee, "Shall We Have a Censorship of the Stage?" *Jewish Woman* 7, 2 (April 1927); New York Society for the Suppression of Vice *Annual Report 1926*; *New York Times*, March 7, 1927, p. 11; *New York Evening Post*, March 8, 1927, clipping in scrapbook MWEZ+n.c.17,072, Lincoln Center. For examples of the argument that the play taught "the utter horror and tragedy of vice," see the *Daily Mirror*, February 17, 1927, p. 2; *New York World*, November 16, 1926, p. 17, and February 4, 1927, p. 11; *New York Herald Tribune*,

February 21, 1927, p. 15; *New York Telegraph*, February 11, 1927 and *New York Herald-Tribune*, February 20, 1927, both in *The Captive* clipping file, Lincoln Center. For a very interesting discussion of the response to *The Captive* and its audience, see Hamilton, *When I'm Bad I'm Better*, chapter 4.

69. Decision of Justice Mahoney in *Liveright v Banton*, in Box 3352, LaGuardia Collection, Mayors' Papers; October 1926 Executive Secretary's Report, Box 2, Folder 9, Sumner Papers.

70. January 1927 Executive Secretary's Report, Box 2, Folder 9, Sumner Papers.

71. The similarities in the broad outlines of the plot may be more than coincidence, for West wrote *The Drag* after noting the commercial success of *The Captive*. It is published in Schlissel, *Three Plays by Mae West*. On *The Drag*, see Hamilton, *When I'm Bad I'm Better*, chapters 3 and 4. See Chauncey, *Gay New York*, on the use of the terms *fairy* and *gay* in the years prior to 1930. On the actors' alleged sexual identity, see Curtin, *"We Can Always Call Them Bulgarians,"* pp. 84 and 97–98; *New York World*, February 1, 1927, p. 1.

72. For example, simultaneously with the uproar over *The Drag* the play *New York Exchange* featured Harold Minger playing a character variously described as "a perfumed insect" and a "fag" in reviews, as well as Doris Underwood who portrayed "a mannish villager with a good heart." Although this play came under police supervision, apparently its theme (the play concerned a gigolo) rather than these characterizations offended them. Notably, the play was advertised as a "male Captive," but again this referred to the gigolo character and seems only to have been an advertising ploy to capitalize on the publicity about *The Captive*. See January 1, 1927, "Synopsis," *New York News*, January 9, 1927; and *New York Times*, January 1, 1927, in "New York Exchange" clipping file, Lincoln Center; unidentified clipping in scrapbook MWEX+n.c. 18,709, Lincoln Center. Plays featuring gay men were one aspect of what George Chauncey has identified as a "pansy craze" to hit New York's nightlife in the 1920s. See Chauncey, *Gay New York*, chapter 11.

73. *New York World*, February 10, 1927, p. 1; *New York Daily Mirror*, February 10, 1927, p. 2; *New York Times*, February 10, 1927, p. 1.

74. *New York American*, April 27, 1926, in "Sex" clipping file, Lincoln Center.

75. *New York Herald-Tribune*, February 16, 1927, p. 1; *New York Times*, February 17, 1927, p. 1, March 29, 1927, p. 27, April 6, 1927, p. 1.

76. *New York World*, February 11, 1927, p. 4, and February 13, 1927, p. 1; *New York Times*, February 13, 1927, p. 1. Indeed, the prospect of *The Drag* was greeted with horror not only by reformers and politicians but by many theater people as well. Assuming that the play would bring in its wake the passage of the censorship legislation being touted by Hearst, these groups closed ranks to ensure that *The Drag* never opened on Broadway. New York police observed its out-of-town tryouts; the district attorney warned he would prosecute the play if it was produced in New York City; representatives of organizations of actors, playwrights, and producers conferred about preventing the opening; and, possibly most important, no theater manager would agree to rent a playhouse to stage the production. See the *New York Times*, January 28, 1927, p. 14, and February 2, 1927, p. 1; *New York Daily Mirror*, February 2, 1927, p. 2; *New York World*, February 4, 1927, p. 1, February 5, 1927, p. 1, February 10, 1927, p. 1, February 13, 1927, p. 1; *New York Herald-Tribune*, February 1, 1927,

p. 20; *Evening Post*, February 1, 1927, in "Censorship, Stage, U.S., 1920–1929" clipping file, Lincoln Center. West's adeptness for capturing public attention is described in Hamilton, *When I'm Bad I'm Better*.

77. Curtin, *"We Can Always Call Them Bulgarians,"* pp. 60–62, 86–87, 101. On state motion picture censorship, see chapter 1, this volume.

78. *Halsey v The New York Society for the Suppression of Vice*, 234 N.Y. 1, reprinted in De Grazia, *Censorship Landmarks*, pp. 71–74. Thus, the aspect of the Hicklin Rule permitting categorization of a work as obscene based on an isolated passage had already eroded substantially in New York courts. The Wales Law was an effort to shore it up. It is worthy of note that a similar provision, applicable to printed materials, was a key aspect of the so-called Clean Books Bill, for which anti-obscenity activists and clerics lobbied during the mid-twenties. That bill never passed. See Boyer, *Purity in Print*.

79. Federal authorities had similar powers with respect to any establishment the owner of which was convicted of violating laws prohibiting liquor sales, and Banton drew upon his experience in enforcing Prohibition by including this provision.

80. Assistant District Attorney James G. Wallace to editor, *New York Times*, April 17, 1927, 7:14.

81. The Wales Law was used in an attempt to prohibit discussions of homosexuality in print as well. When New York City officials sought to prohibit the distribution of Radclyffe Hall's novel *The Well of Loneliness* in 1928, a city magistrate refused to dismiss the complaint against the book's publishers, citing the law's passage as evidence of the Legislature's intent that courts protect "the weaker members of society from corrupt, depraving and lecherous influences." He countered the defendants' argument that the book "be judged by the mores of the day" with the observation that "the community, through this recent legislation, has evinced a public policy even more hostile to the presentation and circulation of matter treating of sexual depravity. The argument, therefore, that the mores have so changed as to fully justify the distribution of a book exalting sex perversion is without force." *People v Friede et al.*, reprinted in De Grazia, *Censorship Landmarks*, pp. 78–79. However, city officials were unable to obtain a conviction when they brought the book's publishers to trial.

82. *New York Sun*, March 19, 1930, in "Censorship — Stage — U.S. — 1930" clipping file, Lincoln Center; *New York Times*, April 4, 1930, p. 1. The play is published in Schlissel, *Three Plays by Mae West*. See also Hamilton, *When I'm Bad I'm Better*, chapter 6; Curtin, *"We Can Always Call Them Bulgarians,"* chapter 7.

83. Evidence was also introduced that a cast member had told the police that there were many gay men in the cast. See clippings in "Censorship — Stage — United States — 1930" file, Lincoln Center, including *New York Sun*, March 19, 1930, and April 2, 1930; *New York American*, March 29, 1930, and April 1, 1930; and an unidentified scrap (perhaps *Daily Mirror*, March 22, 1930); *Zit's Theatrical Weekly*, April 12, 1930.

84. *New York Times*, April 4, 1930, p. 1. West closed the play after three performances when she had failed to obtain an injunction prohibiting New York police from interfering with it. Despite the lack of a conviction, she decided not to revive the production. At trial the jurors voted seven to five in favor of acquittal, but after the trial eleven of them

took the extraordinary step of writing a letter to New York Governor Franklin D. Roosevelt, urging that some preexhibition censorship scheme be instituted. This contradiction between their verdict and their feelings about the play has several possible explanations. It may be that the jurors felt that the penalties exacted by the Wales Act were too harsh. In addition, prosecutors may have encountered difficulty translating "effeminate" behavior into homosexual identity, providing support for George Chauncey's suggestion that, at least for men, popular and expert perceptions of the signs of homosexual identity were shifting from a concern with inappropriate gender behavior to sexual object choice. Hamilton also points out that the eighteen-month delay before coming to trial hindered the prosecution. *New York Times*, April 4, 1930, p. 1, and April 16, 1930, p. 13; *New York Herald*, April 4, 1930, in "Censorship — Stage — United States — 1930" file, Lincoln Center; "Theatre Regulation in New York City," Box 3568, LaGuardia Collection, Mayors' Papers; Chauncey, "From Sexual Inversion to Homosexuality"; Hamilton, *When I'm Bad I'm Better*, chapter 6.

85. Simon Gantillon, *Maya*, script held at Lincoln Center.

86. *New York Times*, February 25, 1928, p. 10, February 27, 1928, p. 21, February 28, 1928, p. 18, February 29, 1928, p. 28; *New York Telegraph*, February 26, 1928; *New York World*, February 29, 1928, both in "Maya" clipping file, Lincoln Center; *Brooklyn Eagle*, February 25, 1928; *New York Daily News*, February 26, 1928, both in MWEZ+n.c. 16,879, Lincoln Center. The Shubert organization, which owned the theater, evicted the production by invoking a clause that they had inserted into their contracts after passage of the Wales Law, permitting them to eject a play "if there [was] any public objection on moral grounds." See *New York Herald-Tribune*, February 26, 1928, in "Maya" clipping file, Lincoln Center.

87. Very frequently authorities had only to observe a production and ask for changes to regulate the stage effectively. See "Theatre Regulation in New York City," n.d., Box 3568, LaGuardia Collection, Mayors' Papers. Sometimes they resorted to raids without actual prosecution to attain their goals. On action against *My Girl Friday*, see the *New York Times*, February 16, 1929, p. 1, February 17, 1929, p. 15, March 3, 1929, p. 13; on *Sisters of the Chorus* see the *New York Times*, June 20, 1929, p. 19; on *Earl Carroll's Vanities*, see the *New York Times*, July 10, 1930, p. 1, August 13, 1930, p. 1; *New York Herald-Tribune*, July 16, 1930, and August 13, 1930, both in "Censorship — Stage — United States — 1930" file, Lincoln Center; and *New York Catholic News*, August 16, 1930, p. 4; on *Bad Girl*, see the *New York Times*, September 20, 1930, p. 15, and November 8, 1930, p. 20. The 1930 production of *Frankie and Johnnie* proved an exception to this pattern, when the play's tryout in Queens was raided and authorities proceeded to trial. Although initially the cast was convicted of violation of obscenity statutes, that conviction was later overturned. See the *New York Times*, September 11, 1930, p. 1, November 22, 1930, p. 21, March 4, 1932, p. 17; *New York Herald-Tribune*, September 13, 1930; and *New York American*, October 10, 1930, both in "Censorship — Stage — United States — 1930" file, Lincoln Center; for the decision overturning the conviction, see *People v Wendling*, 258 N.Y. 451, 180 N.E. 169. For a summary of some of these actions, see "Theatre Regulation in New York City," n.d., Box 3568, LaGuardia Collection, Mayors' Papers.

88. *New York Post*, November 6, 1944, clipping in vol. 2546, ACLU.

89. These plays include *Winter Bound*, produced in 1929, and the most famous "lesbian" play of the period, Lillian Hellman's *The Children's Hour*, which appeared in 1933. Neither of these plays prompted suppression by municipal authorities or even a great deal of protest on the part of anti-obscenity activists. I would argue that this is because they did not follow the conventions of the plot I have laid out here. Most important, neither of these plays acknowledged mutual sexual desire between two women. On both of these plays, see the discussion in Curtin, *"We Can Always Call Them Bulgarians."*

90. Baker, *Trio*, p. 151. While I have been unable to find a copy of the play, descriptions suggest that it followed the novel by Dorothy Baker from which it was adapted. My discussion of its plot is based on the novel, and all quotes are from the 1943 edition. The novel was adapted for the stage by Baker and her husband Howard Baker.

91. *New York Times*, February 26, 1992, p. D21.

92. See chapter 2, this volume.

93. N.d. press release, Box 3351, LaGuardia Collection, Mayors' Papers; *New York Times*, February 25, 1945, p. 36.

94. Transcript of March 1, 1945 League of New York Theatres meeting; n.d. "Report by Osmond K. Fraenkel," both vol. 2638, ACLU.

95. William Vaughan to LaGuardia, Box 3351, LaGuardia Collection, Mayors' Papers.

96. February 26, 1945, Eugene Lerner to LaGuardia, Box 3351, LaGuardia Collection, Mayors' Papers. See also, for example, letters from Ellis Baker, Mrs. W. L. Shinnick, Siegfried P. Stiefel, Aaron H. Esman, E. T. Daniels, Robert G. Tomkins, and Richard Lester, Box 3351, LaGuardia Collection, Mayors' Papers.

97. Frank Nosoff to LaGuardia, Box 3351, LaGuardia Collection, Mayors' Papers.

98. Estelle P. Levy to LaGuardia, Box 3352; see also Carrie S. Broadwin to LaGuardia, Box 3351; both LaGuardia Collection, Mayors' Papers.

99. E. T. Daniels to LaGuardia, Box 3352, LaGuardia Collection, Mayors' Papers.

100. March 1, 1945, LaGuardia to Russel Crouse, Box 3351, LaGuardia Collection, Mayors' Papers. See also March 1, 1945, Harry L. Bowlby to LaGuardia, Arthur Leonard to LaGuardia, Box 3351; March 20, 1945, Harry L. Bowlby, Box 3352; March 2, 1945, Mrs. A. E. Bonbrake to LaGuardia, Box 3629; all LaGuardia Collection, Mayors' Papers.

101. March 1, 1945, Harry L. Bowlby to LaGuardia, Arthur Leonard to LaGuardia, J. Francis A. McIntyre to Paul Moss, Geoffrey O'Hara to LaGuardia, Arch Remayne to LaGuardia, Box 3351; Sermon of William F. Rosenblum, Thomas A. Madden to Paul Moss, Norman Vincent Peale to LaGuardia, March 20, 1945, Harry L. Bowlby to LaGuardia, Box 3352; both LaGuardia Collection, Mayors' Papers.

102. On medical and psychological discourses about homosexuality, see Chauncey, "From Sexual Inversion to Homosexuality"; Robinson, *The Modernization of Sex*; Lawrence Birken, *Consuming Desire: Sexual Science and the Emergence of a Culture of Abundance, 1871–1914* (Ithaca: Cornell University Press, 1988); Hale, *Freud and the Americans*. For an avidly pro-Freudian study of the exploration of Freudian ideas in theatrical productions, see W. David Sievers, *Freud on Broadway: A History of Psychoanalysis*

and the American Drama (New York: Hermitage, 1955). On the uses of the concept of repression, see Simmons, "Modern Sexuality and the Myth of Victorian Repression."

103. On concerns about female sexuality related to women's entry into the military, see Meyer, "Creating G.I. Jane."

104. For example, actress Margaret Webster publicly protested the play's fate, although she was silent about her own lesbian identity. On the formation of these communities, see Chauncey, *Gay New York*; D'Emilio, *Sexual Politics, Sexual Communities*; Faderman, *Odd Girls and Twilight Lovers*; Elizabeth Lapovsky Kennedy and Madeline Davis, *Boots of Leather, Slippers of Gold: The History of a Lesbian Community* (New York: Routledge, 1993); Bérubé, *Coming Out Under Fire.*

105. Among scores of letters see, for example, those from members of the cast of "A Bell for Adano," Anthony T. Bartuski, Noel Mills, Mrs. G. Klonsky, Mrs. W. L. Shinnick, Elliot Fishbein, Al Aranoff, and Vera Saphire, Box 3351; and letter from Mrs. Lawrence H. Pike, Box 3352; both LaGuardia Collection, Mayors' Papers; *New York Times*, February 26, 1945, p. 21, February 28, 1945, p. 28, and March 4, 1945, 2:1.

106. Sergeant Melvin Parks to LaGuardia, and Arnold Epstein to LaGuardia, Box 3351; see also Pvt. John A. L. Davis to LaGuardia, Box 3352; both LaGuardia Collection, Mayors' Papers.

107. *New York Times*, March 8, 1945, p. 1; *New York Daily News*, January 31, 1946; and *Variety*, March 20, 1946, both in "Censorship — Stage — U.S. — 1940–1949" clipping file, Lincoln Center.

108. March 2, 1945, Mrs. A. E. Bonbrake to LaGuardia, Box 3629; February 27, 1945, Mary Nolan Bonbrake to Paul Moss, Box 3351; both LaGuardia Collection, Mayors' Papers.

109. March 16, 1945, M. Bonbrake to LaGuardia, Box 3352, LaGuardia Collection, Mayors' Papers.

110. Indeed, Mary Bonbrake refers tantalizingly to a "little group" in Forest Hills who shared her puzzlement: "Our little group out here cannot understand the application of the Wales Act." It may be that the "group" was affiliated with the Catholic Theatre Movement, for she sent a copy of one of her letters to an official of the CTM. March 16, 1945, Mrs. A. E. Bonbrake to LaGuardia, Box 3352, LaGuardia Collection, Mayors' Papers.

111. Curtin, *"We Can Always Call Them Bulgarians,"* p. 266.

4. The Shifting Contours of Anti-obscenity Activism

1. Pascoe, *Relations of Rescue*; DuBois and Gordon, "Seeking Ecstasy on the Battlefield"; Ruth Bordin, *Woman and Temperance: The Quest for Power and Liberty, 1873–1900* (Philadelphia: Temple University Press, 1981); Odem, *Delinquent Daughters*; Parker, *Purifying America.*

2. On maternalism, see Koven and Michel, *Mothers of a New World*; Ladd-Taylor, "Toward Defining Maternalism," and *Mother-Work*; Gordon, *Pitied But Not Entitled*; Parker, *Purifying America*; Skocpol, *Protecting Soldiers and Mothers.*

3. Scott, "Women's Voluntary Associations"; D'Emilio and Freedman, *Intimate Matters*, especially chapters 10 and 11; Cott, *The Grounding of Modern Feminism*, especially chapter 1. For a survey of the feminist movement in New York City, see Adickes, *To Be Young Was Very Heaven*.

4. The National WCTU's emphasis on "pure" culture suggests that this may have been less true outside New York City, but even members of the WCTU relied mainly on maternalist arguments to explain their anti-obscenity activism. See Parker, *Purifying America*, passim. See also Beisel, *Imperiled Innocents*, p. 73, on women's role in anti-obscenity rhetoric.

5. *New York Times*, April 15, 1935, p. 14, and September 13, 1926, p. 18; *New York Catholic News*, March 15, 1924, p. 9.

6. *New York Times*, April 29, 1937, p. 1, July 16, 1930, p. 25; see also October 8, 1922, 2:5.

7. *New York Catholic News*, February 21, 1925, p. 4, November 7, 1942, p. 1; see also the *New York Catholic News*, May 12, 1917, p. 3; n.d. *New York Tribune* clipping in "The Demi-Virgin" clipping file, Billy Rose Theatre Collection, Lincoln Center Library for the Performing Arts (hereafter cited as Lincoln Center). More general condemnations of women for sustaining immoral productions by their attendance can be found in "Statement of Acting Mayor Murray Hulbert on Theatre Regulation," Box 195, John Hylan Collection, Mayors' Papers Collection, Municipal Archives, Department of Records and Information Services, City of New York (hereafter cited as Mayors' Papers); Committee on Drama Report, Year Book of the New York State Federation of Women's Clubs (1912), Box 6, New York State Federation of Women's Clubs Collection, Elmira College (hereafter cited as NYSFWCC); *New York Times*, February 23, 1910, p. 6, June 27, 1910, p. 2, September 12, 1913, p. 10, June 3, 1926, p. 25, September 13, 1926, p. 18, April 15, 1935, p. 14, May 23, 1935, p. 27; *New York Catholic News*, March 31, 1917, p. 4.

8. *New York Evening Bulletin*, February 20, 1925, in "A Good Bad Woman" scrapbook, Lincoln Center; *New York Catholic News*, November 7, 1942, p. 10; *New York American*, December 2, 1923 (quoting from *The Voice* of the Methodist Episcopal Board of Temperance, Prohibition and Morals), and December 7, 1923, in "Censorship — Stage — U.S. — New York" scrapbook, Lincoln Center.

9. *New York Times*, December 23, 1942, p. 22; *New York Catholic News*, October 31, 1925, p. 1. See also New York Society for the Suppression of Vice *Annual Report, 1919*, pp. 12–13; *New York American*, November 28, 1923, in "Censorship — Stage — U.S. — New York" scrapbook, Lincoln Center; *New York Times*, April 6, 1921, p. 19, March 22, 1942, p. 50; *New York Catholic News*, October 11, 1930, p. 1, and December 26, 1942, p. 3.

10. Eileen Boris, "The Power of Motherhood: Black and White Activist Women Redefine the 'Political'" in Koven and Michel, *Mothers of a New World*, p. 231. See this anthology generally on maternalist activism.

11. Emilie D. Martin to John Purroy Mitchell, Proceedings, New York City Board of Aldermen, October 18, 1910, pp. 115–116, New York Municipal Research Library (hereafter cited as Proceedings).

12. *New York Times*, March 5, 1925, p. 21, and December 16, 1930, p. 4.

13. The New York State Federation of Women's Clubs lobbied for the appointment of

two women to the Commission. See New York State Federation of Women's Clubs *Yearbook* (1922), p. 69. Governor Miller later denied promising to appoint a woman, stating that "I don't believe in making appointments on sex lines. . . . We have eliminated sex distinction . . . when it comes to public affairs." His public pronouncement suggests the complexities of gender politics after women were enfranchised, especially since Miller was an opponent of women's rights and feminism. The film "reviewers" employed by the state to make recommendations to commission members were also women. See the *New York Times*, March 4, 1921, p. 11, May 15, 1921, p. 1, July 21, 1921, p. 17. Similar attitudes were reflected in the assignment in Pittsburgh of four policewomen to the task of reading all magazines sold in the city, with the aim of identifying objectionable periodicals. See *New York Times*, July 13, 1915, p. 6.

14. "The News Letter" (October 1923), Box 6, NYSFWCC. For other examples of arguments appealing to women as the guardians of the young, see n.d. clipping "Strong Resolutions Passed" in 1903–1910 Scrapbook, and January 31, 1923, Minutes, Box 6, NYSFWCC; "A Misrepresentation," *General Federation Magazine* (July 1918); *New York Times*, May 2, 1910, p. 5, November 23, 1913, 3:6, February 24, 1925, p. 11, December 3, 1925, p. 27, June 3, 1926, p. 25; *New York Journal*, April 29, 1937, clipping in vol. 962, American Civil Liberties Union Papers, Seeley G. Mudd Library, Princeton University (hereafter cited as ACLU). Correspondents urging New York mayors to close immoral theatrical productions often identified themselves to be mothers as a way of signifying their interest in the issue of obscenity. See, for example, n.d. letter from "A mother of two boys" and n.d. letter from "Mrs. M.L. — A Mother," Box 3629, LaGuardia Collection, Mayors' Papers; also see Elsie McCormack to editor, *New York Times*, January 21, 1927, p. 14, and Mary L. Smith to the Board of Aldermen, Proceedings, November 14, 1911, p. 143.

15. For an overview of some of "the paradoxical legacies of maternalism" see Koven and Michel, "Introduction," *Mothers of a New World*, pp. 1–42.

16. This dynamic will be discussed further in chapter 5.

17. Simmons, "Modern Sexuality and the Myth of Victorian Repression."

18. On Sumner, see Boyer, *Purity in Print*, p. 30; also "Manuscripts — Autobiography," vols. 1–3, Box 1, John Saxton Sumner Papers, State Historical Society of Wisconsin Archives (hereafter cited as Sumner Papers). Comstock and Sumner apparently had a stormy relationship. See "Diary 1915," Box 1, Sumner Papers.

19. New York Society for the Suppression of Vice *Annual Report, 1929*, p. 6.

20. May 1916 Executive Secretary Report, Box 2, Folder 5, Sumner Papers.

21. New York Society for the Suppression of Vice *Annual Report, 1916*.

22. May 2, 1917, Resolution, "NYSSV Miscellaneous Papers" file, Box 3, Folder 8; "Manuscripts — Autobiography," vol. 3, Box 1; December 1921 Executive Secretary Report, Box 2, Folder 7; all in Sumner Papers.

23. Boyer, *Purity in Print*, especially chapters 4 and 5.

24. "Suppose It Happened to Your Boy or to Your Girl?" Box 3, Folder 10, Sumner Papers; New York Society for the Suppression of Vice *Annual Reports* for the years 1929, 1935, and 1936.

25. Sumner frequently proclaimed his opposition to the "principle of censorship." See, for example, the *New York Times*, July 25, 1926, 4:10.

26. New York Society for the Suppression of Vice *Annual Report, 1926*, p. 7; see also the *Annual Report, 1920*, p. 4.

27. "Suppose It Happened to Your Boy or to Your Girl?" Box 3, Folder 10, Sumner Papers; New York Society for the Suppression of Vice *Annual Report, 1917*, p. 10.

28. See, for example, "Repeal the Special Police Powers of the New York Vice Society" pamphlet, vol. 508, ACLU.

29. October 11, 1954, Louis Haggerty to John Sumner, Box 1, Folder 2, Sumner Papers. The decline in individual complaints to the society can be seen in the Executive Secretary Reports in the Sumner Papers.

30. Historian Hugh McLeod numbers among the many forces that may have contributed to declining church influence around the turn of the century "a tendency for leisure to become the emotional centre for many people's lives, and as such a kind of alternative religion." See Hugh McLeod, "Secular Cities? Berlin, London, and New York in the Later Nineteenth and Early Twentieth Centuries" in Bruce, *Religion and Modernization*, p. 61. The extent to which the process of "modernization" induces a decline in religiosity and strengthening of secular institutions and values has long been debated by scholars. For an overview of this debate see Bruce, *Religion and Modernization*; see also Peter Berger, *The Sacred Canopy* (Garden City: Doubleday, 1967); Roger Finke and Rodney Stark, "Religious Economies and Sacred Canopies: Religious Mobilization in American Cities, 1906," *American Sociological Review* 53 (1988): 41–49; Marty, *The Irony of It All*, pp. 153–154.

31. *New York Times*, December 21, 1908, p. 2, March 5, 1915, p. 18, January 9, 1917, p. 12, October 5, 1925, p. 24; *New York World*, December 21, 1908, p. 16; *New York Catholic News*, May 12, 1917, p. 3, August 23, 1929, p. 3, December 16, 1933. For examples of criticisms of clergy, see Hearing Transcript, Box MGB51, George McClellan Collection, Mayors' Papers; *Daily Mirror*, November 18, 1930, in "Censorship — Stage — U.S. — 1930" scrapbook, Lincoln Center; *New York Tribune*, December 2, 1930, clipping in vol. 385, ACLU; *New York Times*, February 23, 1925, p. 5, December 22, 1931, p. 14, July 19, 1934, p. 20; September 4, 1940, Reverend Norman Vincent Peale to LaGuardia, Box 3569, LaGuardia Collection, Mayors' Papers.

32. There is a surprising paucity of historical scholarship analyzing this relationship, and such questions are just beginning to attract attention from scholars. For a comparative analysis of the importance of regulation of sexuality and the body within Judaism worldwide, see Eilberg-Schwartz, *People of the Body*. David Biale provides a historical overview of sexual regulation within Judaism, but one that emphasizes "high culture" debates rather than actual sexual practice or popular views, in *Eros and the Jews*. John Maynard approaches the topic from the perspective of literary criticism in *Victorian Discourses*. See also Gardella, *Innocent Ecstasy*; Eric Fuchs, *Sexual Desire and Love: Origins and History of the Christian Ethic of Sexuality and Marriage*, trans. Marsha Daigle (New York: Seabury, 1983).

33. Maynard, *Victorian Discourses*, pp. 26–28, 16; Gardella, *Innocent Ecstasy*, p. 37;

Biale, *Eros and the Jews*; Edward Parrinder, *Sex in the World's Religions* (London: Sheldon, 1980); Howe, *World of Our Fathers*.

34. July 18, 1934, William F. Rosenblum to Clifton R. Read, vol. 694, ACLU.

35. On Protestant clerics' changing attitudes toward the theater see Richard Wightman Fox, "The Discipline of Amusement" in Taylor, *Inventing Times Square*, pp. 83–98.

36. *New York Catholic News*, November 25, 1916, p. 1.

37. *New York Times*, August 12, 1930, p. 1; *New York Catholic News*, September 7, 1940, p. 22. The White List was published weekly in New York City's diocesan newspapers, including the *New York Catholic News* and the *Brooklyn Tablet*.

38. Walsh, *Sin and Censorship*; Black, *Hollywood Censored*; Facey, *The Legion of Decency*. During the 1930s the Catholic hierarchy also instituted a boycott of sex magazines that was administered through the National Office (later, Organization) for Decent Literature.

39. Catholic Theatre Movement representatives claimed that they sometimes successfully asked for changes in offending Broadway productions, but such efforts were not the focus of their activism.

40. Griffin, "American Catholic Sexual Ethics."

41. *New York Catholic News*, February 18, 1928, p. 6, August 6, 1927, p. 18.

42. Griffin, "American Catholic Sexual Ethics;" Dolan, *The American Catholic Experience*, pp. 221–228; Gardiner, *Catholic Viewpoint on Censorship*, pp. 20–29, 65. For an example of this reasoning see *New York Catholic News*, February 18, 1928, p. 6.

43. *New York American*, June 19, 1930, clipping in "Censorship — Stage — U.S. — 1930" scrapbook, Lincoln Center.

44. *New York Catholic News*, October 12, 1929, p. 1. See also the *New York Catholic News*, December 8, 1923, p. 1, and August 23, 1929, p. 3, on theater; *New York Catholic News*, August 6, 1927, p. 18, on literature; *New York Catholic News*, January 7, 1933 [page number illegible], on magazines and burlesque; *New York Journal*, April 29, 1937, clipping in vol. 962, ACLU, on burlesque; *New York Herald-Tribune*, December 13, 1937, in "Catholic Theatre Movement" clipping file, Lincoln Center, on motion pictures and theater.

45. *New York Times*, March 16, 1925, p. 21, August 11, 1930, p. 1, February 12, 1934, p. 17, February 28, 1934, p. 21, December 13, 1937, p. 24; *New York Catholic News*, October 12, 1929, p. 1, February 3, 1934, July 14, 1934, p. 5; *New York Herald-Tribune*, December 13, 1937, in "Catholic Theatre Movement" clipping file, Lincoln Center. The pledge adopted by the Legion of Decency had its antecedent in the Catholic Theatre Movement, which in 1923 encouraged Catholics to sign a pledge to avoid "plays, moving pictures, and all exhibitions offensive to Christian faith and morals." *New York Catholic News*, March 3, 1923, p. 7.

46. Timothy J. Meagher, "Introduction," in Meagher, *From Paddy to Studs*, pp. 1–25; McLeod, "Catholicism and the New York Irish."

47. Catholic and Protestant clergy offered strong support for the Clean Books Bill, which would facilitate criminal prosecution of printed materials; Rabbi Stephen Wise, on the other hand, spoke out against it, and few Jews endorsed the legislation. On the campaign for the bill, see Boyer, *Purity in Print*, chapter 5.

48. Dolan, *The American Catholic Experience*, especially pp. 350–352. See also Halsey, *The Survival of American Innocence*; David J. O'Brien, "Catholicism and Americanism," in Edward R. Kantowicz, ed., *Modern American Catholicism, 1900–1965* (New York: Garland, 1988), pp. 98–115; Purcell, *The Crisis of Democratic Theory*.

49. Kathleen M. Blee, *Women of the Klan: Racism and Gender in the 1920s* (Berkeley: University of California Press, 1991), discusses the prominence of assertions of moral depravity in the anti-Catholicism of the 1910s and 1920s. See also Kenneth Jackson, *The Ku Klux Klan in the City, 1915–1930* (New York: Oxford University Press, 1965).

50. *New York Catholic News*, May 22, 1937, p. 3; *New York Times*, May 17, 1937, p. 11. For other examples of the Knights' activism in this area, see the *New York Times*, February 28, 1911, p. 6, August 8, 1924, p. 16, March 5, 1934, p. 13, July 27, 1937, p. 24, April 4, 1938, p. 6; *New York Catholic News*, February 24, 1934, September 7, 1940, p. 22; April 21, 1937, Thomas J. Scanlon to Fiorello LaGuardia, Box 3399; March 5, 1945, Thomas A. Madden to Paul Moss, Box 3352; both LaGuardia Collection, Mayors' Papers. On the Knights of Columbus, see Kauffman, *Faith and Fraternalism*; Dohen, *Nationalism and American Catholicism*; Meagher, "Introduction," p. 13.

51. On Jews as primitives, see Jonathan D. Sarna, "Jewish-Christian Hostility in the United States: Perceptions from a Jewish Point of View," in Robert N. Bellah and Frederick C. Greenspan, *Uncivil Religion: Interreligious Hostility in America*, pp. 5–22 (New York: Crossroad, 1987), especially p. 13.

52. On the role of Jews in American entertainment industries, see Gabler, *An Empire of Their Own*; May and May, "Why Jewish Movie Moguls"; Colin Shindler, "Jews and American Showbusiness," *Listener* 111 (3 May 1984): 10–11. Lary May and Robert Sklar have debated the date by which Jews were "in control" of the motion picture industry, May arguing that Jews did not dominate until after the end of World War I, Sklar contending their rise to power came earlier. For the case of New York City, the early importance of Jews as exhibitors and theater owners supports Sklar's interpretation. See Robert Sklar's review of *Screening Out the Past*, *American Historical Review* 86 (October 1981): 945; and Sklar and May's subsequent exchange, *American Historical Review* 87 (June 1982): 913–914.

53. Bristow, *Prostitution and Prejudice*, p. 46.

54. David A. Gerber, "Cutting Out Shylock: Elite Anti-Semitism and the Quest for Moral Order in the Mid-Nineteenth-Century American Marketplace," in Gerber, *Anti-Semitism in American History*, pp. 201–232. See also Sarna, "Jewish-Christian Hostility in the United States."

55. Gilman, *The Jew's Body*; MacLean, "The Leo Frank Case Reconsidered."

56. See Bristow, *Prostitution and Prejudice*; Egal Feldman, "Prostitution, the Alien Woman, and the Progressive Imagination, 1900–1915," *American Quarterly* 19 (Summer 1967): 192–206.

57. *American Hebrew*, April 8, 1921, p. 566.

58. *New York Catholic News*, October 1, 1927, p. 2; *New York Times*, September 27, 1927, p. 16. An example of a less nuanced condemnation of Jewish immorality can be found in

the pamphlet "Jew Movies Urging Sex Vice," Box 65, National Board of Review of Motion Pictures Collection, Rare Books and Manuscripts Division, New York Public Library, Astor, Lenox and Tilden Foundations (hereafter cited as NBRMPC). The undated pamphlet (probably mid-1920s), which reprints an article originally found in the "patriotic" periodical the *American Standard*, added Catholics to the list of those corrupting American youth, condemning "Jew-Jesuit" motion picture producers, directors, theater owners, and managers.

59. May 3, 1937, Horace C. Smith to LaGuardia, Box 3190, LaGuardia Collection, Mayors' Papers; "Jail the Beast" cartoon [1923 *New York Journal?*], scrapbook MWEZ+n.c. 6521, Lincoln Center; *New York Times*, February 26, 1927, p. 15; *New York Catholic News*, September 7, 1940, p. 22; March 10, 1945, Harry L. Bowlby to LaGuardia, Box 3352, LaGuardia Collection, Mayors' Papers. See also New York Society for the Suppression of Vice *Annual Report, 1919* for statistics delineating religious affiliation for those arrested on obscenity charges. The society used the increase in arrests of "Hebrews" to demand laws limiting immigration. A similar point regarding the meaning of references to "shekels" is made by Couvares and Peiss, "Censoring the Movies," p. 12.

60. *Zit's Entertainment Weekly*, December 29, 1934, p. 1; *New York Catholic News*, July 14, 1934, p. 5; *New York Times*, July 9, 1934, p. 1. See also the *New York Times*, March 13, 1922, p. 18, in which Rabbi Wise reveals that he asked Jewish theatrical producer A. H. Woods to close *The Demi-Virgin* "for the good reputation of his race"; and the *New York Catholic News*, March 10, 1934, p. 2, for similar views by Rabbi Morton Goldberg of Fall River, Massachusetts. On similar Jewish attempts to use voluntary organizations to control vice and crime among Jews, see Arthur A. Goren, *New York Jews and the Quest for Community* (New York: Columbia University Press, 1970), especially chapters 7 and 8.

61. Testimony of Samuel Marcus, Burlesque Hearing Transcript, Box 242, James J. Walker Collection, Mayors' Papers. Marcus was referring to Minsky's claim that he kept a kosher household. See also June 17, 1937, "A Good Jewish Subject" to Mayor LaGuardia, Box 3399, LaGuardia Collection, Mayors' Papers.

62. On *The God of Vengeance* generally see chapter 3, this volume, and Curtin, *"We Can Always Call Them Bulgarians,"* chapter 1. On the Jewish response to the play, see *New York Times*, March 8, 1923, p. 8, May 29, 1923, p. 2; "'The God of Vengeance': Is the Play Immoral" in "The God of Vengeance" Programme file, Lincoln Center; February 16, 1931, Harry Weinberger to Forrest Bailey, vol. 516, ACLU; Erdman, "Jewish Anxiety in 'Days of Judgment'"; Zosa Szakjowski, *Jews, Wars, and Communism*, vol. 2 (New York: Ktav, 1974), pp. 142–147. On Jewish concerns regarding transitions from the Yiddish theater to Broadway, see Ellen Schiff, "Shylock's *Mishpocheh*: Anti-Semitism on the American Stage," in Gerber, *Anti-Semitism in American History*, pp. 79–99.

63. Marty, *The Noise of Conflict*, p. 137. A few non-Reform rabbis spoke out on these questions in the period prior to 1945. Israel Goldstein was the leader of Congregation B'nai Jeshurun, a Conservative congregation, but one that has been described as "just this side of Reform." Orthodox rabbi Herbert S. Goldstein also participated in these debates upon occasion, but Goldstein differed greatly from other New York Orthodox lead-

ers in insisting upon the importance of social action. See Marcus and Peck, *The American Rabbinate*; Aaron I. Reichel, *The Maverick Rabbi: Rabbi Herbert S. Goldstein and the Institutional Synagogue* (Norfolk, Va.: Donning, 1984).

64. Howe, *World of Our Fathers*; Marty, *The Noise of Conflict*, pp. 123–145; Moore, *At Home in America*; Berrol, "In Their Image."

65. See the essays in Stevens, *Rabbinic Authority*, especially Harold I. Saperstein, "The Origin and Authority of the Rabbi," pp. 15–27, and Walter Jacob, "The Source of Reform Halachic Authority," pp. 31–36; David Polish, "The Changing and the Constant in the Reform Rabbinate," in Marcus and Peck, *The American Rabbinate*, pp. 173–251.

66. On Reform Judaism's stress on individual autonomy, see Walter Jacob, "The Source of Reform Halachic Authority"; and Polish, "The Changing and the Constant." A useful brief discussion of the contradictions between tradition and modernity for Jewish leaders can be found in Meyer, "Tradition and Modernity Reconsidered," pp. 465–469. On Reform rabbis' sexual liberalism, see Meyer, *Response to Modernity*, pp. 312–313.

67. [1931] pamphlet on National Council for Freedom from Censorship, Box 38, NBRMPC; January 30, 1931, Sidney E. Goldstein to Forrest Bailey, vol. 516, ACLU; *New York Times*, January 21, 1932, p. 37; January 22, 1932, Gordon W. Moss to Rabbi Sidney E. Goldstein, vol. 508, ACLU. Rabbi Goldstein's career can be traced in J. C. Schwarz, ed., *Religious Leaders of America*, vol. 2 (New York: n.p., 1941), p. 434, and John Simons, ed., *Who's Who in American Jewry*, vol. 3 (New York: National News Association, 1938), p. 365.

68. Testimony of Dr. Sidney E. Goldstein, Burlesque Hearing Transcript, p. 45, Box 242, James J. Walker Collection, Mayors' Papers. Jews were also prominent in the distribution of magazines through New York's newsstands, but they were not so centrally identified with the entire industry as were the Minskys with burlesque.

69. October 18, 1932, NCFC Minutes, vol. 516, ACLU. Goldstein's continuing campaign against New York's burlesque theaters can be traced in the *New York Times*, June 27, 1934, p. 14, March 22, 1942, p. 50, December 2, 1942, p. 27; unidentified clipping "Burlesque Assailed in New Affidavits," Box 3629, LaGuardia Collection, Mayors' Papers; *New York Catholic News*, June 30, 1934, p. 5. His participation in the Interfaith Committee on Decency is noted in the *New York Times*, July 10, 1934, p. 1.

70. Goldstein, *The Synagogue and Social Welfare*, p. 267.

71. June 5, 1936, Clifton Read to Members, Box 38, NBRMPC.

72. For examples, see the *Watchman-Examiner*, March 31, 1921, p. 390; *New York Times*, March 8, 1922, p. 1, October 9, 1928, p. 34, December 22, 1931, p. 14, November 28, 1934, p. 25, February 27, 1936, p. 23, May 23, 1938, p. 2, June 16, 1938, p. 19; *New York Catholic News* March 1, 1924, p. 1, April 2, 1927, p. 4, September 13, 1930, p. 4; "Suggested program for Interfaith Committee on Decency," and October 5, 1934, statement of Greater New York Federation of Churches, both vol. 694, ACLU.

73. *New York Catholic News*, March 3, 1945, p. 8. For similar arguments, see *New York Times*, March 8, 1922, p. 1, March 22, 1925, p. 23, February 4, 1927, p. 17, December 22, 1931, p. 14, March 5, 1934, p. 13, June 16, 1938, p. 19; clipping titled "Indecent Features of Plays Ruled Out" in Scrapbook MWEZ +n.c.6521, Lincoln Center; *New York Catholic News*, February 10, 1923, p. 3, March 1, 1924, p. 1, March 17, 1945, p. 10; October 5, 1934, Statement

of the Greater New York Federation of Churches, vol. 694; and April 4, 1938, John J. Mc-Clafferty to Mrs. H. Rice, vol. 1077; both ACLU. While, as far as I can ascertain, the term *moral majority* was not used during this period, references to an "anti-moral minority," and the drawing of a distinction between an immoral "minute minority" and "moral minded persons" who were presumably in the majority raise striking parallels to later antipornography discourse.

74. *New York Times*, February 21, 1927, p. 19; *New York Herald*, November 22, 1923; and *New York American*, December 2, 1923, both in "Censorship — Stage — U.S. — New York" scrapbook, Lincoln Center. See also New York Society for the Suppression of Vice *Annual Report, 1919*; *New York Times*, April 3, 1932, p. 19.

75. Cooney, *The American Pope*, especially pp. 108–110, 196–202.

76. *New York Catholic News*, March 28, 1942, p. 10, November 7, 1942, p. 10. See also *New York Catholic News*, December 26, 1942, p. 3, and March 3, 1945, p. 8.

77. *New York Catholic News*, March 1, 1924, p. 1, May 1, 1926, p. 15, September 30, 1933, p. 11, *New York Times*, March 2, 1925, p. 15.

78. *New York Times*, March 8, 1922, p. 1, March 22, 1925, p. 23; *New York Catholic News*, September 13, 1930, p. 4; *New York World*, November 17, 1930, clipping in vol. 385, ACLU; *New York Catholic News*, February 10, 1923, p. 3, March 7, 1925, p. 1.

79. *New York Times*, February 18, 1924, p. 1, March 2, 1925, p. 15, March 22, 1925, p. 23, March 4, 1926, p. 1, March 7, 1927, p. 11, April 3, 1927, p. 21, August 13, 1930, p. 21, July 16, 1934, p. 11; *New York Catholic News*, March 1, 1924, p. 1; *New York Daily Mirror*, November 18, 1930, clipping in "Censorship: Stage: US: 1930" file, Lincoln Center; *Federal Council Bulletin* (March 1920), pp. 54–55; Rabbi William F. Rosenblum sermon typescript, and March 5, 1945, Thomas A. Madden to Paul Moss, both Box 3352, LaGuardia Collection, Mayors' Papers.

80. *New York World*, November 17, 1930, and December 20, 1930, clippings in vol. 385, ACLU; *New York Times*, March 8, 1922, p. 1, March 13, 1922, p. 18, May 11, 1927, p. 28; *New York Herald-Tribune*, February 26, 1931, clipping in "Censorship: Stage: US: 1930" file, Lincoln Center. Very rarely, the use of such reasoning allowed clerics to support proposals for preexhibition government censorship of adult media. In 1927, for example, Catholic and fundamentalist Protestant clergy supported a bill that would require preproduction censorship of all Broadway scripts by the State Department of Education.

81. March 5, 1945, Thomas A. Madden to Paul Moss, Box 3352, LaGuardia Collection, Mayors' Papers.

82. *New York Catholic News*, December 25, 1920, p. 7; pamphlet attached to March 8, 1921, Charles A. McMahon to President, Motion Picture Directory Co., Box 37, NBRMPC; *New York Catholic News*, March 1, 1924, p. 1, September 17, 1927, p. 5, January 5, 1929, p. 4.

83. McNickle, *To be Mayor of New York*; Steven P. Erie, *Rainbow's End: Irish-Americans and the Dilemmas of Urban Machine Politics, 1840–1985* (Berkeley: University of California Press, 1988).

84. Paul Boyer notes that Catholics were especially strong supporters of the Clean Books Bill in the 1920s, a statewide measure that would have established more lenient

standards for obtaining violations of obscenity statutes in the case of printed matter. The bill never passed. Their support for this state-level legislation fits in with the New York Catholic hierarchy's general pattern of distrusting federal regulation while advocating local and state regulation. The bill did not, however, establish prepublication censorship. See Boyer, *Purity in Print*, chapter 5.

85. Sarna, "Christian America or Secular America?" p. 19; Handy, *Undermined Establishment*, p. 69; Howe, *World of Our Fathers*, p. 379. For a related argument explaining contemporary Jewish liberalism on the issue of pornography, see Wald, *Religion and Politics in the United States*, pp. 75–82.

86. See July 18, 1934, William F. Rosenblum to Clifton R. Read, and "Suggested Program for Interfaith Committee on Decency," both vol. 694, ACLU.

87. See, for example, *New York Catholic News*, July 14, 1934, p. 5, July 20, 1940, p. 22, November 1, 1941, p. 3, December 4, 1943, p. 17; July 16, 1940, Reverend Edward J. Hogan to Fiorello LaGuardia, Box 3569, LaGuardia Collection, Mayors' Papers.

5. Doing Things the American Way

1. On the preference among settlement house and social workers for "constructive" recreation reform, see Perry, *Belle Moskowitz*, chapter 3; Cavallo, *Muscles and Morals*; Peiss, *Cheap Amusements*, chapter 7.

2. The actions of the League for Political Education and the Ethical Culture Society can be found in January 1916 Report of the National Board of Censorship, Box 170, National Board of Review of Motion Pictures Collection, Rare Books and Manuscripts Division, New York Public Library, Astor, Lenox and Tilden Foundations (hereafter cited as NBRMPC); *New York Times*, March 25, 1916, p. 13, February 8, 1927, p. 12, March 31, 1931. For anticensorship positions by the New York City Federation of Women's Clubs, see May 1916 W. M. Covill to William McGuire, Box 64, NBRMPC; June 20, 1916, Report to the General Committee, Box 120, NBRMPC; January 15, 1934 [Mrs. Morrie Ryskind], to Mrs. Charles H. Savin, vol. 693, American Civil Liberties Union Papers, Seeley G. Mudd Library, Princeton University (hereafter cited as ACLU); *New York Times*, April 19, 1934, p. 27 and June 27, 1934, p. 21; *New York Herald-Tribune*, January 30, 1931, clipping in "Censorship — Stage — U.S. — 1930" scrapbook, Billy Rose Theatre Collection, Lincoln Center Library for the Performing Arts (hereafter cited as Lincoln Center).

3. For examples of the Women's City Club's opposition to censorship see *New York Times*, May 1, 1921, 8:2, February 15, 1925, p. 27, February 25, 1925, p. 1; March 13, 1942, Juliet M. Bartlett to Fiorello LaGuardia, Box 3629, LaGuardia Collection, Mayors' Papers Collection, Municipal Archives, Department of Records and Information Services, City of New York (hereafter cited as Mayors' Papers); January 2, 1923, Alice B. Evans to Corresponding Members of the National Committee for Better Films, Box 95, NBRMPC; Perry, "Training for Public Life," p. 39. On the Women's City Club generally see Perry, "Training for Public Life," pp. 28–45. On Belle Moskowitz see Perry, *Belle Moskowitz*. For an example of Dorothy Kenyon's influence, see November 2, 1936, Dorothy Kenyon to Roger Baldwin, vol. 878, ACLU. For an interesting analysis of another Women's City

Club, see Flanagan, "Gender and Urban Political Reform." The National Council on Freedom from Censorship will be discussed at greater length later in this chapter.

4. On *The Inside of the White Slave Traffic*, see chapter 1, this volume. Similarly, when owners of the film *Birth Control* (produced by Margaret Sanger) went to court to contest the license commissioner's suppression of the film, they introduced an affidavit in support of their motion picture on behalf of prominent feminist Henrietta Rodman. See *New York Times*, May 10, 1917, p. 11. In prohibiting exhibition of *Birth Control*, license commissioner George Bell justified his action on the grounds that the film "promote[d] class hatred," but this does not explain a pattern of action against films about white slavery, birth control, and venereal disease; see *New York Times*, July 14, 1917, p. 7; *New York Dramatic News*, May 12, 1917, clipping in Box 32, NBRMPC.

5. The controversy over *The Fight* and *The Lure* can be followed in the following articles in the *New York Times*: September 5, 1913, p. 9, September 7, 1913, 2:3, September 9, 1913, p. 2, September 10, 1913, p. 1, September 12, 1913, p. 11, September 13, 1913, p. 20, September 17, 1913, p. 9, September 18, 1913, p. 10, October 7, 1913, p. 13, October 13, 1913, p. 9, October 15, 1913, p. 11, October 30, 1913, p. 7. There is tantalizing but unsubstantiated evidence that women also led the protest against city closure of *Maya*, a play about prostitution, in 1928. An article in the *New York Telegraph*, February 28, 1928, observed that there had been a "flood of protests from New York society women, clubwomen and literary folk." Helen Arthur, the play's producer, was a member of the feminist group Heterodoxy. See the "Maya" clipping file, Lincoln Center.

6. Cott, *The Grounding of Modern Feminism*, p. 42. On the relationship between feminism and the sexual revolution, see Gordon, *Woman's Body, Woman's Right*; DuBois and Gordon, "Seeking Ecstasy on the Battlefield"; Schwartz, *Radical Feminists of Heterodoxy*; Ellen Kay Trimberger, "Feminism, Men, and Modern Love: Greenwich Village, 1900–1925," in Snitow, Stansell, and Thompson, *Powers of Desire*, pp. 131–152; Rupp, "Feminism and the Sexual Revolution."

7. Boissevain is quoted in *New York Times*, February 4, 1914, p. 8. On Crystal Eastman, see Blanche Wiesen Cook, "Female Support Networks and Political Activism: Lillian Wald, Crystal Eastman, Emma Goldman," in Nancy F. Cott and Elizabeth H. Pleck, eds., *A Heritage of Her Own* (New York: Simon and Schuster, 1979), pp. 412–444; Blanche Wiesen Cook, ed., *Crystal Eastman on Women and Revolution* (New York: Oxford University Press, 1978); and Sochen, *The New Woman in Greenwich Village*. Leila Rupp describes Alva Belmont's views on sex in "Feminism and the Sexual Revolution," pp. 300–301. Catt is quoted in Gordon, *Woman's Body, Woman's Right*, p. 238.

8. Frances Perkins's observations of New York City in the 1920s could also be applied to the previous decade and convey the overlapping networks within New York's progressive community: "The people who did anything were few in number, so that no matter what they did, whether it was art, music, the drama, social work, religion, they all touched each other sooner or later." Perkins herself demonstrates how these networks overlapped in the 1910s. In 1914 she spoke at a "feminist mass meeting" organized by Heterodoxy, a feminist group founded by Marie Jenney Howe. Its members also included Helen Arthur, Inez Milholland Boissevain, Crystal Eastman, Fannie Hurst, and Henri-

etta Rodman (all of whom were active in anticensorship activities). Perkins was an early leader of the Women's City Club, as was Howe. The latter's husband, Frederic Howe, was the director of the National Board of Censorship of Motion Pictures for several years. Perkins is quoted in Ware, *Partner and I*, p. 144; Heterodoxy membership can be found in Schwartz, *Radical Feminists of Heterodoxy*.

9. *New York Times*, September 12, 1913, p. 10, September 18, 1913, p. 10, September 7, 1913, 2:3.

10. On the debates over increased regulation, especially federal censorship, see Feldman, *The National Board of Censorship*, pp. 66–75 and 89–111; and Inglis, *Freedom of the Movies*, pp. 68–73.

11. On the better films movement, see Rosenbloom, "Progressive Reform, Censorship, and the Motion Picture Industry," especially pp. 58–59; Couvares and Peiss, "Sex, Censorship, and the Movies," especially pp. 25–26. See also Hanson, "Catheryne Cooke Gilman"; Jowett, *Film*, p. 129.

12. To avoid confusion, in the discussion that follows I will refer to this group as the National Committee for Better Films throughout.

13. January 4, 1916, Adele F. Woodard to Orrin Cocks, Box 19; June 15, 1916, Minutes, Box 95; September 14, 1916, Minutes, Box 126; all NBRMPC. On the founding of the National Committee on Films For Young People, see Minutes for May 9, 1916, June 15, 1916, September 14, 1916, Box 126, NBRMPC. Its members are listed in January 6, 1917, Orrin Cocks to "my dear friend," Box 95, NBRMPC.

14. Kathryn Kish Sklar, "The Historical Foundations of Women's Power in the Creation of the American Welfare State, 1830–1930," in Koven and Michel, *Mothers of a New World*, pp. 63–65; Blair, *The Clubwoman as Feminist*; Scott, *Natural Allies*, especially chapters 5 and 6.

15. *General Federation Magazine* (April 1918).

16. December 4, 1917, n.a. article [on state censorship efforts], Box 140, NBRMPC.

17. "Motion Picture Survey," *General Federation Magazine* (April 1918); Blair, *The Clubwoman as Feminist*, p. 112. On women's political activism in the period before 1920, see Baker, "The Domestication of Politics"; Flanagan, "Gender and Urban Political Reform"; Monoson, "The Lady and the Tiger"; Kathleen D. McCarthy, "Parallel Power Structures: Women and the Voluntary Sphere" in McCarthy, *Lady Bountiful Revisited*, pp. 1–31; McGerr, "Political Style and Women's Power"; Sklar, "The Historical Foundation of Women's Power"; Scott, *Natural Allies*. The case against overemphasizing 1920 as the defining moment in American women's political history is also stated in Cott, *The Grounding of Modern Feminism*, p. 85 and passim.

18. "Motion Picture Survey," *General Federation Magazine* (April 1918).

19. For board members' belief that women's clubs advocated motion picture censorship, see June 21, 1916, William McGuire to George Eastman, Box 24; February 25, 1916, Helen Varick Boswell to Mrs. Ackerman, Box 27; n.d. press release [re: Mary Gray Peck], Box 41; "Report Regarding Publicity for March and April, 1917," Box 97; February 24, 1916, Report of the Committee on Education and Publicity, Box 120; "The Relation of the National Board of Censorship to Motion Picture Regulation," Box 172; all NBRMPC.

20. "Report Regarding Publicity for March and April, 1917" and "The National Committee on Films for Young People, Summary, Report, Recommendations," Box 97; May 23, 1917, Report to the General Committee, Box 120; February 3, 1917, Orrin Cocks to Madam President, and March 9, 1918, Editor of the Bulletin to Madam, Box 95; all NBRMPC.

21. N.d. press release [re: Mary Gray Peck], Box 41; September 14, 1916, Minutes, National Committee on Films for Young People, Box 126; September 18, 1916, Orrin Cocks to William McGuire, and October 15, 1916, Mary Gray Peck to Orrin Cocks, Box 41; all NBRMPC.

22. September 18, 1916, Orrin Cocks to W. D. McGuire, Box 41; September 14, 1916, Minutes, National Committee on Films for Young People, Box 126; June 21, 1916, William McGuire to George Eastman, Box 24; n.d. press release [re: Mary Gray Peck], Box 41; all NBRMPC.

23. September 18, 1916, Orrin Cocks to William McGuire; September 25, 1916, Orrin Cocks to Mary Gray Peck; n.d. Statement, all Box 41, NBRMPC.

24. 5 February 1917 Mary Gray Peck to W.D. McGuire, Box 41, NBRMPC.

25. Indeed, the timing of Peck's hiring — fund-raising for the position began two months after the 1916 Biennial — suggests that her lecture tour was a response to the agitation for censorship evidenced by clubwomen there. See also Budd, "Film Censorship and Public Cultures."

26. "The Responsibility of the National Board," speech contained in June 5, 1916, Spring Conference transcript, Box 86, NBRMPC.

27. *General Federation of Women's Clubs Magazine* 15, 7 (July 1916), p. 17; Proceedings of the Thirteenth Biennial Convention, Box 0301–3–1/3, General Federation of Women's Clubs Archives, Washington D.C. (hereafter cited as GFWC); *General Federation Magazine* (April 1918), p. 11; June 21, 1916, William McGuire to George Eastman, Box 24, NBRMPC.

28. Proceedings of the Thirteenth Biennial Convention, Box 0301–3–1/3, GFWC; February 25, 1918, Mary Gray Peck to W. D. McGuire, Box 41; May 23, 1917, Report to General Committee, Box 120; both NBRMPC; *General Federation of Women's Clubs Magazine* (May 1917); *General Federation Magazine* (September 1918 and January 1919). The Report of the Special Committee on Motion Pictures appears in the Proceedings of the 1916 Biennial Convention; however, since the committee was appointed at that convention and all other sources agree that it made its report in 1917 at a General Federation Council meeting in New Orleans, I presume that it was included in the Proceedings after the fact. Further, reports differ as to whether committee members resigned or were dismissed. Unfortunately, the minutes from the 1917 council meeting could not be located at the General Federation of Women's Clubs Archives.

29. May 23, 1917, Report to General Committee, Box 120; "Report Regarding Publicity for March and April 1917," Box 97; both NBRMPC; Proceedings of the Fourteenth Biennial Convention, Box 0301–3–1/3, GFWC; *General Federation Magazine* (June and July, 1918).

30. Mrs. Bessie Leach Priddy, "The Civics Department and Motion Pictures," *General*

Federation Magazine (January 1919), pp. 14 and 15. Ruth Inglis attributes this quote to Mrs. Guy Blanchard in *Freedom of the Movies*, p. 78, but the byline is Priddy's. For the argument that both better films work and legalized censorship were necessary, see Florence Butler Blanchard, "The September Symposium and Legalized Censorship," *General Federation Magazine* (January 1919), p. 16.

31. Mrs. O. I. Woodley, "The Club Woman's Point of View," *General Federation Magazine* (January 1919), p. 25. See the articles on motion pictures in this issue for this line of reasoning.

32. Mrs. B. F. Langworthy, quoted in "PTA Scores Film Councils," September 9, 1934, *Washington Herald* clipping, Box 37, NBRMPC. See also January 31, 1923, Mrs. Charles E. Merriam to National Committee for Better Films, Box 34; October 11, 1923, Mrs. A. H. Reeve to Alice B. Evans, Box 37; "The Better Films Movement in 1924," Box 98; "Resolutions of Protest Against the Film Lists of the National Committee for Better Films," Box 150; October 25, 1934, Report of the Better Films National Council, Box 95; all NBRMPC. On the WCTU's approach to film regulation, see Parker, *Purifying America*, chapter 5.

33. See Rosenbloom, "Progressive Reform, Censorship, and the Motion Picture Industry"; and Couvares and Peiss, "Sex, Censorship, and the Movies."

34. "The National Board of Review — who composes it, what are its functions, why does it pursue its work" typescript (March 1921), Box 170, NBRMPC.

35. "Report Regarding Publicity for March and April, 1917, Box 97; see also n.d. press release, Box 41; 1917 typescript and "Better Motion Pictures in Your Community," both Box 97; "Membership Charter," Box 98; "Points for an Address," Box 151; "Better Films and Community Development," Box 170; May 1921 *Film Progress*, Box 96; all NBRMPC.

36. January 8, 1916, William McGuire to Helen Varick Boswell, Box 25, NBRMPC.

37. N.d. press release, Box 41; "Better Films and Community Development," Box 170; *Film Progress* (February and May 1921), Box 96; "Better Motion Pictures in Your Community," Box 97; all NBRMPC. The quote is from "Better Films — The New Year" in *Affiliated Committees for Better Films Bulletin* (September 1917), Box 96; see also "The Motion Picture and the Family," Box 140; both NBRMPC.

38. Blanchard, "The September Symposium and Legalized Censorship," p. 15.

39. Leff and Simmons, *The Dame in the Kimono*; Sklar, *Movie-Made America*; Jacobs, *The Wages of Sin*. A list of women's organizations that cooperated with the Committee on Public Relations can be found in *General Federation News* (November 1922).

40. On the motion picture code see Walsh, *Sin and Censorship*; Leff and Simmons, *The Dame in the Kimono*; Facey, *The Legion of Decency*; Sklar, *Movie-Made America*; Couvares, *Movie Censorship and American Culture*. Women's clubs' participation in better films work during the 1920s is noted in Jowett, *Film*. It is important to note that Catholic women in the International Federation of Catholic Alumnae were integral to the everyday functioning of the Legion of Decency, at least for a time.

41. On opposition to the Comstock Act, see Gordon, *Woman's Body, Woman's Right*, pp. 167–170, 212–214; D'Emilio and Freedman, *Intimate Matters*, pp. 161–164, 232–233. In the early twentieth century lawyer Theodore Schroeder launched a campaign to convince jurists and citizens that obscenity ought never be regulated by the government. On

Schroeder, see Wertheimer, "Free-Speech Fights," chapter 5; Rabban, "The Free Speech League"; Boyer, *Purity in Print*, pp. 41–43. Not until the 1890s did defendants in obscenity prosecutions even begin to raise first amendment guarantees of free speech as a defense, and their arguments were routinely rejected by American courts. For an overview of legal treatments of obscenity in the pre-World War I period, see Schauer, *The Law of Obscenity*; Wertheimer, "Free-Speech Fights"; Gibson, "The Supreme Court and Freedom of Expression."

42. *Mutual Film Corporation v Industrial Commission of Ohio*, 236 U.S. 230, reprinted in De Grazia, *Censorship Landmarks*, pp. 59–63; see also Jowett, "'A Capacity for Evil.'"

43. The traditional account of the emergence of free-speech theory is that it occurred in the postwar period as a response to government repression of dissent, that it was represented in the abandonment of the "bad tendencies" test and the substitution of the "clear and present danger" test, and that its primary theoretician was Zechariah Chafee. See, for example, Hall, *The Magic Mirror*, pp. 262–264; Murphy, *The Shaping of the First Amendment*. Graber has reevaluated Zechariah Chafee's role in this process in *Transforming Free Speech*. Recently, a number of scholars have traced the roots of free-speech doctrine to the period prior to World War I. See Rabban, "The Emergence of Modern First Amendment Doctrine"; Anderson, "The Formative Period of First Amendment Theory"; Wertheimer, "Free-Speech Fights," especially chapters 4 and 5.

44. On the role of the ACLU in this process, see Walker, *In Defense of American Liberties*. In "The Free Speech League" Rabban emphasizes that the ACLU refused to include obscenity in its free speech agenda at the beginning of the 1920s, arguing that it was actually quite conservative in this regard.

45. For reports of the activities of a series of anticensorship committees, see *New York Times*, April 7, 1921, p. 20, December 24, 1921, p. 7, August 27, 1922, 3:1, December 17, 1923, p. 11. In *Purity in Print* Paul Boyer places the formation of an anticensorship coalition somewhat later in the 1920s, identifying its origins in the fight against the Clean Books Bill. My evidence indicates that at least some of the organizations he describes, such as the Authors' League, were already taking steps toward anticensorship activism in the first years of the decade.

46. February 11, 1930, Langdon W. Post to Forrest Bailey, vol. 431, and October 22, 1930, letters to Franklin D. Roosevelt and Louis Waldman, vol. 430; both ACLU.

47. Although I have found no direct evidence, I suspect that Dramatists' Guild member Elmer Rice may have had a direct role in the creation of the Committee Against Stage Censorship and, later, the National Council on Freedom from Censorship. Rice was an early member and a strong presence in the group, and the Committee Against Stage Censorship was originally founded during a dispute between the guild and Actors Equity over voluntary regulation; it sided with the guild. See December 10, 1930, press release, "Union Offers Aid in New York Censorship Fight," vol. 404b, ACLU.

48. Information on the formation of the NCFC can be found in vols. 463 and 516, ACLU; see also November 6, 1931, Hatcher Hughes to National Board of Review, Box 38, NBRMPC. Apparently, the funds for the creation of the Committee Against Stage Censorship were furnished by Mary Ware Dennett in the wake of her prosecution on ob-

scenity charges. See Walker, *In Defense of American Liberties*, pp. 83–85; Boyer, *Purity in Print*, p. 241. As these authors note, the ACLU became interested in obscenity issues in 1929, after Arthur Garfield Hays and Morris Ernst became co-counsel for the organization. Anticensorship attorney Edward De Grazia misleadingly states that the ACLU did not take up obscenity as a policy matter until the 1940s. See *Girls Lean Back Everywhere*, 75n.

49. See, for example, November 6, 1931, Hatcher Hughes to National Board of Review, Box 38, NBRMPC; February 15, 1932, Minutes, Joint Meeting of the ACLU Board of Directors and the National Council on Freedom from Censorship, vol. 516, ACLU.

50. N.d. press release entitled "Dramatists Fight Censorship," vol. 404b; *New York Herald-Tribune*, December 2, 1930, December 10, 1930; and *New York World*, December 10, 1930, clippings in vol. 385; *New York Herald-Tribune*, January 25, 1931, clipping in vol. 604; all ACLU; *New York Times*, December 2, 1930, p. 30, December 14, 1930, 9:1, October 7, 1931, p. 28; January 28, 1931, Forrest Bailey to Professor Hatcher Hughes, vol. 516, ACLU. Significantly, Elmer Rice was an early critic of the play jury system. In 1922 he condemned the plan, suggesting that the play jury was a form of censorship that was equally as dangerous to artistic innovation as "official" censorship. See *New York Times*, January 29, 1922, 6:1.

51. March 29, 1931, News Release, February 15, 1932, Minutes of a joint meeting of the ACLU Board of Directors and the NCFC, January 28, 1931, Forrest Bailey to Professor Hatcher Hughes, vol. 516; June 5, 1936, Clifton Read to Members, vol. 878; letters dated June 1936 from various NCFC members to Henry Imre Kohn, vol. 900; "Repeal the Special Police Powers" pamphlet, vol. 508; "Statement . . . on the recent agitation against the movies," vol. 677; all ACLU; n.d. National Council on Freedom from Censorship pamphlet, "Censorship Covers Up But Does Not Cure," Box 38, NBRMPC.

52. N.d. National Council on Freedom from Censorship pamphlet, "Censorship Covers Up But Does Not Cure," Box 38, NBRMPC.

53. July 2, 1931, [Roger Baldwin] to Upton Sinclair, vol. 516, June 10, 1936, Alexander Lindey to Henry Imre Kohn, vol. 900, both ACLU. See also *New York Herald-Tribune*, October 1, 1930, clipping, vol. 385; [July 16, 1934] Statement by the National Council on Freedom from Censorship, vol. 677; February 13, 1931, H. L. Mencken to Forrest Bailey, vol. 516; [March 27, 1936] typescript, "Conference with Commissioner of Licenses," vol. 877; all ACLU; letters to LaGuardia from Mr. and Mrs. Ross, Jesse Zunser, Harold Kiviat, and Miss H. Hummel et al., all Box 3351, LaGuardia Collection, Mayors' Papers.

54. Law partners Morris Ernst and Alexander Lindey represented both Mary Ware Dennett in *United States v Dennett* and Random House, the defendant in *United States v One Book Called "Ulysses."* The Dennett case was decided before the NCFC was formed, while Ernst was ACLU co-counsel; both men also became active in the NCFC. The Dennett case established as precedent in New York the "dominant effect" test (that is, the requirement that a work must be considered in its entirety in order to judge its obscenity). Each case had influence far beyond the jurisdictional boundaries of the Second Circuit Court of Appeals. The opinions for both cases are reprinted in De Grazia, *Censorship Landmarks*, pp. 83–86, and 94–101. See Schauer, *The Law of Obscenity*, pp. 27–29, for

analysis of the ways in which these and other New York cases prefigured the standards for judging obscenity established in 1957 by the U.S. Supreme Court in *Roth v. United States*.

55. Walker, *In Defense of American Liberties*, p. 83.

56. April 22, 1932, J. J. Schalet to Gordon Moss (two letters), vol. 604, ACLU.

57. Transcript of meeting to discuss response to *Trio* [March 1, 1945], p. 31, vol. 2638, ACLU. In addition, insisting on a jury trial mandated that indictment proceed by Grand Jury, which would make it even more difficult to bring a case to trial.

58. For examples of the demand for trial by jury in obscenity prosecutions see March 29, 1931, News Release, and July 2, 1931, [Roger Baldwin] to Upton Sinclair, vol. 516; April 16, 1936, Henry Moskowitz to F. H. LaGuardia, and "Conference with Commissioner of Licenses" (March 27, 1936), vol. 877; "Memorandum of a Meeting Held at the Town Hall Club," vol. 1077; n.d. clipping, *New York World-Telegram* [authored by Frederick Woltman], vol. 2348; June 10, 1943, [Elmer Rice] to Ronald Jump, vol. 2435; "Report by Osmond K. Fraenkel," [1945], vol. 2638; all ACLU; March 3, 1942, Howard Lindsay et al. to Fiorello LaGuardia, Box 3629; February 28, 1945, Gilbert Seldes to LaGuardia, Box 3351; March 2, 1945, Russel Crouse to Fiorello LaGuardia, and [March 3, 1945] Telegram, "owners and operators of legitimate theatres" to Fiorello LaGuardia, Box 3352; all LaGuardia Collection, Mayors' Papers; February 19, 1946, John Haynes Holmes and Roger N. Baldwin to William O'Dwyer, Box 123, William O'Dwyer Collection, Mayors' Papers; March 18, 1932, Gordon Moss to Wilton Barrett, and Memorandum in support of abolition of state motion picture censorship [1934], Box 38, NBRMPC; *New York Times*, January 12, 1943, p. 20, March 8, 1945, p. 1. For a different interpretation of understandings of the jury in anticensorship thought, see Gurstein, *The Repeal of Reticence*, p. 207.

59. On constructions of "liberty" and "freedom" in American history, see Kammen, *Spheres of Liberty*; Rodgers, *Contested Truths*, pp. 213–214.

60. *New York Times*, December 23, 1942, p. 22, and February 1, 1942, p. 45; *New York Catholic News*, December 26, 1942, p. 3. Anti-obscenity activists used similar arguments. For examples, see the *New York Times*, December 2, 1941, p. 17; *New York Catholic News*, November 7, 1942, p. 1; February 27, 1942, "A Friend" to LaGuardia, n.d. Mr. Benson to LaGuardia, March 25, 1942, John A. O'Brien to LaGuardia, Box 3629, LaGuardia Collection, Mayors' Papers.

61. March 3, 1942, Howard Lindsay et al. to LaGuardia, Box 3629, LaGuardia Collection, Mayors' Papers. See also "Says Mayor Aims to Censor Theaters," February 24, 1942, *New York World-Telegram* clipping, vol. 2348, ACLU; March 16, 1942, Frank Gillmore to Paul Moss, Box 3629, LaGuardia Collection, Mayors' Papers; *New York Times*, February 22, 1942, p. 29, February 25, 1942, p. 21, March 18, 1942, p. 28, March 30, 1942, p. 21.

62. N.d. Board of Governors, Association of Theatrical Agents and Managers to LaGuardia, March 5, 1945, Mrs. A. H. Bergson to LaGuardia, n.a. n.d. postcard to LaGuardia, n. d. Alexander H. Cohen to LaGuardia, n.d. Miss Helen Beal to LaGuardia, n.d. L. Arnold Weissburger to LaGuardia, Box 3351; March 7, 1945, Mrs. Ira Hinsdale to LaGuardia, and n.d. Glory Harris to LaGuardia, Box 3352; both LaGuardia Collection, Mayors' Papers.

63. The quotes are from letters to LaGuardia from Al Aranoff, Harold Kramer, and Anthony T. Bartuski, Box 3351, LaGuardia Collection, Mayors' Papers. Boxes 3351 and 3352 contain letters, postcards, and telegrams from hundreds of New Yorkers. While some of these were sent by organizations that had long been active in the anticensorship campaign, many came from individuals who appear to have had no formal connection to the entertainment industry or to the anticensorship coalition.

64. On the constitution of authority in democratic societies, see Joshua Cohen, "Procedure and Substance in Deliberative Democracy" in Benhabib, *Democracy and Difference*, pp. 95–119; Connolly, "Modern Authority and Ambiguity"; Lincoln, *Authority*. For a compelling interpretation of the issues of citizenship and sexuality in the contemporary U.S., see Berlant, *The Queen of America Goes to Washington City*.

65. On the jury as a model of direct democracy, see Abramson, *We, the Jury*; Constable, *The Law of the Other*. On definitions of citizenship, see Dietz, "Context is All"; Pocock, "The Ideal of Citizenship Since Classical Times."

66. *United States v. One Book Called "Ulysses"*, 5 F. Supp. 182 (1933), reprinted in De Grazia, *Censorship Landmarks*, pp. 94–96.

67. Women were awarded the right to sit on juries in New York state in *Gerry v Volger*, 298 N.Y.S. 433, 252 A.D. 217. Women's participation in the citizens' play jury is documented in *New York Times*, March 22, 1925, 9:6, June 8, 1926, p. 1, November 16, 1926, p. 11; *New York World*, November 16, 1926, p. 17.

68. See Muncy, *Creating a Female Dominion*; Molly Ladd-Taylor, "Hull House Goes to Washington: Women and the Children's Bureau," in Noralee Frankel and Nancy S. Dye, eds., *Gender, Class, Race, and Reform in the Progressive Era* (Lexington: University Press of Kentucky, 1991), pp. 110–126; Koven and Michel, *Mothers of a New World*, especially the essays by Sklar, Boris, Michel, and Ladd-Taylor; Gordon, *Pitied But Not Entitled* and "Social Insurance and Public Assistance"; Skocpol, *Protecting Soldiers and Mothers*; Ware, *Partner and I*.

69. Gordon, *Pitied But Not Entitled*; Gwendolyn Mink, "The Lady and the Tramp: Gender, Race, and the Origins of the American Welfare State," in Gordon, *Women, the State, and Welfare*, pp. 91–122; Barbara J. Nelson, "The Origins of the Two-Channel Welfare State: Workmen's Compensation and Mothers' Aid," also in Gordon, *Women, the State, and Welfare*, pp. 123–151; Ware, *Partner and I*.

70. For examples, see the numerous telegrams from female burlesque employees to Mayor LaGuardia in Box 3190; an anonymous letter (marked received February 26, 1942) to LaGuardia in Box 3629; both LaGuardia Collection, Mayors' Papers; *New York World-Telegram*, February 27, 1942, in "Burlesque 1940–1949" clipping file, Lincoln Center.

71. Webster's resignation is noted in an undated *New York Herald-Tribune* clipping, Box 3351, LaGuardia Collection, Mayors' Papers, and in Curtin, *"We Can Always Call Them Bulgarians,"* p. 276. At the time of the *Trio* incident she was involved in a ten-year relationship with actress Eva Le Gallienne. Her sexual identity is discussed in Robert A. Schanke, *Shattered Applause: The Lives of Eva Le Gallienne* (Carbondale: Southern Illinois University Press, 1992), and is also obliquely referred to by director Herman Shumlin, quoted in Curtin, *"We Can Always Call Them Bulgarians,"* p. 201. One anonymous

correspondent used Webster's sexuality to justify his or her opposition to *Trio*. This person wrote Mayor LaGuardia: "It may interest you to know Margaret Webster is a woman who has abnormal relationships with women. Please Mr. Mayor fight Trio." February 5, 1945, "a friend" to LaGuardia, Box 3351, LaGuardia Collection, Mayors' Papers.

72. Joan B. Landes, "The Performance of Citizenship: Democracy, Gender, and Difference in the French Revolution" in Benhabib, *Democracy and Difference*, p. 296. Also relevant here are considerations of authority's gender. See, for example, Jones, "What Is Authority's Gender?"

Conclusion

1. *New York Times*, May 14, 1911, p. 13, April 18, 1920, 6:5, May 11, 1920, p. 17, September 29, 1921, p. 2, February 20, 1926, p. 19, May 30, 1928, p. 13, July 16, 1928, p. 25, March 30, 1942, p. 15.

2. On criticism of the Legion of Decency, see Walsh, *Sin and Censorship*, pp. 110, 164, 172.

3. Breazeale, "In Spite of Women"; Theodore Peterson, *Magazines in the Twentieth Century* (Urbana: University of Illinois Press, 1964), p. 355; D'Emilio and Freedman, *Intimate Matters*, p. 302. On *Playboy*, also see Ehrenreich, *The Hearts of Men*, chapter 4.

4. U.S. House of Representatives, *Investigation of Literature*, pp. 9–12; Lockhart and McClure, "Literature, the Law of Obscenity, and the Constitution," especially pp. 302–304; D'Emilio and Freedman, *Intimate Matters*, p. 280.

5. Gilbert, *A Cycle of Outrage*, pp. 144–145.

6. May, *Homeward Bound*.

7. Charles H. Keating, quoting from a May 1956 Internal Security Report to the Senate Judiciary Committee, in U.S. House of Representatives, *Mailing of Obscene Matter*, p. 74; "Brain Washing: American Style," reprinted in U.S. Senate, *Hearings Before the Subcommittee to Investigate Juvenile Delinquency*, p. 35.

8. D'Emilio, *Sexual Politics, Sexual Communities*; U.S. House of Representatives, *Obscene Matter Sent Through the Mail*, p. 19.

9. U.S. Senate, *Obscene and Pornographic Literature*, p. 8.

10. U.S. House of Representatives, *Hearings Before Select Committee*, p. 217.

11. Information about clubwomen's activities can be found in issues of the *General Federation Clubwoman* from 1954 through 1960. The Colorado claim is in the October 1955 issue, p. 10. On the "traditional" family, see Stephanie Coontz, *The Way We Never Were: American Families and the Nostalgia Trap* (New York: Basic, 1992).

12. Gilbert, *A Cycle of Outrage*, p. 40.

13. Psychiatrist Fredric Wertham, who played an important role in mobilizing this activism, appealed explicitly to mothers on these grounds. See for example, Wertham, *Seduction of the Innocent*, pp. 396–397. On concerns about the media, see Gilbert, *A Cycle of Outrage*, especially chapters 2, 4 and 6. On cold war-era criticism of mothers, see May, *Homeward Bound*.

14. Gilbert, *A Cycle of Outrage*, pp. 105–106.

15. Wertham, *Seduction of the Innocent*, pp. 13, 326. Wertham did not trouble to comment on how a drawing of a gorilla was more real than a stuffed gorilla.

16. Ibid., pp. 13, 329.

17. Ibid., p. 91.

18. Ibid., pp. 175–187. Similar testimony about the relationship between pornography and the proliferation of perversions was offered in congressional hearings during the decade. For example, when the Senate Subcommittee to Investigate Juvenile Delinquency investigated pornographic materials, they heard from Dr. George Henry about pornography's ability to turn individuals to a wide range of fetishes, including high-heel, leather and rubber, and lingerie, as well as bondage and sadomasochism, and from Dr. Benjamin Karpman, who testified about spanking, sadomasochism, and homosexuality, among other practices. See *Obscene and Pornographic Literature*, pp. 9–13.

19. Wertham, *Seduction of the Innocent*, pp. 189–193.

20. Quoted in *Mailing of Obscene Matter*, p. 26; *Obscene Matter Sent Through the Mail*, p. 49.

21. U. S. Senate, *Control of Obscene Material*, p. 8.

22. *Hearings Before the Select Committee on Current Pornographic Materials*, pp. 267, 285, 363; *Hearings Before the Subcommittee to Investigate Juvenile Delinquency*, p. 188.

23. Judge Curtis Bok in *Commonwealth v Gordon*, 66 D. & C. 101 (1949), reprinted in De Grazia, *Censorship Landmarks*, pp. 150–165; Lockhart and McClure, "Literature, the Law of Obscenity, and the Constitution." Overviews of these changes can be found in Lockhart and McClure, "Literature, the Law of Obscenity, and the Constitution"; Blanchard, "The American Urge to Censor"; and De Grazia, *Girls Lean Back Everywhere*.

24. *Joseph Burstyn, Inc. v. Wilson*, 343 U.S. 495 (1952), reprinted in De Grazia, *Censorship Landmarks*, pp. 180–192.

25. *Butler v Michigan*, 352 U.S. 380 (1957), reprinted in De Grazia, *Censorship Landmarks*, pp. 301–302.

26. See, for example, Lockhart and McClure, "Literature, the Law of Obscenity, and the Constitution." At this time, however, even these authors distinguished between obscenity and pornography, characterizing pornography as "indefensible" and not entitled to constitutional protection.

27. The appeal to prurient interest was here defined as having a "tendency to excite lustful thoughts." *Roth v. United States*, 354 U.S. 476 (1957), reprinted in De Grazia, *Censorship Landmarks*, pp. 290–300.

28. Quoted in Richard Kuh, *Foolish Figleaves?* p. 43.

29. Section 22-A was first passed at the urging of Fiorello LaGuardia's administration in 1941 and was amended in 1954 upon the recommendation of the New York State Joint Legislative Committee to Study the Publication of Comics.

30. *Kingsley Books Inc. v. Brown*, 354 U.S. 436 (1957), reprinted in De Grazia, *Censorship Landmarks*, pp. 265–268; Kuh, *Foolish Figleaves*, pp. 43–46.

31. *Obscene Matter Sent Through the Mail*, pp. 1, 8; *Control of Obscene Material*, p. 5.

32. *Obscene Matter Sent Through the Mail*, p. 3; *Mailing of Obscene Matter*, pp. 3–4 and passim; see also *Obscene Matter Sent Through the Mail*, pp. 27–28, for a report of a

Chicago law prohibiting the dissemination to minors of materials that have the effect of "substantially arousing sexual desires in persons under the age of 17 years."

33. *Obscene Matter Sent Through the Mail*, pp. 29–33; see also p. 3–4, 45; U.S. House of Representatives, *Circulation of Obscene and Pornographic Material*, pp. 3, 31.

34. *Mailing of Obscene Matter*, pp. 55–56. In fact, the statute permitted prosecution not only at the point of deposit or delivery but at any point along the way; however, after its passage the Post Office Department indicated it planned only to prosecute at the deposit or delivery point. See *Control of Obscene Material*, pp. 10, 71.

35. *Control of Obscene Material*, p. 40.

36. *Circulation of Obscene and Pornographic Material*, p. 3; *Control of Obscene Material*, p. 46.

37. De Grazia, *Girls Lean Back Everywhere*, pp. 552, 559; Jules Witcover, "Civil War Over Smut," *Nation*, May 11, 1970, pp. 550–551; *The Report of the Commission on Obscenity and Pornography* (Washington, D.C.: GPO, 1970), p. 1 (hereafter cited as *Report*); see also Blanchard, "The American Urge to Censor," pp. 813–816; Kendrick, *The Secret Museum*, pp. 213–219.

38. "Odd Man In," *Newsweek*, September 21, 1970, p. 44; *Report*, pp. 51, 387; Witcover, "Civil War Over Smut," p. 552; "Porno Politics," *Nation*, November 9, 1970, pp. 452–453; "Is Smut Good for You?" *Time*, October 12, 1970, p. 19; "Porno Report Becomes Political Football," *Publishers Weekly*, October 12, 1970, p. 34; "Pornography and Politics," *Newsweek*, August 17, 1970, p. 81.

39. *Report*, p. 47.

40. Ibid., p. 48.

41. Ibid., pp. 196–197, p. 49.

42. Ibid., pp. 51–52.

43. Parker, *Purifying America*, p. 216.

44. *Report*, p. 385. On the increasing reliance on social scientific evidence of harm, see Gurstein, *The Repeal of Reticence*.

45. *Report*, pp. 66–67. Like all of their proposed legislation (the commission also drafted a law prohibiting public display of sexually explicit material), this model ordinance governed only pictorial representations of sex, not words.

46. Ibid., p. 386.

47. Ibid., pp. 419–420, emphasis original.

48. Ibid., pp. 464, 535–536.

49. Ibid., p. 549.

50. Quoted in De Grazia, *Girls Lean Back Everywhere*, p. 569; see also Blanchard, "The American Urge to Censor," pp. 816–817. Interestingly, the majority report of the President's Commission on Obscenity and Pornography criticized the *Roth* standard on exactly these grounds: that among Supreme Court justices there was no consensus about which community's standards should be consulted. See p. 314.

51. The *Report*'s authors relied here on the 1969 *Stanley v Georgia* decision, which recognized a right to private possession of pornography. See especially pp. 304–307.

52. Kendrick, *The Secret Museum*, p. 234.

53. *Attorney General's Commission on Pornography Final Report* (Washington, D.C.: GPO, 1986), chapter 5 (hereafter cited as *Final Report*).

54. See the individual statements by Henry Hudson, Diane Cusack, James Dobson, and Bruce Ritter.

55. Indeed, the members of the Meese Commission commented on this absence, taking it as a sign of changes in the pornography industry itself: "No clearer measure exists of the radical shift in the issues confronted by the Commission on Obscenity and Pornography in 1970 and those facing this one than the problem of child pornography." The Commissioners also charged, incorrectly, that their predecessors had recommended the "repeal of all laws restraining distribution of sexually explicit materials to children." See *Final Report*, p. 595.

56. *Report*, pp. 19, 24, 53.

57. Ibid., p. 201.

58. Diana E. H. Russell with Laura Lederer, "Questions We Get Asked Most Often," in Lederer, *Take Back the Night*, pp. 10–11.

59. MacKinnon, *Toward a Feminist Theory of the State*, p. 196.

60. Variations of the ordinance were passed in Minneapolis, where it was vetoed by the mayor, and Indianapolis. It was declared unconstitutional in *American Booksellers Association Inc. v. Hudnut*, 771 F.2· 323 (7th Cir. 1985), aff'd mem. 106 S.Ct. 1172 (1986).

61. There is a voluminous literature on the feminist antiporn movement and the so-called feminist porn wars. Some important texts include Burstyn, *Women Against Censorship*; Mary Caputi, *Voluptuous Yearnings: A Feminist Theory of the Obscene* (Lanham, Md.: Rowman and Littlefield, 1994); Dworkin, *Pornography*; Caught Looking Collective, *Caught Looking*; Gubar and Hoff, *For Adult Users Only*; Leidholdt and Raymond, *The Sexual Liberals and the Attack on Feminism*; MacKinnon, *Feminism Unmodified*; MacKinnon, *Toward a Feminist Theory of the State*; MacKinnon, *Only Words*; Segal and McIntosh, *Sex Exposed*. An interesting analysis of MacKinnon's approach to pornography can be found in Gates, "To 'Deprave and Corrupt.'"

62. Vance, "The Meese Commission on the Road."

63. *Final Report*, p. 52.

64. Ibid., p. 78.

65. Ibid., pp. 755–756.

66. There is much debate about how to describe those within feminism who take different positions about pornography: *sexual liberals, sex radicals, antipornography, propornography, radical feminists, cultural feminists, procensorship, anticensorship*. My use of this term here reflects antipornography feminists' self-designation and is not intended as an argument that antipornography feminists are the "true" radicals.

67. Vance, "The Meese Commission on the Road," p. 80.

68. *Final Report*, pp. 769–772.

69. Ibid., p. 769.

70. Ironically, it was on exactly this basis that three of the four women members of the commission dissented from its report. Commissioners Judith Becker, Ellen Levine, and Deanne Tilton-Durfee protested against "any judgmental and condescending efforts

to speak on women's behalf as though they were helpless, mindless children" and defended "the rights of all citizens to participate in legal activities if their participation is truly voluntary." *Final Report*, p. 194.

71. Actually, the feminist anti-porn analysis constitutes *all* viewers of pornography as vulnerable: male viewers who like earlier burlesque patrons may be led to commit acts of sexual violence and female viewers who are taught oppressive models of femininity and terrorized by the images that men force them to watch.

72. Concern with protection of children was used to justify passage of the Communications Decency Act in 1996. Those provisions of the act criminalizing the transmission of "indecent" or "patently offensive" messages to minors were held unconstitutional by the U.S. Supreme Court. See *Reno v ACLU*, 117 S.Ct. 2329 (1997).

73. This, of course, is only one of many problematic implications of the contemporary feminist antipornography movement identified by anticensorship feminists. For another perspective on the problems of claiming citizenship from the status of victim, see Berlant, *The Queen of America Goes to Washington City*. A different analysis of the ways that feminist antipornography activism refigured the vulnerable viewer (or the "young person") can be found in Kendrick, *The Secret Museum*, pp. 227–239.

74. *Final Report*, chapter 7.

SELECTED BIBLIOGRAPHY

MANUSCRIPT COLLECTIONS

Columbia University, New York, N.Y.
    Rare Book and Manuscript Library
        Frank Smithwick Hogan Papers
        Society for the Prevention of Crime Papers
    Oral History Research Office
        Morris L. Ernst Interview, Socialist Movement Project
Elmira College, Elmira, New York
    New York State Federation of Women's Clubs Collection
General Federation of Women's Clubs Archives, Washington, D.C.
    General Federation of Women's Clubs Collection
Library of Congress, Washington, D.C.
    Manuscript Division
        John Purroy Mitchel Papers
        Mae West Papers
        New York Society for the Suppression of Vice Records
    Motion Picture, Broadcasting, and Recorded Sound Division
Municipal Archives, Department of Records and Information Services, City of New York
    Mayors' Papers
        William J. Gaynor Collection
        John F. Hylan Collection
        Fiorello H. LaGuardia Collection
        George B. McClellan Collection
        William O'Dwyer Collection
        James J. Walker Collection
    City Council Collection
    New York County District Attorneys Collection
Municipal Reference Library, City of New York
    Board of Aldermen Proceedings, 1906–1945
    City of New York Department of Police Annual Reports, 1906–1957
    Court of Special Sessions Annual Reports, 1911–1960
    City of New York Department of Licenses Annual Reports, 1904–1956
    Annual Report of the Domestic Relations Court, City of New York, 1940
    Cosby's Code of Ordinances of the City of New York
    General Ordinances of the City of New York, 1906
    Administrative Code of the City of New York, 1938

New York State Penal Code, 1940
    Laws of New York, 1941
New York Historical Society, New York, N.Y.
    Women's Municipal League Records
New York Public Library, New York, N.Y.
    Rare Books and Manuscripts Division
        Committee of Fourteen Papers
        National Board of Review of Motion Pictures Collection
    Jewish Division
        New York Board of Jewish Ministers, President's Report, 1927
    Women's Municipal League, *Bulletin*, 1909–1913
New York Public Library Annex
    Forty-Second Street Property Owners and Merchants Association, *Activities*, 1936
    New York Society for the Suppression of Vice Annual Reports, 1909–1945
    "Sex Offenses in New York City: A Study by the Staff of the Citizens Committee on
        the Control of Crime in New York," 1938
New York Public Library at Lincoln Center, New York, N.Y.
    Billy Rose Theatre Collection of the Performing Arts Research Center
        Clippings, Scrapbooks, and Programme Files
        National Board of Review of Motion Pictures Records
        Minsky Papers on Appeal
New York University, Robert F. Wagner Labor Archives, New York, N.Y.
    Actors' Equity Association Records
    American Guild of Variety Artists Records
    Associated Actors and Artists of America Records
Players' Club, Walter Hampden-Edwin Booth Theatre Collection, New York, N.Y.
    Chuck Callahan Burlesque Collection
Princeton University, Seeley G. Mudd Manuscript Library, Princeton, N.J.
    American Civil Liberties Union Archives
State Historical Society of Wisconsin, Madison, Wisc.
    John Saxton Sumner Papers

NEWSPAPERS AND MAGAZINES

American Hebrew, 1909–1925
American Mercury, 1927
Christian Advocate, 1920–1927, 1941–1943
Churchman, 1926–1937
Federal Council Bulletin, 1918–1945
General Federation Clubwoman, 1954–1960
General Federation Magazine, 1914, 1917–1930

Jewish Woman, 1921–1931
Nation, 1970, 1986
Newsweek, 1970, 1986
New York Catholic News, 1916–1945
New York Dramatic News, 1909–1917
New York Herald-Tribune, 1919–1937
New York Times, 1900–1945
New York World, 1926–1930
Publishers Weekly, 1970, 1986
Theatre Magazine, 1923
Time Magazine, 1970, 1986
Variety, 1908, 1916, 1946
Watchman-Examiner, 1920–1930
Zit's Entertainment Weekly, 1930–1937

PUBLISHED PRIMARY SOURCES

Addams, Jane. *The Spirit of Youth and City Streets.* Urbana: University of Illinois Press, 1972 [1909].
Asch, Sholem. *The God of Vengeance.* Trans. Isaac Goldberg. Boston: Stratford, 1918.
Attorney General's Commission on Pornography. *Final Report.* Washington, D.C.: GPO, 1986.
Baker, Dorothy. *Trio.* Boston: Houghton Mifflin, 1943.
Bourdet, Edouard. *The Captive.* Trans. Arthur Hornblow Jr. New York: Brentano's, 1926.
"Censorship for Moving Pictures." *Survey,* April 3, 1909, pp. 8–9.
Chase, William Sheafe and Frank L. Dyer. "The Great Debate: Shall the Plays Be Censored?" Brooklyn: Motion Picture Magazine, n.d.
Collier, John. "Cheap Amusements." *Survey,* April 11, 1908, pp. 73–76.
——. "Film Shows and Lawmakers." *Survey,* February 8, 1913, pp. 643–644.
Davis, Michael, Jr. *The Exploitation of Pleasure.* New York: Russell Sage Foundation, 1911.
Fosdick, Raymond B. *A Report on the Condition of Moving Picture Shows in New York.* New York: n.p., 1911.
Goldstein, Sidney E. *The Synagogue and Social Welfare.* New York: Bloch, 1955.
Hays, Arthur Garfield. *Let Freedom Ring.* New York: Liveright, 1937.
McAdoo, William. *When the Court Takes a Recess.* New York: Dutton, 1924.
McDermott, John Francis and Kendall B. Taft, eds. *Sex in the Arts: A Symposium.* New York: Harper, 1932.
"The Morals of the Movies." *Outlook,* June 29, 1914, pp. 387–388.
Nathan, George Jean. "The Theatre." *American Mercury,* March 1927, pp. 373–374.
National Board of Censorship of Motion Pictures. *Standards of the National Board of Censorship of Motion Pictures.* [New York]: n.p., n.d.

Oberholtzer, Ellis Paxson. *The Morals of the Movie*. N.p., Jerome S. Ozer, 1971 [1922].

Perlman, William J., ed. *The Movies on Trial*. New York: MacMillan, 1936.

President's Commission on Obscenity and Pornography. *Report*. Washington, D.C.: GPO, 1970.

Schroeder, Theodore. *"Obscene" Literature and Constitutional Law*. New York: n.p., 1911.

Tevis, Charles V. "Censoring the Five-Cent Drama." *World Today* (1910), pp. 1132–1139.

U.S. Congress. House. *Circulation of Obscene and Pornographic Material*. Washington, D.C.: GPO, 1960.

——. House. *Hearings Before the Select Committee on Current Pornographic Materials*. Washington, D.C.: GPO, 1953.

——. House. *Investigation of Literature Allegedly Containing Objectionable Material*. Washington, D.C.: GPO, 1953.

——. House. *Mailing of Obscene Matter*. Washington, D.C.: GPO, 1958.

——. House. *Obscene Matter Sent Through the Mail*. Washington, D.C.: GPO, 1959.

——. House. Committee on Education. *Motion Picture Commission Hearings*. Washington, D.C.: GPO, 1914 and 1916.

——. Senate. *Control of Obscene Material*. Washington, D.C.: GPO, 1960.

——. Senate. *Hearings Before the Subcommittee to Investigate Juvenile Delinquency*. Washington, D.C.: GPO, 1954.

——. Senate. *Obscene and Pornographic Literature and Juvenile Delinquency (Interim Report)*. Washington, D.C.: GPO, 1956.

Wertham, Fredric. *Seduction of the Innocent*. New York: Rinehart, 1954.

Young, Donald Ramsey. *Motion Pictures: A Study in Social Legislation*. Philadelphia: Westbrook, 1922.

SECONDARY SOURCES

Abramson, Jeffrey. *We, the Jury: The Jury System and the Ideal of Democracy*. New York: Basic, 1994.

Adickes, Sandra L. *To Be Young Was Very Heaven: Women in New York Before the First World War*. New York: St. Martin's, 1997.

Agnew, Jean-Christophe. *Worlds Apart: The Market and the Theatre in Anglo-American Thought, 1550–1750*. New York: Cambridge University Press, 1986.

Allen, Frederick Lewis. *Only Yesterday: An Informal History of the 1920s*. New York: Harper and Row, 1931.

Allen, Robert C. *Horrible Prettiness: Burlesque and American Culture*. Chapel Hill: University of North Carolina Press, 1991.

——. "Motion Picture Exhibition in Manhattan, 1906–1912: Beyond the Nickelodeon." In Gorham Kindem, ed., *The American Movie Industry*, pp. 12–24. Carbondale, Ill.: Southern Illinois University Press, 1982.

Anderson, Alexis J. "The Formative Period of First Amendment Theory, 1870–1915." *American Journal of Legal History* 24 (1980): 56–75.

Armour, Robert A. "Effects of Censorship Pressure on the New York Nickelodeon Market, 1907–1909." *Film History* 4 (1990): 113–121.

Baker, Paula. "The Domestication of Politics: Women and American Political Society, 1780–1920." *American Historical Review* 89 (June 1984): 620–647.

Bayor, Ronald. *Neighbors in Conflict: The Irish, Germans, Jews and Italians of New York City, 1929–1941*. 2d. ed. Urbana: University of Illinois Press, 1988.

Beisel, Nicola. *Imperiled Innocents: Anthony Comstock and Family Reproduction in Victorian America*. Princeton: Princeton University Press, 1997.

Bendroth, Margaret Lamberts. *Fundamentalism and Gender, 1875 to the Present*. New Haven: Yale University Press, 1993.

Benhabib, Seyla, ed. *Democracy and Difference: Contesting the Boundaries of the Political*. Princeton: Princeton University Press, 1996.

Berlant, Lauren. *The Queen of America Goes to Washington City: Essays on Sex and Citizenship*. Durham: Duke University Press, 1997.

Berrol, Selma C. "In Their Image: German Jews and the Americanization of the *Ost Juden* in New York City." *New York History* 63, 4 (October 1982): 417–433.

Bérubé, Alan. *Coming Out Under Fire: The History of Gay Men and Women in World War II*. New York: Free, 1990.

Biale, David. *Eros and the Jews: From Biblical Israel to Contemporary America*. New York: Basic, 1992.

Black, Gregory D. *Hollywood Censored: Morality Codes, Catholics, and the Movies*. New York: Cambridge University Press, 1994.

Blair, Karen J. *The Clubwoman as Feminist: True Womanhood Redefined, 1868–1914*. New York: Holmes and Meier, 1980.

Blanchard, Margaret A. "The American Urge to Censor: Freedom of Expression Versus the Desire to Sanitize Society — From Anthony Comstock to 2 Live Crew." *William and Mary Law Review* 33 (1992): 741–851.

Boyer, Paul. *Purity in Print: The Vice Society Movement and Book Censorship in America*. New York: Scribner's, 1968.

——. *Urban Masses and Moral Order in America, 1820–1920*. Cambridge: Harvard University Press, 1978.

Brandt, Allan M. *No Magic Bullet: A Social History of Venereal Disease in the United States Since 1880*. Rev. ed. New York: Oxford University Press, 1987.

Breazeale, Kenon. "In Spite of Women: *Esquire* Magazine and the Construction of the Male Consumer." *Signs* 20, 1 (1994): 1–22.

Bristow, Edward J. *Prostitution and Prejudice: The Jewish Fight Against White Slavery, 1870–1939*. Oxford: Clarendon, 1982.

Brodie, Janet Farrell. *Contraception and Abortion in Nineteenth-Century America*. Ithaca: Cornell University Press, 1994.

Broun, Heywood and Margaret Leech. *Anthony Comstock: Roundsman of the Lord*. New York: Boni, 1927.

Brownlow, Kevin. *Behind the Mask of Innocence*. New York: Knopf, 1990.

Bryan, George B. *American Theatrical Regulation, 1607–1900: Conspectus and Texts*. Metuchen, N.J.: Scarecrow, 1993.

Bruce, Steve, ed. *Religion and Modernization: Sociologists and Historians Debate the Secularization Thesis*. Oxford: Clarendon, 1992.

Buckley, Peter G. "The Culture of 'Leg-Work': The Transformation of Burlesque After the Civil War." In James Gilbert, ed., *The Mythmaking Frame of Mind: Social Imagination and American Culture*, pp. 113–134. Belmont, Cal.: Wadsworth, 1993.

Burnham, John C. "The Progressive Era Revolution in American Attitudes Toward Sex." *Journal of American History* 59 (March 1973): 885–908.

Burstyn, Varda, ed. *Women Against Censorship*. Vancouver: Douglas and McIntyre, 1985.

Butsch, Richard, ed., *For Fun and Profit: The Transformation of American Culture, 1890–1930*. Philadelphia: Temple University Press, 1990.

Byrnes, Timothy. *Catholic Bishops in American Politics*. Princeton: Princeton University Press, 1991.

Carnes, Mark C. and Clyde Griffen, eds. *Meanings for Manhood: Constructions of Masculinity in Victorian America*. Chicago: University of Chicago Press, 1990.

Carrow, Milton M. *The Licensing Power in New York City*. South Hackensack, N.J.: Rothman, 1968.

Carson, Mina. *Settlement Folk: Social Thought and the American Settlement Movement, 1885–1930*. Chicago: University of Chicago Press, 1990.

Cassady, Ralph, Jr. "Monopoly in Motion Picture Production and Distribution: 1908–1915." In Gorham Kindem, ed., *The American Movie Industry: The Business of Motion Pictures*, pp. 25–75. Carbondale: Southern Illinois University Press, 1982.

Caught Looking Collective. *Caught Looking: Feminism, Pornography, and Censorship*. Seattle: Real Comet, 1988.

Cavallo, Dominick. *Muscles and Morals: Organized Playgrounds and Urban Reform, 1880–1920*. Philadelphia: University of Pennsylvania Press, 1981.

Chauncey, George, Jr. "From Sexual Inversion to Homosexuality: The Changing Medical Conceptualization of Female 'Deviance.'" In Kathy Peiss and Christina Simmons, eds., *Passion and Power: Sexuality in History*, pp. 87–117. Philadelphia: Temple University Press, 1989.

——. *Gay New York: Gender, Urban Culture, and the Making of the Gay Male World, 1890–1940*. New York: Basic, 1994.

Churchill, Allen. *The Theatrical Twenties*. New York: McGraw-Hill, 1975.

Coben, Stanley. "The Assault on Victorianism in the Twentieth Century." *American Quarterly* 27 (December 1975): 604–625.

Cohalan, Rev. Msgr. Florence D. *A Popular History of the Archdiocese of New York*. Yonkers: U.S. Catholic Historical Society, 1983.

Connelly, Mark. *The Response to Prostitution in the Progressive Era*. Chapel Hill: University of North Carolina Press, 1980.

Connolly, William E. "Modern Authority and Ambiguity." *Nomos XXIX: Authority Revisited*, pp. 9–27. New York: New York University Press, 1987.

Constable, Marianne. *The Law of the Other: The Mixed Jury and Changing Conceptions of Citizenship, Law, and Knowledge*. Chicago: University of Chicago Press, 1994.

Cooney, John. *The American Pope: The Life and Times of Francis Cardinal Spellman*. New York: Times, 1983.

Corio, Ann with Joseph DiMona. *This Was Burlesque*. New York: Madison Square, 1968.

Cott, Nancy. *The Grounding of Modern Feminism*. New Haven: Yale University Press, 1987.

Couvares, Francis G. "The Good Censor: Race, Sex, and Censorship in the Early Cinema." *Yale Journal of Criticism* 7, 2 (1994): 233–251.

——. *The Remaking of Pittsburgh: Class and Culture in an Industrializing City, 1877–1919*. Albany: State University of New York Press, 1984.

Couvares, Francis G., ed. *Movie Censorship and American Culture*. Washington, D.C.: Smithsonian Institution Press, 1996.

Cross, Robert D. "The Changing Image of the City Among American Catholics." In Timothy J. Meagher, ed., *Urban American Catholicism: The Culture and Identity of the American Catholic People*. New York: Garland, 1988.

Curtin, Kaier. *"We Can Always Call Them Bulgarians": The Emergence of Lesbians and Gay Men on the American Stage*. Boston: Alyson, 1987.

Czitrom, Daniel. "The Politics of Performance: Theater Licensing and the Origins of Movie Censorship in New York." In Francis G. Couvares, ed., *Movie Censorship and American Culture*, pp. 16–42. Washington, D.C.: Smithsonian Institution Press, 1996.

——. "The Redemption of Leisure: The National Board of Censorship and the Rise of Motion Pictures in New York City, 1900–1920." *Studies in Visual Communication* 10, 4 (1984): 2–6.

DeBerg, Betty A. *Ungodly Women: Gender and the First Wave of American Fundamentalism*. Minneapolis: Fortress, 1990.

deCordova, Richard. "Ethnography and Exhibition: The Child Audience, the Hays Office, and Saturday Matinees." *Camera Obscura* 23 (May 1990): 91–107.

D'Emilio, John. *Sexual Politics, Sexual Communities: The Making of a Homosexual Minority in the United States, 1940–1970*. Chicago: University of Chicago Press, 1983.

D'Emilio, John and Estelle B. Freedman. *Intimate Matters: A History of Sexuality in America*. New York: Harper and Row, 1988.

De Grazia, Edward. *Girls Lean Back Everywhere: The Law of Obscenity and the Assault on Genius*. New York: Random House, 1992.

De Grazia, Edward, ed. *Censorship Landmarks*. New York: Bowker, 1969.

Demastes, William W. *Beyond Naturalism: A New Realism in American Theatre*. Westport, Conn.: Greenwood, 1988.

Denning, Michael. "The End of Mass Culture." *International Labor and Working-Class History* 37 (1990): 4–18.

Dietz, Mary. "Context Is All: Feminism and Theories of Citizenship." *Daedalus* 116, 4 (1987): 1–24.

Dohen, Dorothy. *Nationalism and American Catholicism*. New York: Sheed and Ward, 1967.

Dolan, Jay P. *The American Catholic Experience: A History from Colonial Times to the Present*. Garden City: Doubleday, 1985.

——. "Catholic Attitudes Toward Protestants." In Robert N. Bellah and Frederick E. Greenspan, eds., *Uncivil Religion: Interreligious Hostility in America*. New York: Crossroad, 1987.

Dolan, Jill. "'What, No Beans?' Images of Women and Sexuality in Burlesque Comedy." *Journal of Popular Culture* 18, 3 (Winter 1984): 37–47.

Douglas, Ann. *The Feminization of American Culture*. 2d ed. New York: Doubleday, 1988.

——. *Terrible Honesty: Mongrel Manhattan in the 1920s*. New York: Farrar, Straus and Giroux, 1995.

Duberman, Martin Bauml, Martha Vicinus, and George Chauncey Jr., eds. *Hidden from History: Reclaiming the Gay and Lesbian Past*. New York: New American Library, 1989.

DuBois, Ellen Carol and Linda Gordon. "Seeking Ecstasy on the Battlefield: Danger and Pleasure in Nineteenth-Century Feminist Thought." *Feminist Studies* 9, 1 (Spring 1983): 7–25.

duCille, Ann. "Blues Notes on Black Sexuality: Sex and the Texts of Jessie Fauset and Nella Larsen." *Journal of the History of Sexuality* 3, 3 (1993): 418–444.

Durham, Frank. *Elmer Rice*. New York: Twayne, 1970.

Dworkin, Andrea. *Pornography: Men Possessing Women*. New York: Dutton, 1989.

Ehrenreich, Barbara. *The Hearts of Men: American Dreams and the Flight from Commitment*. Garden City: Anchor, 1983.

Eilberg-Schwartz, Howard, ed. *People of the Body: Jews and Judaism from an Embodied Perspective*. Albany: State University of New York Press, 1992.

Ellis, Richard J. *American Political Cultures*. New York: Oxford University Press, 1993.

Epstein, Barbara. *The Politics of Domesticity: Women, Evangelism, and Temperance in Nineteenth Century America*. Middletown: Wesleyan University Press, 1981.

Erdman, Harley. "Jewish Anxiety in 'Days of Judgment': Community Conflict, Anti-semitism, and the *God of Vengeance* Obscenity Case." *Theatre Survey* 40, 1 (May 1999): 51–74.

Erenberg, Lewis A. "From New York to Middletown: Repeal and the Legitimization of Nightlife in the Great Depression." *American Quarterly* 38, 5 (Winter 1986): 761–778.

——. *Steppin' Out: New York Nightlife and the Transformation of American Culture, 1890–1930*. Westport, Conn.: Greenwood, 1981.

Ewen, Elizabeth. "City Lights: Immigrant Women and the Rise of the Movies." *Signs* 5, 3 (1980): S45-S65.

Facey, Paul W. *The Legion of Decency: A Sociological Analysis of the Emergence and Development of a Social Pressure Group*. New York: Arno, 1974.

Faderman, Lillian. "The Morbidification of Love Between Women by Nineteenth-Century Sexologists." *Journal of Homosexuality* 4, 1 (1978): 73–89.

——. *Odd Girls and Twilight Lovers: A History of Lesbian Life in Twentieth-Century America*. New York: Penguin, 1991.

Feldman, Charles Matthew. *The National Board of Censorship (Review) of Motion Pictures, 1909–1922.* New York: Arno, 1977.

Fisher, Robert. "Film Censorship and Progressive Reform: The National Board of Censorship of Motion Pictures, 1909–1922." *Journal of Popular Film* 4, 2 (1975): 143–156.

Flanagan, Maureen A. "Gender and Urban Political Reform: The City Club and the Woman's City Club of Chicago in the Progressive Era." *American Historical Review* 95, 4 (October 1990): 1032–1050.

Fogarty, Gerald P. *The Vatican and the American Hierarchy from 1870 to 1965.* Stuttgart: Anton Hiersemann, 1982.

Foster, Jeannette. *Sex Variant Women in Literature.* 2d ed. Baltimore: Diana, 1975.

Franzway, Suzanne, Dianne Court, and R. W. Connell. *Staking a Claim: Feminism, Bureaucracy, and the State.* Cambridge: Polity, 1989.

Freedman, Estelle. "'Uncontrolled Desires': The Response to the Sexual Psychopath, 1920–1960." In Kathy Peiss and Christina Simmons, eds., *Passion and Power: Sexuality in History*, pp. 199–225. Philadelphia: Temple University Press, 1989.

Freund, Ernst. *The Police Power: Public Policy and Constitutional Rights.* Chicago: Callaghan, 1904.

——. *The Growth of American Administrative Law.* St Louis: Thomas Law, 1923.

Frug, Gerald E. "The City as a Legal Concept." *Harvard Law Review* 93, 6 (April 1980): 1059–1154.

Gabler, Neal. *An Empire of Their Own: How the Jews Invented Hollywood.* New York: Crown, 1988.

Gardella, Peter. *Innocent Ecstasy: How Christianity Gave America an Ethic of Sexual Pleasure.* New York: Oxford University Press, 1985.

Gardiner, Harold C., S.J. *Catholic Viewpoint on Censorship.* Garden City: Hanover, 1958.

Gates, Henry Louis, Jr. "To 'Deprave and Corrupt.'" *New York Law School Law Review* 38 (1993): 401–442.

Gerber, David A., ed. *Anti-Semitism in American History.* Urbana: University of Illinois Press, 1986.

Gibson, Michael T. "The Supreme Court and Freedom of Expression from 1791 to 1917." *Fordham Law Review* 55 (1986): 263–333.

Gilbert, James. *A Cycle of Outrage: America's Reaction to the Juvenile Delinquent in the 1950s.* New York: Oxford University Press, 1986.

Gilfoyle, Timothy J. *City of Eros: New York City, Prostitution, and the Commercialization of Sex, 1790–1920.* New York: Norton, 1992.

——. "The Moral Origins of Political Surveillance: The Preventive Society in New York City, 1867–1918." *American Quarterly* 38 (1996): 637–652.

Gilman, Sander. *The Jew's Body.* New York: Routledge, 1991.

Ginzburg, Lori D. *Women and the Work of Benevolence: Morality, Politics, and Class in the Nineteenth-Century United States.* New Haven: Yale University Press, 1990.

Gordon, Linda. *Pitied But Not Entitled: Single Mothers and the History of Welfare.* Cambridge: Harvard University Press, 1994.

———. "Social Insurance and Public Assistance: The Influence of Gender in Welfare Thought in the United States, 1890–1935." *American Historical Review* 97, 1 (1992): 19–54.

———. *Woman's Body, Woman's Right: A Social History of Birth Control in America*. New York: Grossman, 1976.

Gordon, Linda, ed. *Women, the State, and Welfare*. Madison: University of Wisconsin Press, 1990.

Graber, Mark. *Transforming Free Speech: The Ambiguous Legacy of Civil Libertarianism*. Berkeley: University of California Press, 1991.

Griffin, Leslie. "American Catholic Sexual Ethics, 1789–1989." In Stephen J. Vicchio and Sister Virginia Geiger, ed., *Perspectives on the American Catholic Church, 1789–1989*, pp. 231–252. Westminster, Md.: Christian Classics, 1989.

Gubar, Susan and Joan Hoff, eds. *For Adult Users Only: The Dilemma of Violent Pornography*. Bloomington: University of Indiana Press, 1989.

Gurstein, Rochelle. *The Repeal of Reticence: A History of America's Cultural and Legal Struggles Over Free Speech, Obscenity, Sexual Liberation, and Modern Art*. New York: Hill and Wang, 1996.

Hale, Nathan G. *Freud and the Americans: The Beginnings of Psychoanalysis in the United States, 1876–1917*. New York: Oxford University Press, 1971.

Hall, Kermit L. *The Magic Mirror: Law in American History*. New York: Oxford University Press, 1989.

Halsey, William M. *The Survival of American Innocence: Catholicism in an Era of Disillusionment, 1920–1940*. Notre Dame: University of Notre Dame Press, 1980.

Hamilton, Marybeth. *When I'm Bad I'm Better: Mae West, Sex, and American Entertainment*. Berkeley: University of California Press, 1997.

Hammack, David C. *Power and Society: Greater New York at the Turn of the Century*. New York: Russell Sage Foundation, 1982.

Hampton, Benjamin B. *History of the American Film Industry*. New York: Dover, 1970 [1931].

Handy, Robert T. *A Christian America: Protestant Hopes and Historical Realities*. 2d ed. New York: Oxford University Press, 1984.

———. *Undermined Establishment: Church-State Relations in America, 1880–1920*. Princeton: Princeton University Press, 1991.

Haney, Robert. *Comstockery in America: Patterns of Censorship and Control*. New York: DeCapo, 1974 [1960].

Hanley, Lawrence F. "Popular Culture and Crisis: King Kong Meets Edmund Wilson." In Bill Mullen and Sherry Lee Linkon, eds., *Radical Revisions: Rereading 1930s Culture*, pp. 242–263. Urbana: University of Illinois Press, 1996.

Hansen, Miriam. *Babel and Babylon: Spectatorship in American Silent Film*. Cambridge: Harvard University Press, 1991.

Hanson, Cynthia A. "Catheryne Cooke Gilman and the Minneapolis Better Movie Movement." *Minnesota History* (Summer 1989): 202–216.

Higham, John. "The Reorientation of American Culture in the 1890s." In John Higham, *Writing American History*. Bloomington: Indiana University Press, 1973.

Howe, Irving. *World of Our Fathers*. New York: Harcourt Brace Jovanovich, 1976.

Hunt, Lynn, ed. *The Invention of Pornography: Obscenity and the Origins of Modernity, 1500–1800*. New York: Zone, 1993.

Inglis, Ruth A. *Freedom of the Movies: A Report on Self-Regulation from the Commission on Freedom of the Press*. Chicago: University of Chicago Press, 1947.

Jacobs, Lea. *The Wages of Sin: Censorship and the Fallen Woman Film, 1928–1942*. Madison: University of Wisconsin Press, 1991.

Jones, Kathleen B. "What Is Authority's Gender?" In Nancy J. Hirschmann and Christine Di Stefano, ed., *Revisioning the Political: Feminist Reconstructions of Traditional Concepts in Western Political Theory*, pp. 75–93. Boulder, Col.: Westview, 1996.

Jowett, Garth. "'A Capacity for Evil': The 1915 Supreme Court Mutual Decision." *Historical Journal of Film, Radio, and Television* 9, 1 (1989): 59–78.

——. *Film: The Democratic Art*. Boston: Little, Brown, 1976.

Kammen, Michael. *Sovereignty and Liberty: Constitutional Discourse in American Culture*. Madison: University of Wisconsin Press, 1988.

——. *Spheres of Liberty: Changing Perceptions of Liberty in American Culture*. Madison: University of Wisconsin Press, 1986.

Kasson, John. *Amusing the Million: Coney Island at the Turn of the Century*. New York: Hill and Wang, 1978.

Kauffman, Christopher J. *Faith and Fraternalism: The History of the Knights of Columbus, 1882–1982*. New York: Harper and Row, 1982.

Kendrick, Walter. *The Secret Museum: Pornography in Modern Culture*. New York: Viking, 1987.

Kessner, Thomas. *Fiorello H. LaGuardia and the Making of Modern New York*. New York: McGraw-Hill, 1989.

——. *The Golden Door: Italian and Jewish Immigrant Mobility in New York City, 1880–1915*. New York: Oxford University Press, 1977.

Koven, Seth, and Sonya Michel, eds. *Mothers of a New World: Maternalist Politics and the Origins of Welfare States*. New York: Routledge, 1993.

Kuh, Richard. *Foolish Figleaves? Pornography in — and out of — Court*. New York: Macmillan, 1967.

Kuhn, Annette. *Cinema, Censorship, and Sexuality, 1909–1925*. New York: Routledge, 1988.

Ladd-Taylor, Molly. *Mother-Work: Women, Child Welfare, and the State, 1890–1930*. Urbana: University of Illinois Press, 1994.

——. "Toward Defining Maternalism in U.S. History." *Journal of Women's History* 5, 2 (1993): 110–113.

Laufe, Abe. *The Wicked Stage: A History of Theatre Censorship and Harassment in the United States*. New York: Ungar, 1978.

Lederer, Laura, ed. *Take Back the Night: Women on Pornography*. New York: Bantam, 1982.

Leff, Leonard J. and Jerold L. Simmons. *The Dame in the Kimono: Hollywood, Censorship, and the Production Code from the 1920s to the 1960s.* New York: Grove Weidenfeld, 1990.

Leidholdt, Dorchen and Janice G. Raymond, eds. *The Sexual Liberals and the Attack on Feminism.* New York: Pergamon, 1990.

Levine, Lawrence. "American Culture and the Great Depression." *Yale Review* 74 (Winter 1985): 196–223.

——. *Highbrow/Lowbrow: The Emergence of Cultural Hierarchy in America.* Cambridge: Harvard University Press, 1988.

Lincoln, Bruce. *Authority: Construction and Corrosion.* Chicago: University of Chicago Press, 1994.

Lindsley, James Elliot. *This Planted Vine: A Narrative History of the Episcopal Diocese of New York.* New York: Harper and Row, 1984.

Lockhart, William B. and Robert C. McClure. "Literature, the Law of Obscenity, and the Constitution." *Minnesota Law Review* 38, 4 (1954): 295–395.

Loth, David. *The Erotic in Literature.* New York: Julian Messner, 1961.

McCarthy, Kathleen D., ed. *Lady Bountiful Revisited: Women, Philanthropy, and Power.* New Brunswick, N.J.: Rutgers University Press, 1990.

McGerr, Michael. "Political Style and Women's Power, 1830–1930." *Journal of American History* 77, 3 (December 1990): 864–885.

MacKinnon, Catherine. *Feminism Unmodified: Discourses on Life and Law.* Cambridge: Harvard University Press, 1987.

——. *Only Words.* Cambridge: Harvard University Press, 1993.

——. *Toward a Feminist Theory of the State.* Cambridge: Harvard University Press, 1989.

MacLean, Nancy. "The Leo Frank Case Reconsidered: Gender and Sexual Politics in the Making of Reactionary Populism." *Journal of American History* 78, 3 (1991): 917–948.

McLeod, Hugh. "Catholicism and the New York Irish, 1880–1910." In Jim Obelkevich, Lyndal Roper, and Raphael Samuel, eds., *Disciplines of Faith: Studies in Religion, Politics and Patriarchy,* pp. 337–350. London: Routledge and Kegan Paul, 1987.

McNickle, Chris. *To Be Mayor of New York: Ethnic Politics in the City.* New York: Columbia University Press, 1993.

Mangan, J. A. and James Walvin, eds. *Manliness and Morality: Middle-Class Masculinity in Britain and America, 1800–1940.* New York: St. Martin's, 1987.

Marcus, Joseph Rader and Abraham J. Peck, eds. *The American Rabbinate: A Century of Continuity and Change, 1883–1983.* Hoboken, N.J.: Ktav, 1985.

Marcus, Steven. *The Other Victorians.* New York: Basic, 1966.

Marty, Martin. *The Irony of It All, 1893–1919.* Vol. 1, *Modern American Religion.* Chicago: University of Chicago Press, 1986.

——. *The Noise of Conflict, 1919–1941.* Vol. 2, *Modern American Religion.* Chicago: University of Chicago Press, 1991.

May, Elaine Tyler. *Homeward Bound: American Families in the Cold War Era*. New York: Basic, 1988.

May, Lary. *Screening Out the Past: The Birth of Mass Culture and the Motion Picture Industry*. Chicago: University of Chicago Press, 1983.

May, Lary and Elaine Tyler May. "Why Jewish Movie Moguls: An Exploration in American Culture." *American Jewish History* 72, 1 (September 1982): 6–25.

Maynard, John. *Victorian Discourses on Sexuality and Religion*. New York: Cambridge University Press, 1993.

Meagher, Timothy J., ed. *From Paddy to Studs: Irish-American Communities in the Turn of the Century Era, 1880–1920*. New York: Greenwood, 1986.

Mennel, Robert M. *Thorns and Thistles: Juvenile Delinquents in the United States, 1825–1940*. Hanover, N.H.: University Press of New England, 1973.

Merritt, Russell. "Nickelodeon Theaters, 1905–1914: Building an Audience for the Movies." In Tino Balio, ed., *The American Film Industry*, pp. 59–79. Madison: University of Wisconsin Press, 1976.

Meyer, Leisa D. "Creating G.I. Jane: The Regulation of Sexuality and Sexual Behavior in the Women's Army Corps During World War II." *Feminist Studies* 18, 3 (Fall 1992): 581–601.

Meyer, Michael A. *Response to Modernity: A History of the Reform Movement in Judaism*. New York: Oxford University Press, 1988.

——. "Tradition and Modernity Reconsidered." In Jack Wertheimer, ed., *The Uses of Tradition: Jewish Continuity in the Modern Era*. New York: Jewish Theological Seminary of America, 1992.

Meyerowitz, Joanne. *Women Adrift: Independent Wage Earners in Chicago, 1880–1930*. Chicago: University of Chicago Press, 1988.

Minsky, Morton and Milt Machlin. *Minsky's Burlesque*. New York: Arbor House, 1986.

Mitchell, Brian C., ed. *Building the American Catholic City: Parishes and Institutions*. New York: Garland, 1988.

Mollenkopf, John Hull, ed. *Power, Culture, and Place: Essays on New York City*. New York: Russell Sage Foundation, 1988.

Monoson, S. Sara. "The Lady and the Tiger: Women's Electoral Activism in New York City Before Suffrage." *Journal of Women's History* 2, 2 (Fall 1990): 100–135.

Moore, Deborah Dash. *At Home in America: Second Generation New York Jews*. New York: Columbia University Press, 1981.

Mumford, Kevin J. "'Lost Manhood' Found: Male Sexual Impotence and Victorian Culture in the United States." *Journal of the History of Sexuality* 3, 1 (1992): 33–57.

Muncy, Robyn. *Creating a Female Dominion in American Reform, 1890–1935*. New York: Oxford University Press, 1991.

Murnion, Philip J. *The Catholic Priest and the Changing Structure of Pastoral Ministry: New York, 1920–1970*. New York: Arno, 1978.

Murphy, Brenda. *American Realism and American Drama, 1880–1940*. Cambridge: Cambridge University Press, 1987.

Murphy, Paul. *The Shaping of the First Amendment, 1791 to the Present.* New York: Oxford University Press, 1991.

Nasaw, David. *Children of the City: At Work and Play.* New York: Oxford University Press, 1985.

Nelson, William E. "Criminality and Sexual Morality in New York, 1920–1980." *Yale Journal of Law and the Humanities* 5, 2 (1993): 265–341.

Nevins, Allan and John A. Krout, eds. *The Greater City: New York, 1898–1948.* New York: Columbia University Press, 1948.

Noll, Mark A., ed. *Religion and American Politics: From the Colonial Period to the 1980s.* New York: Oxford University Press, 1990.

Odem, Mary E. *Delinquent Daughters: Protecting and Policing Adolescent Female Sexuality in the United States, 1885–1920.* Chapel Hill: University of North Carolina Press, 1995.

Parker, Alison M. *Purifying America: Women, Cultural Reform, and Pro-Censorship Activism, 1873–1933.* Urbana: University of Illinois Press, 1997.

Pascoe, Peggy. *Relations of Rescue: The Search for Female Moral Authority in the American West, 1874–1939.* New York: Oxford University Press, 1990.

Peiss, Kathy. *Cheap Amusements: Working Women and Leisure in Turn-of-the-Century New York.* Philadelphia: Temple University Press, 1986.

——. "Commercial Leisure and the 'Woman Question.'" In Richard Butsch, ed., *For Fun and Profit: The Transformation of American Culture, 1890–1930,* pp. 105–117. Philadelphia: Temple University Press, 1990.

Peiss, Kathy and Christina Simmons, eds. *Passion and Power: Sexuality in History.* Philadelphia: Temple University Press, 1989.

Perry, Elizabeth Israels. *Belle Moskowitz: Feminine Politics and the Exercise of Power in the Age of Alfred E. Smith.* New York: Oxford University Press, 1987.

——. "'The General Motherhood of the Commonwealth': Dance Hall Reform in the Progressive Era." *American Quarterly* 37, 5 (1985): 719–733.

——. "Training for Public Life: ER and Women's Political Networks in the 1920s." In Joan Hoff-Wilson and Marjorie Lightman, ed., *Without Precedent: The Life and Career of Eleanor Roosevelt.* Bloomington: Indiana University Press, 1984.

Pivar, David J. *Purity Crusade: Sexual Morality and Social Control, 1868–1900.* Westport, Conn.: Greenwood, 1973.

Platt, Anthony. *The Child Savers: The Invention of Delinquency.* 2d ed. Chicago: University of Chicago Press, 1977.

Pleck, Elizabeth H. and Joseph H. Pleck, eds. *The American Man.* Englewood Cliffs, N.J.: Prentice-Hall, 1980.

Pocock, J. G. A. "The Ideal of Citizenship Since Classical Times." *Queen's Quarterly* 99, 1 (1992): 33–55.

Poggi, Jack. *Theater in America: The Impact of Economic Forces, 1870–1927.* Ithaca: Cornell University Press, 1968.

Purcell, Edward A., Jr. *The Crisis of Democratic Theory: Scientific Naturalism and the Problem of Value.* Lexington: University Press of Kentucky, 1973.

Rabban, David M. "The Emergence of Modern First Amendment Doctrine." *University of Chicago Law Review* 50 (1983): 1205–1355.

—— "The Free Speech League, the ACLU, and Changing Conceptions of Free Speech in American History." *Stanford Law Review* 45 (November 1992): 47–114.

Rabinovitz, Lauren. "Temptations of Pleasure: Nickelodeons, Amusement Parks, and the Sights of Female Sexuality." *Camera Obscura* 23 (May 1990): 71–89.

Ramsaye, Terry. *A Million and One Nights: A History of the Motion Picture.* 2 vols. New York: Simon and Schuster, 1926.

Randall, Richard S. *Censorship of the Movies: The Social and Political Control of a Mass Medium.* Madison: University of Wisconsin Press, 1968.

Rischin, Moses. *The Promised City: New York's Jews, 1870–1914.* Cambridge: Harvard University Press, 1962.

Robinson, Paul. *The Modernization of Sex.* New York: Harper and Row, 1976.

Rod, David K. "Trial by Jury: An Alternative Form of Theatrical Censorship in New York, 1921–1925." *Theatre Survey,* 26, 1 (1985): 47–61.

Rodgers, Daniel T. *Contested Truths: Keywords in American Politics Since Independence.* New York: Basic, 1987.

—— "In Search of Progressivism." *Reviews in American History* 10, 4 (December 1982): 113–132.

Rosen, Ruth. *The Lost Sisterhood: Prostitution in America, 1900–1918.* Baltimore: Johns Hopkins University Press, 1982.

Rosenbloom, Nancy J. "Between Reform and Regulation: The Struggle Over Film Censorship in Progressive America, 1909–1922." *Film History* 1, 4 (1987): 307–325.

—— "In Defense of the Moving Pictures: The People's Institute, the National Board of Censorship, and the Problem of Leisure in Urban America." *American Studies* 33, 2 (Fall 1992): 41–60.

—— "Progressive Reform, Censorship, and the Motion Picture Industry, 1909–1917." In Larry Bennett and Ronald Edsforth, eds., *Popular Culture and Political Change in Modern America,* pp. 41–59. Buffalo: State University of New York Press, 1991.

Rosenwaike, Ira. *Population History of New York City.* Syracuse: Syracuse University Press, 1972.

Rosenzweig, Roy. *Eight Hours for What We Will: Workers and Leisure in an Industrial City, 1870–1920.* Cambridge: Cambridge University Press, 1983.

Rupp, Leila J. "Feminism and the Sexual Revolution in the Early Twentieth Century: The Case of Doris Stevens." *Feminist Studies* 15, 2 (Summer 1989): 289–309.

Ryan, Mary P. "The Projection of a New Womanhood: The Movie Moderns in the 1920s." In Jean E. Friedman and William G. Shade, eds., *Our American Sisters: Women in American Life and Thought.* 3d ed. Lexington, Mass.: Heath, 1982.

Sarna, Jonathan D. "Christian America or Secular America? The Church-State Dilemma of American Jews." In Richard John Neuhaus, ed., *Jews in Unsecular America.* Grand Rapids: Eerdmans, 1987.

Schauer, Frederick F. *The Law of Obscenity.* Washington, D.C.: Bureau of National Affairs, 1976.

Schlissel, Lillian, ed. *Three Plays by Mae West*. London: Nick Hern, 1997.

Schwartz, Judith. *Radical Feminists of Heterodoxy: Greenwich Village, 1912–1940*. Lebanon, N.H.: New Victoria, 1982.

Scott, Anne Firor. *Natural Allies: Women's Associations in American History*. Urbana: University of Illinois Press, 1991.

——. "Women's Voluntary Associations: From Charity to Reform." In Kathleen D. McCarthy, ed., *Lady Bountiful Revisited: Women, Philanthropy, and Power*, pp. 35–54. New Brunswick, N.J.: Rutgers University Press, 1990.

Segal, Lynne and Mary McIntosh, eds. *Sex Exposed: Sexuality and the Pornography Debate*. New Brunswick, N.J.: Rutgers University Press, 1993.

Shaw, Frederick. *The History of the New York City Legislature*. New York: Columbia University Press, 1954.

Simmons, Christina. "Companionate Marriage and the Lesbian Threat." *Frontiers* 4, 3 (1979): 54–59.

——. "Modern Sexuality and the Myth of Victorian Repression." In Kathy Peiss and Christina Simmons, eds., *Passion and Power: Sexuality in History*, pp. 157–177. Philadelphia: Temple University Press, 1989.

Singal, Daniel Joseph. "Toward a Definition of American Modernism." *American Quarterly* 39, 1 (Spring 1987): 5–26.

Sklar, Robert. *Movie-Made America: A Cultural History of American Movies*. New York: Vintage, 1975.

Skocpol, Theda. *Protecting Soldiers and Mothers: The Political Origins of Social Policy in the United States*. Cambridge: Harvard University Press, 1992.

Skowronek, Stephen. *Building a New American State: The Expansion of National Administrative Capacities, 1877–1920*. New York: Cambridge University Press, 1982.

Sloan, Kay. *The Loud Silents: Origins of the Social Problem Film*. Urbana: University of Illinois Press, 1988.

Smith-Rosenberg, Carroll. *Disorderly Conduct: Visions of Gender in Victorian America*. New York: Oxford University Press, 1985.

Snitow, Ann, Christine Stansell, and Sharon Thompson, eds. *Powers of Desire: The Politics of Sexuality*. New York: Monthly Review, 1983.

Snyder, Robert W. *The Voice of the City: Vaudeville and Popular Culture in New York*. New York: Oxford University Press, 1989.

Sobel, Bernard. *A Pictorial History of Burlesque*. New York: Putnam's, 1956.

Sochen, June. *The New Woman in Greenwich Village, 1910–1920*. New York: Quadrangle, 1972.

Staiger, Janet. *Bad Women: Regulating Sexuality in Early American Cinema*. Minneapolis: University of Minnesota Press, 1995.

Stansell, Christine. *City of Women: Sex and Class in New York, 1789–1860*. Urbana: University of Illinois Press, 1987.

Stevens, Elliot L., ed. *Rabbinic Authority: Papers Presented before the Ninety-first Annual Convention of the Central Conference of American Rabbis*. New York: CCAR, 1982.

Susman, Warren I. *Culture as History*. New York: Pantheon, 1984.

Sutton, John. *Stubborn Children: Controlling Delinquency in the United States*. Berkeley: University of California Press, 1988.

Taylor, William R., ed. *Inventing Times Square: Commerce and Culture at the Crossroads of the World*. New York: Russell Sage Foundation, 1991.

Valverde, Mariana. *The Age of Light, Soap, and Water: Moral Reform in English Canada, 1885–1925*. Toronto: McClelland and Stewart, 1991.

Vance, Carole S. "The Meese Commission on the Road." *Nation*, August 2/9, 1986, pp. 78–79.

Wainscott, Ronald H. "Attracting Censorship to the Popular Theatre: Al Woods Produces Avery Hopwood's *The Demi-Virgin*." *Theatre History Studies* 10 (1990): 127–140.

Wald, Kenneth D. *Religion and Politics in the United States*. New York: St. Martin's, 1987.

Walker, Samuel. *In Defense of American Liberties: A History of the ACLU*. New York: Oxford University Press, 1990.

Walsh, Frank. *Sin and Censorship: The Catholic Church and the Motion Picture Industry*. New Haven: Yale University Press, 1996.

Ware, Susan. *Partner and I: Molly Dewson, Feminism, and New Deal Politics*. New Haven: Yale University Press, 1987.

Wertheimer, John. "Mutual Film Reviewed: The Movies, Censorship, and Free Speech in Progressive America." *American Journal of Legal History* 37 (1993): 158–189.

Zeidman, Irving. *The American Burlesque Show*. New York: Hawthorn, 1967.

UNPUBLISHED PAPERS AND THESES

Budd, Mike. "Film Censorship and Public Cultures: The National Board of Review and Women's Voluntary Associations, 1909–1950." Paper presented at the American Studies Association Annual Meeting, Washington, D.C., 1997.

Budke, Timothy Daniel. "Assessing the 'Offense of Public Decency': The Advent of Censoring Particular Dramas on the New York Stage, 1890–1905." Diss. University of Missouri-Colombia, 1989.

Cerillo, Augustus. "Reform in New York City: A Study of Urban Progressivism." Diss. Northwestern University, 1969.

Couvares, Francis G. and Kathy Peiss. "Censoring the Movies: The Problem of Youth in the 1920s." Paper presented at the Organization of American Historians Annual Meeting, Reno, Nevada. 1988.

——. "Sex, Censorship, and the Movies: The National Board of Review, 1909–1922." Unpublished paper.

Dressler, David. "Burlesque as a Cultural Phenomenon." Diss. New York University, 1937.

Fisher, Robert. "The People's Institute of New York City, 1897–1934: Culture, Progressive Democracy, and the People." Diss. New York University, 1974.

Johnson, Richard Christian. "Anthony Comstock: Reform, Vice, and the American Way." Diss. University of Wisconsin, 1973.

McFadden, Margaret. "'Give Him the Ooh-la-la': Gender and Sexuality in the Comic Popular Culture of the 1930s." Paper presented at the Ninth Berkshire Conference on the History of Women, Vassar College, 1993.

Parker, Alison M. "'That Organized Disrespect Toward Women': Living Pictures and Theatrical Censorship at the Turn of the Century." Paper presented at the Ninth Berkshire Conference on the History of Women, Vassar College, 1993.

Skolnick, Richard Stephen. "The Crystallization of Reform in New York City, 1890–1917." Diss. Yale University, 1964.

Wertheimer, John W. "Free-Speech Fights: The Roots of Modern Free-Expression Litigation in the United States." Diss. Princeton University, 1992.

INDEX